Suleiman the Magnificent

Translated from the French by Matthew J. Reisz
Edited by Jana Gough

Originally published in France as *Soliman le Magnifique* by
Librairie Arthème Fayard in 1989.

First published in the United States of America in 1992 by
New Amsterdam Books
by arrangement with Librairie Arthème Fayard.

Library of Congress Cataloging-in-Publication Data is available.

ISBN 1-56131-039-5

Typeset by Contour Typesetters, Southall, London
Printed in Great Britain by Redwood Press Limited, Melksham, Wiltshire

Suleiman the Magnificent

André Clot

NEW AMSTERDAM
NEW YORK

In memory of my father and mother

Contents

Preface

The main object of this book is to bring back to life a man, an empire and an era relatively close to us in time and yet little known. Indeed, for many people, they seem at least as alien as the states and sovereigns of antiquity and the Middle Ages. I would have liked to provide a fuller understanding of the most powerful of Ottoman sultans, and especially of the men, institutions, economy and individual countries which made up his great empire, but for various reasons I decided to restrict myself to broad-brush descriptions. I hope, however, that educated readers will be encouraged to go deeper into the study of Turkish history and civilization. They certainly deserve such attention. (Turkish studies in France have produced a whole catalogue of remarkable works to which, as the Bibliography testifies, I have often turned for inspiration.)

I should like to express my gratitude to the people who have helped me carry out the work for this book. In first place comes Professor Louis Bazin, Director of the Institute of Turkish Studies at the University of Paris III, who encouraged me to take on the project, opened many doors and then was kind enough to read the finished product and provide many learned comments. Jean-Louis Bacqué-Grammont, head of research at the Centre National de Recherche Scientifique (CNRS) and an eminent specialist on Iranian and Ottoman history, provided me with many documents and books and also took the trouble to look over the text and suggest many amendments. Abidin and Güzin Dino gave advice which clarified a wide variety of issues and obtained some very useful texts and translations for me.

I must also express my thanks to Fernand Braudel, who gave me the opportunity to use documents at the Simancas Archives, and to Emmanuel Le Roy Ladurie for valuable guidance about the problem of climate in the sixteenth century.

A Note on Pronunciation

For Turkish names, a simplified form of spelling has been adopted which will pose no problems for the English-speaking reader. The only exceptions are the following:

c pronounced *j* as in *jam*
ç pronounced *ch* as in *church*
ğ not pronounced; lengthens the preceding vowel
ş pronounced *sh* as in *shall*

(Words that have an accepted English form, such as pasha, have retained this spelling.)

At the Dawn of the Golden Century

I who am the Sultan of Sultans, Sovereign of Sovereigns, Distributor of Crowns to Monarchs over the whole Surface of the Globe, God's Shadow on Earth, Sultan and Padishah *of the White Sea and the Black Sea, of Rumelia and Anatolia, of Karaman and the countries of Rum, Zulcadir, Diyarbekir, Kurdistan, Azerbaijan, Persia, Damascus, Aleppo, Cairo, Mecca, Medina, Jerusalem and all Arabia, Yemen and many other lands that my noble forebears and illustrious ancestors . . . conquered by the force of their arms and that my August Majesty has also conquered with my blazing sword and victorious sabre . . .*

Letter from Suleiman to Francis I of France

1453: Mehmed II enters Constantinople. 1492: Columbus discovers America and the Catholic Kings capture Grenada from the Moors. 1519: Charles V is elected Emperor of Germany. 1520: Luther is condemned for heresy.

Whatever dates and events we choose to mark the start of modern times in the West, one crucial fact stands out: after an extended crisis which struck Europe in the 14th and 15th centuries and shook medieval civilization to its foundations, the feudal age was utterly dead. The age of states was born amid economic and social change unprecedented since the end of the Roman Empire. It represented almost a new civilization, a veritable renaissance or rebirth.

The crisis of the two previous centuries, the most serious the West had known for a millennium, affected most of the Old World. In the wake of disaster all over Europe brought by wars and peasant revolts, the Black Death arrived from the Black Sea port of Caffa and spread its own share of suffering, misery and insecurity. The Christian nations presented a sad spectacle: conflict between France and England, and between the King of France and Dukes of Burgundy; the Hussite wars and the collapse of imperial authority in Bohemia; chaos and guerrilla warfare in Central

Europe and the Scandinavian countries; decadence and anarchy in Italy and Spain; an unprecedented schism within the Church. Yet this was not all. A new danger was soon to appear on the horizon in Central Europe – the Ottomans.

If the Old World had continued in its conflicts and errors, nothing could have prevented the people always described as 'barbarians' (although the term had long ceased to be appropriate) from overrunning the West. History is littered with the bodies of once rich and powerful states which have collapsed under the weight of their internal quarrels, offering an easy prey to conquerors or bold adventurers.

Yet this time, at the moment when all seemed lost, Europe recovered. The Battle of Castillon (1453) put an end to the Hundred Years' War. The huge epidemics which had caused such damage in the previous century died down. Prosperity and security returned. The return to peace was accompanied by a recovery similar to that of the 12th and 13th centuries. Populations began to increase (numbers doubled in France between 1450 and 1560), deserted villages were repopulated and towns expanded. Agriculture increased its yields as new, mainly industrial forms of cultivation were introduced. More and more land was given over to wine-growing and animal husbandry.

Industrial processes improved existing products or created new ones in metalwork, glassware, light drapery, silk and linen. Iron, silver and copper mining, spurred on by the demands of industry, took off. Mines abandoned since Roman times were brought back into operation. (The Habsburg fortunes were based on the mines they operated or used as security for loans.) Printing and hence also paper making took off. With the return of peace, trade in products of every kind started to flow again on the traditional trade routes: within Europe, and from the Orient by way of Venice or Eastern Europe to Poland, Western Europe and the Baltic states. Yet now there was also increasing trade from the Atlantic ports to Central Europe and the North. Fairs held on set dates and large banking organizations eased the flow of capital. The monetary economy expanded, along with resort to credit facilities.

This renewal in every aspect of Western life, reflected in art and literature, spurred on the ambitions of the sailors who set off to explore the world. Europeans were soon to discover other civilizations, which in turn learned of the existence of countries such as France, Spain and Italy, located on the edges of the huge continent which separated the two great oceans. The *Grand Siècle* – the Great (16th) Century – was essentially a century of encounters.

Yet it was also a century of great heads of state, of kings and emperors who left an indelible mark on it. The sovereigns of the 14th and 15th centuries struggled first to ensure the survival of their states, and then to secure their own positions by weakening the great feudal lords. In France, England, Italy and Portugal, kings and princes at the end of the 15th century brought under control the dukes and barons who encroached on their power. The great landowning dynasties like the Bourbons in France would be around for a long time, yet their battle was hopeless: the ancient notion of sovereignty inherited from Roman law and revived by Philippe le Bel's jurists was destined to prevail.

Things were very different in Central and Eastern Europe, where the nobility not only prevented the emergence of modern states but greatly contributed by their disorderliness to the success of the Turkish forces and the loss of national independence. Everywhere else, even in the papal states, sovereigns used similar means to maintain their powers within and outside their territories; few serious challenges were forthcoming.

States of every kind require an armed force capable of ensuring their neighbours will respect their wishes. Feudal armies were no longer suited to the great states which were coming into being. The techniques of war, which had developed rapidly since the invention of artillery, now required experts. A French decree of 1439 laid down that the army belonged to the king and that no others were permitted. In 1445 the king was granted 20 permanent cavalry regiments. Three years later, the infantry was organized into irregular companies of bowmen which were replaced by 7 legions of 6,000 men under Francis I. The French artillery was soon to become one of the best in Europe. Like the rulers of the Italian republics, the king also recruited mercenaries.

Spain established a form of regular military service with a new unit known as a *coronelia*, made up of 12 companies of pikemen, harquebusiers and cavalry. Together they formed the *tercio*, a formidable force. Armies became and remained permanent, although an increasing drain on resources.

Throughout the Middle Ages, kings lived by coining money, on their feudal and seigneurial rights, and on revenues from landed estates. The development of armies, international politics and royal ambitions made such means insufficient. Throughout Europe, sovereigns adopted the same solution: permanent and regular taxes levied on their subjects. The

Estates General in France were called upon less and less to vote in taxes and, from the time of Charles VII, governments levied the *taille* and *aides* directly. Francis I reorganized his finances by creating a treasury to centralize all state revenue.

In England, by contrast, where the king failed to make the taillage permanent, Henry VII fell back on forced loans from the nobility. Henry VIII confiscated clerical property – the reform of the Church was a way of getting rich. In Spain the possessions of Jewish and Muslim 'Infidels' were confiscated. Before gold started to pour in from the New World, money also came from the sale of indulgences, thanks to a 'crusading papal bull', and the income of the great chivalric orders. Everywhere in Europe, money lenders – whom we would call bankers – advanced money to sovereigns.

Another general development in Europe as kings and princes reinforced their powers over their subjects was the creation of a new system of administration based on functionaries. Although they almost always came from a humble background, recruited among the clergy or lesser nobility, they propped up the ambitions of sovereigns and reinforced their prerogatives. In Spain, France and, with the Star Chamber, in England, the powers of the king's councils increased while representative institutions were progressively enfeebled. With the exception of Venice, the Italian states were either true monarchies such as Naples or closer to monarchies than republics (Milan, Florence). Everywhere absolutism was triumphant, as an inexorable result of the need to concentrate power in a Europe dominated by international politics and economics – and where great ambitions were soon to come face to face.

Whether it is just a historical accident or a reflection of an age of strength and renewal, states almost all over Europe, the Orient and even India were ruled by powerful personalities for over a hundred years. Such men were warrior chiefs, diplomats, administrators, often artists yet always ambitious – and rarely weighed down by scruples. None ever reproached his rivals with their terrible crimes – massacre, disembowelment, kidnap, plunder, oaths betrayed as soon as made – since he knew he had committed just as many. None ever confused religion – to which they ostentatiously proclaimed their adherence – with morality. The 16th century was an age of iron.

1509: Henry VIII comes to the throne of England. 1515: Francis I becomes King of France. 1516: the accession of Charles V in Spain. Four years later, Suleiman puts on the sword of Osman. These four men dominated Europe and much of the inhabited earth for nearly half a century, united in their desire to increase their power by any means, and particularly by war. All four were warrior princes yet claimed to be fervent lovers of peace – when it served their interests.

The oldest, Henry VIII, was no cardboard cut-out king. 'A potentate to his fingertips', according to one biographer (who compared him to Rockefeller), Henry was interested only in power. He went as far as establishing his own religion – not even God would stand in his way. Of his six wives, two were handed over to the executioner, two more cast aside. Yet this cultivated Blue Beard, artist, Erasmus-like humanist and archetypal Renaissance prince made of England a rich and powerful country which at one point held the balance of power in Europe. Both Francis I and Charles V tried in turn to gain Henry's favour, yet for a long time he skilfully and opportunistically managed to manoeuvre between them. How different from the early years of Henry VII's reign, when a penniless country was surrounded by plotters! Half a century later, Elizabethan England sparkled with health and riches.

Facing the English ogre across a Channel which has often seemed wider than an ocean was the dazzling Francis I of France, 'as handsome a prince as any in the world', the knightly king, gallant and charming, with his own special touch of gaiety and joy. The *beau seizième siècle* is essentially his. The Renaissance was bursting forth in every field: artists, scholars, great writers who celebrated human dignity and at last gave man his rightfully pre-eminent place. Castles sprouted on the banks of the Loire and the king, open to every innovation, summoned painters and sculptors to his court and founded the Collège de France. Yet Francis was also a man of great political vision and bold ambitions. 'He had', according to Lavisse, 'an exact sense of the kingdom's interests; in the struggle with Charles V, he revealed his energy and skill on more than one occasion; he knew how to win allies; he dared appeal for help to the Turks when he needed to defend French independence or grandeur. In all these ways, he expressed his freedom of mind and clarity of vision . . . In a quarter century full of dangerous external developments, our country carried through crucial social, economic, intellectual and moral changes which helped set her course for the future.'

The third great figure in a Europe opening up to the outside world was Charles V of Spain – often known as Charles Quintus – Francis's rival and adversary. Henry and Francis were both generous-spirited live wires and enthusiastic womanizers. Charles was sullen, slow and reticent, with a hanging jaw. Little inclined to study in his youth, he was addicted only to the most ignoble of vices: gluttony. Yet this unappealing exterior hid a lively imagination, an unyielding doggedness, a wise and scheming mind and a constitution equal to every trial. The somewhat melancholy young man was to become one of the keenest participants in the European struggle for power. Of boundless ambition, he wanted to become emperor, bought outright the votes of the seven electors – and triumphed. As a result, the 150 million gold francs he borrowed from the Fugger banking dynasty had an incalculable long-term impact on the continent, although the empire itself – 'a construction too great for the strength of a single man' – did not survive his death.

Yet would the century present such a lively and colourful scene – so full of intricate diplomacy, sword thrusts, stories of adventure and openings to new countries and new ideas – if it were not for great sovereigns like Ivan III ('Ivan the Terrible'), who brought all the Russian lands under his sway, like the Sophy,[1] Shah Ismail, or like Babur and Akbar in India? For the countries to the East of Europe, the 16th century also signified increasing contact with the outside world, the creation of unified states, new intellectual horizons. It was then that Russia was born of fire and the sword – although also with the help of Greeks and Italians called up by Ivan III. It was then that Shah Ismail, grandson of an Emperor Comnenus from Trabzon, a boy of dazzling beauty with something 'grand and majestic' in his eyes yet also of appalling cruelty, recreated Iran as a political unit all the way from Bactria to Fars. An exquisite civilization emerged from the fusion of Shiite Islam[2] and the earlier artistic and intellectual traditions of Iran, together with influences from China and Italy. Its refinement and elegance achieved supreme expression under Shah Abbas. Later, when Babur seized Delhi in 1526, he was to graft it onto the trunk of existing Indian art to create the Moghul renaissance. It reached its apogee before the end of the century under his grandson Akbar.

An Iron Race

These kings and emperors, or at least the European ones, were successors to generations of sovereigns who had long fought to retain or, more often, extend their territories. The Middle Eastern rulers, comparative latecomers, who were destined like Suleiman to achieve unparalleled power and glory, made a sudden appearance on the scene when they crushed and conquered parts of the Eastern Roman Empire. We can hardly imagine today the shock of the Turks arriving at the gates of Europe, or the fear they continued to inspire into the 18th century and beyond, among a populace which saw them as barbarians with knives between their teeth.

For almost ten centuries, the Turks, 'one of the iron races of the ancient world',[3] had waged war on the steppes of Upper Asia. Having set out from the Altay mountains and the Orkhon and Selenge basins, the first Turks history has been able to identify – the Tabghach (*To-Pa* in Chinese) – occupied Northern China in the 5th century and then blended into the native population. A hundred years later, other Turks conquered first Mongolia and then Turkestan. Masters of an immense empire extending from Korea to Iran, they used the Sogdian alphabet, a predecessor of the runic script.[4] This empire disappeared when its founder, Bumin, died in 552. It then split in two: Bumin's son Muhan ruled over the Eastern Frontier Region, to the East of the Tien Shan in Mongolia; to the West, on the steppes of Siberia and Transoxania, the emperor's second-born son, Istami, became khan of the Western Frontier Region.

The inscriptions at Orkhon, carved around 730, preserve for us in powerful poetic language the memory of that great adventure: 'O Turkish chiefs! O Oguz! O people, listen! As long as the sky has not fallen and the earth has not split open, who will be able to destroy the institutions of your country, O Turkish people? . . . I did not become the sovereign of a rich people but of a hungry, naked and wretched people. We agreed, my younger brother, the Prince Koltegin, and I, not to allow the glory and renown our father and uncle won for our people to perish. For love of the Turkish people, I have neither slept at night nor rested by day . . . and now my brother Koltegin is dead. My soul is filled with anguish, my eyes can no longer see, my mind no longer think. My soul is in torment . . . My ancestors subjugated and pacified many peoples in every corner of the world, making them bow their heads and bend their knees before them. From the mountains of Khinghan to the Gates of Iron, the power of the Blue Turks extended . . .'[5] This empire, in its turn, collapsed in 740.

Meanwhile the first group of people, the Western Toukiues, were replaced for a century by the Uighurs. The Uighur Empire borrowed from outer Iran (the Iran of the oases of Turfan and Beshbalik) its artforms and Manichaean religion and became more and more civilized. Then it was overcome by the Kirghiz and disappeared, only to be reborn as a Buddhist state in Chinese Turkestan. To the West, the Turkish tribes converted to Islam. It is from this world, ceaselessly warring and ceaselessly changing, that the Ghaznavids, the Ghourids and the Seljuks[6] would soon emerge.

The 'iron race' had set out long ago from the depths of Asia, and wandered from the Caspian to the Pacific, crossed deserts and valleys, founded empires, taken up and abandoned religions. Now, on the harsh steppes of Anatolia, they found a country with a climate much like that of Central Asia and put an end to their wanderings. The Seljuk Empire was formed, with its great chiefs (Alp Arslan, Melikshah) and great administrators (Nizam al-Mulk), and then shattered into rival principalities. It was then, at the start of the 13th century, that the Osmanli or Ottomans appeared.

According to legend, Suleimanshah, the chief of the tribe from which the line of Osman descends, fled before the Mongol invasion of Khorasan in Eastern Anatolia, but then, when the wave of invaders led by Genghis Khan ran out of steam, decided to return to Iran. He was drowned in the Euphrates on the way back. Two of his sons, Dundar and Ertugrul, considered this a bad omen and turned East, towards the part of Central Anatolia inhabited by the Seljuk Turks. They are said to have arrived unexpectedly at the scene of a battle between combatants they did not recognize. Ertugrul decided to intervene on the side which seemed to be losing. This was Alaeddin, sultan of Konya, who was engaged in a desperate struggle with the Mongols. When he won an unexpected victory, he offered Ertugrul a fiefdom in the region of Sogut (between Bursa and Eskişehir) as a reward. Thus the Ottoman era began.

This legend is rather too good to be true. Put together much later, in the 15th century, it was inspired by popular stories about the life of the Seljuk prince Suleiman Kutlumuş, his son Kiliç Arslan and the flight from the Mongols of Celaleddin Rumi, the founder of the Mevlevi order. The most reliable sources lead one to believe that the small group of men who gave their name to one of the most powerful empires in human history were descendants of *gazi* (Muslim fighters who formed numerous communities on the borders of Islam to ward off the Infidels, just as the *akritai*[7] protected the Byzantine Empire). The struggle against the Christians was always critical for the Ottomans – the day it was abandoned marked the start of the empire's decline.

These *gazi* – 'instruments of the religion of Allah, the sword of God' – were established in the Islamic parts of the Orient and, from the 9th century, in Khorasan and Transoxania. Turks were always dominant in the *gazi*, which attracted unemployed wanderers, heretics fleeing persecution and even Christians in search of loot. They sacked Sebaste (Sivas) and Iconium (Konya). Later, Turks who had remained outside the Seljuk Empire often joined *gazi*. The Mongol invasion, which made the Seljuks vassals of the Il-Khanid Empire (founded by Hulegu, grandson of Genghis Khan), increased the westward migration of the Turkish tribes. In search of territory, they too joined *gazi* and attacked the Byzantines.

It was then that an event with incalculable consequences occurred: the eastern defences of Byzantium collapsed. The Latin-speakers of the Fourth Crusade left Constantinople (which they had held since 1204) and the Emperor Michael Palaeologus returned. The empire's centre of gravity moved West. The *akritai*, who were hostile to the Palaeologus dynasty, made no attempt to hold the frontiers.

The *gazi* leaped into the breach and each tried to carve out from the spoils of the Byzantine Empire a territory as large as its armed forces could control. Anatolia split into several principalities based on *gazi*. The chiefs who had led them to victory founded dynasties. Some collapsed almost at once, but many survived far longer. Their links with the Seljuks of Konya (who had nominally taken over from the great Seljuk dynasty of Iran) were very loose; they were not in any real sense vassal states. The *beys* of Aydin, Karaman and Menteş, with territory bordering the Aegean, gained immense wealth from piracy. The Osmanli *bey*, on the other hand, possessed none of their advantages: his territory was situated in the North-West of Anatolia on the borders of the Turco-Byzantine area, far from the sea and fruitful sources of pillage. But Osman and his successors lacked neither skill nor audacity in seizing every favourable opportunity.

Osman revealed his genius as a politician by immediately laying the foundations of a state, largely inspired by the example of the Seljuks, with their traditions, guilds and culture inherited from the older Muslim world and the Iranian-Sassanid Orient. He seized Nicaea in 1301, after defeating the army sent against him by the Emperor of Byzantium. As his fame increased, he attracted to himself not only brigands and deserters but intellectuals, artists and the cultivated elite of the towns. Theologians and jurists (the *ulema*) provided the basis for the administration and brought with them a spirit of tolerance characteristic of Muslim dealings with Jewish and Christian Infidels. Schools of theology modelled on the Seljuk *medrese* soon opened in Iznik (Nicaea) and Bursa (Brusa). By the end of the 14th century, while other principalities were still wasting their energies on costly rivalries, the Ottoman Turkish state was born. Soon it proved its superiority in the whole of Anatolia, and then on the other side of the Propontis, in Europe.

It was the Byzantines themselves who provided the opportunity, when John VI Cantacuzenus asked for the help of Osman's son Orhan in his struggle against John V Palaeologus and even offered him his daughter Theodora in marriage.[8] A few years later, in 1354, Orhan captured the fortress of Gallipoli, on the European shore, when an earthquake had caused it to collapse. Since he already controlled positions on the Asian side, he was now able to cut off Constantinople from its European possessions whenever he wished.

The Christian world was alarmed. There was talk of a new crusade – not to save Jerusalem, but to deliver the capital of Byzantium from the Turkish menace. Even a reunion of the Roman and Orthodox Churches was discussed . . . But it was too late. The Balkans and Europe itself were in total disorder. The Serbian, Byzantine and Bulgar Empires fought among themselves. The rivalry between Genoa and Venice in the Eastern Mediterraean was fiercer than ever. The Byzantine Empire, its forces quite spent, was open to capture.

Fate – known in the Orient as 'the will of Allah' – decided that a bold and cunning sultan, Murad I, should be ruler of the Ottomans at the crucial moment. Having succeeded Orhan in 1362, it was he who set in motion the occupation of the Balkans. In a matter of years he led his troops from Marmara to the shores of the Adriatic. With Bulgaria conquered and Hungary under threat, Europe was frightened. Every month the Turkish 'hordes' increased in size. Attracted by adventure and the chance of loot, many men, most of them Greeks, joined the sultan's service. Local populations, long oppressed by Serbian and Bulgarian feudal lords and by religious orders, put up little resistance to the Turkish occupation. The Catholic Church was suppressed, to the delight of Orthodox Christians. Many soldiers who had fought in the ranks of the Serbian and Bulgarian armies joined the Ottoman side when offered grants of land and exemption from taxes. Nobles allowed to retain their fiefdoms agreed to serve in the Turkish cavalry.

After the capture of, first, Gallipoli and then Demotika and Edirne (Adrianople) in 1362, the Christian powers made a vain attempt to react. Urban V's appeal for a new crusade fell on deaf ears, since neither France nor England, caught up in the Hundred Years' War, responded. Only Count Amédée of Savoy set out and recaptured Gallipoli, but, alone against Murad, he was soon forced to beat a retreat and return to Italy. Murad won victory after victory and, on 15 June 1389, crushed the Serbian army of Prince Lazar at Kossovo (the Field of the Blackbirds). Murad himself was assassinated; Lazar, taken prisoner, was executed. The Turks occupied the Balkans; they were to control the area for five centuries.

Murad's successor, Bayezid *Yildirim* (or 'The Thunderbolt'), continued Murad's conquests at an even more irresistible pace. In 1393 he annexed the area of Bulgaria around the Danube, then Thessaly and Wallachia. At last, the Christian nations made a supreme effort. Sigismund, King of Hungary, called for a crusade. For once (but it was to be the last time), the response was favourable from both the English and the French. At the head of the French army were John the Fearless, Admiral Jean de Vienne, Marshal Boucicault, the Count of La Marche and Philippe d'Artois. The Grand Master of the Order of Saint John of Jerusalem took part along with the Elector Palatine. Each side brought about 100,000 men to the field. The armies met on the lower Danube near Nicopolis, which the Christian armies had besieged. Against the advice of Sigismund, who wanted to wait for a Turkish offensive, the French nobility impatiently launched an attack. They managed to break through the first two Turkish lines but were too exhausted to exploit their advantage. The Turkish cavalry and janissaries (the best corps of the day) easily surrounded the French horsemen and, after several hours when the result seemed uncertain, the Serbian contingents of the Turkish army joined battle and tipped the balance.

Bayezid soon won over the few surviving independent emirates and decided to seal the fate of Constantinople. In the event, the town was saved, for a considerable period of time, not by the Christians, but by another Turkish conqueror. This was Timur Leng ('Timur the Lame') from the depths of Central Asia and known to us as Tamerlane.

It was at Ankara, in the heart of Anatolia, that the armies of Bayezid and Tamerlane met in 1402. Although the emirs defeated by the Ottomans had often joined Tamerlane, their troops had sometimes joined Bayezid. As with the Serbs at Nicopolis, it was they who decided the result of the battle. When they saw the combat hanging in the balance, they were finally swayed by loyalty to their princes and thus changed sides to fight with Tamerlane. Bayezid's army was defeated and he was taken prisoner.

The Christian powers failed to seize the chance they had been offered by fate. With the Turkish Empire crippled by defeat and the sons of

Bayezid at loggerheads, reconquest of the Balkans was possible. Nobody moved. In a few years, Mehmed I *Çelebi* ('the Lord'), one of Bayezid's sons, eliminated his brothers Isa, Suleiman and Musa. He brought back order and stability to the empire. First Mehmed I and then Murad II (who succeeded him in 1421) returned to a policy of expansion. Their main aim and purpose was crystal clear: the conquest of Constantinople.

Again the Christians wanted to halt the Turkish advance. Ladislas Jagiellon, King of Hungary, and John Hunyadi, voivode (or governor) of Transylvania, gave way to the pleas of the Pope and the Emperor of Byzantium and invaded the Ottoman Empire. In 1444 they laid siege to Varna. Murad II crushed the Christian armies in a surprise attack with 40,000 men while his enemies still believed him to be 100 leagues away. Ladislas and Giulio Caesarini, the Papal Legate, were left dead on the field of battle. Emperor John VIII of Byzantium, seeing that his turn would come too, tried to win over the sultan with valuable gifts – although this naturally proved unsuccessful. His successor, Constantine Dragases, in a supreme effort to gain the support of the Latin nations, announced a union of the two churches. This only enraged the hardline members of the Orthodox Church, who made their own the formula pronounced by one of the empire's leading dignitaries: 'Better the Turkish turban than the tiara of the Pope ruling in Constantinople.'

At all events, it was too late. Mehmed II, who had succeeded Murad II in 1451, took pains to isolate Byzantium by making peace with John Hunyadi, with Venice, Genoa and even the Knights of Rhodes. Constantine Dragases's appeals to the Christians fell on deaf ears. Europe left Byzantium to its fate. Now only a shadow of its former glory, Constantinople was quite unable to avoid falling into the hands of the Ottomans.

The siege began on 6 April 1453; by 29 May, it was all over. The courage of the Greeks was of no avail in the face of the Turks' modern weapons – war machines and above all huge cannons – the six-to-one Ottoman superiority and Mehmed's determination. The last Byzantine Emperor perished sword in hand and the garrison was massacred. In the evening, Mehmed took part in the prayers in Saint-Sophia – now turned into a mosque. The *gazi* warrior was on the throne of the Caesars and from there he would set forth across Europe and Asia in the pursuit of further conquest.

The Greatest Army in the World

The year 1453, therefore, marks the end of the Roman Empire. No one can fail to be amazed by the almost constant successes of the Ottoman armies, which developed in less than two centuries from a small group of fighters who waged war around their *gazi* in Eastern Anatolia into a force whose power reached the shores of the Bosphorus and the palace of Justinian's successors. How can we explain that extraordinary advance which continued until the day when a counter-thrust before Vienna checked forever the Ottoman invasion of Europe?

First of all, complete anarchy had engulfed the Byzantine Empire, the Balkans and Asia Minor. If the empire had still been ruled by Justinian, Basil II or Alexis Comnenus, Turkish history would have come to an end with the Seljuks. Strong Serbian or Bulgar Empires would also have held the invaders back. But neither North nor South of the Balkan peninsula were there any such empires. Byzantium, after a period of revival under the Comnenus dynasty, had been taken and occupied by the Fourth Crusade. Although Constantinople had been recovered from the Latins in 1261, it was now hardly more than a pile of ruins. When they came to power, the Palaeologus dynasty found themselves at the head of a reduced and exhausted empire. Religious and class conflicts as well as sordid intrigues had enfeebled it. Byzantium had essentially defeated itself.

Exactly the same internal disputes and unwillingness to join forces were to be seen in the Serbian and Bulgar Empires. From time to time they woke up and found another city taken – Kossovo, Nicopolis, Varna – largely because of the frivolous life-styles of the Christian ights. The empires crumbled into the domains of rival feudal lords, where oppressed populations were happy to be ruled by anyone who would lighten their burden even slightly. 'The serfs welcomed the Islamic armies for the same reasons that they later welcomed the French revolutionary armies.'[9] The Ottomans were skilful enough to rule with justice and moderation. Even when the people did not truly support Turkish domination, the Turks' spirit of religious tolerance soon made them accepted.[10] It was this which led to the *pax Ottomanica* described by Toynbee.

The Ottomans were the only people to bring powerful, well trained and equipped military forces against the brave but also dissolute local knights and their undisciplined hangers-on. All contemporary witnesses declare that, for at least two centuries, the Turkish army was the most powerful in the world. The administration developed out of the army and was for a long time essentially part of it. In time of war, almost everybody became part of the army which, until the end of the reign of Suleiman, was led by the sultan himself. Many of the leading dignitaries of the state were military commanders. 'Governing and waging war were the two main aims – internal and external – of a single institution controlled by the same group of men.'[11]

The discipline of the sultan's army terrified the West. At a time when European troops were equipped and armed in haphazard fashion and often obeyed or disobeyed according to momentary whims and deserted at the first opportunity, the Turkish soldiery possessed all the qualities which make armies invincible: courage, discipline and almost fanatical loyalty. Ambassador Ghiselin de Busbecq[12] often wrote about this in his *Letters*:

'One or twice a day on campaign, the Turkish soldiers drink a beverage made of water mixed, when available, with a few spoonfuls of flour, a little butter, spices and a piece of bread or ration of biscuit. Some of them take with them a little bag of powdered dried beef which they use in the same way as flour. Sometimes they also eat the meat of their dead horses . . . All this will convey to you how patiently and abstemiously the Turks confront difficult times and wait for better days. How different are our soldiers, who despise ordinary food and want delicacies (like thrush and pipit) and *haute cuisine* even on campaign! If we don't give them food like that, they mutiny and bring suffering on themselves; if we do give them such food, they still bring suffering on themselves. Each man is his own worst enemy and has no more deadly adversary than his own intemperance, which kills him off even if the enemy doesn't . . . I dread to think what the future holds for us when I compare the Turkish system to ours.'

Describing the camp of a campaigning army where he spent three months, Busbecq noticed the silence reigning there, the absence of quarrels and acts of violence, and how clean it all was. No one was drunk, because the soldiers had only water to drink; their food was a sort of gruel of turnips and cucumbers seasoned with garlic, salt and vinegar. A hearty appetite was their only sauce, he added humorously.

Paolo Giovio, an Italian chronicler of the age of Suleiman, summarized his opinion of the Turkish army as follows: 'Their discipline is far more just and strict than that of the ancient Greeks and Romans. There are three reasons for their superiority over us in battle: they immediately obey their commanders; they never worry about the possibility of losing their lives; and they can survive without bread and wine on a little barley and water.'[13] It only remains to add that, at a time when provisioning was unknown in Europe, the Ottoman army's supply lines were very well organized.

The permanent army was made up of slaves of the Porte[14] (*kapikulu*). Two forces formed part of it: the Porte *sipahi* (cavalry) and the janissaries, the most illustrious corps in the Turkish army. The janissaries were formed at the start of the Osmanli era and were about 5,000 in number in the 15th century, 12,000 under Suleiman. They are sometimes given a significance they did not really possess, at least on the battlefield, since at no time did they make up the whole Turkish army or anything like it. Their role was usually to join battle after the enemy had faced attack from the cavalry and irregulars and artillery bombardment. Their fresh forces would then often tip the balance.

Their political influence, on the other hand, was immense and their demands – particularly dangerous in that they were inspired by a powerful *esprit de corps* – more than once forced the sultan to change his plans. No sultan could take power without granting a large accession gift agreed after long negotiations and much argument. By siding with a particular claimant to the throne, the janissaries decided the fate of the empire on several occasions. They gave much help to Murad II in his triumph over his rivals and it was thanks to them that Selim I, Suleiman's father, defeated his brother Ahmed in 1511.

They terrified the population of Istanbul. 'Above all, don't let any of your people get into quarrels with the janissaries,' the Porte functionaries advised foreign ambassadors, 'because we would be quite unable to do anything for you or for them.' When bands of janissaries entered a district, the shopkeepers immediately shut up shop. It was usually impossible to stop them ransacking a city after it had surrendered, as happened in Rhodes in 1521 and at Buda in 1529 despite the promises and express orders of Suleiman. During the Persian campaign of 1514, when the army was advancing with great difficulty in the region of Araxe, Selim, for all his ruthlessness, was compelled to make an about-turn. The janissaries went so far as to pierce the sultan's tent with their lances in order to force him to go back towards the capital. Thus, if they sometimes complained when long periods of peace deprived them of booty, they also sometimes forced the sultan to cut short a war.

Their devotion knew no limits, their loyalty was absolute. Only too ready to sacrifice their lives for the sultan, in battle they formed a completely solid line of defence around him. To give expression to the link which united him with his elite troops, Suleiman enlisted in one of their companies and was paid like an ordinary soldier. His successors did exactly the same.

Compelled to be celibate and subject to strict training and iron discipline, the janissaries showed matchless strength and skill in handling their weapons. When they trooped by in silence, they deeply impressed European visitors. 'One would have thought them friars,' remarked Busbecq, in his account of an audience with Suleiman at Amasya. They were so still and rigid, he continued, that from a distance one could not tell if they were men or statues. A Frenchman called du Fresne-Canaye compared them with monks. Bodyguards of the sultan and his greatest asset in battle, the janissaries were fanatical Muslims – although all of them, at least in the 16th century, were of Christian origin. They were, in fact, slaves of the sultan recruited by means of the *devşirme* system – that is, chosen from among the provincial children who did not possess the intellectual ability to become civil servants.

This *devşirme* or conscripting of Christian children dated far back into the Ottoman past. When the sultan decided to collect some children in this way, a commission, including an official and a janissary, was nominated for each province (*sancak*). It went to each village, summoned all the boys aged between 8 and 20 and then, under the authority of a judge (*kadi*) and the *sipahi*, picked out those whose intellectual and physical abilities made them good potential soldiers or administrators. They were always from peasant families and were never only sons. Once the boys had been gathered together in the large towns, they were sent to Istanbul in groups of 100. The most promising (the *içoğlanlari*) were then directed to the palaces of Galata Saray or Ibrahim Pasha, in the capital, or to those of Manisa and Edirne. The others – the *Turk oğlanlari* – went to work in the fields on Anatolian farms before being enrolled in the *yeniçeri* or janissaries (see Appendix 3).

Under Suleiman and his successors, therefore, the system of *devşirme* supplied both the elite troops – the janissaries and the *sipahi* of the Porte – and all the administrators up to and including the Grand Vizier. All were slaves of the sultan; at a time when birth meant everything in Europe, their advancement depended solely on merit. No earlier regime, not even the Abbasid caliphs or the Mamluks, had created such a successful and large-scale slave state. From the beginning of the Ottoman Empire, slaves were educated to become officers and administrators; but it was not until the time of Mehmed II that the sultans learnt the lessons of the rebellions which had shaken the empire in the early 15th century and concluded that only slaves with indissoluble ties to their rulers could safely be entrusted with executive power. Despite the protests of well-born Turks, the system continued to develop until, at the time of its apogee under Suleiman, all the Grand Viziers without exception were Islamicized Christian slaves.

Ten Sultans Born for Conquest

The Turkish army also owed its almost uninterrupted successes to the men who commanded it: the Ottoman sultans. 'No European dynasty produced ten sovereigns of such remarkable talents in two and a half centuries.'[15] All possessed the qualities which turn men into conquerors: a talent for command, organizational ability, and the diplomatic skills shown by Osman and Orhan, the founders of the empire. Murad I, one of the dominating figures of the 14th century, was a wise and cunning warrior chief; Mehmed I rebuilt the state after the disastrous defeat at Ankara; Murad II defeated the last Christian coalition at Varna; and Mehmed II, conqueror of Constantinople, was – with Suleiman – the most powerful figure in Turkish history.

Mehmed II aimed at nothing less than world power. Considered a butcher and the Antichrist by the Christians, he was acclaimed by the Turks as their greatest leader. Under his authority, the whole world would be united. He realized the age-old Islamic dream of avenging Moawiya[16] – the first Omayyad caliph, who had been forced to lift his siege of Constantinople in 677 – and wanted to go further, to outdo Caesar and Alexander the Great. His death at the age of 52 probably saved Europe from conquest. At the time he controlled the whole Balkan peninsula and Trabzon in Asia, the last scrap of the Byzantine Empire to be wrenched from the Comnenus family. Apart from the principality of Zulcadir, the whole of Anatolia to the Euphrates was his, as were the southern Crimean ports. His two setbacks – at Belgrade and Rhodes – were avenged by Suleiman, his greatgrandson. Before that could happen, two other sultans, a skilled politician and a great warrior chief, had laid the foundations for Suleiman's string of major victories.

Bayezid II, the son of the Conqueror, was as deeply religious as his father was sceptical and dissolute. He even destroyed or sold in the bazaar all the Italian works of art Mehmed had brought to the palace. He felt no great enthusiasm for war beyond what was politically necessary. His first struggle was with his brother Cem, who took refuge with the Knights of Rhodes after his defeat in Anatolia and became a sort of hostage of the Christian princes and the Pope. Fearing that the enemy powers could use

Cem as a weapon against the Ottoman Empire, Bayezid embarked on no major offensives but put his energies into organizing the administration and developing the economy. Later sultans reaped the fruits of his efforts.

In 1495, Cem died in mysterious circumstances near Naples.[17] This brought an end to the long truce which had confined Turkish military activities to routine operations in Moldavia and the area around the Danube. A war with Venice erupted at once, since the two powers were rivals in the Adriatic and the Republic dominated the coast.[18] The Christians were amazed to see ships flying the sultan's flag cutting through the Adriatic for the first time and were soon defeated in several sea battles. Mehmed II had started to build up a fleet, but Bayezid now had a far larger one,[19] making the Ottomans more than a match for their adversaries.

The days when Venice could lay down the law unopposed in the Mediterranean were numbered. Lepanto surrendered to the sultan; Modon, Koron and Navarino were captured. By land, the Ottoman units of Bosnia devastated Venetian possessions as far as Vicenza. In Dalmatia and in the Aegean too, the Republic suffered major setbacks. At the end of 1502, Venice was compelled to sign a humiliating peace treaty, agreeing to give up some of the places occupied by the Ottomans and to pay tribute for Zante. It meant an end to the Venetians' domination of the seas, although they retained their commercial privileges.

The Ottoman Empire was now a major power in the Mediterranean, the equal at sea of the nations who would for so many years be its enemies or allies: the Spanish, the French, the Venetians, and later the English and the Dutch. Its conquests in the Peloponnese could be used for further advances to the West and the North; soon privateers also joined the Turkish side, bringing ships and unparalleled experience at sea. It was during the reign of Bayezid that the Ottomans took their place on the European stage. In the Italian Wars, the Porte took the side of Milan and Naples against the French and Venetians. A few decades later, the French allied themselves with the sultan: what had once been a tiny kingdom on the steppes was now a major player in the European balance of power. It was the intelligent political manoeuvring of Bayezid II which had prepared the way.

Selim the Grim ruled only from 1512 to 1520 – but what a reign! Those few brief years saw so many decisive events – Egypt and Syria conquered, the Sophy defeated – which had so lasting an impact on the destiny of the empire that it is hard to assess Selim's personal contribution. Only a few months after he had eliminated his enemies and his father and then defeated the last of his brothers, Selim prepared to attack Shah Ismail, the Safavid sovereign of Persia.

In a short space of time, Ismail had become the clear leader of a heretical sect formed of a strange mixture of Islamic, Kurdish, pre-Islamic and Turkish elements. Relying on the support of the Kizilbaş, fanatical Turkomans who were violently opposed to the sultan because he had encroached on their privileges (particularly with regard to taxes), Ismail had extended his territory from Eastern Anatolia as far as Baghdad and the Amu-Darya. He had stirred up revolts even in the Aegean region and had supported Ahmed, Selim's brother, after the death of Bayezid.

There was thus every reason for Selim to try and eliminate such a dangerous enemy: a heretic of the worst kind, a trouble-maker in the Ottoman Empire and a potential ally of the European powers, which were always ready to seize any chance to destroy the enemy of Christianity. Even under Bayezid, Ismail had offered troops to the Senate of Venice to support an attack on the Ottomans. That offer had, as it happens, been refused, but they or another enemy power could certainly accept a similar offer in the future. Before taking to the field, Selim eliminated this danger by renewing a peace treaty with Venice. He also got the chief *ulema* (the *şeyhulislam*) to issue a judgement (*fetva*) condemning Shah Ismail and his supporters. The Kizilbaş chiefs of Anatolia were immediately arrested and executed. Then, at the head of his army, the sultan set out for Azerbaijan.

The war was no military parade. Selim's troops mutinied several times and he came close to defeat. In the end, though, Shah Ismail joined battle at Chaldiran, in the region between Tabriz and Lake Van. On 23 August 1514, the Ottomans' firearms gave them victory and Shah Ismail was crushed. His successors in the 16th and 17th centuries were never again willing to face the Ottomans in pitched battle.

Selim had won an immense victory. His prestige was re-established in Anatolia. But the Safavid danger had been averted rather than destroyed. Unable to root it out completely, the sultan proceeded instead, with his customary ruthlessness, against the Shiites[20] of Anatolia; he took control of the few remaining areas he had not yet conquered (the principality of Zulcadir) and which gave him access to Syria, the route to the South. Finally, he subdued the Kurdish lords, who still upheld Safavid authority. In 1515, therefore, the Ottomans controlled all the principal trading and strategic routes towards Iran, the Caucasus and the Levant.

The next year, Selim decided to seal the fate of the Mamluk Empire. Learning that the sultan of Cairo, Kansuh al-Ghouri, had joined forces with the Safavids and that an army led by the Mamluk sultan had already left Cairo, Selim set out on 5 June 1516. Five weeks later, he met up with the troops led by the Grand Vizier Sinan Pasha. He ordered his men to make for Kansuh's army, which had already marched North out of Aleppo. The battle took place on 24 August at Marj Dabik. The Mamluks were defeated and their sultan killed. Four days later, Selim entered Aleppo and, in the presence of Caliph al-Mutawakil,[21] the last of the Abbasids, took for himself in the Great Mosque the title of 'Protector of the Two Sacred Sanctuaries' (Mecca and Medina) which had been claimed by the Mamluk sultans up to that time. On 9 October he reached Damascus and made Syria an Ottoman province – it was to remain so for four centuries. Now the road through the Nile valley was open to the Turkish conqueror.

When he had set out to fight the Ottomans, Kansuh had left Tuman Bey, one of the most respected Mamluk dignitaries, as his regent in Cairo. On the death of Kansuh, Tuman declared himself sultan and proceeded to improve Cairo's defences. He also constructed an entrenched camp at Ridanya, which was protected with guns and ditches lined with spears. This cunning stratagem might well have proved successful if Mamluk deserters had not revealed it to Selim. He therefore changed his plans and started the battle with an exchange of artillery. The poor quality of the Mamluk cannons proved disastrous, and the ensuing mêlée soon turned to the Ottomans' advantage. Tuman ordered his troops to retreat to Cairo, which he hoped to defend more easily with the whole population in arms behind the strong city walls.

The battle was fierce, the city conquered one house at a time. It lasted three days and nights as more and more corpses piled up in streets red with blood. On 30 January 1517, the Mamluks surrendered. Tuman managed to escape and led 4,000 horsemen in an attack on the Turkish forces South of Alexandria. Taken prisoner, he was brought back to Cairo and hanged at one of the city gates. Selim was master of Egypt. He appointed a governor and accepted the surrender of the Arab emirs, the Druze chiefs and the Christian lords of Lebanon. He reduced the customs duties and excessive rates of taxation which the Mamluks had imposed.

Now Selim, the successor of the Mamluks, was also master of the Eastern Mediterranean. He received the keys to the Holy Cities and the submission of the Sharif of Mecca. This event, which was to have profound consequences, opened a new era in Ottoman history. From now on, the sultan in Istanbul was not just the ruler of a frontier state but the sovereign chosen by God to protect the whole Islamic world. His prestige outshone by far that of all the other Muslim leaders, who were duty bound to submit to him just as he was now obliged to defend Islam against its enemies.[22]

Selim's successors were able to reap the political benefits of this change; Suleiman was the first to call himself 'Inheritor of the Great Caliphate', 'Possessor of the Exalted Imamate' and 'Protector of the Sanctuary of the Two Revered Holy Cities'. Ottoman jurists laid down the principle that the sultan had a right to the titles of Imam and Caliph because it was he who maintained the Faith and defended the *Şeriat* (Islamic law). Fresh obligations were thus incumbent upon the sultan of Constantinople – and the first was to extend the dominance of the House of Osman over the whole world of Islam.

The greatest of the *gazi* warriors, the sultan now had a responsibility constantly to advance the frontiers and laws of orthodox Sunni Islam. Religion acquired a more and more important place in the administration of the Ottoman state. In the following centuries, religion came to be controlled by a caste which, eager to retain its privileges, often acted as a barrier to the modernization of the empire. Because they always remained in contact with the earliest urban civilizations and the major currents of Islamic theology and law, and had exclusive dealings with the great Sunni religious centres, the Ottomans fought ceaselessly against every form of heresy. Yet by shutting out the Shiites in this way, they cut themselves off still further from their Asiatic origins and the civilizations of the steppes with which they had once been so closely linked.

Ottoman control of the countries of the Levant and the Nile naturally brought them pre-eminence and prestige in the Muslim world. But it also did much more. It put them in contact with the Red Sea and the Indian Ocean. It gave them greater access to the Mediterranean and North Africa and the economic and financial means which a great power needs to set out on a policy of conquest and expansion.

Selim and his successors now controlled transit centres which were among the richest in the known world. Portuguese penetration into the area, as we shall see,[23] sometimes acted as a considerable nuisance in the trade between India, Malaysia and the islands of the Indian Ocean, on the one hand, and the major commercial centres of the Red Sea and Eastern

Mediterranean, on the other. But such trade never came to a complete standstill. Money coming in from customs duties and various taxes levied on the passage of spices, cloth and precious goods continually made a large contribution to the resources of the Ottoman treasury. Thanks to taxes, tribute payable by local chiefs and the Ethiopian and Sudanese gold carried along the Nile, the sultans' revenues doubled within a few years. Almost to the end of his reign, Suleiman financed without difficulty major military campaigns and countless monuments.

After his return from the Levant, Selim spent two further years in Istanbul. He reorganized the administration and *devşirme* system of recruitment with the same feverish activity and authoritativeness that he showed in all his activities. His major concern, however, was to modernize and build up his fleet. He built a new arsenal at Kasimpasha on the Golden Horn and enlarged those of Gallipoli and Kadirga. When Barbarossa offered to put his ships and corsairs at his disposal, he accepted without hesitation. That decision was destined to have a profound effect on the fortunes of the Ottoman Empire at sea.

When Selim died in 1520, almost all the countries to the South of the Danube – Wallachia, Moldavia and Rumelia – were already under Ottoman control. Albania and the Peloponnese had been annexed by the sultan, and the khan of Crimea was his vassal. In the Orient, the Mamluks had been crushed and Shah Ismail defeated – no further dangers remained. With the strongest army of its day and a flourishing economy, the Ottoman Empire was about to experience the reign of its most glorious sultan: Suleiman.

Part One
The Sultan of Sultans

1
The *Padishah*'s First Triumphs

Suleiman I – 'the Magnificent' to Europeans, 'the Lawgiver' to the Turks – was born in Trabzon (Trebizond), on the shores of the Black Sea, probably on 6 November 1494. In the very same year, his father, Prince Selim, took over as governor of the province, which had been conquered from the Comneni about three decades earlier by Mehmed II. Thanks to its position between the Greek world, the Caucasus and the Islamic countries, this major market town at the crossroads of several caravan routes had long enjoyed prosperity and finally collapsed more as a result of internal squabbles than from Muslim attacks. Abandoned by his allies, David, the last emperor, made over the keys of the city to the sultan on 15 August 1461. He was taken as a prisoner to Istanbul and executed a few years later.

The Shadow of the Father

The governorship of the province of Trabzon (which had been the last Byzantine territory in Asia) was of particular importance because of its proximity to Safavid Iran, which put out a constant stream of Shiite and anti-Ottoman propaganda throughout Eastern Anatolia. It was here that Selim spent fifteen years and thus became aware of the threat to the empire the heresy represented.

The former capital of the Comneni was a beautiful town spread over a series of hills which overlooked the sea and were separated by deep ravines. The last Byzantine emperors had built churches – some of them still survive – colonnades, markets and luxurious dwellings, all surrounded by a strong city wall. The imperial palace dominated the town, and it was probably here that Selim resided and that Suleiman was born.

We know hardly anything about the childhood of the future sultan, because nothing marked his father out as heir to the throne. Suleiman himself also seems to have had brothers who were executed much later.[1] There was thus no reason for Ottoman chroniclers to relate the childish exploits of Suleiman in particular, and stories of the early years of royal princes were, in any case, hardly one of their specialities. Besides, they knew little more about them than we do.

His mother, Hafsa Hatun, is believed to have been the daughter of Mengli Giray, the khan of the Crimean Tartars. The khans married Circassian women fairly often, which explains Suleiman's Circassian features. She was apparently as intelligent as she was beautiful and was 17 years old at the time of Suleiman's birth. She was also the last of the sultan's royal wives; those who succeeded her were mostly slaves. Through her, the blood of Genghis Khan ran in Suleiman's veins since the Crimean khans were descended from Jochi, the eldest son of the conqueror of Asia.

Suleiman's childhood no doubt resembled that of all the other princes of the House of Osman – and most of the children of the upper classes – at the time. In his earliest years, he was looked after exclusively by his mother and her women servants. When he reached the age of 7, his father took personal control of his education. Selim was far from tender-hearted, and it is safe to assume that he brought up his son with great severity. A *hoca*,[2] well known for his wisdom and piety, also oversaw his studies.

His teachers taught him the Koran, reading and writing, arithmetic and music. They introduced him to physical exercise such as archery, which played a major role in the life of a young man. Around the age of 11, after being circumcised, he left his mother and the women's quarters. A residence, servants and a budget were allotted to him. A tutor (*lala*) looked after his intellectual and physical education. Like all well-born young Turkish men of his age, Suleiman will have read the best-known books of the day: *The History of the Forty Viziers, The History of Sinbad the Philosopher, Kalila and Dimna* (the famous novel of Indian origin), *The 1,001 Nights* translated into Turkish and the chronicle of *Seyyid Battal*

(Battal the Valiant), a real person, descended from the Prophet, whose courageous and adventurous life formed the basis of one of the earliest Anatolian Islamic epics. He certainly learnt Arabic, Mohammed's language, and Persian. Since he possessed a gift for languages, he also proved able, when he became sultan, to converse with the members of his entourage who were of Balkan origin. In Ottoman society, princes were taught how to work with their hands: like his father, Suleiman learnt the skills of the goldsmith.

When he reached the age of 15, his grandfather Sultan Bayezid II, as was the established custom for Ottoman princes, appointed him as a provincial governor (*sancakbey*). The governorship of Karahisar (Şebinkarahisar[3]) was thus granted to him, but his uncle Ahmed – then heir to the throne – considered this small town to be too close to Amasya, where he himself was governor; Suleiman was therefore sent to Bolu. Then Ahmed pointed out that Bolu was on the road from Amasya to Istanbul, and it detracted from his dignity for his brother's son – and thus his rival – to be appointed there. He was particularly afraid that on the day the throne became vacant, Suleiman might cut off his route to the capital. Finally, on 6 August 1509, the young prince left for Caffa (Theodosiya) in the Crimea, where he was to spend three years.

Caffa had long been a major Genoese trading post. It was there that some of the produce of India and Iran – spices, silk, cotton – ended up, whence they were transported by sea to the Mediterranean and sold all over Europe. It also possessed the dismal privilege of having been the starting point for the Black Death, which was brought by caravan from Central Asia around 1345 and then spread by way of Genoa throughout Europe, claiming millions of victims. Mehmed II had conquered the town, along with the rest of the Crimea in 1475, and had kept the khan, Mengli, in power there as a vassal of the Ottoman Empire. Some years later, his daughter had married one of Mehmed's grandsons – Selim, the father of Suleiman.

The Law of Fratricide

Bayezid had not intended that Selim in particular, rather than one of his other sons, should inherit his empire. When the problem of succession arose, his five living sons all laid claim to the throne. Ahmed, the eldest, was a skilful politician, loved by the people though hardly by the janissaries. Korkud, more of a poet and a mystic than a soldier, was also unpopular with the janissaries. Selim, on the other hand, had their support, because of his tastes and the military talent he had already shown in attacking the Safavids. Soon the other two brothers died, leaving Ahmed, Korkud and Selim to fight it out. They each prepared for battle by obtaining governorships of provinces near Istanbul, so they could intervene rapidly when the succession crisis occurred. Selim assured himself of the support of the Crimean Tartars whose khan was his father-in-law. It was there that Suleiman came to his aid.

It took three years of fighting for Selim to achieve victory. Korkud revolted against his father in Asia, as did Selim in Europe. Defeated at Edirne, he had to seek refuge in the Crimea. At this point, however, Ahmed took up arms in turn and the sultan called on Selim, who brought about a spectacular intervention of the janissaries to compel Bayezid to give up his throne. The old sultan abdicated and set off to retire in Demotika, his place of birth. Death surprised him *en route*, a death by natural causes 'helped along', it is said, 'by poison'.

Once Selim had become sultan, he had Korkud and the children of his other brothers strangled, then defeated Ahmed in battle and had him killed in the same way. It is said that when Korkud learnt of the sentence he sent his brother a poem accusing him of cruelty. The new sultan read it, apparently, with tears in his eyes.

After all these executions the House of Osman consisted only of the sultan himself and his children. There were several daughters, of whom one married the Grand Vizier Lutfi Pasha, another the vizier Mustafa Pasha, and a third, Hadice, married Ibrahim Pasha (who became Grand Vizier under Suleiman); there was only a single son, Suleiman – it is safe to assume that there had been other sons[4] who had already been executed.

Suleiman was now 17. His father appointed him Governor (*kaymakam*) first of Istanbul and then of Sarukhan (Manisa) on the Aegean Sea. He was to remain there until his accession to the throne except at the time of the Iranian campaign, when his father gave him governorship of Edirne and then Istanbul. At Manisa, his main task was to fight banditry. The internal disputes which preceded and accompanied Bayezid's abdication had deeply shaken that prosperous region, even though it was very close to the capital. It was Suleiman who managed to restore law and order. He thus acquired experience of government and administration which would prove very useful, particularly when he had to draw up the codes of law – *Kanunname* – which bear his name.

At Manisa, he was safe from the rage and suspicions of his fearsome father. It is said that Selim tried to do away with him by sending him a poisoned shirt, but that his mother made sure a page put it on instead; the unfortunate servant collapsed at once. No reliable source confirms this story, although Selim was certainly capable of anything.

Selim died suddenly while travelling from Istanbul to Edirne. The few people who were witnesses or learnt of his death – the Grand Chamberlain, the chief treasurer – all agreed to keep it a secret until Suleiman arrived. They convinced the viziers and other leading dignitaries to do the same. If news of the sovereign's decease had been widely broadcast, the janissaries would probably have caused a good deal of disorder, which the new sultan could have suppressed only with great difficulty and at great cost. A messenger was sent to Suleiman. The young prince is said to have waited for confirmation of the news before setting off for the capital, where the Grand Vizier Piri Pasha had preceded him. He was afraid that it was just a subterfuge of his father's which could cost him his life. When the janissaries were finally informed, they threw their bonnets on to the ground in grief but did not cause any trouble. The funeral cortège then set off for Constantinople.

On Sunday 30 September 1520, Suleiman arrived at Uskudar (Scutari), on the Asiatic coast of the Bosphorus. He immediately set out on three galleys, which took him and his entourage to the Seraglio where the Grand Vizier was waiting for him. The next morning, at dawn, the *şeyhulislam*, the *ulema* and the other chief dignitaries came to pay homage to him in the *Divan* (or council) chamber, then the new sultan went to Edirne Kapi to rejoin the funeral cortège. He followed it on foot as far as the fifth hill and ordered that a mosque be built there in honour of his father, who would rest in peace in a neighbouring tomb.

Like the Heavenly Dew . . .

The first act of Suleiman's reign, as usage demanded, was to make an accession gift to the janissaries. They each asked for 5,000 *akçe*[5] (aspers). In fact, they received 3,000 but their pay was increased. The other soldiers also received gratuities and pay rises. The dignitaries who had taken his side when he was heir to the throne were recompensed too. The new sultan wished to make clear at once that his would be a reign of justice and tolerance.

The eight years under Selim had been a long reign of terror. He was intelligent, cultivated (some of his verses count among the most beautiful in Ottoman poetry), a bold conqueror and a skilful politician, but he far outdid early members of the House of Osman in his willingness to execute people on all sides. He almost certainly hastened on his father's end and executed all the males in his family, apart from Suleiman. 'Is it not permitted to put to death two-thirds of the inhabitants of the empire for the greater good of the remaining third?' he once asked the Grand Mufti, who refused to give his approval to a sentence condemning to death 400 traders who had not obeyed his edict forbidding commerce with Persia.

After this long bloodbath, Suleiman's first acts of clemency appeared 'like the heavenly dew on a sunny plain'. The sultan immediately ordered the release of 600 notables and Egyptian traders deported to Istanbul by his father. Foreign merchants whose goods had been confiscated were indemnified. Persian traders and artisans brought to Turkey after the Battle of Chaldiran were allowed to return home. Freedom of trade with Iran was re-established. Within weeks, the arbitrary decisions of Selim and his entourage were abrogated and those responsible punished. The chief admiral (*kapudan pasha*), Cafer Bey – known as 'the Bloodthirsty' because of his acts of cruelty – was hanged. From the first days of his reign, Suleiman made everybody understand that his empire would be governed with a firm but just hand. 'My sublime commandment,' he wrote to the Governor of Egypt, 'as inescapable and as binding as fate, is that rich and poor, town and country, subjects and tribute payers – everyone must hasten to obey you. If some of them are slow to accomplish their duty, be they emirs or fakirs, do not hesitate to inflict on them the ultimate punishment.'

When he put on the sword of Osman in 1520, Suleiman was 25. We possess several descriptions of him at the time, including one by the Venetian ambassador, Bartolomeo Contarini: 'He is tall but thin, with a delicate complexion. His nose is a little too long, his features fine and his nose aquiline. He has the shadow of a moustache and a short beard. His general appearance is pleasing, although he is a little pale.'[6] This verbal portrait corresponds fairly closely with the profile drawn by Albrecht Dürer in 1526. Dürer, who never actually met him, based his picture on descriptions which the Venetians had given him. Another picture by Hieronymus Hopfer of a slightly later date is almost exactly the same as Dürer's, although it shows the opposite profile. These portraits are also fairly close to the picture reproduced on the cover of this book, in which Suleiman appears slightly older.[7] All reveal a hooked nose above a short upper lip, a prominent chin and small ears. His neck is long and thin. There is also a striking resemblance between Suleiman and his great-grandfather,

Mehmed the Conqueror, whose portrait by Gentile Bellini[8] survives. Suleiman's expression is severe, and this is emphasized by his habit of wearing his turban very low, just above his eyes. His calm and sang-froid are the complete opposite of his father's violent and irritable personality. His attitude is distant and possesses a natural majesty very fitting in a *padishah* who, like his grandfather, had world rule in mind.

The new sultan was a pious Muslim, but completely unfanatical. His attitude towards the Shiites, at least at the beginning of his reign, makes this quite clear. He was also tolerant towards Christians, as the Islamic religion demands, provided they carried out their obligations, such as paying taxes. Apart from that, the religion of his non-Islamic subjects was a matter of complete indifference to him.

When Suleiman came to power, the Ottoman Empire enjoyed enormous wealth and an unrivalled position in the Islamic world. With the Mamluk Empire crushed and Egypt and Syria annexed, the *padishah*'s prestige as caliph and protector of the Holy Cities was immense. The treasures of the sultans of Cairo and the revenues of both Egypt and Syria now belonged to him. The Safavids were no longer a threat – at least for the time being – and the defeats inflicted on the Venetians by sea, towards the end of Bayezid's reign, made it clear to the Christian powers that the Turks would prove a formidable adversary. Selim had managed to make the Turkish army the greatest of its time. Furthermore, Suleiman was no novice in the art of governing men, since he had already spent some ten years at the head of various provinces.

Thus, a future of immense promise already stretched out before the young sultan, the tenth of his dynasty – and ten, the number of fingers on two hands and of Mohammed's companions, is considered a perfect number by Muslims. Suleiman's name had been given to him at birth by opening the Koran at random – but was it not the name of one of the rulers of antiquity most venerated in the Orient, the King Solomon to whom God had granted, as to David, 'Wisdom and Knowledge'?[9]

The First Rebellion in the Empire

Suleiman had taken precautions to deal with all possible rivals in advance. There were none left in the imperial family since Selim's great massacres. The janissaries were happy with the money they had received and the promises they had been given and the population and traders were delighted to see a young man on the throne blessed with so many remarkable qualities. The established authority was quite secure in

Istanbul and the neighbouring provinces. It was in Egypt, unexpectedly, that a rebellion broke out. In the Orient as in Europe, there was no shortage at that time of men desperately eager for power. It was fairly easy for a strong personality to get hold of money and men in an attempt to take control of a principality here or there. A leading dignitary of the Porte tried to do just that.

When Selim had conquered Egypt, an emir called Canberdi al-Ghazali had betrayed Tuman, the Mamluk sultan, to the advantage of the Ottomans. In return, Ghazali had been appointed Governor of Syria. But he was no more sincerely committed to the sultan of Constantinople than he had been to the sultan of Cairo. He started by occupying the citadel of Damascus, then Beirut, Tripoli and all the coast between them. He then proposed to the Governor of Egypt, Hayra Bey, that they should join forces. 'Certainly!' replied the latter. 'Seize Aleppo and everything will be easy. I will send you some of my troops.' But, at the same time, he revealed Ghazali's plan to Suleiman. Ghazali fell straight into the trap. He laid siege to Aleppo for a month and a half with 15,000 horsemen and 8,000 archers, but without success. Meanwhile, the troops the sultan had sent on forced marches under the command of Ferhad Pasha arrived. Ghazali lifted the siege and turned back towards Damascus. He proclaimed himself sultan. But Ferhad Pasha had now reached the walls of the city with 40,000 horsemen and a large force of artillery. Ghazali, seeing that all was lost, joined battle, but since the Ottoman army was eight times stronger, he was decisively defeated; he died a few days later while being pursued.

The government of Syria was given to Ayas Pasha, the *ağa* (chief) of the janissaries under Selim I. Meanwhile, Ferhad Pasha turned back to Aksaray, in Central Anatolia, where he could keep an eye on the movements of the Safavid army. Shah Ismail had been informed in advance about the imminent rebellion by Ghazali, to whom he had made promises and encouraging noises. Indeed, he had rapidly assembled troops in case the success of the plot gave him a chance to avenge Chaldiran. All his efforts, however, came to nothing and he therefore sent a message to Suleiman congratulating him on his success in Syria, as Oriental protocol required.

After a few years relations between the two empires again became tense. Suleiman constantly had to keep in mind the presence on his eastern flank of an adversary who could launch an attack at any time. At the start of his reign, he showed great skill in dealing with Ismail – so that no conflict could arise there while he was occupied with fighting in Europe.

The Enemy of Charles V

Suleiman sat very secure on his throne; it was now that the western policy of the Ottomans began to take shape. The young sultan had prepared himself for this for a long time. As heir to the throne he had taken immense pains to learn about the policies of the major European states and about their sovereigns, armies and commercial relations. He made efforts to meet the foreign envoys, particularly the Venetian *bailo* (or representatives in Constantinople). The capital of the empire was a very important trading centre at the crossroads of two continents, and in the 16th century, as today, intelligence-gathering flourished there. Almost all the people who surrounded the sultan were Islamicized Christians, Slavs, Greeks or Albanians. 'A chancellery using Slavonic languages functioned alongside one which used Turkish and Greek.'[10] The royal Seraglio was thus very open to the outside world, and well informed about what was happening in Europe as well as Asia, thanks to the network of spies which the Porte retained in many places such as Venice.

The sultan knew that in 1519 – only two years earlier – the death of Maximilian had led to a bitter contest for the crown of the Holy Roman Empire between Francis I of France and the Habsburg king, Charles V. The latter – whom Suleiman always referred to as 'the King of Spain' and never recognized as emperor – managed to win this contest by borrowing vast sums of money in bills of exchange from the Fugger firm of financiers. But the sultan also knew that the election of Charles made pressure for a new crusade far stronger in Europe and that, despite the failure of successive schemes launched by the Pope and various sovereigns, there was a real danger that the whole of Christendom might unite against him.[11] The Lateran Council which met in 1512–17 discussed a new crusade and Leo X's Papal Bull *Postquam ad universalis* had also encouraged princes and sovereigns to prepare for a Holy War against the Turks.

The Great Lord in Constantinople was not afraid. Certainly the weak, poor and divided states of old Europe had given way to kingdoms possessing great military power, vast finances and many men who lacked neither courage nor resolution. But his own forces were far superior to those of any of these states taken separately. The countries of Europe were also divided by many religious disputes – the Reformation had just begun in earnest – which increased still further their lack of unity. Nonetheless, the idea of a crusade was always present. Whatever their disagreements, the Christian kings and princes were agreed on one thing: they wanted to make war against the Turks.

For Suleiman, the danger was all too real. At the head of Christian Europe, now, was Charles V, who as Holy Roman Emperor wore the crowns of Spain, the Two Sicilies, the Low Countries and Austria. An instransigent Catholic, he believed that his first duty was to unite the other sovereigns and lead them in a combat against the Infidels. Like the rest of Europe, he had thought that Suleiman was in his element at court and not on the battlefield. But Charles quickly discovered that the young prince, who had lived so long in the shadow of his terrible father, was deeply ambitious and a soldier of great ability, and this made him all the more convinced that a crusade was necessary.

On one side, therefore, we have Suleiman who saw a Europe ruled by powerful sovereigns who dreamed of destroying him; on the other are Charles V and the kings and princes longing for a chance to fall on the Turks and drive them back into Asia. The sultan, fired by ambition and his sense of his duty as a *gazi*, was led to fight almost ceaselessly to increase the territory of Islam and to reduce the danger that Christendom constantly posed for him; meanwhile, the Europeans fought to try and stop the conquering Infidel in his tracks, to expel him from their continent and, if possible, to destroy him. This broad picture is obviously lacking in nuances: as the events unfolded day by day, things were, of course, rather less simple.

In the Mediterranean, there were many fierce disputes over the control of the North African ports. Throughout his reign, Charles V tried to establish the Spanish frontier on the southern side of the Mediterranean, faithful to the idea of Isabella the Catholic who always claimed that the *Reconquista* would be complete only when the Western Mediterranean had become 'a Spanish lake'. At least for the moment, however, the main theatre of operations was elsewhere. Charles soon became convinced that, now Selim's eastern interlude had come to an end, the Ottomans would continue their thrust towards the North – into Europe.

What obstacle or barrier could be put in their way? Charles decided to entrust the defence of Central Europe to his brother Ferdinand, who shared with him the heritage of Maximilian. In 1521, he married Ferdinand to Anne, the sister of King Lewis of Hungary; the following year, King Lewis himself married Ferdinand's sister. Charles's aim was for Ferdinand to become King of Hungary (and Bohemia) if Lewis died without issue; thus he would be able to extend his empire to the frontiers of the Slavonic world. This was a very feeble response to the Turkish danger, especially since Charles soon found himself caught up in Spain by the revolt of the Comuneros and in Germany by the storms of the Reformation – a most unexpected source of help to the Turks.

Charles was often in disagreement with his brother about the Turkish threat. His main objective was to re-establish Christian unity within the Holy Roman Empire, which was then in utter disarray. His dynastic aims centred on Burgundy and Italy, which his enemy for thirty years, Francis I, also claimed. His means were limited, as those of Maximilian had been and as those of the Habsburgs would always be. He remained completely deaf to the appeals of Pope Adrian VI, who asked him to make a two-year truce on his western flank so as to prepare for war against the Turks; in the same way, he almost always pushed aside the appeals of his brother. Totally preoccupied with European affairs and the religious disputes which, as a sincere Christian, obsessed him, Charles never had the opportunity to set in motion a full-scale confrontation with the Ottomans. He dreamed of retaking Constantinople at the head of a great Christian crusade, but it was a dream which neither he nor his successors realized. It was to be Suleiman's good fortune that he too never had the opportunity to push his ambitions as far as he wished: to meet Charles on the battlefield, defeat him and occupy Vienna and Rome.

The almost permanent conflict which broke out between the Ottomans and the Christian world in about 1520 lasted until the end of the century. The whole of Europe and the Middle East was involved: Venice and Genoa were directly concerned because of their possessions nearby and across the seas and therefore schemed without really committing themselves to either side; France soon understood the great advantage in having an eastern ally to protect it against the Germano-Spanish danger; while the Protestant princes of Germany were in two minds: tempted to profit from the Turkish counterweight in their struggles with the Catholic Emperor yet worried by the idea of making use, even indirectly, of the help of the Infidels. Finally, there was the Safavid dynasty in Persia, the political and religious enemy of the Ottomans. Such was the great power game which continued until the Battle of Lepanto – and even beyond, to the Turkish imperial peace of 1606.

The Conquest of Belgrade

At the end of the 14th century, the Bulgar and Serbian Empires had ceased to exist; in the following century, the Byzantine Empire had also collapsed; this left the kingdom of Hungary as the major enemy of the Ottomans in Eastern Europe. Under John Hunyadi and his son Matthias Corvinus, the country had played a full role as a bulwark against the Infidels. Corvinus had even drawn up plans to launch a crusade to expel the Turks from the Balkans. Since then, however, Hungary had been much weakened. The nobles elected a mediocrity, Ladislas Jagiellon, when Corvinus died. His successor, Lewis II, was equally ineffectual. Neither took advantage of the absence of the Ottomans in Persia and Egypt to put their country in order and prepare for war. Although the peace treaty signed in 1503 had not been openly violated, conflict had never ceased between the sultan's pashas and the King of Hungary's feudal lords. A single incident set the sparks ablaze: an envoy sent from Constantinople to demand payment of the annual tribute that Suleiman had proposed in return for a renewal of the peace treaty was assassinated by the Hungarians. The sultan was absolutely furious – and used the incident as an ideal pretext to start a war.

Preparations in Constantinople took up the whole winter of 1520. The *sipahi* of each province and irregular troops were called up. Requisition orders for the local guilds, provisions and animals were sent along the whole route the army was to follow. Roads and bridges were repaired.

Suleiman's objective was Belgrade, the gate-way to the countries around the Danube. Once the fortress there had been captured, the valleys of the Danube, the Sava and the Tisza would take his armies straight to Vienna and Buda. In the previous century, Mehmed II had been defeated before Belgrade; it was that disaster which Suleiman was determined to avenge.

Six weeks before the date fixed for the departure of the army, two of the six horse-tail banners (*tuǧ*), insignia of the supreme power, were raised in the first court of the imperial palace. When that period had elapsed, the banners were carried in solemn state to Davud Pasha, the first encampment outside Istanbul, where the janissaries, the other regiments and the team of artisans who always accompanied the army on campaign were assembled.

Everything made it clear to the Hungarians that a new wave of Turkish invaders was imminent. They sought help from their fellow Europeans, who failed them completely: Venice, which was about to conclude a highly advantageous commercial treaty with the Porte; the Pope, who had other worries; the King of Poland; the Holy Roman Emperor – all found different excuses not to intervene. And indeed the Diet of Worms did have more important concerns: the very month when the Hungarian envoy asked for help, Luther had broken off all ties with the Catholic Church. Other things were far more pressing in Germany than the Turkish menace. Emperor Charles advised King Lewis of Hungary to gain time by signing a truce with the sultan – sound advice, if Suleiman had been thinking along the same lines, but that was very far from being the case.

On 6 February 1521, Suleiman left Constantinople for his first great expedition in full military array. The sultan's departure for war was always an imposing spectacle – a demonstration of power designed to impress other kings and emperors when their ambassadors reported back to them. The 6,000 horsemen of the imperial guard headed the procession. Mounted on thoroughbreds, with saddles and trappings sparkling in the sun, they were sumptuously dressed in velvet and silk and resplendent with gold. With bows on their shoulders, they carried in their right hand a short sword, and arrows and a shield in their left. There was a mace in their saddle while a scimitar embossed with jewels girded their chest. Black feathers floated above a head-dress of light blue cotton, but none of the helmets nor the armour in which so many Christian knights had perished or been taken prisoner. Behind them came the janissaries, all soberly dressed in uniforms of the same colour. They wore a tall bonnet with felt hanging down at the back and a feather or a spoon fixed on top. The whole troop marched past in silence.

Then came the palace dignitaries, the imperial guard and the footsoldiers, bow in hand. Stable boys led out magnificent horses with glittering harnesses. They preceded the sultan, who rode a splendid courser on such occasions. Dressed in a robe of embroidered silk, Suleiman wore on his head a tall turban surmounted with a spray of diamonds and precious stones. Three pages followed him, carrying a water-bottle, a cloak and a coffer. At the rear came the eunuchs in the sultan's private service and the noble guard: two hundred young men chosen from the sons of the great Turkish families or the vassals of the sultan. In battle, they would fight to the death to protect Suleiman.

The long line of Turkish troops always advanced in strict order. They raised camp at dawn and stopped at noon in a place chosen in advance, where everything had been prepared before the arrival of the sultan and his entourage. In the centre was the sultan's tent, as sumptuous as his palace suites, with those of the Grand Vizier and other leading dignitaries nearby. Sheets of cloth painted to look like walls were placed round this area, and the troops of the imperial house – the janissaries and Porte *sipahi* – camped outside. Further away were the provincial *sipahi* and the other troops. They would set off again the next morning. All the soldiers were ruled by an iron discipline which amazed the Christians: compensation was given for any damage to property; provisions were duly paid for; marauders were immediately executed.

By way of Edirne and Plovdiv, the army rapidly reached Sofia, where the vizier Ferhad Pasha soon arrived with several thousand camels carrying cannons and ammunition. The Christians of Sofia, Semendra and Vidin had to provide 10,000 wagons of wheat and barley. It was thus a very powerful army which moved North: one unit, commanded by Ahmed Pasha, made for Sabac on the river Sava; another aimed for Transylvania under Mehmed Mihaloğlu; a third column led by the Grand Vizier, Piri Pasha, took the direct route towards Belgrade. Suleiman met up with the troops marching towards Sabac.

Piri Pasha had been encamped before Belgrade for several weeks when Suleiman arrived with the rest of the army. Batteries were immediately set up on the island situated at the confluence of the Danube and the Sava. These were used for continual bombardment of the citadel, the usual Ottoman tactic. For three weeks, assaults succeeded each other in rapid succession but to no effect. Then, on the advice of a French or Italian 'renegade', Suleiman ordered that the fortress's largest tower be blown up. Several hundred Hungarians and Serbs heroically fought on, until 'religious hatred' – the former were Catholic and the latter Orthodox – led the Serbs to surrender on the condition that their lives would be spared. Most of the Hungarians were massacred. The Serbs, on the other hand, were taken to Constantinople and established nearby, on the site of ancient Pera, in the middle of a forest – still known today as the Forest of Belgrade – on the European shores of the Bosphorus. The main church in Belgrade, meanwhile, was turned into a mosque, where Suleiman recited the first Friday prayer.

Rumours of the successes of the Ottoman army spread rapidly across Europe. Envoys from Venice, Russia and Ragusa (present-day Dubrovnik) were the first to offer their congratulations to the sultan, yet the fall of one of the major strongholds of Eastern Europe, the bulwark of Christendom and 'gateway to Hungary', filled the Christian powers with fear and anxiety for the future. Thirty years later, Ghiselin de Busbecq, Ferdinand I's perceptive ambassador to Istanbul, would write: 'The capture of Belgrade was at the origin of the dramatic events which engulfed Hungary. It led to the death of King Lewis, the capture of Buda, the occupation of Transylvania, the ruin of a flourishing kingdom and the fear of neighbouring nations that they would suffer the same fate . . . These events should have taught the Christian princes to strengthen their fortifications and fortresses if they did not wish to perish. The Turkish armies are like powerful rivers swelled by rain which cause infinite destruction when they find ways of undermining the dikes which hold them back and rush into the breach . . . Thus the Turks, when they have broken through the barriers which contain them, unleash waves of devastation beyond comprehension.'

Not many years later, Suleiman again marched into the Danube territories. Once more, the Christians presented a spectacle of complete disunity and, defeated yet again, Hungary ceased to exist.

The Knights Expelled from Rhodes

Without losing time – hardly a year had passed since his accession to the throne – Suleiman prepared another expedition in a totally different direction: Rhodes. In doing so, he proved himself decisively to be a man quite unlike the incompetent voluptuary the Europeans had at first imagined.

In 1480, Mehmed the Conqueror had been defeated before the island ruled by the Knights of Saint John. Forty years later, Suleiman had even more reasons for wanting to put an end to the Order's domination of the Mediterranean. Installed in Rhodes since their departure from Saint John of Acre at the end of the 13th century, the warrior monks had built up a powerful military base from which to rove the neighbouring seas. Since they often plundered the coast of Asia Minor and Syria, they posed a permanent threat to the communication routes between Constantinople and Alexandria, which carried most of the trade between Egypt and the rest of the empire. Turkish commercial vessels were stopped, their cargo seized and crews taken prisoner. Muslim pilgrims who took the sea route to Mecca constantly ran the risk of being arrested, killed or taken into slavery. Christian corsairs, on the other hand, were given refuge and help by the Knights, who had even supported Canberdi al-Ghazali at the time of his recent revolt.

Suleiman decided to finish once and for all with this powerful menace situated only some 16 kilometres from the coast of Asia Minor. The second vizier, Mustafa Pasha, and Kurdoğlu Musliheddin Reis (a renowned sailor in whom he had great confidence) both urged him to undertake such an expedition at the first opportunity.

Suleiman soon ascertained that none of the Christian states would come to the aid of the Knights. Nobody in Europe, even less than at other times, was willing to sacrifice a single man, and far less a ship, to defend the island.

Only Francis I, if he had been able, would willingly have given help to the Knights. But circumstances prevented this at every opportunity. In 1518, he had sent Prégent de Bidoux and Chanoy to Rhodes on a mission to 'find out about and understand the Turk's plans, war against him, and inflict destruction and damage on him'. The next year, as the exact danger became clearer, he sent a small fleet to the Levant under the command of Chanoy, but he was killed in attacking Beirut. In June 1521, Philippe Villiers de l'Isle Adam was elected Grand Master of the Order of Saint John; before leaving France, he had a meeting with Francis, who promised to help him. But although the king did indeed almost immediately give orders to Bernardin to set out for the island with several ships, they were soon needed in the fight against Spain when war broke out with Charles V only a few weeks later. The new Grand Master could no longer hope for anything from the French king, who suffered defeat after defeat, nor, indeed, from Charles, who was also tied up in the skirmishing and the many problems posed by Luther's revolt and the agitation for social reform in Germany.

Suleiman had nothing to fear, except perhaps from Venice, the only state in the region with a fleet powerful enough to worry him. But while the shipyards of the Golden Horn were accelerating their production of Ottoman ships, the ambassador of the Republic, Marco Memmo, signed a treaty in thirty articles which was greatly to the advantage of Venetian trading interests. Certain terms of this treaty were incorporated 15 years later in the first 'capitulations' – or, rather, the first treaty – with France.[12] The Venetians, willing to make any concessions to safeguard their trade in the Mediterranean, agreed to pay the Porte a tribute of 10,000 ducats to retain possession of Cyprus and 5,000 ducats for Zante. They did send a squadron to observe the movements of the Turkish fleet, but it was ordered to return to base as soon as it was clear that Cyprus was not threatened. Thus the Christian powers of Europe, including the impoverished Pope Adrian VI, abandoned the Knights of Saint John to their fate.

Knowing that he would have to confront no enemy other than the Order itself, Suleiman wrote a letter (as Islamic law required) calling on Villiers de l'Isle Adam to surrender.[13] Four days later, Mustafa Pasha, appointed commander-in-chief (*serasker*) of the expedition, left Istanbul with a fleet – of 700 ships, according to the Ottoman historian Haci Halifa, 300 according to more reasonable estimates – carrying 10,000 men and heavy artillery. On the 18th of the same month, the sultan left Uskudar by the overland route with 100,000 men (many more, according to Christian sources). On 2 July, the *beylerbey* (governors) of Rumelia and Anatolia, Ayas Pasha and Kasim Pasha, met up with him at Kutahya; on the 28th, the huge army arrived at Marmaris, opposite Rhodes, where Suleiman disembarked, greeted, the chroniclers tell us, by all the siege artillery:[14] more than 100 guns 'including 12 immense cannons, the two most powerful of which shot boulders 11 to 12 palms in circumference'! The sultan inspected the installations and ordered the start of the operation.

The iron discipline which ruled among the Knights made the Order a formidable power. The defences of the town were divided into seven bastions, each put under the control of a 'nation'.[15] To the North, the assailants facing the French and German sectors were commanded by the *beylerbey* of Rumelia, Ayas Pasha; the third vizier, Ahmed Pasha, had to attack the sectors defended by the Knights of Spain and Auvergne. To the East, opposite the vizier and *serasker* Mustafa Pasha was the English bastion, where the attackers brought to bear the main brunt of their assault. The sultan pitched his tent there, on the heights of San Stefano, overlooking the sea. In front of the Provençal bastion to the South was the *beylerbey* of Anatolia, Kasim Pasha; next to him, facing the Italian bastion, was the Grand Vizier Piri Pasha. The Grand Master, Villiers de l'Isle Adam, had set up his general quarters near the church of Saint Mary the Victorious, not far from the port. He led about 7,000 men, including 650 Knights and 300 Genoese and Venetian sailors. The rest of his troops were very varied: they included the islanders themselves, who were provided with arms and eager to fight but not particularly experienced. A talented engineer and gunner from Lombardy, Gabriele de Martinengo, also fought alongside the Knights, but their supply of gunpowder and ammunition was quite insufficient to sustain a long siege.

On 1 August, the *beylerbey* of Rumelia opened hostilities. Twenty-one cannons simultaneously attacked the German bastion, which was commanded by a Knight called de Waldner, while 22 others aimed at the Saint Nicholas tower. Forty-two pieces of artillery were pointed at the English bastions and 50 at the Italian. All opened fire together, creating an absolutely infernal noise. On 4 September, a mine made a large breach in the English bastion. The assailants poured in and a terrible battle ensued, in the course of which, according to Bâtard de Bourbon, 2,000 Turks were killed. Six days later, another assault was equally inconclusive, but the defenders of the city lost the commander of their artillery, Guyot de Marsalhac. Attacks followed each other in quick succession without breaking the Knights' powers of resistance. Each time, they pushed back Ottoman assaults through breaches which the mines had made in their walls. Suleiman was determined to finish the job, while the Grand Master tried to gain time. He still hoped that the Christian powers might come to his aid.

On 23 September, Suleiman gave the orders for a general assault. The heralds cried out: 'Tomorrow, the assault! The stones and the soil belong to the *padishah*, but blood and booty will come to the conquerors!' At dawn, mines broke open more gaps in the city walls and the janissaries attacked all the bastions at once. On all sides they were forced back. That was the most terrible day of the whole siege. On that day, Bâtard de Bourbon notes, the whole town – the cloth and the laity – fought with extraordinary heroism. Women, showing contempt for every danger, brought bread and wine to the combatants or heavy stones to throw from the ramparts on to the heads of the assailants. According to Fontanus,[16] a Greek woman whose lover had been killed on the English bastion covered her children with kisses, stabbed them and threw them into the flames, saying: 'Neither in life nor in death will the Turks be able to violate you!' Then, wrapping the bloody coat of the man she had loved around her, she rushed into battle sword in hand and was immediately struck down.

The combat went on all day yet resulted in nothing but countless dead on both sides. The Turks had lost 45,000 men. Suleiman was furious at the setback and decided that the responsibility for it belonged to Ayas Pasha, who was immediately arrested and deprived of his rank. The next morning, when the sultan had calmed down again, he released Ayas and gave his post back to him. The main victim of the defeat was *serasker* Mustafa Pasha, the husband of Suleiman's sister, who was replaced immediately by Ahmed Pasha, the third vizier. Mustafa was sent to Egypt as Governor.

On 12 October, the Ottomans made a new attempt on the town, this time against the English bastion. But the *ağa* of the janissaries was wounded and Suleiman stopped the fighting. Two months of murderous fighting went by. On 30 November, an attack against the Spanish and Italian bastions left 3,000 Turkish dead. Ahmed Pasha decided to use only war machines and artillery for the time being. Ten days later, Suleiman offered to negotiate with the Grand Master: if the town was made over to him in three days, the garrison could go free; if they refused, 'not even the cats' would be spared. The Chapter of the Order, which had decided to surrender because the reserves of gunpowder and ammunition were running low, said that the offer did not give them time to consult with the whole population. Suleiman recommenced his bombardment and planted more mines. Villiers de l'Isle Adam – known as Mighali Masturi (Grand Master) by the Ottomans – tried to influence the sultan by a quite different method: he sent two Knights into the Turkish camp bearing a letter written by Suleiman's grandfather, Bayezid II, to the Grand Master, assuring him that the Order would keep Rhodes. *Serasker* Ahmed Pasha replied only by tearing the letter to shreds and sending them back with two Christian prisoners whose noses and ears he had cut off.

Villiers de l'Isle Adam decided at last to capitulate, 'deprived of hope and of the help we had called on so many times'.[17] A Knight and two islanders brought his terms to Suleiman, who accepted them: the Order would depart within twelve days, leaving fifty hostages (half of them Knights and half islanders) and the Turks would retreat a mile from the town. For five years, the Christians remaining in Rhodes would be exempt from taxes and from the *devşirme* (conscription of children into the imperial service). Suleiman was certainly sincere in promising that the island would be spared, but the janissaries managed to enter the town without arms and committed every possible kind of outrage: 'They proceeded to the great church of Saint John, where they scratched the frescos, broke up the tombs of the Grand Masters, scattered the ashes of the dead, dragged the crucifix in the dust, turned the altars upside-down. All these acts of extreme impiety were committed on Christmas morning.'[18] And yet the janissaries were soldiers very largely of Christian origin.

Next morning, Villiers de l'Isle Adam repaired to the sultan's camp, since Suleiman had let him know that he wished to see him. The Grand Master arrived at Suleiman's tent at dawn and was made to wait a long time, in the rain and snow, before being admitted to kiss the sultan's hand.

It was the first Wednesday since the capture of the city and the viziers and other dignitaries were solemnly granted an audience to congratulate Suleiman on his victory. At last Villiers de l'Isle Adam was introduced. The two men remained looking at each other in silence for a long time. Suleiman spoke first, 'consoled the Grand Master by saying it was the fate of princes to lose towns and provinces' and assured him he could freely leave the island whenever he wished. 'I am really distressed to have thrown that old man out of his palace,' Suleiman confided to the Grand Vizier.[18] On 1 January 1523, Villiers de l'Isle Adam came to kiss the sultan's hand again and offered him four golden vases. At midnight, he embarked with the survivors of the siege: fewer than 200 Knights and 1,600 soldiers. Several years later, the Order was re-established on Malta, granted them by Charles V, where they remained until the Napoleonic wars.

News of the fall of Rhodes was greeted with grief and consternation all over Europe. Cyprus was still in Venetian hands – but for how long? And what about the other islands of the Dodecanese? The danger was getting closer – soon nothing would remain of the Christian possessions in the Orient. The Doge of Venice, the only Christian prince to whom Suleiman had announced his victory, sent congratulations; we can easily guess what his true feelings were. The fall of Rhodes meant he would face terrible battles in the near future. He strengthened the defences in Cyprus and started to build up his fleet. What else could he possibly do?

The Cannons of the Mighty Turk

Thanks to his magnificent artillery, the sultan of Constantinople now controlled the most powerful and modern military machine in the known world; the Christian nations, well aware of the fact, were terrified. The enormous Turkish guns, often built with the help of Christians who knew the most up-to-date techniques, were famous throughout Europe. The Ottomans also bought cannons in Europe or used those they had captured from their Christian enemies: between 1521 and 1541, according to F. Braudel, 5,000 guns were taken in battle in Hungary. Francis I even sent some cannons to Suleiman at the time of his Hungarian expedition in 1543. Gun carriages had been introduced into Turkey by Marrano immigrants from Spain, but most of the gunnery was produced within the empire: in the Tophane (or foundry) district of Istanbul, which has retained the name to this day and where the gunners' barracks were also situated; and in other foundries and units scattered throughout the provinces. There were about a thousand artillerymen in all, plus specialists in mines, mortars and bombs, units involved in the transport of cannons (*topçu başi*), and so on.

It was their artillery power which assured Ottoman superiority over the rest of the Islamic world. We have seen Selim I relying on firearms to take control of Egypt and Syria. A few years later in Persia, Ottoman cannons pounded Tabriz for eight successive days until the city fell. For a long time, the Ottomans kept completely up-to-date with the latest developments in military science: their decline began when they refused to admit that the armaments which had won so many victories for them in the past had become obsolete.

But this was still a long way in the future in the early 16th century. No fortress could hold out against the cannons of the mighty Turk, nor any army against the regiments of janissaries or the squadrons of Porte *sipahi*, still less against the immense cavalry of the provincial *sipahi* or *timariotes*.

These *timariotes* were feudal knights or vassals subject to dismissal, who formed part of a complex feudal system: in return for the revenue from a plot of land (normally received in the form of a tax from the person who actually cultivated it), they were obliged to take up arms for the sultan whenever they were called upon.

The number of men and kind of equipment the *timariote* had to bring with him on campaign varied with the size of the *timar*. If the *timar* consisted in an annual income above 4,000 *akçe*, the *sipahi* had to be accompanied by a soldier in a coat of mail (*cebelu*); above 15,000 *akçe*, by a further man for each additional 3,000 *akçe*. A *subaşi* (captain or city governor) supplied one man for every 4,000 *akçe*, and the *sancakbey* (superior officer or district governor) one for every 5,000 *akçe*. The *sipahi* had to be armed, usually with a bow, a sword, a mace, a lance and a shield. Above a certain income (30,000 *akçe* for the *subaşi*, 50,000 for the *sancakbey*), he was also required to provide armour for his horse (*gecim*) made of very thin steel and in any case far lighter than that of Christian knights (there is one on display in the Metropolitan Museum in New York). He also had to bring with him tents (the number and kind depended on the revenue from his endowment). The leading *timariotes* brought tents with them which were used for many different purposes: as a treasury, kitchen, saddlery store, etc.

Thus all the equipment needed on campaign was determined in advance and the commanders knew exactly what forces and *matériel* they could count on when they mobilized the army. Some of the *timariotes*, with revenues of several hundred thousand *akçe*, brought whole squadrons with them. Under the command of the *subaşi*, all these men would assemble round the *bey*'s flag on an agreed day; when mobilization had thus been completed, the *bey* took command of the troops and led them to the muster, where they passed in review before the sultan. They were something between 50,000 and 200,000 in number and formed the light cavalry of the army, which drew up on the wings in the battle formation.

This *timar* system was based on the fundamental principle of the Ottoman Empire: land belonged to the state, but individuals were granted use of it in return for services rendered. The *timar*, in theory, were given by the Porte to soldiers who had distinguished themselves in combat. The *sancakbey* or *beylerbey* proposed somebody and, if the Porte agreed, drew up an attestation: the man's name was placed on a register, along with the size of the endowment.[19] A son could inherit his father's *timar*, with the administration's permission, only if he belonged to the military class or was one of the sultan's slaves (*kul*). But, at least in the early days, such inheritance was not automatic and there was no danger of creating a privileged class or embryo nobility in this way.

The *timar* could also be taken back from the title holder if he failed in his duties of service, did not present himself when the army mobilized or if he was guilty of treason, desertion, or misdemeanours such as criminal offences, impiety or ill treatment of his peasants (*reaya*). In other words, the endowment did not belong to him – he had constantly to deserve it (see Appendix 5).

More prestigious but fewer in number were the knights of the Porte, also called *sipahi* or *Alti Boluk Halki* (the Men of the Six Regiments). In the first rank were the *sipahi* or *sipahioğlan*, where the young men co-opted by the *devşirme* system who were considered more suited to military life than civil administration were sent (although this in no way prevented them from obtaining high rank in either the army or government). Next came the *silahdar*, who shared with the *sipahioğlan* the task of protecting the sultan during battle. Two other divisions, both divided into left and right sections, the *ulufeci* and the *gureba* (foreigners in the service of the Ottomans), were stationed on the outskirts of Constantinople and other towns. Each unit had an *ağa*, to whom the men were responsible. As opposed to the *sipahi timariotes*, the mounted soldiers received a fixed salary. At the time of Suleiman, there were about 15,000 of them, armed with bows, scimitars, lances and battle-axes.

More numerous – 30,000 in peacetime – were the *akinci*, the horsemen stationed near the frontiers in Europe. In time of war they were often joined by adventurers greedy for loot or, sometimes, by men who hoped to attract the attention of the commanders by some striking feat and be taken on as regular soldiers or even receive a *timar*. They lived on booty from raids into enemy territory or taxes they levied directly. The *azab* – about 12,000 in peacetime, three times as many during hostilities – helped defend the fortresses or served in the navy; they too were conscripted and drew a salary. The *derbentçi* were also local troops, responsible for guarding roads and fortresses, protecting caravans and maintaining bridges. Divided into units of 25–30 men who served in turn, they were paid by grants of land or exemption from taxes. Known also as *martolos* in Europe, they guarded the forts along the Danube and in Hungary when Suleiman had conquered the area.

Against such a force, so formidable in its day, the Christians had only badly armed and badly paid troops. German soldiers were no longer willing to fight in Hungary, where the wine was bad and the bread tasted like chalk. Lewis of Hungary and Ferdinand of Habsburg, terrified, feared the worst. They sent constant messages to Charles V, begging him to make peace on his western flank and to come to the aid of the countries of Eastern and Central Europe, especially Hungary. But the emperor wanted to deal with Francis first of all and impose on him his peace terms. Only afterwards would he turn to Hungary; for the moment, Italy and the religious disputes were far more important than the area around the Danube. It was as if Charles thought Suleiman incapable of carrying out a lengthy expedition far from his home base. He was not entirely mistaken, yet it was his brother Ferdinand and Lewis who saw things as they really were: if he did not come to help them, their kingdoms were doomed.

The Handsome Favourite

A few months after his return from Rhodes, Suleiman appointed as Grand Vizier Ibrahim, a Greek with whom he had long been on extremely friendly terms.

What an extraordinary and romantic career! A son of a fisherman still under 30 years of age when he attained the highest positions in the most powerful empire of his time, husband of the sultan's sister and almost his equal – only to be cut down one night, at the height of his prestige, caught in the trap laid by the mute servants of the Seraglio!

The man called Makbul (the favourite) and Maktul (the assassinated) by chroniclers was born in 1493 in Parga, a small village on the Adriatic coast opposite Corfu. Captured during a raid, he was offered to Suleiman by a Porte dignitary at Caffa. According to another, more plausible, account, pirates had captured him and sold him to a widow in Manisa, who, struck by the young man's intelligence and talents, had taught him many things. Desperately eager for instruction, he learnt to speak Italian, Turkish and Persian as well as his native Greek and played with supreme skill on an instrument like a violin. He was educated in the palace school in Istanbul and became a page in Suleiman's service when the latter was Governor of Manisa.

His vivacity and good looks – he was tall and thin – soon attracted the attention of the young prince. He rose through the ranks with astonishing speed, since Suleiman, of much the same age, soon offered him his friendship. When he became emperor, Suleiman made Ibrahim his chief falconer and then chief of the sultan's bedchamber (*has oda başi*), one of the most important posts in the Ottoman hierarchy. The slave who held that position was in constant contact with the emperor, guarded him in his sleep and accompanied him everywhere. One of the three seals of the empire was conferred on him. With the two other, inferior, *oda başi*, he had total charge of the sultan's personal service.

We can easily imagine how an intelligent and attractive young man made use of every occasion to increase his intimacy with the master of the empire. When they were not together, they sent each other letters from one pavilion of the Seraglio to another. They would go for walks together, unescorted, in the palace gardens or take boat trips with a single oarsman on the Bosphorus or Golden Horn. Such intimacy between a sultan and one of his slaves had never been seen before. Indeed, it was considered such a scandal that chroniclers kept silent about a relationship which, in their view, tarnished the sultan's glory. Most of the evidence we have comes from foreign visitors, notably the Venetian ambassador. Slavery in the Ottoman Empire was not quite what we might imagine, since the slaves of powerful men often had opportunities to attain riches and honour. Nonetheless, the sultan's intimacy with Ibrahim was considered by public opinion to go too far.

Even the Grand Vizier himself was anxious about the rapidity of his rise to power. Baudier, a 17th-century chronicler, tells us that Ibrahim asked the sultan not to promote him to such an important position: since he was able to live in ease and tranquillity, his services had already been adequately recompensed. Suleiman praised his modesty but insisted on granting him the highest honours. As long as he reigned, whatever the circumstances, Ibrahim would never be put to death. 'And yet,' Baudier adds, 'the condition of kings, like that of other people, is constantly changing; and favourites are often proud and ungrateful. This was what led Suleiman to forget his promise and Ibrahim to fail in loyalty and duty.'[20]

In June 1523, Ibrahim was appointed Grand Vizier: at the head of government, the administration and the army (apart from the janissaries). No other post in the Ottoman Empire conferred so much honour and power or offered so many opportunities for material enrichment. As the sultan's deputy, the Grand Vizier possessed even more extended powers in times of war and could take certain major decisions without consultation. Everything had to be submitted to him.

Primus inter pares, Ibrahim soon obtained power infinitely greater than that of the other viziers. The empire was far too vast for Suleiman to bear the heavy responsibilities alone. For thirteen years, he had the same confidence in Ibrahim as in himself. Even when his favourite had left the scene, the habit had taken root: the sultan continued to make over to his Grand Vizier all decisions for which he was not personally responsible.

'Chief slave' of the sultan and pivot of the state, the Grand Vizier was surrounded with respect and honours almost equal to those of Suleiman himself. Like the *padishah*, he attended Friday prayers in a solemn procession. On holidays, the leading functionaries came to congratulate him. He was escorted to see the sultan with the *çavuş başi* (or chief of protocol); he received the chief functionaries and governors at a set time and held a *Divan* (or council) in his palace, just like his master. He had the right of precedence over all the top dignitaries, apart from the *şeyhul-islam* – or chief of the *ulema* – whom protocol considered as his equal (see Appendix 6).

Soon the sultan conferred another honour on Ibrahim: he made him *beylerbey* of Rumelia.[21] This title gave the court favourite authority over all the Turkish territories in Europe and, in time of war, the command of all the troops in the region. It was he who had to assemble all the provincial *sipahi* (the *timariotes*) when Suleiman called them up. The *beylerbey* of Rumelia (like the one in Anatolia, who had similar responsibilities) had immense revenues at his disposal, which only increased his huge salary as Grand Vizier. Furthermore, there were constant presents from the sultan, from the functionaries – or those who wished to become functionaries – and from foreign envoys who hoped to obtain concessions in return.

Powerful and rich, Ibrahim had built for himself the most sumptuous palace ever seen in Constantinople. This was near the Seraglio at the edge of the Hippodrome (At Meydani). It was here that his marriage to Hadice Hanim, the sultan's sister, took place. Both Turkish and foreign chroniclers were equally struck by the splendour of the festivities and the signs of deep friendship Suleiman bestowed on his favourite.

A throne covered in velvet and golden embroidery was set up for the sultan near the Hippodrome. The festivities commenced when a message – carried by the second vizier and the *ağa* of the janissaries – was taken to Suleiman, inviting him to take part in the ceremonies. They received 'the most sumptuous gifts' to thank them and heard from the mouth of the *padishah* the most high-flown speech in praise of Ibrahim. A series of banquets 'of the greatest magnificence' were offered to the army chiefs and dignitaries. On the ninth day – the day before the bride was due to be brought from the Seraglio to be married – Suleiman went to visit Ibrahim in his palace between two 'walls' suspended from the windows, hangings of silk and gold cloth. He made the Mufti Ali Cemali and the royal tutor, Şems Effendi – later to be dismissed on grounds of ignorance – sit by his side and listened to 'jousting matches' on literary and scientific subjects between the most famous intellectuals of Istanbul. The esquire trenchant had a table laid for the Grand Vizier alone and then for all the *ulema*. They 'were later sent away bearing elaborate sweets and jams as presents'. On his return to the Seraglio, Suleiman was told of the birth of a son – the future Selim II – which had occurred on the anniversary of the conquest of Constantinople. Two days later, the procession of 'the bridal palms' took place and the sultan again honoured Ibrahim by visiting his palace. There, after taking part in dances, races, archery contests and other entertainments, he listened to the hymns composed in honour of the Grand Vizier and his imperial spouse.

Further Troubles in the Empire

Ibrahim's elevation to the post of Grand Vizier was the indirect cause of a rebellion which, if it had succeeded, could have had incalculable consequences. It was not the first time, nor the last, that a leading dignitary revolted and tried to take over a province in order to create an independent state and even, perhaps, overthrow the sultan. On this occasion, however, the danger was very serious, since the rebellion was started in Egypt, which had only recently become a part of the Ottoman Empire, by Ahmed Pasha, the second vizier and an exceptionally skilful and enterprising man.

The Grand Vizier Piri Pasha had been relieved of his post and replaced by Ibrahim. Ahmed had been instrumental in the dismissal of Piri, since he coveted the post for himself. When he failed to obtain it, he realized he would never do so. He knew he could never dislodge Ibrahim either and decided to resign instead. He asked to be made Governor of Egypt; Suleiman agreed at once – although he soon came to regret the decision.

As soon as he got to Cairo, Ahmed started plotting. He won over to his side several Mamluk dignitaries and made contact with the Pope and the Grand Master of the Knights of Saint John of Jerusalem, to whom he promised, if the Christians sent him a fleet, that he would expel the Turkish garrison from Rhodes. He also asked for the assistance of Shah Ismail of Persia. While waiting for help from these rather unlikely quarters, Ahmed dealt with the janissaries stationed in Cairo: all were massacred. He took for himself the title of sultan and had money minted and prayers recited in his name. The rebellion had a good chance of success, but the Mamluks and Arab chiefs who had initially supported him then decided to abandon him. Eventually, Ahmed was assassinated.

Several other revolts followed. One in early 1524 failed when the main conspirators were discovered. A rather more serious rebellion, led by a Mamluk called Canim Kaşifi, managed to assemble several thousand men in the Nile delta, and the Turkish governor had to send in janissaries and artillery. Canim was killed and the rebellion collapsed.

Clearly all was not well in Egypt. The constant succession of rebellions, fanned by popular discontent, was worrying. Although all these revolts directed at the Turkish occupying forces had failed so far, some day one of them was likely to succeed. Rapid intervention was therefore necessary. Only one of the leading dignitaries of the Porte, according to Suleiman, was absolutely trustworthy and capable of dealing with the disturbances in Egypt and Syria: Ibrahim.

Suleiman was keen for the Grand Vizier's mission to meet with a resounding success. He gave him 500 janissaries and 2,000 foot soldiers and accompanied him as far as the Princes Isles (Kizil Adalar) in the Sea of Marmara. He was to be absent for a year.

The *padishah*'s envoy appeared to the peoples among whom he travelled more as a sovereign in his own right than a minister sent on a mission. He went first to Aleppo and Damascus, where Ghazali's recent revolt was still not totally crushed. Ibrahim rapidly reorganized the two provinces with immense skill. Officers and functionaries were beheaded. Changes were made in the administration Selim had instituted and the country was divided into three regions ruled by governors based in Damascus, Aleppo and Tripoli. Then the Grand Vizier made his triumphal entry into Cairo, which 'far surpassed all memories of the magnificence of earlier sultans': pages dressed in golden fabrics, soldiers and janissaries 'richly attired' and Ibrahim himself mounted on a horse whose trappings – a gift from Suleiman – were worth more than 150,000 ducats.

Everything had been planned to give the population a striking image of the new rulers who had taken over from the age-old Mamluk authorities. The still rebellious tribes were subdued and their chiefs hanged or decapitated. Anyone with injustices to complain of was invited to come forward, and debtors were released from prison. Regulations were drawn up concerning rates of tax, the administration of justice, payment of state servants, the maintenance of order – and even the price of sugar cane. Heavy penalties (often death) were laid down for anybody who broke these rules or for functionaries who abused their authority. For the first time in Egypt, checks and balances were instituted between the governor (*beylerbey*), the *beys*, the janissaries and the Arab tribes. Thanks to this system, the power of the *beylerbey* was limited by the *beys* who kept him under control.

Until the beginning of the 19th century, Egypt and Syria remained secure. In only a few months, Ibrahim had shown himself to be a masterly politician and an invaluable servant of the state. His reputation only increased still further.

2
The Magnificent Sultan in His Splendour

Back in Istanbul, Ibrahim found a difficult situation. Suleiman had just, with some difficulty, put down a revolt by the janissaries. When he had extended a hunting trip in the region of Edirne, a rumour had gone round that he would be away for a long time and would therefore undertake no further military campaigns in the near future. The janissaries had shown their displeasure by ransacking the Jewish quarter and the palaces belonging to Ibrahim and other leading dignitaries. Suleiman immediately returned to Istanbul and showed his authority. He killed three of the ringleaders with his own hands, and the other janissaries fell back into line. He then distributed money and passed severe sentences: the *ağa* (or general) of the janissaries and the *ağa* of the *sipahi*, as well as several officers, were executed. During the whole course of his reign, the janissaries never again revolted against his authority.

In what direction was the *padishah* going to launch his next attack? Towards Persia or Hungary? When Shah Tahmasp succeeded Ismail to the Persian throne, Suleiman had sent him a letter, ostensibly of congratulation, which is very revealing of his feelings towards him and the immense pride which animated 'God's shadow on earth': 'If there still remained a spark of honour and ardour in a personality corrupted by

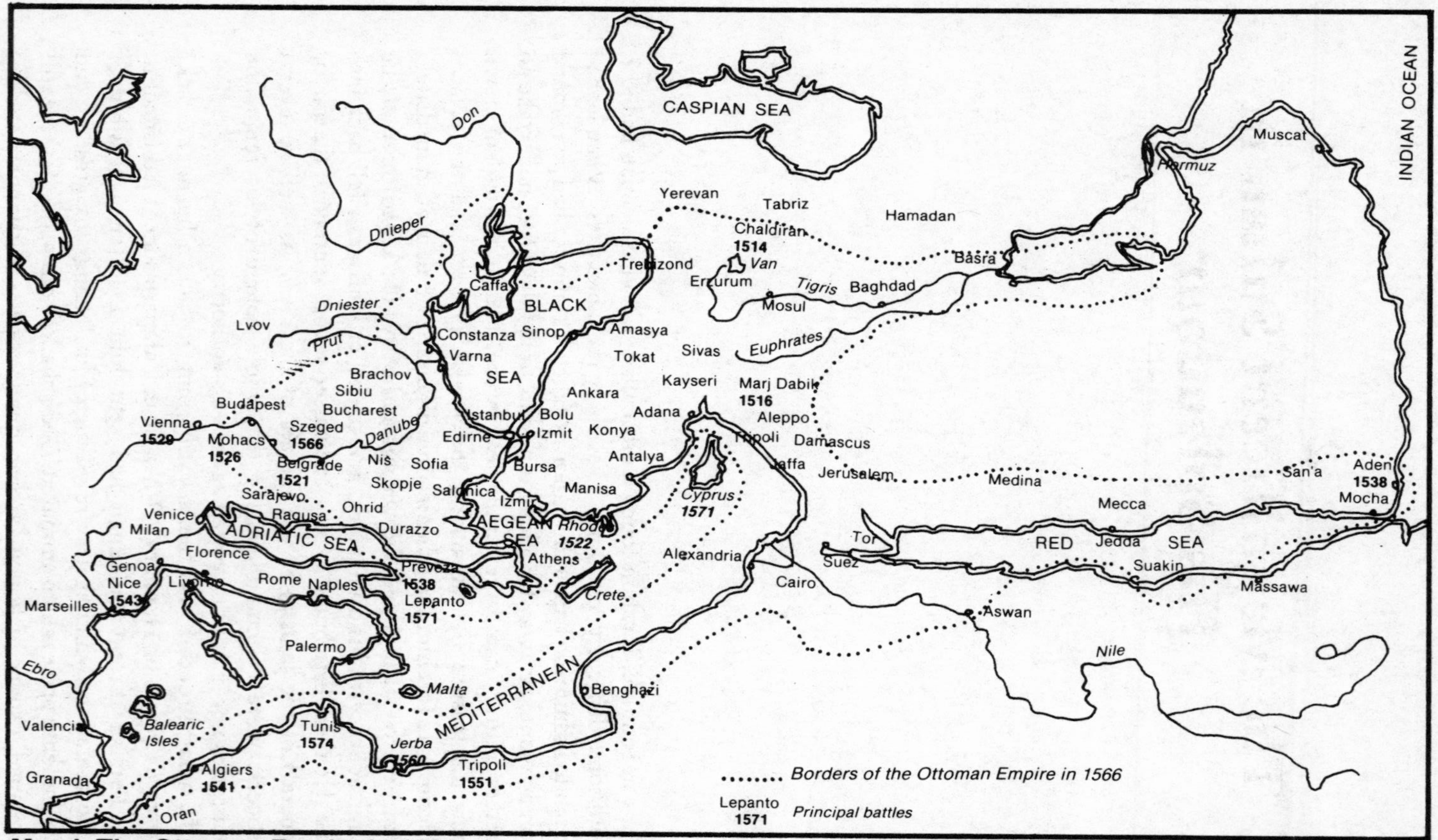

Map I. The Ottoman Empire in 1566

error, you would long ago have vanished. I have decided to bear arms to Tabriz and into Azerbaijan and to pitch tent in Iran and Turan, at Samarkand and in Khorasan. If I have put off executing this plan, it was because I had diverted my attention to my triumphant campaigns against the Hungarians and Francs, against Belgrade and Rhodes, the greatest fortresses on earth and the wonders of the world. Before the immense hordes, huge as mountains, of my army take over your land, ravage your country and kill off your family, bow your head, take off your crown and put on a monk's habit, like your ancestors before you . . . If you want to come and beg a crust of bread at my door for the love of God, I will be happy to oblige and you will lose nothing of your country. But if you continue to act with the pride of Pharoah and the madness of Nimrod, if you keep to the path of error, soon the click of sabres and lances and the boom of cannons will tell you that the hour of your defeat has arrived. And then, even if you bury yourself in the earth like an ant or take flight like a bird, I will keep you in my sights and, with the grace of God, seize on you and rid the world of your poisonous presence . . .'[1]

At the same time as this letter, Suleiman executed a group of Persians detained in Gallipoli. And so the matter rested, for a few years.

Throughout the winter of 1525–6, preparations for battle proceeded apace, although nobody knew whom they were directed at. Great efforts were lavished on the artillery, which had proved so vital to the Turkish armies in the past. Shipyards were put to work. By spring, everything was ready and Suleiman had made up his mind where to attack: Hungary.[2]

The sultan had many reasons to undertake such a campaign – the same reasons which had inspired his moves against Belgrade and would often lead him into further expeditions against the Christian countries: his duty as a *gazi* to enlarge the territory of Islam; his ambition to create a universal monarchy; and his sense of the role he had been allotted by God. His peers and rivals – the great sovereigns who represented a constant threat – were the rulers of Spain, Charles V, and those of France and England, not the Sophy of Iran, a mere despised heretic, or the Muscovite prince (whose country would play no role on the international scene until the time of Ivan the Terrible, thirty years later). Europe was his field of battle. He had almost undertaken a major campaign in Italy against 'the King of Spain', when Francis I, imprisoned by Charles V after the defeat at Pavia, asked for his help. But the plan fell through when Francis was released. It is not, therefore, really accurate to say that it was the King of France who urged the sultan to attack Hungary and who thus bears responsibility for the terrible disaster that befell the Christians at Mohacs.

Mohacs, or the Great Victory

Before setting off on campaign, Suleiman made sure that there were no threats to peace elsewhere. Since his victory at Rhodes, he had maintained good relations with Venice – the Most Serene Republic would cause him no problems. Ragusa, which had just received further privileges from the Ottomans, was not a menace either. Shah Tahmasp was plotting with Charles V, but was in no position to go to war. Wallachia had been subdued after enormous complications: a former monk called Radul, elected by the boyars, had been confirmed in his position as prince after his rival Vlad had been deposed and exiled to Constantinople. As for Charles himself, the League of Cognac, recently formed to fight against him, meant that he had enough troubles at home and was in no way tempted to intervene in the East.

Suleiman knew that Hungary was more divided than ever. The peasants lived in such misery that they looked upon the Turks as liberators. John Zapolyai was plotting to win the crown and the Magyar nobles were so anti-German that they demanded the expulsion of all the Germans in the king and queen's entourage at the very time when the country most needed the emperor's help. Some of the Hungarians shared Luther's view that the Turkish successes were a just punishment for social injustices and the corruption of the Roman Church.

On Monday 21 April 1526, at the head of 100,000 men and 300 cannons, the sultan left Istanbul by the Adrianople gate. He was accompanied by Grand Vizier Ibrahim, the other viziers Mustafa and Ayas, the Porte dragoman Yunis Bey and many dignitaries. The army followed the river valleys so as to avoid mountain crossings and thus marched North-West towards Belgrade. Bad weather made the journey between Philippopolis (Plovdiv) and Niš very difficult. Storms and heavy rain had swollen rivers, swept away bridges and made roads impassable. Discipline, always perfect in the Ottoman army, was reinforced and soldiers who had trampled on sown fields or let their horses loose in them were executed. Even judges, Suleiman reports in his journal,[3] were hanged. When they arrived at Sofia, the Grand Vizier was ordered to make straight for Petrovaradin and lay siege to the town while the sultan went to Belgrade to meet up with the *sancakbey* of Bosnia and Herzegovina and their troops. The khan of the Crimean Tartars, Saadet Giray, was also there. Mines soon defeated the fortress of Petrovaradin and the Grand Vizier is said by chroniclers to have brought the heads of 500 defenders when he came to announce the news to the sultan. The Ottomans, for their part, had lost only 25 men.

The expedition followed the course of the Danube towards Buda. The Ottomans captured Ilok and then Eszek (Osijek), where Suleiman had a bridge built to cross the river Drava. It was 332 metres long and 2.4 wide and was finished in five days. Turkish bridge-builders played as important a role on such expeditions as the janissaries and artillery. When the troops had crossed the river, Suleiman had the bridge destroyed – so the soldiers would have no thoughts of retreat. Then, across marshes and peat-bogs, the army reached the Mohacs plain, about 20 kilometres from the confluence of the Danube and the Drava. It was there that the King of Hungary, Lewis II, was waiting to cut off the road to Buda.

As had happened so many times before, the Christians failed to unite. Lewis had begged for aid from the whole of Europe. 'If help from your majesty does not arrive soon, my kingdom is lost,' he wrote to the King of England, who did nothing. He tried with equal lack of success to get the Shah of Persia to act as a diversion by tying up Turkish forces in the East. Charles V, then in Spain, turned a deaf ear to his appeals: all his troops were not enough to deal with the dangers posed by the League of Cognac, which incited part of Europe and the Pope against him. Ferdinand, aware of the threat, had made a pathetic cry for help to the German Diet at the beginning of the summer, but this insisted that Charles should first convoke a general council to settle the religious problem. When it at last decided to send 24,000 men to Hungary in return for a promise that such a council would be held in eighteen months' time, it was too late: the disaster had already occurred.

Even the Hungarian nobles – on whom the defence of the country depended – mobilized without enthusiasm. Those who could stayed at home. They had no desire to strengthen the position of the king, whose privileges they hoped to snatch away, nor of the Habsburgs. Divided into supporters of the Palatine Bathory and those of Verboeczy, they proved unable to join forces even on the battlefield! Such nobles forced the king to join battle without waiting for John Zapolyai's contingents or the Croatians from Frangipani (30,000 to 40,000 men in all). A monk called Paul Tomori, Bishop of Kalocsa, who had most reluctantly been appointed commander-in-chief, now hoped to obtain all the glory of a great victory for himself. He had absolute confidence in the Hungarian cavalry, which was cased in steel from head to foot, both horses and men. He had quite forgotten the superiority of the far lighter and quicker Turkish cavalry. Even more significant, he had forgotten the artillery. With no allied troops to support them, 30,000 Hungarians faced more than twice as many Turks on the field of battle. The Turks obeyed an iron discipline, the Hungarian knights obeyed no one. Their chances were made even less promising in that they failed to construct any defence works and picked a battle site which favoured the deployment of the enemy forces far more than their own. Bishop Perenyi predicted that 20,000 Hungarian martyrs would soon be going to paradise – which proved to be an underestimate.

At noon, on the eve of the battle, Suleiman held a council of war. The general of the *akinci* suggested that they should not make a direct head-on attack on the Christian cavalry but should open the ranks, let them through and attack them from the sides. Suleiman agreed to this strategy, which probably determined the outcome. Ibrahim then passed the troops in review, promised them large quantities of loot and took up position in the front line at the head of the Rumelian troops. Behind him were the Anatolian troops with the sultan and the artillery.

On 29 August, at about 3 o'clock in the afternoon, battle commenced with a round fired by the enemy artillery. The Hungarian cavalry charged first, with Perenyi and Tomori at the head, just as the Turks had hoped. The Rumelian troops bore the brunt of the attack and fell back to the Anatolians. The tactic suggested by the general was then put into effect: the *akinci* opened ranks and the Hungarians rushed in to try and reach the sultan and capture him. The *akinci* attacked them from right and left. The Turkish historian Kemalpashazade[4] described the combat in the following, highly poetic, style: 'When the *akinci* joined the attack in impetuous waves, a sea of blood began to be stirred up in seething waves. Their red head-dresses made the battlefield a bed of tulips . . . Shields cracked like the heart of a rose, helmets filled with blood like the lips of a rose-bud. Mists of blood rising like a purple cloud to the horizon were like a rosy sky above the head of victory's betrothed . . .'

The Hungarian knights fought extremely valiantly. A group of 22 of them came very close to Suleiman, who ran the greatest risk of his life. Several of his bodyguards were killed and he owed his safety to the presence of mind of the janissaries, who surrounded him and hamstrung the assailants' horses. The sultan himself fought with courage. Arrows and lances hit him, only to bounce off his breastplate.

The Turkish artillery then joined battle. At the very moment when Lewis, at the head of his remaining squadrons, came near the rampart formed by his guns tied together with chains, all the Turkish cannons opened fire. The Hungarian knights were crushed. The *akinci* followed those who had not been killed by the cannon-balls. 'The two armies fought and attacked each other ferociously. The flashing swords shone to the distant Orient. The wooden arrows, lances and javelins stoked the fires of war. The breastplates cut by scimitar blades looked like nets ripped to pieces by a swordfish.'

The combat continued like this until evening. The Hungarian artillery, manned by inexperienced gunners, played almost no part. The cavalry, heroic but poorly commanded and ill-disciplined, had borne the whole brunt of battle. Kemalpashazade paid homage to Paul Tomori, the Hungarian commander-in-chief: 'Like cast iron, the more the battle struck him, the more he steeped himself in it and drew strength from it. Like a viper or an elephant, he held his own against the claws of combat or the stones cast in battle. Covered with wounds, like a mad dog he recovered himself. When he rushed into the attack, impetuous as the Nile, he uttered screams like the trumpeting of elephants when tigers and lions flee before them . . .'

The Hungarians dispersed in all directions. Many got stuck in the marshes, including King Lewis: 'Burned by the brand of shame, the rebel had dashed into the river with horse and arms and increased the number of those who were destined to die by fire and water . . .' Suleiman's victory was total.

It was too late to pursue the scattered fugitives, and the Ottomans decided to spend the night on the field of battle: 'Until midnight the fanfares rang out in honour of victory.' The next day, Suleiman surveyed the scene of battle with Ibrahim and the second vizier and then, seated on a golden throne in a red tent, received the congratulations of the leading dignitaries and handed out many rewards for service. Two thousand heads, including those of the seven Hungarian bishops, were laid out in a pyramid before the sultan's tent. The number of enemy dead was reckoned at 30,000, including 4,000 knights. Hungary never recovered from this crushing defeat, caused by internal disputes, the mad temerity of its military chiefs and their total inability to make use of their artillery.

The victory at Mohacs increased still further the prestige of the Grand Vizier and the sultan's affection for him. Suleiman in person placed on his turban a heron's feather decorated with diamonds 'whose shadow covered him like the wing of Felicity'. The eyewitnesses all agree on the courage and martial prowess the sultan's favourite had revealed in battle. Kemalpashazade assigns to him credit for victory: 'The achievement of that astounding victory, tragic to the Infidels yet one of the most glorious for Islam, was due to the warlike emir, the ever-prudent vizier Ibrahim Pasha, whose lance was like the beak of the falcon of vigour and whose sword, thirsty for blood, was like the claws of the lion of bravery.' The historian compares him with 'the sun which shoots its rays over the universe', to a lion 'eagerly pursuing its prey' and to a cypress tree 'sprouting swords from its trunk'. Such hyperbole reflected the views of the dignitaries around Suleiman: an extraordinary future lay before the Grand Vizier, now almost an equal of the sultan. But the most powerful man in the empire was also the most exposed, as became clear to everybody, less than ten years later.

Suleiman wrote in person to his mother to tell her about his great victory. Letters were sent to Istanbul and to the provincial governors, always with the same text: the sultan recounted at length in colourful, poetic style the army's march towards the Danube, the preparations and the combat itself. He heaped high praise on Ibrahim, 'the hero who revealed all his innate valour.' 'God's munificence,' he declared in the peroration, 'has granted to my glorious army a victory such as none of the earlier sultans, nor the all-powerful khans, nor even the companions of the Prophet, have ever achieved. What remained of the godless nation has been rooted out. Glory to God, the Lord of the World.' It was indeed in just such terms that the Islamic world interpreted his triumph. Like his ancestors on the frontiers, Suleiman had joined battle for the glory of the faith of Mohammed. 'That great victory was one of Islam's greatest. Down to our own days, no *padishah* has won a similar triumph.'[5]

Without delay, Suleiman ordered the army to depart; on 10 September, they pitched camp before Buda. The sultan took up residence in the royal palace and immediately announced that no damage was to be done to the inhabitants and their possessions. This order was largely ignored. Irregular troops ransacked and set on fire part of the town. Ibrahim tried in vain to stop this. Scenes of pillage and even murder continued for several weeks in neighbouring towns. Kemalpashazade himself tells us that 'the *akinci* threw themselves on the piles of treasure and wove rubies red as tulips into crowns; the janissaries were so weighed down with loot that their caps looked like lilies full of gold'.

Before leaving Buda, Ibrahim gave orders for all the guns, the castle treasures and the bronze statues of Hercules, Diana and Apollo[6] to be put on board the boats. He also took away with him the library which had belonged to the former king, Matthias Corvinus, one of the most valuable of its day. The Hungarian nobles came to surrender to Suleiman.

At the end of November, the sultan entered Constantinople to immense popular acclaim. He had left only a single garrison at Petrovaradin. The war had been merely a punitive expedition and a defeat for the Christians, yet conquest would not be long delayed.[7]

The victory at Mohacs had an immense impact in Europe. No one had come to help the King of Hungary, but everybody was distressed. In fact, nobody except a few Cassandras had really believed, even after the fall of Belgrade, that the Ottomans would penetrate so deeply into Central Europe and capture Buda. Both Catholics and Protestants saw the battle as a sign of divine providence punishing the Christians for their sins. More perceptive onlookers knew that the real causes were quite different: the divisiveness, selfishness and cowardice of Christian Europe, 'reduced to the status of a European canton by the disputes between the Christian princes which became fiercer with every day that passed'.[8]

Suleiman Appoints the King of Hungary

King Lewis had been killed, the cavalry decimated, Buda burnt to the ground and the whole country ravaged – but these were not all the problems the Hungarians faced. The country was also torn apart by a dynastic dispute which would play a central role, less than twenty years later, in its loss of independence. If the nobles were unable to unite on the battlefield against the great enemy of Christianity, they were also divided when it came to electing a king.

Ferdinand of Habsburg, Charles V's brother, was married to Anne, the sister of the former King Lewis; from the very day after the defeat at Mohacs, he put forward his claim to the throne.[9] Most of the Hungarian nobility, however, preferred to be ruled by a local prince – an outsider was far more difficult to control – and therefore elected the voivode of Transylvania, John Zapolyai, whose marriage had linked him with the Jagiellons of Poland. But Ferdinand nonetheless retained many supporters and, before the end of the year, he too was elected and crowned. Hungary had two kings!

Everyone who feared the increasing power and influence of the Habsburgs naturally took Zapolyai's side: Francis I, in particular, supported him with large subsidies, as well as the princes of Bavaria, Pope

Clement VII, the Venetians and the King of England. Yet the help they offered was more often verbal than substantial and before long Ferdinand's troops had expelled Zapolyai from Buda. When he was subsequently defeated at Tokaj, he took refuge in Poland. Now there was nobody who could help – except Suleiman, who held the balance of power in the Danube territories.

Thus, at the end of December 1527, Zapolyai's envoy, Jerome Laski, arrived in Constantinople. A skilful diplomat, 'equally talented as a writer and a swordsman', Laski first made sure of the support of Ibrahim and the representative of the Venetian Republic, Luigi Gritti.[10] A natural son of Doge Andrea Gritti, he was a man 'cunning, flattering, greedy, ambitious and depraved'[11] who had soon acquired a good deal of influence over Ibrahim. Thanks to these powerful advocates, Laski's plans made rapid progress, especially since he had been wise enough to assure the neutrality of the other viziers with lavish gifts. At first Ibrahim addressed him in blunt terms: 'We have killed the king and taken over his residence – the kingdom is ours. It is crazy to believe that a crown makes a king. Gold and precious stones do not confer power – one can only rule by the sword. What is won by the sabre is defended with the sabre. But if your master takes the hand of ours and recognizes him as his lord, then he shall gain his kingdom and help which will enable us to reduce to dust Ferdinand and his friends; we will flatten their mountains under the feet of our horses. We Turks talk little but act effectively. When the time comes, we will come and make of Buda a new Constantinople.'

Several weeks went by, with Laski sparing no effort – or money – to obtain what he wanted. At last Suleiman offered him an official audience. His decision had been made: Zapolyai would be King of Hungary. He preferred to have as King of Hungary the ruler of one weak country, who would always be at his mercy, rather than an ambitious Habsburg, shored up by all the countries, men and resources of the Holy Roman Empire. Zapolyai would be a vassal, Ferdinand an enemy. 'I receive with goodwill', he said to Laski, 'your king's submission to me, whose states, acquired by war and the sword, have hitherto belonged to me and not to him. I hereby make them over to him and further intend to give him the kind of military assistance against the Austrian Ferdinand which will allow him to sleep in peace.' Laski swore 'by the living God, by Jesus the Redeemer who is also God, that his king would be the friend of Suleiman, the enemy of his enemies'.[12] Shortly afterwards, Gritti became the representative of the King of Hungary and, on 28 February 1528, the

Porte signed a treaty promising 50 cannons and 500 hundredweight of gunpowder to Zapolyai for his first campaign against Ferdinand.

The Habsburg claimant soon learnt of the success of his enemy's mission. It had taken him totally by surprise and he hastened to send his own legation in turn to Constantinople. But he was far less skilful than Zapolyai and his envoys were far from possessing Laski's talents. Hobordansky, who led them, was under instructions to lay claim to all the territories captured from Hungary, including Belgrade! He presented these demands with a total ineptness which immediately shocked the Turks. 'How does your master dare to call himself most powerful when face to face with the emperor of the Ottomans, under whose shadow all the other Christian powers take refuge?' asked Ibrahim. 'Which other powers?' retorted Hobordansky. 'France, Poland, Venice, Transylvania', replied Ibrahim. The ambassador then listed the possessions Ferdinand wanted to have returned. 'Why not Constantinople as well?' Ibrahim asked with irony.

Greatly irritated by the tone and excessive claims of the Austrian delegation, Suleiman gave orders for them to be kept under house arrest, where they remained for nine months. They were then released and given a present of 200 ducats each, before being received by the sultan. The language he used to them hardly augured well: 'Your master has yet to experience what I am like as a friend and neighbour – but he soon will. Tell him that I will come to find him in full force and I think I will be able to return to him with my own hands what he lays claim to. He should get everything ready to receive us.' Hobordansky proudly replied that Ferdinand would receive him with great joy as a friend but also knew how to deal with his enemies.

The diplomats left while Suleiman and Ibrahim hastened ahead with their military preparations. This time, they wanted to crush their only worthy adversary, 'the self-proclaimed emperor' Charles V, who had until then always managed to escape their clutches; after that, they would carry the Turkish standards to Vienna.

There was, in reality, little chance that they would ever meet. Charles had made over to his brother the duchies of Tyrol, Carinthia, Styria, Carniola and Austria, and it was Ferdinand who had the heavy responsibility of defending the territories around the Danube while the Habsburgs were tied up with costly disputes in Europe. By land, Ferdinand had to deal with the Turks, while Charles only retained responsibility for the defence of the Mediterranean – which, as we shall see, caused him a good deal of anxiety. Only once in his forty-year reign did he visit Vienna, when in 1532 he took command of the armies which faced a new Turkish offensive. Destiny never brought the Holy Roman Emperor and the Leader of the Faithful face to face.

Vienna in Danger

For the third time in eight years, Suleiman marched North at the head of his troops. He had appointed Ibrahim as *serasker* or supreme commander of the army and given him three fur-lined ceremonial cloaks, eight horses with rich trappings and a ninth laden with swords, bows, a quiver sparkling with jewels, six horse's tails and seven standards (instead of the usual four). Of these standards, one was white, one green, one yellow, two red and two striped – all intended to obtain for the campaign the favourable influence of the seven planets.

On 10 May 1529, the expedition left Istanbul with the customary ceremonial and display. Suleiman advanced among thousands of janissaries, *sipahi* and *akinci*, while the artillery, administrators and commissariat followed in perfect order behind. As on previous campaigns to the North, rivers overflowing their banks considerably slowed down the army's progress, and they took two months to reach Belgrade. A bridge on the river Maritsa had been washed away. Floods often submerged the camp and many soldiers were drowned. The army experienced the same difficulties on the Morava and the Sava and then in crossing the Drava, at Eszek. They arrived at last at Mohacs, where the memory of the great Ottoman victory seemed to fill the air and where Zapolyai was due to meet up with the sultan.

The ceremony was magnificent. The Grand Vizier advanced towards the king, followed by 500 janissaries and the same number of *sipahi*. Zapolyai had 6,000 knights with him. Then a solemn audience took place, during which Suleiman recognized Zapolyai as King of Hungary in the presence of the leading court and military dignitaries. Janissaries surrounded the tent where the *Divan* was held. Behind them were the *sipahi* and Rumelian troops. Zapolyai advanced, escorted by Turkish officials. The sultan took three steps forward and the king kissed his hand and was invited to sit down. A miniature of that time shows us the young sultan seated on a throne giving back to John Zapolyai, who is wearing an honorary caftan he has just been given, the Hungarian crown (the Saint Etienne crown), which had fallen into Turkish hands. Before departing, Suleiman addressed kind words to the king and made over to him gifts of three horses harnessed in gold and four caftans made of gold brocade. The Christian ruler of Hungary had just become the vassal of the sultan of Constantinople. Not long afterwards, Suleiman was to declare: 'That kingdom belongs to me and I have installed my servant there. I gave him the kingdom and can take it back if I wish, for it is entirely my right to dispose of it – and of its inhabitants, my subjects – as I see fit.' Hungarian independence was a pure fiction.

Three days after leaving Mohacs, Suleiman and his army took up position before Buda, which had now been occupied by Ferdinand's supporters. In the Turkish camp was Antonio Rinçon, the ambassador of Francis I, who had brought 40,000 crowns for Zapolyai in payment for his alliance with the King of France. The siege was brief. On the fifth day, the Ottomans carried off one of the city gates. On the next day, they launched a full-scale attack and the enemy surrendered. The janissaries were not allowed to ransack the town. They therefore snatched many inhabitants to sell as slaves and massacred the Austrians. 'We could see so many heads cut off it was impossible to calculate the number,' reported a witness.

A week after the capture of the city Zapolyai was solemnly installed on the throne of Hungary. The second-in-command of the janissaries presided over the ceremony. In refusing to take part or even send a vizier, Suleiman wished to make clear the small importance he attached to his vassal, the nominal chief of a satellite kingdom he was soon going to incorporate into his empire.

As autumn approached, Suleiman ordered his troops to make straight for Vienna. His firm intention was to capture the city before the bad weather started and to spend the winter there. The distance was relatively short and, on 27 September, the 120,000 men and 28,000 camels of the Ottoman army reached the city. In the heart of Europe, before the walls which would see – or so he passionately hoped – the defeat of 'the King of Spain', Suleiman had never been more worthy of the title 'Magnificent'.

He pitched camp near the village of Semmering. Columns with golden capitals surrounded his tent and gold brocade embellished the interior. Around it were ranked the 12,000 janissaries; behind, the *beylerbey* of Anatolia with the Asian troops. Further away at his sides were the Grand Vizier Ibrahim, the Governor of Bosnia, who commanded the front line, and the Serbian governor with the rearguard, the Rumelian troops. The artillery consisted of 300 culverins and cannons. Unfortunately, the bad weather had delayed the arrival of the biggest guns, and this proved highly significant during operations.

Within the city were 20,000 men and 72 cannons, commanded by Philip, the Palatine of Bavaria, Count Nicholas of Salm and the Baron of Roggendorf. The troops were made up of soldiers from the empire, Bohemia, Spain, Styria, Lower Austria as well as Viennese civilians 'wild with ardour at the thought of fighting the Turks'. Ferdinand had preferred to remain in Linz, where he could organize help, if necessary, and keep in contact with his brother, Charles V. Both prepared for the worst: if Vienna fell, it would mean a long campaign against the Turks through the whole of Germany.

The whole Christian world was aware of the danger, which concerned not only far-away Hungary and the Lower Danube but the very heart of Europe. This time, the German Protestants were ready to fight. Charles V had threatened them with sanctions if they abandoned Ferdinand at such a crucial moment. But Luther was quite willing to help the emperor and his brother, and the Protestants did not try, as Ferdinand had feared, to exploit Habsburg difficulties by creating a diversion in Germany.

The defence of the city had been organized with remarkable skill. While Suleiman had lost a month because of incessant rain and flooding, Ferdinand and the Viennese had taken measures which were to prove, rather to their surprise, extremely effective. The walls had been repaired and reinforced, the houses around them destroyed, munitions and supplies stocked up in large quantities, and provisions for fire-fighting prepared. All the gates of the city, except one, were blocked up.

The siege proceeded with the usual sequence of bombings, sorties, massacres, beheadings, acts of heroism and treason. On 7 October, 800 imperial troops attempted a sortie to catch the Turks near the Carinthian gate from behind. The operation was badly executed and ended in disaster. Most of the soldiers took flight, but the Turks pursued them and, by the evening, 500 Christian heads were piled up as a trophy. The Ottomans were by then only inches away from breaking into Vienna and blasted the city for three successive days. Their mines even opened up a large breach in the walls, but for some reason they did not seize the chance to rush in.

Bad weather had now arrived, ammunition and supplies were running low and the janissaries were beginning to complain. Suleiman held a meeting of viziers and army chiefs and it was decided to launch one final major assault. 'Courage was re-awakened by gold and promises': 1,000 *akçe* were promised to each janissary, with 30,000 for the first to get over the ramparts. On 14 October, three columns threw themselves furiously into the breach near the Carinthian gate. Another assault took place in the afternoon. No breakthrough occurred. Every attempt was broken by the unshakeable resistance of the troops commanded by Nicholas of Salm. It had proved impossible to capture Vienna in a sudden attack and the siege had to be lifted. Suleiman gave orders for departure.

Before raising camp, Suleiman held a *Divan* to distribute the promised rewards. Ibrahim received a sabre decorated with jewels, four caftans and five purses of gold. The janissaries received their 1,000 *akçe*.[13] Suleiman presented his retreat as a decision taken to spare his men and the enemy, and turned his defeat into an act of magnanimity. He let everybody know that he had only wanted to meet Charles V and Ferdinand face to face – they had always escaped him – and had never intended to take Vienna. The Turkish historian Mehmed Zaim is no doubt nearer the truth: 'The occupation of the castle at Vienna did not succeed. Since it was snowing on the victorious army before Vienna, his majesty the blessed *padishah* turned round and set off again for home.'

The Viennese also understood what the result of the battle meant. Salvoes of artillery and ringing of bells greeted the departure of the Turks, while the sultan's army was constantly harassed in revenge for the dangers the besieged Viennese had faced and the extortion widely practised throughout Austria and Styria by the *akinci* during the siege. At Buda, Zapolyai kissed the sultan's hand and congratulated him on his 'victorious campaign'. He received as thanks ten caftans and three horses with golden harnesses. Two months later, after a difficult journey through snow and flooded roads, during which men and many animals died, Suleiman re-entered Istanbul.

The setback before Vienna of the powerful Turkish army makes clear just how far an expedition from the Orient, however disciplined and well commanded, could go at the dawn of the modern age. In earlier times, hordes of knights armed only with lances and light bows could cross whole continents without needing to think about arms or supplies. With the progress of military technology armies had always to take with them, on difficult – and often non-existent – roads, cannons, large quantities of cannon-balls and wagons full of every kind of *matériel*. Suleiman's convoys spread out over dozens and dozens of kilometres.

Having left Istanbul on 10 May, Suleiman did not reach Belgrade before mid-July – two months to march 1,500 kilometres! He only reached Vienna on 27 September, at the start of the bad weather. 'It has snowed from the evening to noon the following day,' it is written in his journal for 14 October; it was this which led, two days later, to his decision to turn home. He had only had twenty days available to take a powerfully defended city. He ought to have left Istanbul earlier in the year and departed later from Vienna. But bad weather was a permanent problem – the level of rainfall was very high in the first half of the 16th century – and winters came early. A campaign lasting a whole year was quite impossible in a climate as harsh as that of Central or Eastern Europe. Even if Rhodes only surrendered at the end of December, in the Balkans one had to turn back earlier. From mid-September, one had to begin preparing for the home journey – otherwise the janissaries became angry and epidemics attacked troops and animals. For several centuries, it was its climate and distance from Constantinople far more than the prowess of its generals which saved Europe from the Turks.

The Vienna campaign had not proved a success for the sultan. Francis I, however, gained from it indirectly. Charles V had signed the Treaty of Barcelona with the Pope in the spring of 1529, which made him the protector of Italy. He thus had his hands free and was able to turn his attention against the French. Only the attack on Vienna prevented this. To fight on two fronts was impossible: he could not combat the King of France and deal with the Turkish menace at the same time. In the Treaty of Cambrai – the Ladies' Peace – he gave Burgundy back to France, which, in return, renounced all its claims in Italy. He desired peace in Europe so as to form an anti-Turkish coalition. He failed to achieve this, and the next ten years saw instead an almost permanent conflict between Charles, pursuing his imperial dreams, and those who opposed him: Henry VIII, Francis I and Suleiman.

The Merry Sultana and the Magnificent Sultan

Suleiman was now 35 years old. Despite the setback at Vienna, the Ottoman Empire was at its peak and the sultan at the height of his glory. Nothing had yet come to cast a shadow on the happiness of 'the master of his time', *Padishah*, the Caliph of God's Prophet and the Leader of the Faithful. In 1530, he had two intimates: the Grand Vizier Ibrahim, who never left his side, and one of his wives, Hurrem Sultan, known in Europe as Roxelane.

We know little about the princes of the House of Osman and even less about the women, thousands of whom lived over the centuries in the

Turkish sovereign's Harem. Apart from a few indiscretions by leading dignitaries which Western travellers and diplomats snapped up, we know virtually nothing not only about the anonymous women who just passed through or died in the Harem but even about those who lived there, had an important place and were the mothers of princes and princesses. Of some, whose intrigues made them talked about, we know the names and nothing else, such as the famous Koşem Sultan. Their whole life slipped by within the walls of Topkapi or the Old Seraglio without leaving any traces.

Roxelane is much better known to us, although many obscurities remain, starting with the circumstances of her birth. According to a Polish tradition, she was the daughter of a poor priest from Rohatyn in Ruthenia, on the Dniester, a region bordering on Hungary, Moldavia and Poland. She was born Alexandra Lisowska and carried off by Tartars, who made frequent raids into Poland, sold to Ibrahim and given as a present to Suleiman. This story, however, is not confirmed in any sources.

The nickname she was given of 'Roxelane' means 'the Russian woman' and not 'the Red-head'. Fairly short – *non bella ma grassiada*, according to Bragadino, the Venetian ambassador – her playful temperament had won her the nickname of *Hurrem* (the merry woman). Certainly intelligent and crafty, she used 'her seductions and talents' to inspire an exclusive passion in the sultan. She is said to have sung and played on the guitar nostalgic Slav songs, but her influence over Suleiman must have owed more to the fact that she bore him four sons than to her musical gifts. She soon gained complete control of the sultan's heart. Bragadino tells us that when someone offered some beautiful young girls to Suleiman, she made such a scene he had to send them away: 'If those girls or any others had stayed in the Seraglio, she would have died of grief.' According to Busbecq, Ferdinand's ambassador, Roxelane retained Suleiman's affection 'by love charms and magical means'.

When Roxelane arrived at the palace, the chief sultana (*kadin*) was a woman called Gulbahar, probably of Tartar origin, who had borne Suleiman a son called Mustafa. Roxelane eliminated her rival in a scene which, according to the Venetian ambassador, turned into a real battle. Her hair was torn out and her face scratched, and she said that she could not appear before Suleiman in such a state. From that day on, Suleiman had nothing more to do with Gulbahar (she left the Harem with Mustafa when he was appointed provincial governor in Manisa).

When a fire did great damage to the Old Seraglio, Roxelane used the opportunity to ask for permission to live in the new palace – known to us as Topkapi – the centre of political life and the sultan's court, where he also had an apartment. She brought with her a crowd of eunuchs, black and white, servants and domestics; once installed there, she stayed. The Harem and the state were no longer separate; the consequences of this were to prove deplorable.

A little later, she sealed her triumph by marrying Suleiman, although the court did not approve and none of the Ottoman chroniclers even mention it. But Busbecq describes the dowry Suleiman bestowed on her, and in Turkish law it was that which legitimized a union.

The marriage is also reported in the *Journal of the Genoese Bank of Saint George*: 'A most extraordinary event took place this week in the town, absolutely unprecedented in the history of the sultans. The Great Lord Suleiman has taken for his empress a woman called Roxelane, of Russian origin, amid much rejoicing. The ceremony took place in the Seraglio and the festivities surpassed anything we have ever witnessed. There was a public procession, gifts exchanged, all the main roads lit up gaily at night, much music and celebration. The houses are decked in garlands. A platform put up in the Hippodrome let Roxelane and the court take part in a tournament of knights and a long procession of wild beasts, with giraffes so tall their necks reached the sky . . . Everybody is talking about the marriage, but nobody is sure what it means . . .'[14]

Hurrem Sultan had started to influence her husband before her marriage and continued to do so until her death. Her effect on him may indeed have been exaggerated, for Suleiman was far from being feeble or easily swayed and took sole responsibility for his acts, good and bad, during a 46-year reign. She was, however, jealous of Suleiman's intimacy with his favourite and argued for war with Venice in 1537, even though Ibrahim was opposed to it. Foreign ambassadors never failed to bring gifts to her, and many leading dignitaries owed their appointment to her. She advanced the career of Rustem, the husband of her daughter Mihrimah, and never ceased to protect him. She was also involved without question, as we shall see, in the murder of Mustafa.

Roxelane was probably not Suleiman's evil genius, although some have taken great pleasure in depicting her thus. The only genuine criticism one can make is that she helped create the system of rule by favourites and courtiers which was soon to enfeeble the empire so disastrously.

The Supreme *Gazi*

In his maturity, Suleiman remained youthful, thin and rather frail. Yet his arm, according to Bragadino, was very strong 'and he is said to be capable of bending the tightest bow'. The Venetian ambassador added that his character was both fiery and melancholy and that he did not relish work, because, he noted, 'he has handed over the empire to the Grand Vizier: neither the sultan nor any of the courtiers take any decisions without Ibrahim, yet Ibrahim does everything without consulting the Great Lord or anyone else'.

Leader of the Faithful, Protector of the Holy Cities, by the will of God who had placed him in the seat of the Great Caliphs, Suleiman had a very elevated sense of his Islamic role. He was the 'Exalted Caliph' to whom the whole Islamic world had to submit, the Supreme *Gazi* who had replaced the last of the Abbasids as God's Lieutenant on earth. His duties as a *gazi*, inherited from ancestors who fought on the frontier between the Muslim and Christian worlds, now had to be exercised over the whole face of the earth.

Sincerely religious, Suleiman was convinced that God was on his side. Before the Battle of Mohacs, he uttered an impassioned prayer which history has preserved. At Buda, he did not hesitate to humbly join in carrying the bier of one of his companions. Although he took a very liberal attitude towards non-Muslims, he showed great severity to the Shiite heretics. He did not go quite as far as his father, who supposedly massacred 40,000 Shiites, but he unequivocally condemned their supporters. He had nothing but disdain for the Shah of Persia, who had split off from Sunni orthodoxy. For this reason, although for political reasons as well, he dreamed of crushing him once and for all.

In the great Suleimaniye library in Istanbul are to be seen eight copies of the Koran copied out by Suleiman in person. The sultan loved to take part in discussions between theologians or arguments about this or that obscure point in the Koran or *hadith*; although, unlike Mehmed II, who is said by Spandugino to have burnt candles before holy relics, he took no interest in learning about other religions. 'Suleiman's favourite pastime', the French traveller Antoine Geuffroy reports, 'was to read books about philosophy and his faith. He was so learned on such topics that even his Mufti would not be able to teach him anything.'

He was no religious fanatic. He showed the tolerance laid down in the Koran towards 'the peoples of the Book' as long as they do not take up arms against Muslims. The Ottoman Empire guaranteed the life, liberty and property of the *dhimmis* and Suleiman respected the agreements made with the *millets* without restrictions or excessive ferocity. He refused to permit Francis I to re-establish a church in Jerusalem which had been turned into a mosque, since Islam did not allow him to abandon a mosque once prayers had been said there; but, to show that his reasons were purely religious, he added that the Christians could keep all the oratories and establishments presently in their possession and that 'nobody would oppress them or torment them in any way whatsoever'.[15]

In old age, Suleiman banned the drinking of wine, in which he had earlier indulged moderately. He used plates of silver and gold on one occasion when he received a Persian embassy, but when jurists made it clear to him that such luxury was incompatible with his religion, he gave orders that only china plates were to be used for all meals in the palace. A few years before his death, even these were abandoned and clay plates became obligatory.

The Duty of Justice

Suleiman was guided all his life by religion. He advanced the borders of the empire further than any other sultan, and he gave to the Turks, in every field, a quite unparalleled glory; yet in the history of his own country he has gone down with the name of the Lawgiver (*Kanuni*).

God had given the people a master, who thus – according to ancient Oriental tradition – had a duty: to bring about the reign of justice. 'Justice forms the foundation of a powerful state,' said the Sassanid Chosroes (Khosrow I). And the *Siyasetname*, the treatise on government by the Seljuk vizier Nizam al-Mulk, says: 'The world can live in unbelief but not in injustice.' A celebrated Near Eastern saying known as 'the circle of equity' also sums up the double duty of states to assure justice and the wellbeing of their subjects: 'No state without an army, no army without money, no money without contented subjects, no subjects without justice; without justice no state.'

This meant justice between subjects but also, and more important, the justice shown by the authorities towards their subjects. The sultan's first duty was to protect them against the abuses of his representatives. Since the earliest times, the sovereign had to judge between the people and his functionaries. On set days, he listened to the grievances of his people and passed a final judgement, often executing the guilty party. In theory, anybody could stop the sultan in the street to submit his grievances to him.

In an Islamic state, the sultan was the defender of the *Şeriat* or Holy Law. Based on the Koran and the traditions about Mohammed, this had been codified in the 8th century by the great jurists of the school of Abu Hanifa (to which Turkish law belonged) and could not be altered. But the sultan also possessed a right of interpretation which permitted him to supplement the *Şeriat* by decrees (or *kanun*) when the circumstances or development of the Muslim community demanded it. This principle of the *orf* was admitted by theologians and first used by Mehmed II who, at the time of the conquest of Constantinople, published laws and decrees dealing with taxes, the penal code, and the organization of the court and government. By then, the Ottoman state had become an empire and its various organs had to be defined and strengthened.

A century later, the House of Osman ruled over three continents and, as successor to the Abbasids and to the Mamluks of Cairo, controlled an empire whose frontiers included states peopled by almost every known race and religion. The central task of Suleiman and his jurists was therefore to organize the administration, harmonize the legislation, and protect and control all the new subjects of his empire.

The great-grandson of the Conqueror had a very elevated sense of justice. All his contemporaries, even Christians, were agreed on this. A Frenchman called Guillaume Postel spoke of 'his humanity, justice and fidelity'. In the inscription above the door of the Suleimaniye mosque, he put the title 'propagator of the imperial laws' after his name. In the following century, when the empire faced many stern trials, Suleiman's time was remembered as a golden age; decadence had followed from forgetting the laws of the great sultan. Suleiman's acts of justice were recalled – and embellished in the telling. Even the execution of his two sons, once time had revealed the overall pattern behind these events, seemed like acts of justice: both had broken the laws of the empire, rebelled and caused many innocents to lose their lives. They had deserved punishment and Suleiman had made wise use of his unlimited powers.

Suleiman and those who worked with him – Ebusuud, a legal expert, and Kemalpashazade, the chief *ulema* – accomplished an immense task: sorting out the legislation for the whole empire. The decrees they laid down each dealt with only a single province and usually concerned fiscal arrangements, property rights and regulations about the army. Thus each province (*sancak*) had virtually a law code (*Kanunname*) of its own. The other codes, the *Kanun-i-Hukuk*, consisted of laws applicable in all places and at all times. These laws, which were often issued in response to questions raised or a report the sultan had received, were later integrated into the *Kanunname* of the empire, consisting in the code, drawn up by Mehmed II and Suleiman's own decrees. The *Kanunname* was thus constantly modified, rather as English law develops as precedents are established.

The sultan retained all powers and he was the only person who could exercise them. This was not always easy in so vast and dispersed an empire. Governors, *sipahi* and *beys* were controlled by nobody – or only from a great distance – and they could abuse their authority to the detriment of the defenceless *reaya* but at no great risk to themselves. One of Suleiman's main concerns was to prevent the men he had invested with authority from exceeding their legitimate powers. All his legislation was of an extreme severity designed to achieve this. 'No one has the right to exercise authority over land or population without the express mandate of the sultan. No one can exact taxes greater than those officially decided upon, nor forced labour and fines which have not been fixed by law.' One of the main aims of the *Kanun-i-Osmani* was to protect subjects against the local military classes. Many decrees ended in the following terms: 'If a subject brings a complaint to you against the *beys*, other military officials or tax collectors, you must prevent them from committing acts of injustice. If you think you are not able to do so, you must immediately let it be known to my Porte. If you do not, it is you who will be punished. My chief desire is to maintain the people in peace and wellbeing, the country in prosperity.'[16]

The law also protected the population against the many people who might be tempted to exploit them or stir up trouble, from the shopkeepers, cheats and speculators to agitators and thieves. Judges and police officers had to impose fixed penalties, neither more nor less, or they themselves would be liable to punishment. Everything was laid down in great detail: a fine of 200 *akçe* for a broken tooth if the offender was a rich man, 30 *akçe* if he was poor. Someone who stole a donkey, a horse or an ox would have his hand cut off or could pay off the theft with a fine of 200 *akçe*. To snatch off a Muslim's turban in an angry movement was fined 1 *akçe*. False witnesses and counterfeiters were to have a hand chopped off, and this time there was no redress. A man who tried to kiss a woman by force had to pay a fine of 1 *akçe* per kiss, and so on.

Suleiman established some very important regulations as well as measures which seem amusing today but nonetheless reflect the sultan's constant concern to protect his people from injustice. Pastry-cooks had to put a fixed proportion of butter in their cakes; the price of sweets had to depend on the price of the honey and almonds they were made of; not more than a 10% profit was allowed on the sale of dried fruit; restaurants had to pay a fine if the thickness of the tin on their bronze utensils was insufficient; owners of Turkish baths had to keep them hot enough and employ skilful and clean staff... The legislator even went so far as to lay down that beasts of burden must be treated with moderation.

Suleiman's successors were to pass equally detailed regulations about the making and selling of products. According to the rules drawn up by Mehmed IV, which consisted of over 600 articles, sorbets had to be made with musk and rose water, and yoghurt without water or starch; candle-makers were not allowed to use dirty or smelly grease; cereals for sale could not include straw, millers were not permitted to steal any grain for themselves or even to bring up chickens in a mill – 'If they want to know the time, they need only keep a cock . . .'[17]

Any man could come direct to the sultan to demand justice. In early Ottoman times it happened fairly frequently, but in the 16th century recourse was made to him only in exceptional circumstances. The *Divan* then acted as the supreme tribunal, before which the plaintiff came to put his grievances, which were usually concerned with abuses by the authorities particularly concerning taxes. It also functioned as a high court which passed judgement in the absence of the accused, who was usually a leading dignitary. If he was found guilty, a *çavuş* was sent with an execution order and he brought back the severed head to show it had been carried out.

Day-to-day legal judgements, in Istanbul as in the provinces, were the concern of the *kadi*, who were appointed after study in a *medrese*.[18] Unlike the leading administrators and most of the army chiefs they were Muslims by birth and received a course of instruction which lasted fifteen or twenty years and could lead eventually to the summit of the hierarchy: the post of *şeyhulislam*, equal in rank to the Grand Vizier's. The *şeyhulislam* issued the *fetva*, the written responses to questions about religious law. He also had to nominate the *kadi* in the 16th century, who were all placed under his authority. Below him in the hierarchy came the two *kazasker* (army judges) for Anatolia and Rumelia. Their responsibilities were later extended to include those of the civil judges who served under them. Pillars of the state, they ranked just below the viziers.

The *kadi* of Istanbul was the chief judge, and after him came the judges of other towns: 200 in Europe, as many in Asia, about 30 in Egypt. Below them were the *naib*, judges of districts, villages or small towns, who had studied at the *medrese* for a shorter time or did not have enough supporters to become *kadi*.

A single judge presided in court. He had to apply the *Şeriat* and the *kanun* within very wide limits of discretion (all the wider in that the *kadi*'s functions required him to lay down as well as interpret the law). Appointed by the sultan in his wisdom, directly responsible to him, and receiving his orders directly from him, the *kadi* controlled all aspects of administration, including taxes. He made sure that the sultan's orders, in every field, were carried out. He informed the sultan about any illegal act committed by any of his administrators. Of the three chief officials in each province – the *sancakbey* (commander of the troops), the *subaşi* (police chief) and the *kadi* – it was the *kadi* who had most influence. The *kadi* had no need to pay any attention to the observations of the *beylerbey*, who could merely pass on to the Porte his comments about the *kadi*'s conduct: in the Ottoman Empire, the judiciary was superior to the rest of the government, and its representatives took precedence over the others.

Despite inevitable abuses in an empire which extended over such an immense area, justice under Suleiman functioned in the most efficient manner possible. The Europeans were astounded by the rapidity and equity of the system. Guillaume Postel, who visited the empire twice between 1535 and 1550, spoke of this on several occasions. He praised the speed and honesty of Turkish justice, which he compared with the 'immorality' and corruption of French tribunals. Speaking of the window by which Suleiman could take part in trials before the *Divan*, the French traveller wrote: 'If I only dared say what I think! May it please God that a guardian angel could make the same thing happen at the court of the True Christian King, so he could see and hear all the judges behaving like sovereigns and spinning out trials. We would not see the talents of two or three hundred men who laugh as they steal from everyone and find a thousand ways of turning the law into a spider's web of complexities.'[19] Vincent Le Blanc from Marseilles, who visited Turkey in 1579, was astonished that 'the Christian and the Jew are as free as the Turk to put forward the least complaint, without needing the eloquence of a lawyer to defend the truth . . . Being far less partisan, the administration of justice is also carried out more honestly.'[20]

The Greatest Monarch in the World

'A born sovereign, of a distant majesty and impressive in the centre of a brilliant court,' Suleiman had been confirmed in his belief that he was the greatest monarch of his day by victories at Belgrade, Rhodes and Mohacs and his expedition right to the heart of Christian Europe. A flourishing economy enabled him to make lavish gifts, surround himself with the most precious objects, and to keep a large entourage in style. As soon as he had come to the throne, he set in motion a building programme which transformed Constantinople[21] and left its mark on all the large towns of the empire.

The celebrations he held were dazzling, like those of the great Oriental emperors such as Chosroes and Haroun al-Rashid. The summit of splendour was reached in the festivities for the circumcision of his sons, Princes Mustafa, Mehmed and Selim. First, he sent a leading dignitary as envoy to Venice, to invite the Doge as a 'friend of the Porte', the only European ruler considered worthy of the honour. That ambassador extraordinary appeared before the Venetian senate dressed in gold brocade and expressed in terms of eloquent friendship his master's desire to see the sovereign of a friendly state by his side on such a joyful occasion. The Doge excused himself on grounds of old age, but sent Luigi Mocenigo as his envoy extraordinary as well as Pietro Zeno, the permanent ambassador. Both have left accounts of the festivities.

On the morning of 27 June 1530, Suleiman rode to the Hippodrome, where a throne had been set up below a canopy 'dazzling with gold'. Surrounded by viziers, *beylerbey* and the *ağa* of the janissaries, he received the congratulations and gifts of the leading dignitaries and, on the following day, those of the former viziers, the Kurdish emirs and the Venetian ambassadors. 'The gifts', the latter reported, 'surpassed in magnificence anything we had seen up to then': shawls and Indian muslin, the finest cloths of Greece and Venetian velvet, silver plates full of gold pieces, gold cups encrusted with jewels, lapis-lazuli discs, Chinese porcelain, Russian furs and Arab mares. The sultan was also offered Mamluks and young boys, Ethiopian and Hungarian slaves. Shortly afterwards, mock battles were held: an assault was made on two wooden towers, which were set alight amid fireworks and fanfares. The following days, acrobats, musicians, clowns and jugglers gained great applause. On the fourteenth day, leading dignitaries went in procession to fetch the three young princes who were to be circumcised, and competitions in public speaking and discussions about religious doctrine were held. One of the *ulema* is said to have been so mortified when he failed to find a reply that he died. Then the circumcision ceremony took place, finishing in the traditional way with the guests coming to kiss the sultan's hand and congratulate him. Celebrations concluded with horse races on the plain of the Sweet Waters, beyond the Golden Horn.

These festivities were undoubtedly the most sumptuous of Suleiman's reign, or perhaps in Ottoman history. Yet many others took place throughout the year and on every occasion: religious festivals, the sultan's departure for war and (always victorious) return, the presentation of new ambassadors. Mehmed II, after taking Constantinople, had established a hierarchy of titles and ceremonial partly inspired by Byzantium. Suleiman developed and formalized all this, and the *Kanun-i-Teşrifat* (or *Book of Ceremonies*) laid down the order of precedence, the list of dignitaries who had to take part in each ceremony, and even the colour of the turbans they had to wear. Indeed, headgear was treated at great length: the sultan alone wore a high turban, decked with two heron's feathers, while the viziers' were less tall but had gold bands on the top; the state functionaries' turbans were like the sultan's although not as tall, while the janissary officers wore a sort of cap with feathers on.

Many foreign ambassadors have left accounts of their presentation to the Great Lord and their amazement before such splendour. Ghiselin de Busbecq's description is one of the most striking: 'The sultan was sitting on a very low couch covered in carpets and cushions of exquisite workmanship. His bow and arrows were just next to him. Chamberlains held our arms, a precaution which had been established when a Croat who wished to avenge the death of his master, the Serbian tyrant, had asked for an audience with Murad in order to assassinate him. We gestured to kiss his hand and were led along a wall which faced his seat, being careful never to turn our back on him. There were high-ranking officers, troops of the Imperial Guard, *sipahi* and janissaries in the room . . . Look now at the immense sea of turbans with countless folds of the whitest silk, the bright clothes of every kind and colour, and everywhere the glitter of gold, silver, silk and satin. Words cannot give a clear impression of that strange spectacle: I have never seen a more beautiful ceremony. What most struck me about that crowd was its silence and discipline. The janissaries, lined up apart from the other troops, were so still that I wondered if they were soldiers or statues until I greeted them, as I had been advised, and they all bowed their heads to me.'

Suleiman was passionately interested in things which sparkled and flashed in the light, precious stones and cloths embroidered in gold. None of his predecessors had loved jewels as much as him, the Venetian traveller Sanudo noted. Everything to be seen today in the Topkapi Palace in Istanbul gives only a pale idea of the riches Suleiman had gathered around him. A Venetian goldsmith had made the sultan a sort of golden tiara set with four rubies, as many diamonds, countless pearls, a huge emerald and a turquoise. A contemporary engraving shows him wearing this strange head-dress, down almost over his eyes and covering his neck and ears like a helmet. It is surmounted by a multicoloured plume. In actual fact, the sultan seems never to have worn it, but when he received an ambassador he put it on a chair next to the throne, also dripping with gold and jewels, so as to create an impression.

'Just as there is only one God in heaven, there can be only one empire on earth,' Ibrahim said to Western visitors.

3
From the Danube to the Euphrates

In October 1530, a new diplomatic mission from Ferdinand arrived in Constantinople. It was led by Nicholas Juritchitch, the hereditary chamberlain of Croatia. With him came the Count of Lamberg, a Styrian nobleman. Their brief was to ask Suleiman to give back Hungary – just like Hobordansky's unsuccessful mission of two years earlier, when a high-handed and aggressive approach had only aggravated tension between the two sovereigns.

Habsburg Arrogance

Juritchitch and Lamberg took a quite different line. Ferdinand had no doubt told them to succeed at any price because his position in Hungary was rapidly deteriorating as it became clear that he could neither expel the Turks nor restore the unity of the kingdom. He needed a large supply of troops from the Holy Roman Empire, but he completely failed to obtain them. The nobles who had elected him made it very clear that if they had known that no effort, or practically none, would be made to drive out the Turks, they would not have split with the supporters of Zapolyai. Ferdinand did what he could, but the other Christian states like Austria and Bohemia, unaware of the danger, took little interest in the countries outside the empire such as Hungary. Ferdinand shared with his brother the perennial Habsburg difficulty: shortage of money, greatly aggravated by the debts left by their grandfather Maximilian. Religious disputes made his task even more complicated: certain countries in the empire sympathized with the Lutheran reforms and demanded religious freedom in return for financial support in the struggle against the Turks. Furthermore, Ferdinand was preparing for his election as 'King of the Romans'[1] and had to bring influence to bear on the German electors.

By this time, states were beginning to acquire a stronger and stronger sense of their own identity and argued bitterly in all discussions about subsidies towards the war against the Infidel. The question was constantly on the agenda in the councils of the empire and various other countries, but it was never sorted out. Charles V could do little to help his brother as he was even more taken up with the problems of religion and had also suddenly found Spain and Southern Italy under threat: Barbarossa had taken Algiers and dominated the Central Mediterranean, while Suleiman and Francis I's designs in Italy could not be ignored either.

The first interview between Ferdinand's plenipotentiaries and Ibrahim went badly. Juritchitch and Lamberg could express themselves in German or, if absolutely necessary, Latin, while Ibrahim had only an Italian interpreter. Finally they agreed on Croatian. Ibrahim spoke of Charles V's sack of Rome in the previous year, of the Pope and Francis I, always referring to Charles as 'the King of Spain' and to Ferdinand by his name while refusing to use his titles of 'King of Bohemia and Hungary'. Ferdinand was the Governor of Vienna for the King of Spain and had absolutely no right to Hungary, he told them. Charles thought himself an emperor because he had a crown on his head, but only the sword could truly acquire such imperial titles. Peace could be re-established only if Ferdinand renounced all claims to Hungary and gave up the part of the country he had occupied, and if Charles returned to Spain and left Zapolyai, whom Suleiman had invested King of Hungary, in peace.

The ambassadors thought they could persuade Ibrahim to change his mind by offering money. My master has no need of money, he replied, the Castle of the Seven Towers (where the state treasury was kept) is overflowing with it. Their meeting with the Grand Vizier had led nowhere and they were finally admitted to see Suleiman. In order to impress them, an exceptionally dazzling display was put on at the audience: in the first court of the Seraglio they saw two elephants; six lions and two leopards were chained up in the next. Before the *Divan* room, 3,000 janissaries were assembled, palace guards and bodyguards, wearing golden head-dresses. The ambassadors were received first by the Grand Vizier surrounded by other viziers and leading dignitaries, and then a chamberlain took them to the sultan. Juritchitch again demanded the restitution of the area of Hungary occupied by Zapolyai and insisted on a quick response.

Two days later, they obtained their reply, when they were summoned by the Grand Vizier and told that there was no question of giving back a country 'twice conquered by our arms'. It would have been unbecoming and probably dangerous to insist further: the plenipotentiaries could do nothing but ask to leave.

Their mission had been a complete failure, largely because they had shown absolutely no tact and had revealed only the typical Habsburg arrogance and total ignorance of the personalities and customs of the Orient.

Suleiman had even less desire than usual to make peace. The moment had come to face his only true adversary, Charles V. Circumstances were favourable and 'the King of Spain's' pride, he thought, would bring him up against his great enemy. The sultan declared war on Ferdinand as 'the lieutenant of the King of Spain in Germany', attacking Charles indirectly through his representative. There was only room for one emperor. Charles and his German empire were going to be wiped out.

The German War Against 'The King of Spain'

On 25 April 1532, the sultan set off on a new campaign in the Danube territories. He had with him 100,000 men, including 12,000 janissaries, 30,000 Anatolian soldiers, 16,000 Rumelian soldiers and 20,000 Porte knights, the rest consisting of *akinci*, sappers, pontoneers, etc. As in earlier campaigns, 300 cannons made up his artillery force. At Belgrade, he received 15,000 Tartar reinforcements led by Sahib Giray, the khan's brother. At Eszek, the *sancakbey* brought him further troops. Thus it was at the head of 150,000 to 200,000 men, probably including 100,000 combatants, that Suleiman advanced to meet Charles V.

At Niš, Ferdinand's envoys, the Counts of Nogarola and Lamberg, again came with peace proposals. In vain they offered 25,000 ducats, then 100,000, in return for Suleiman's acceptance of Ferdinand as King of Hungary. Suleiman sent them away with these words: 'The King of Spain has long said that he wants to take on the Turks. Well, by the grace of God, I am now on my way to meet him with my army. If he is great-hearted, let him wait for me on the field of battle and then let the will of God be done. If he has no desire to meet me, let him send a tribute to my imperial majesty.'

He also rejected the request of Rinçon, the King of France's ambassador who had come to Belgrade to ask Suleiman to fight Charles in Italy rather than Germany. Suleiman refused but promised that Barbarossa would help the French in the Mediterranean capture Milan and Genoa.[2] It was too late to change his plans since illness had retained Rinçon at Ragusa. Yet even if he had met with Suleiman in Istanbul before the expedition left, it is doubtful if he could have convinced him to give up his plan of facing the greatest sovereign of Christian Europe in a decisive battle.

Suleiman did not, in fact, meet with Charles V, but the troops of the Holy Roman Empire did participate, for the last time, in the fight against the Turks. Charles had created a brief period of respite for himself by means of an accord signed with the Protestants at Nuremberg: they would help in the struggle against the Turks provided that Charles abandoned (temporarily) the decisions taken at Augsburg (which called on the Protestants to rejoin the Catholic Church and to fight against the sectaries). That accord, signed partly because of the Ottoman danger, gave Charles a breathing space in Germany, which he used to assemble some Spanish and Italian contingents near Vienna for the defence of Austria. (At Vienna, where a new siege was feared, defences had been organized very rapidly.) These troops, few in number, were quite unable to face the powerful army of Suleiman, but they were well used to slow down the progress of the Turks (as always dogged by the changing seasons), and make them lose time before insignificant positions fortified as well as circumstances permitted.

The main battle took place before the fortress of Güns (Köszeg), about 100 kilometres to the South-East of Vienna. Suleiman had easily reduced a series of poorly defended positions in Southern Hungary, but his advance had been delayed and it was only on 9 August that the Turkish army, led by the Grand Vizier, reached the little town of Güns, which was defended by a mere 800 men. They were led by Nicholas Juritchitch, the very man who had headed Ferdinand's mission to Constantinople less than two years earlier. The Turkish artillery pounded the city and mines breached the walls, but to no effect, as every assault was beaten back. On the sixth day of the siege, Suleiman called on Juritchitch to surrender and agree to pay an annual tribute or the immediate sum of 2,000 florins.

Juritchitch replied that he did not have so much money and could not give up a fortress which belonged not to him but to Ferdinand. The summons was three times repeated and three times refused. Ibrahim immediately gave the order for attack.

'The janissaries and *azab* rushed forward and had already planted eight standards on the walls. Only protected by flimsy defences and crushed against the wall, the inhabitants waited for their last hour, when the old people, women and children uttered a cry so pitiful and piercing that the attackers retreated in terror and even left two of their standards in the citizens' hands. This change of fortune occurred so suddenly and seemed so miraculous to both sides that the Turks believed they saw a heavenly knight brandishing a sword against them and the Christians thought they recognized Saint Martin, the doughty patron of Stein on the river Anger.'[3]

Ibrahim was deeply impressed by Juritchitch's brilliant defence of the town and promised him a safe conduct if he came to his camp. Juritchitch, who had lost half his men and had no gunpowder left, agreed. The Grand Vizier received him considerately, asked if his wounds had healed and finally, in the sultan's name, made over the town to him. Gifts were also exchanged.

Shortly afterwards, Suleiman held a solemn *Divan* and was congratulated on the success of his siege – which had in fact made him lose several weeks without achieving anything much. Ferdinand's envoys again asked to be received and again claimed the part of Hungary occupied by Zapolyai, although they had no more success than before and were given a threatening letter for Ferdinand. This, however, was written in gold and azure and put in a purse of gold.

With Güns taken, Suleiman could proceed directly to Vienna, which was feverishly preparing for a new siege. To everyone's astonishment, the Turkish army turned East instead, towards Styria. Was the *padishah* carrying out his plan: to meet Charles in pitched battle, crush him and only then return to capture Vienna (just as he had taken Buda after the Battle of Mohacs)? But Charles was no King Lewis: he was in Vienna and had not left the city. He not only avoided meeting Suleiman in a battle which was likely to turn against him; but, as soon as heard the Turks had changed direction, he decided to leave Vienna (to which he never returned). Ferdinand tried to convince him that it would be easy to recapture Hungary after the Turkish departure, but Charles considered that 'it did not befit his imperial reputation for him personally to direct actions against the retreating Turkish army and that it was neither necessary nor reasonable to maintain such a large army'. The imperial troops would undoubtedly have refused to take the initiative against the Turks in Hungary. 'They are ready to defend only Germany and not to continue the fight in Hungary if the Turks start to turn home.'[4] Charles V left for Italy by way of Carinthia and then returned to Spain.

Suleiman ravaged Styria throughout September: towns fell one after another to the Ottoman army. He encamped before Graz but did not enter the town. He was forced back at Maribor and failed to break into the town. He then continued to Belgrade, where he met up with Ibrahim's army. Yunis Bey, the Porte's interpreter, was sent to Venice bearing a letter for the Doge which read: 'The Great Lord reached the town of Graz, former residence of that miserable fugitive who had fled to save his life and abandoned his unbelieving subjects who were following the Devil's path.' The 'miserable fugitive' was clearly Charles V.

On 18 November 1532, Suleiman entered Constantinople after a six months' absence. For five days bright lights and rejoicing celebrated the happy conclusion of 'the war in Germany against the King of Spain'. In reality, the campaign had ended in a setback. The siege of Güns had lost precious time. Ottoman historians think that the sultan tried to lure Charles V into the area, on to a field of battle very favourable to the deployment of the Turkish cavalry, which would have allowed him to crush the imperial army. Did Charles have wind of the manoeuvre? In any event, the plan failed.

A New Turkish Fleet

The sultan's joyful return to Constantinople was marred by a piece of bad news: the fortress of Koron in Morea[5] had been lost by the Ottomans, snatched by Andrea Doria, Charles V's admiral. It had been defended by a mere 14 cannons. Doria had 150 guns and a fleet made up of 35 capital ships and 88 galleys. He made for Patras, which surrendered, and then inflicted the same fate on the two fortresses which guarded the entrance to the Gulf of Corinth. Doria laid waste to the region and retreated at the approach of winter.

Suleiman and Ibrahim pretended to attach little importance to the loss of these two strongholds. Yet such a Spanish expedition in the Mediterranean, after the occupation of Cherchell and Honein, the port serving Tlemcen (now in Algeria), in 1530–31, made Charles V's determination very clear. It revealed his two main aims: to continue the policy of Ximenez,[6] who had never ceased to claim that Spain's strategic frontier was on the South of the Mediterranean, and to take up, in another form, the idea of a crusade. The Turks were not deceived. Although the fortresses of Koron and the Peloponnese might in themselves only be of secondary importance, they understood that Charles would not stop there and that a second front was going to be opened in the Mediterranean. The occupation of Rhodes had relieved them of the task of defending their lines of communication in the Eastern Mediterranean, but the Spanish and their allies were now going to oppose them throughout the Mediterranean. These forces were commanded by a brilliant admiral, the Genoese prince Andrea Doria, whom Francis I had been foolish enough to let go and who had taken up service with the emperor.[7] Suleiman revealed his military genius when he appointed a highly experienced and extraordinarily bold chief of corsairs as the admiral of his fleet against the formidable Doria. The man, as we shall see, was Khair ad-Din – whom we know better as Barbarossa.

Thus the Ottoman Mediterranean policy, hesitant up until then, becomes clear-cut, as the Turks exploited the experience and courage of the corsairs and their captains. They were involved in an almost continuous confrontation with the Spanish for the whole of Suleiman's and his son's reigns, down to the Battle of Lepanto – over half a century later. The descendants of Turkish tribes from the depths of Asia soon learnt the maritime skills they needed, thanks to the immense resources of money – and wood – possessed by the Ottomans in the 16th century. By the middle of the century, the Ottoman fleet equalled in number those of all the other Mediterranean countries put together. In 1571, at the Battle of Lepanto, 300 ships fought on the Turkish side, yet Venice never had more than 120, Genoa 25, the Pope a dozen, and Spain 50 to 100; France counted for little at sea. 'In the Mediterranean, the second third of the 16th century belonged to the Turks.'[8]

'Peace for Several Centuries'

Turkish setbacks in the Peloponnese and the Gulf of Corinth, although limited, took place at an unfortunate time. The campaign in Central Europe had turned out badly even if it was presented as a success. Above all, Suleiman was soon going to have to launch a new campaign in Persia: he had long wished to restore his authority in Eastern Anatolia and capture Baghdad. But one of the golden rules of the Ottoman Empire was to avoid at all costs fighting on two fronts. The Sublime Porte therefore had to make sure that its European enemies would remain peaceful, particularly since it was known at Constantinople that Charles V and Tahmasp, the new Shah of Iran, were in contact and planning to coordinate their operations against Suleiman.

But Charles V and Ferdinand also needed a respite from war. Difficulties were piling up in Germany. The Protestant princes had formed the Schmalkaldic League, which had just established ties with the Wittelsbachs (who were Catholics) and with Francis I. Charles had had no choice but to backpedal and agree not to cause any annoyance to the dissident princes until the next council had been held. In addition, he and his brother suffered from the usual lack of money.

Thus, the Habsburg Emperor and the Ottoman both needed a breathing space before continuing the long contest which would last, they knew well, for the rest of their lives. When Ferdinand asked to be allowed to send envoys to discuss peace to Constantinople, he therefore received a favourable response. A mission led by Jerome of Zara soon arrived and was offered a truce – to become a genuine peace treaty when Suleiman had received the keys to the town of Gran (Esztergom) from Ferdinand as a sign of his submission to Suleiman's sovereignty. A second embassy arrived with the keys shortly afterwards, together with a letter from Charles V demanding once more the return of Hungary to Ferdinand – in exchange for which, he added, he would give Koron back. These two messages revealed a startling lack of diplomacy – so little had the Habsburg princes learnt from the difficulties of the years gone by.

Negotiations started with the traditional exchange of gifts. The Grand Vizier received a gold medallion decorated with a huge diamond, an even larger ruby and a 'pear-shaped' pearl. Then Ibrahim made a great speech, praising to the skies the power and riches of the Ottoman Empire. Charles's ambassador offered to return Koron in exchange for Hungary but Ibrahim replied that possession of Koron was a matter of complete indifference to them and that they would in any case prefer to reconquer the fortress than obtain it by negotiation. As for Hungary, they had given it to John Zapolyai and he would keep it.

An important incident occurred during the reading of the letter from Charles, when he was referred to, in a long list of titles, as 'King of Jerusalem'. 'How dare he call himself King of Jerusalem?' Ibrahim cried out. 'Does he not know that the Great Lord is master of Jerusalem? Does he mean to steal territories from my master or reveal his lack of respect for him?' He also spoke ironically about the emperor's vain threats: 'He has talked of fighting us, of compelling the Lutherans to convert, but it has all remained a dead letter. It is not worthy of an emperor to undertake something and not accomplish it, to talk but do nothing.'

In the course of these conversations, the Austrian plenipotentiaries were struck by Ibrahim's immense pride when he uttered statements which were almost insulting to Suleiman: 'I can make a sultan of a stableboy. I can give territories to whoever I want without my master making any comment. And when he orders me to do something I don't like, nothing is carried out. It is my will which is accomplished, not his.' Later, those who wanted the sultan to dismiss his favourite had a good deal of evidence like this to put forward.

Finally, the *padishah* granted 'peace for several centuries' to Ferdinand, whom he promised to treat 'like his own son'. The ambassadors had obtained nothing: Zapolyai retained control of Hungary whose frontiers would later be fixed by Gritti[9] in Suleiman's name. Any accords Ferdinand and Zapolyai wished to sign had to be approved by the sultan. The Great Lord, said Ibrahim to the ambassadors before their departure, would be friend of the friends and enemy of the enemies of his son, King Ferdinand. He added that if Charles, King of Spain, wanted peace, he should send an embassy to the Sublime Porte.

The truce Suleiman had signed with Ferdinand committed him to nothing: he had made no concessions and could break it off whenever he wished. But he had made sure of his defences on the European front, which left his hands free for his Persian expedition.

The Conqueror of Baghdad (1534)

Enmity between the Sunni Ottoman sultans and the Shiite Shahs of Iran dated back a long time, as we have seen. The populations of the frontier regions, cut off from the urban and religious centres, had felt the influence, from the 13th to the 15th centuries, of the dervishes,[10] some of them fairly moderate, like the Mevlevis, and others far more heretical (the Hurufi). These heterodox communities, common enough in the early centuries of the empire, considered themselves victims of a central authority which had inflicted restrictions on them, and in particular taxes, they had never experienced before. In the middle of the 15th century, Mehmed II's expropriation of pious bequests and land they owned outright further increased their irritation.[11]

A century later, nothing had changed. These Muslims turned towards the new power of the Safavids, the *şeyh* of Ardabil – Shiite – who would soon dominate Persia for over two centuries. The rivalries between Bayezid's heirs after his defeat, and between the supporters they sought either among the Mamluks or the Safavids, tore the country apart even more. Thus Selim I, when he took power in Constantinople, decided to finish once and for all with the two powers who would otherwise never cease to be a menace to the Ottoman Empire. He succeeded in Egypt but, despite the victory over Ismail at Chaldiran, failed in Iran. The shah had now become a powerful sovereign and an enemy all the more dangerous in that his propaganda proved highly effective among the Shiites of Anatolia and Thrace, who were therefore considered unreliable by the central Ottoman authorities.[12]

Suleiman was also aware of the dangers the Shiite contingents – the Kizilbaş[13] – represented for the empire. He knew of the persecution of Sunnis in Mesopotamia: Sunni notables executed, the tombs of Abu Hanifa[14] (the founder of the religious rituals the Turks used) and Abdulkadir al-Gilani destroyed, Sunni mosques converted into Shiite mosques. The Safavid possessions also represented an obstacle to Turkish ambitions towards the Indian Ocean. The traditional role of the Middle East in trading between South East Asia and Eastern Europe had been put in jeopardy by the Portuguese discovery of the Cape of Good Hope. Such a role could only be sustained if the Ottomans, who had gained control of the Red Sea and Egyptian route in 1517, also had authority over the Gulf and Mesopotamian route (also used to ship products coming from Eastern Asia).[15] Finally, the Safavid possessions prevented the Turks from holding out the hand of friendship, as they wished, towards their Uzbek allies on the other side of Iran.[16]

Suleiman thus had many good reasons for undertaking a campaign against the shah. The war – the 'Two Iraqs Campaign' – lasted for two years. It brought neither defeat nor ruin to the Safavids, but it safeguarded the immense Ottoman possessions in the Middle East, which they were to control for almost four centuries.

The Ottomans found a double pretext to declare war: the treasonable behaviour of the Bey of Bitlis, Şeref Khan, which had worked to the shah's advantage; and the assassination, in Baghdad, of the Safavid governor, who had abandoned the shah's cause and sent Suleiman the keys to the city. The Porte considered itself, the possessor of these keys, as the owner of the city and, when Shah Tahmasp took it over again, believed that he had attacked Suleiman and dragged Baghdad down into the Shiite heresy.

In the autumn of 1533, after long preparations, Ibrahim left for Bitlis and Iranian Azerbaijan as *serasker* (supreme commander of the army). The troops proceeded through Anatolia and then Azerbaijan, encountering many difficulties due to bad weather or the mountainous terrain but few enemy soldiers: before Ibrahim had reached Konya, the head of the rebellious Governor of Bitlis was sent to him by the Governor of Azerbaijan, who had betrayed Tahmasp. Soon afterwards, the commanders of the Safavid fortresses near Lake Van surrendered to the sultan. Ibrahim and his units set out for Aleppo, where they spent the winter. If they had marched on Baghdad instead, they would certainly have captured the city. The Ottomans were already at Kirkuk and Mosul and it is astonishing that they did not grab the chance to realize their ancient ambition of taking control of the Abbasid capital. Was Ibrahim dissuaded from such a plan by the intrigues of his rival Iskender Çelebi, the Minister of Finance, for fear he was being pushed into undertaking a disastrous operation? Did Safavid refugees, to whom governorships had already been promised, put pressure on him? Was he convinced that he could easily capture Qom, Kashan and Ray and then turn to the conquest of Baghdad?

The Ottomans thus set out in the spring towards Tabriz. The Safavid tribal chiefs and garrison commanders submitted in turn and, on 16 July 1534, Ibrahim made his solemn entry into the capital of the Safavid Empire, Tabriz, which Tahmasp had just left. He immediately built a fort and installed a garrison. Suleiman joined up with him two months later. His journey from Constantinople to Azerbaijan had been more like a triumphal march among peoples who came from great distances to pay homage to him. At Tabriz, the emirs of Gilan and Shirvan submitted to him. The latter's son was appointed Governor of Tabriz. The two armies then set out southwards, in the direction of Baghdad.

The time of year made it difficult for the troops to make headway. Many animals died in the Hamadan passes, the guns which could not be transported – 100 out of 300, according to one chronicler – had to be buried, the chariots burned; cannons, on the other hand, were abandoned and used by the Safavids. Bad weather was again the sultan's main problem; the general staff clearly seems to have been unable to deal with the logistical problems. Provisioning an army of 200,000 men was a very difficult task requiring enormous skill. Mistakes had certainly been made: one of the leading Ottoman dignitaries, the *nişanci*, died of hunger during the campaign. Tahmasp used his usual burnt earth technique: the heavy

Ottoman army was quite unable to join battle with the light Safavid cavalry and, as long as they failed to do so, the Turks could never conquer Iran or even establish themselves for long in Azerbaijan.

The shah's troops never appeared and did not even attempt to harass the Turks as they made their difficult crossing of the Zagros mountains before arriving, utterly exhausted, in the Mesopotamian plains. When the Ottomans came within sight of Baghdad, the shah's governors and his troops had already retreated. The Grand Vizier went ahead to take possession of the town; a few days later, on 4 December 1534, the sultan made his entry.

The city of the caliphs was no more than a shadow of its former self. Even in 1184 the Arab traveller, Ibn Jubair, had written: 'Most of its buildings have disappeared and only the glory of its name remains. It looks rather like the faded remains of an encampment, a blurred sea of tracks, a fugitive phantom of the imagination. No longer does its arresting beauty invite troubled spirits to careless idling. Yet its river, the Tigris, remains . . .' In 1437, a century before Suleiman's entry, al-Makrisi remarked: 'Baghdad is in ruins. There are neither mosques, a faithful congregation, calls to prayer nor souks; most of the palm trees are dried out. It cannot be called a town.'

In both these accounts one must bear in mind Arab exaggeration. Even Ibn Jubair talks of 'delicious' gardens and the 'countless' people. Intellectual life had not disappeared, commerce was active, and yet this was far from being the capital that al-Mansour, the second Abbasid caliph, had founded in 762.

In the form of a perfect circle, the 'round city', more often called 'the city of peace' (*medinat al-salam*), had soon become a great urban centre of major commercial and intellectual importance. A surrounding wall with four gates in it formed the only defence. The caliph's residence, a sumptuous palace in the centre of the city, far outshone in luxury and magnificence all the buildings put up by the Sassanids and the Omayyad sovereigns. Only the sacred palace of the emperors of Byzantium could compare with it. It was surmounted by a huge cupola, the 'green cupola', where the caliph received the foreign envoys, who left marvelling at a degree of splendour they had never imagined. Beside the round city was a commercial quarter, where an active and bustling population of very diverse origins – native Aramaeans, Arab conquerors, Iranians, Turks, Jews, Christians, slaves from Russia, Nubia and Turkestan – were in constant contact with each other. The city was an intellectual melting-pot: every opposing view was put forward and all the different tendencies of every religion had their place. The caliphs encouraged the study of science and philosophy. (One of them, al-Mamun, established the translation of the major Greek authors.)

From the reign of Haroun al-Rashid, less than 50 years after its foundation, to the end of the 8th century, Baghdad enjoyed an unprecedented degree of prosperity and influence which it retained for many years, despite the vicissitudes of religious and political disputes. These were a major cause of the decline and fall of the Abbasids. At the end of the 12th century, another Muslim capital, Cairo, supplanted Baghdad, which had been disturbed by more and more violent crises but nonetheless continued for a long time to be very active commercially and intellectually. The arrival on the scene of the Turkish Seljuk sultans – with whom the caliphs shared power and who often ruled alone – and then the 'caliphal renaissance' at the end of the 12th century, again covered in glory a city which retained its prestige in the Islamic world. Yet the invasion of Hulegu, one of Genghis Khan's grandsons, in 1258, reduced the 'city of peace' to the rank of a provincial metropolis. Tamerlane, who had several tens of thousands of its citizens executed, completed its ruin. Finally, the reign of the White Sheep Turkoman princes had further increased the decadence of the town before Shah Ismail came to occupy it.

As the new master of the ancient Abbasid capital, Suleiman was now indeed the legitimate successor of the caliphs. He had brought about the triumph of Sunnism on all sides. His prestige in the Islamic world was constantly increasing. As soon as he had snatched Baghdad from the heretics and entered the city, his first action was to restore the tomb of Abu Hanifa, the founder of the orthodox rite used by the Turks, which had been desecrated by the Safavids; they were even said to have burnt the holy man's remains, yet they were found, miraculously intact. Suleiman also had a mosque and a *medrese* built near the tomb. The tomb of the great Hanbali sage, al-Gilani, was also repaired and work to construct a mosque at Kadhimain rapidly pushed ahead. Suleiman also visited the Shiite holy places: taking both Sunnis and Shiites under his protection, he affirmed the Islamic universalism of the House of Osman.

Having given orders for such works of construction and restoration, the sultan set up a system of Turkish administration in Mesopotamia. A governor was appointed, as in the other provinces of the empire. Garrisons of janissaries and *sipahi* were established in Baghdad and several other towns, the defences of the ancient capital were repaired and reinforced. He instituted a survey of property and distributed fiefdoms.

Soon Baghdad, under the protection of the *pax Ottomanica*, experienced a new period of prosperity. Basra became Ottoman some years later, which took the frontiers of the empire to the Indian Ocean.[17]

On 2 April 1535, the sultan and his army left Baghdad for Tabriz. They took three months to cross Kurdistan and the region of Lake Ourmia. Although it was a good time of year, the march proved difficult and the sultan gave out gratuities to his soldiers when they arrived. He took up residence in the shah's palace. He no doubt believed that he would be able to meet Tahmasp in battle straightaway and finish with the Persian menace once and for all.

But the shah, as always, had retreated with his army. The terrain favoured his strategy, while for Suleiman the distance between his bases made provisioning difficult, not to say impossible. His army was too heavy and not mobile enough to fight an enemy which was so hard to pin down. To set off into the mountains or deserts of Iran would have been madness – the Turkish army would never have returned. Ibrahim's plan to capture the whole Iranian plain as far as Ray, Qom and Kashan could never succeed.

After spending two weeks at Tabriz, Suleiman gave the order for departure. The campaign which had brought great glory to the empire with the capture of Baghdad, but also great losses, could not be prolonged. About 30,000 men had died, mainly of hunger and cold, and 22,000 horses and camels had perished. The troops had neither the morale nor the stamina to face another winter on campaign.

At the beginning of January 1536, Suleiman and Ibrahim were back in Istanbul. On 18 February, Ibrahim signed in the sultan's name the first agreement with France. A month later, the empire and then Europe were amazed to learn of the dramatic end of the all-powerful Grand Vizier.

Ibrahim's Tragedy

In the morning of 15 March 1536, Ibrahim's lifeless body was discovered in the Topkapi Palace, in the bedroom next to the sultan's where he slept. The torn clothes and bloodstains on the walls – they were still to be seen there years later – made clear that he had fought valiantly and that the Seraglio mutes had managed to put the noose round his neck only after a long struggle. His corpse was taken to a dervish monastery behind the arsenal, and buried without any inscription to indicate where the man who had been almost the *padishah*'s equal for thirteen years was buried.

The fall of the all-powerful Grand Vizier in circumstances which soon became known made an enormous impact. There was much speculation about what could have led Suleiman to do away with a man who had for so long been remarkably close to him. But if the sultan spoke of this to his intimates, history has preserved no record of the fact.

Examination of political motives is always very difficult. Had Ibrahim betrayed Suleiman in some way to Charles V or Ferdinand? Yet, quite apart from the fact that no letters indicating his guilt have been found in the Austrian archives, it is hard to imagine the advantage that Ibrahim, who had virtually unlimited power and resources at his disposal, could hope to gain by betraying a country and a man who had given him almost the status of a sovereign. Could he have betrayed the sultan to the shah in return for an immense amount of gold, as Iskender Çelebi, the Minister of Finance, alleged before his execution? Yet Ibrahim was incredibly rich and there is reason to suspect the testimony of a man who revealed an intense hatred for the Grand Vizier who was to bring about his death.

A more likely explanation is intriguing by Roxelane. The ambitious and wilful sultan's wife detested Ibrahim. While he was alive, she could never completely rule Suleiman's mind – and she had not become the first lady of the empire merely to produce dynastic heirs. The death the year before of Hafsa Hatun, the *valide sultan* and mother of Suleiman, had removed a personal rival and a protector of Ibrahim, who now remained the only obstacle. Roxelane probably poisoned the sultan's mind slowly and surely by echoing the slanders about the Grand Vizier retailed by the many envious courtiers and the rumours of the public, which had never felt much affection for an ostentatious and disdainful Christian renegade. Thus, after the Battle of Mohacs, when he brought back three antique sculptures from Buda and set them up in the Hippodrome, the whole of Istanbul was horrified by the infringement of Islamic law. He was even considered an idolator, and the poet Fighani Çelebi wrote a satirical poem about him: 'The world has known two Abrahams: one destroyed idols and the other raised them up again.' Ibrahim was absolutely furious and gave orders for the poet to be marched around the city on a donkey before being strangled. Enemies said that Ibrahim had always remained a Christian despite his conversion to Islam. They quoted the disdain he exhibited for the Holy Places as evidence.

His wife Hadice, the sister of Suleiman, also had little cause to wish him well. Although she had borne him a son, Mehmed Shah, he had greatly annoyed her by taking a second wife called Muhsine.

Harem intrigues and popular rumours on their own, however, would not have been able to win over a man as self-willed as Suleiman. Everything indicates that Ibrahim's own behaviour, particularly some recent errors he had committed, exerted a decisive influence.

Although modest and unsure of himself at the start of his career, he had with time become incredibly arrogant. We have seen the kind of language he used to Ferdinand's ambassadors when they came to negotiate with the Porte. These statements and many others, just as insulting to the *padishah*, were evidently brought to the sultan's notice.

On one occasion, during the Persian campaign, Ibrahim announced that he was taking the title of *serasker sultan*. In Persia, admittedly, provincial governors were indeed known as 'sultan', but for the Turks – and for Suleiman – there could be only one sultan, in Constantinople.

Along with Ibrahim's astounding presumption went the musky intrigue which led to the fall and then execution of the *defterdar* (Minister of Finance) Iskender Çelebi. The Grand Vizier convinced the sultan to deprive him of his post and, since it would be dangerous to let him live, to condemn him to death. He was hanged in the marketplace in Baghdad. Yet the following night Suleiman dreamt about the unfortunate man, who complained of his punishment and threatened to strangle him. The sultan took fright and, apparently, became rapidly convinced of the innocence of his victim and the injustice Ibrahim had made him commit. Perhaps he also remembered in the following weeks the accusations Iskender had made before marching to his death: that Ibrahim was plotting with the Persians and plotting against Suleiman himself.

A day came when Ibrahim's very existence became unbearable to the *padishah*. *Raison d'état* demanded his disappearance, just as we shall later see the sultan's two sons, Mustafa and Bayezid, paying with their lives for rebellion in an empire where every particle belonged to the sultan. This very Asiatic conception of the law allowed Suleiman, for example, to take into his treasury all the wealth of the Grand Viziers or leading dignitaries when they died or were dismissed. Thus, the whole immense fortune amassed by Ibrahim was confiscated by Suleiman.

The Turkish sovereign was in fact a despot whose sacred authority was limited only by the *Şeriat* or law of Mohammed. In practice, however, he also had to take into account the wishes and caprices of the army, particularly the janissaries, and public opinion in Istanbul, which loudly made its presence felt in certain circumstances.

Istanbul[18] was a very big city with a large and diverse population; rumours, true and false, spread all the more rapidly because of their close links with the civil and military personnel of the palace. In times of crisis a mere nothing could often set a spark ablaze. A popular demonstration would lead to a scuffle, and the army would intervene – not always on the side of the rulers.[19] Sometimes the mere fact that the sultan had stayed away too long from the capital provoked discontent: in 1525, when Suleiman prolonged a hunting trip near Edirne, he had to rush back to Istanbul because the janissaries were becoming restive and the citizens were gathering in the streets. The sultans were particularly wary of the religious leaders, *şeyh* and dervishes, who attracted fanatics eager to follow them everywhere. Sometimes rebellion even reached the provinces: peasants took to the roads in a form of passive resistance. Land lay fallow, production fell off – and so did taxes. The rulers then had to pacify the discontented, usually by remission of taxes.

Suleiman also took great care to quash any possible accusations of violating the precepts of Islam. Every Friday, the *padishah* went to say his prayers in solemn state and, on the Feast of the Sacrifice (*Kurban Bayram*), the throats of 3,000 sheep were ritually slit and the meat given to the poor. The departure of the pilgrimage for Mecca was celebrated each year with great festivities. The sultan let no occasion slip to show by his piety that he was the true Leader of the Faithful. The Turkish people, who were deeply committed to their religion, would have rapidly and brutally punished a sultan accused of impiety or violating the *Şeriat*, which had been established once and for all.

In the tragic conclusion to the life of the young and handsome Grand Vizier, it is reasonable to assume that public dissatisfaction with a man who did not conceal, in his later years, his contempt for the religion of Mohammed, who had put up statues in full public view in Constantinople, and whose insane pride – as everybody knew – made him think himself greater than the heir of Osman, exerted a large influence on Suleiman. For all his power, the sultan could not forever remain deaf to the rumours which were spread against the Grand Vizier, even if, as always, they attributed misdeeds to him worse than those he had committed and vices worse than he possessed.

The reverberations, in Turkey and elsewhere, set off by the death of the illustrious favourite eventually died down. Another Grand Vizier,

Ayas Pasha, was appointed and the glorious reign of the sultan known to Europeans as 'the Magnificent' continued. When Ibrahim's properties were seized, his palace by the Hippodrome was turned into a school for pageboys and his gardens at Sutluce on the Golden Horn long became popular as a place for a walk. Now even the tree which was said to mark the place where his remains were buried is long dead; nobody knows any longer where the man lies who thought himself the equal of the greatest sultan of the Ottomans.

The death of Ibrahim and the difficult 'Two Iraqs Campaign' mark the end of the first phase of Suleiman's reign. Youth disappeared from the court with the brutal demise of the sultan's favourite: no confidant or friend would replace the handsome Greek. Those received by Suleiman at the Seraglio or with whom he discussed theology or poetry were subjects whose intelligence and talent he appreciated rather than real friends. From then on, there was always a certain distance between Suleiman and other men, and this only increased with time. He was only truly intimate with Roxelane – his mother, Hafsa Hatun, was dead – and perhaps with his favourite sons, Mehmed and Cihangir. No one else. The strictest protocol was observed in the Seraglio, and when he went out he was surrounded by pomp and ceremony which were dazzling but which also trapped him within his image of inaccessible Oriental sovereign.

The era of great conquests was now over: the capture of Baghdad was the last. Other conquests – in Eastern Anatolia, the Aegean islands, North Africa and the Red Sea – only complete or form the logical sequel to contests already begun. From now on, it seemed as if the empire had reached its natural limits of expansion. Later centuries would witness further great feats of arms bringing more glory to the sultans, provinces lost and recaptured, Grand Viziers ruling the state with a firm and assured hand. Yet nothing would match those years of great conquests and wise rule by the young emperor. If the empire can be said to have had an apogee, it was certainly at that time.

4
The Struggle with Christian Europe

More than fifteen years had gone by since the first Ottoman incursions into Central Europe. With Belgrade and then Buda taken, and Ottoman troops before Vienna, nothing seemed able to halt the sultan's westward advances, towards the European capitals Ibrahim had often told Western envoys that Suleiman could seize whenever he wished. No armies could slow down his progress; only the climate and the distances involved exhausted his troops and always prevented them from making full use of their successes. Suleiman knew better than anyone the limits to which his soldiers could be pushed.

The Catholic emperor was quite clear that no decisive battle against the enemy of Christendom was going to take place in the Danube region. He and his brother Ferdinand were involved in costly wars against the King of England, the King of France and, above all the German Reformers. Charles was still a great believer in the traditional idea of a crusade, which was far more popular in Spain than elsewhere because of the many problems posed by the large population of Moors. The emperor dreamed of expelling the Muslims from Europe once and for all. But he knew that this dream – unless providence intervened – was unattainable. He did not possess the means of realizing it, and nobody in Europe would have accepted the increase in Austrian power and authority a major victory against the Infidels would have given them. Like Suleiman, in the years around 1535, Charles V believed that the decisive events would take place elsewhere, in the Mediterranean.

Spain under the Catholic Kings and Ottoman Europe were not maritime powers at the beginning of the 16th century. When they came to the throne, neither Suleiman nor Charles V had major fleets to put to sea. The successes of the Spanish in Italy, and then against the corsairs from 1500 to 1510, and the conquest of the ports of North Africa by Pedro Navarro were isolated achievements which were not followed up. The Turks, however, had everything they needed to build and equip a powerful fleet: arsenals and numerous well-sheltered ports. They only lacked experienced admirals and superior officers. Although the conquest of Egypt and Syria and then the capture of Rhodes had considerably extended the empire's maritime influence, Suleiman was by no means dominant at sea. The two emperors would indeed have undoubtedly abandoned the Mediterranean to those whose natural element it was – Venice, Ragusa, the corsairs – if they had not received the support, at almost the same time, of the two greatest sea-lords of the era, Andrea Doria and Barbarossa.

The Lords of the Sea

In 1520, Andrea Doria was over 50 and had long experience as a *condottiere*. Genoese by birth and a member of one of the noblest families in Europe – in 1397, a Doria had married the daughter of the Emperor of Constantinople, Manuel Palaeologus – he was the son of a fairly poor galley captain. He served first in Pope Innocent VIII's guard and then, in turn, the Duke of Urbino, Ferdinand King of Naples and his brother Alfonso II, and finally Giovanni de la Rovere. In 1522, as a famous sea captain and the owner of several galleys, he offered his services to Francis I, who accepted them. Almost at once, he defeated Charles's fleet off the coast of Provence. Control of the Mediterranean was almost in the grasp of the French king.

Was Francis just careless or too much under the influence of his chancellor, Duprat? Either way, he seems not to have understood the central role the Mediterranean was going to play, nor the invaluable trump card Doria could be in his struggles against the Austrian dynasty. Doria, for his part, was very attached to his birthplace and extremely vain and would not tolerate Francis's attitude to Genoa nor the way he personally was treated. In 1515, after the Battle of Marignano, Genoa had come under French control. Francis for some reason rapidly gave evidence of his disdain for the proud city. He announced his plan to build up the fortifications around Savona, the rival town, to transfer Genoa's trade there and to grant them the proceeds from the salt-tax. The Genoese asked for help from Doria, who was already disenchanted with the French king for depriving him of his share of the ransom of Hugo de Moncade, the chief of the Spanish squadron he had taken prisoner. Despite the advice of the Marshal of Lautrec, Francis listened to Duprat and sent to Genoa a man called Barbezieux – 'He did not know,' according to Brantôme, 'the meaning of the words sea, port or galley'! – with orders to seize the galleys and person of Doria. 'There are your galleys,' said Doria, pointing out some Provençal galleys which sailed under his colours. 'You can take them; but they belong to me, and I am answerable to no one.'

It was one of those rare days which witnessed a decisive change of fortune. Doria immediately took up service with Charles V, who accepted all his conditions, including the restoration of Genoese autonomy and institutions, with Savona dependent on Genoa. Doria's first action was to expel the French from his native city. They had lost the one man who could have achieved naval supremacy for them.

The Catholic King and Holy Roman Emperor had Doria; the Ottoman sultan had Barbarossa, quite his equal in the arts of war and his clear superior in boldness and trickery.

The son of a Greek potter from Mytilene, Barbarossa (or Khair ad-Din) had converted to Islam, like his brothers Oruç, Elias and Işak and other islanders who preferred roving the seas to fishing for tuna or viniculture. Oruç remained the chief of the clan until his death.

At first, the four brothers operated in the Ionian archipelago: from their bases at Durazzo, in the Gulf of Arta and at Preveza, they attacked Christian shipping and raided villages. In 1501, after an encounter with the Knights of Rhodes, Elias was killed and Oruç taken prisoner. Oruç rowed as a galley slave for the Order of Saint John for four years, until his father paid the ransom to release him.

When Oruç took to sea again, he soon realized that piracy in the Eastern Mediterranean had become less profitable. Venetian and Genoese commerce was slowing down as the republics lost their maritime possessions and as the Turkish fleet started to cruise in the Aegean and Ionian seas. The Barbarossa brothers therefore moved their operations to the Barbary coast, where much of the European trade in the Mediterranean passed.

The Spaniards, since the *Reconquista*, had taken control of most of the fortified positions on the North African coast to protect their communications with Sicily, which supplied them with grain, and to drive away the corsairs who raided their coasts. Many of these corsairs were Moors trying to avenge their expulsion from Spain: like the earlier fighters at the frontiers of the Islamic and Christian worlds, these 16th-century *gazi* carried on a holy war. The Spanish managed to expel them from Mers el-Kebir and then Pedro Navarro occupied most of the other towns. But as time went by, they began to take an interest in the riches of Italy and Atlantic adventure. The corsairs of the archipelago swept into the breach.

The Barbarossa brothers therefore were able to scour the whole North coast of the Maghreb as far as, and beyond, Algiers to the East, and cement relations with the rulers of Tunis, the Hafsids. They became more and more bold: in 1506, Oruç and Khair ad-Din seized a galleon with 500 Spanish soldiers aboard, sent to Gonzalo de Cordova, the viceroy of Naples, by Ferdinand the Catholic. It was certainly in the aftermath of that resounding exploit that Don Garcia de Toledo was given orders to gain a foothold at Algiers (el-Djezair). But when he tried to occupy Jerba, the King of Tunis gave the Barbarossa brothers the task of protecting the island, whose large bay formed a remarkable natural shelter. They moved there and made it into an important centre of resistance.

Occuption of the Maghreb coast followed. Cherchell was captured and then Jijel, although there was a setback at Bougie. In 1516, the sultan of Algiers, Salam al-Tawni, asked Oruç to get rid of the Spanish for him by driving them out of the *peñon*, the fort they had built in front of the city. Oruç pretended to hesitate and then accepted this task. He beleaguered the town with his troops – 300 Turks and Kabyles – by land while his brothers attacked from the sea. He entered Algiers without difficulty, although not the *peñon*, which hardly interested him. With no delay, he acted as master of the city, appropriating the treasury and replacing the sultan's officials with his own. Salam left the city with the warriors of his tribe and then, on Oruç's word of honour, came back. He was soon found dead in his Turkish baths. Oruç lamented the crime louder than anyone else, yet it was he who had strangled the sultan with his own turban. A cortège then led him, on horseback, to the Great Mosque, where he was proclaimed sultan. Algiers belonged to him.

The Barbarossas, who made no secret of their desire to dominate the whole Maghreb, had gained an international reputation. The next year, when the Algerians appealed to the King of Tunis, Hamid the Negro, to help them get rid of their irksome sultan, Barbarossa went to meet Hamid, massacred most of his army and took control of his kingdom. Tlemcen in turn fell after a battle in which the sultan, an ally of the Christians, was killed. The Spanish, who had tried in vain the previous year to recapture Algiers, now wanted to be finished with the Barbarossas at any cost. Charles, not yet Emperor of Germany, sent out an army of 100,000 men under the Marquis of Comares. Their success was complete: the corsairs were outnumbered and Oruç was killed. This news was greeted with immense joy in Spain. Garcia de Toledo was ennobled for having cut off Oruç's head, and his descendants henceforth wore the following coat of arms: 'A shield with the head and crown of Barbarossa and five Turkish heads as border for the said shield.'

Barbarossa: The *Kapudan Pasha* and *Beylerbey* of the Islands

With his three brothers dead, the last surviving Barbarossa, Khair ad-Din, brought undying glory to their name. Oruç had been a brave and cunning adventurer, often cruel but also fair. Khair ad-Din possessed all these qualities and, in addition, a depth of political wisdom and military genius which put him among the ranks of the greatest commanders.

The first sign of his genius was his realization that the Maghreb, divided up by many sultans, petty kings and tribes, would not long remain in Spanish hands. Only a great power, possessing considerable military and financial resources, could succeed where Oruç had failed, and that power would have to be the Ottoman Empire. Before the end of 1518, a few months after Oruç's death, Barbarossa recognized Selim I as his suzerain lord. In return, he received men, arms and equipment for his fleet. Suleiman's father had accepted without a moment's hesitation since the suggestion came at a perfect time, when the Ottomans were determined at all costs to maintain free trade in the Mediterranean at a time when commerce with South-East Asia and the Far East was threatened by the Portuguese Indian Ocean route. Also, at the very moment when Egypt and Syria had been captured, the sultan of Istanbul needed a fleet as powerful as his army. Selim understood immediately what Khair ad-Din's offer meant. In the following year, he sent him 2,000 soldiers and guns on condition that the Turks in his ranks should receive the same pay and enjoy the same rights as the janissaries in Istanbul.

Algiers became an *eyalet* (province of the empire), while Khair ad-Din took the title of *beylerbey* and became the governor.

Thus the Porte, at very little expense, was able to annex a major part of the Maghreb coast; the control of such territories, at the heart of the Mediterranean, offered many strategic possibilities. The European powers, and Spain first of all, were under no illusions: war between the Ottomans and Habsburgs for control of the North African coast would come soon. It was to last the whole of the 16th century.

Several years went by, however, before the Porte made full use of Khair ad-Din and his corsairs. Selim died in 1520 and Suleiman was at first too preoccupied by his wars in Europe to pay any attention, after the capture of Rhodes, to the Central and Eastern Mediterranean.[1] It was only in 1529 that Khair ad-Din – whom we will refer to as Barbarossa from now on – took the offensive by expelling the Spanish from the *peñon*. Algiers became an impregnable fortress. Charles replied by granting Malta and Tripoli to the Knights of Saint John of Jerusalem, who were entrusted with the task of guarding the Sicilian straits. Then he sent Doria to seize Lepanto and the strong fortress of Koron in the southern Peloponnese.

Turkish inferiority at sea was all too clear. The remaining boats from the fleet built to fight Venice at the end of the 15th century by Bayezid II and Selim I – the fleet which had made the Ottomans an important naval power for the first time – were old, insufficient in number and badly captained.

No major political initiatives – with France, among others – were possible without control of the sea. Suleiman, who knew Doria could threaten even the Bosphorus at any moment, decided to appeal to Barbarossa.

At the end of 1533, Barbarossa made an overwhelming impact with his entry into Istanbul at the head of eighteen galleys. Appointed *kapudan pasha* (chief admiral) and *beylerbey* of the islands, he assembled a powerful fleet in a few months – exactly the time of the Two Iraqs Campaign. This proved to be a turning point in the history of the Mediterranean.

A few months later, the Ottomans recaptured Koron and Lepanto. Francis then asked the sultan to make a landing in Italy, but Barbarossa merely started ravaging Calabria and the Neapolitan coast. Fortresses and small towns were pillaged one after another. One night, he secretly disembarked at Fondi to kidnap Giulia di Gonzaga, the wife of Vespasiano Colonna and one of the most famous beauties of the day, whom he wanted to present to Suleiman for his harem. The Grand Vizier Ibrahim is said to have asked him to do this, so that the princess might supplant Roxelane in Suleiman's affections. But 'the divine Giulia, dressed in a nightdress, managed to escape on a horse accompanied by a single knight; she later had him stabbed to death, either because he had been too forward or because he had seen too much during the night'.[2]

Almost immediately after this tragically farcical episode, Barbarossa headed for Tunis, which was then held by Moulay Hassan of the Hafsid dynasty – most famous for having obtained the throne by massacring his forty-four brothers! Since he had shown more interest in enlarging his harem with 400 young boys than in building up his army, he offered only a feeble resistance before fleeing into the desert. With the annexation of Tunis, the Ottomans acquired an even better base than Algiers in the Central Mediterranean.

Tunis in the Hands of Charles V

For Charles V, the danger was quite unbearable. If nothing was done to stop Barbarossa, not only the Eastern Mediterranean and its communication routes, Sicily and Naples, would fall into Infidel hands, but – who knows? the *Reconquista* had taken place hardly fifty years earlier – even Spain could be in jeopardy. More than ever, Isabella the Catholic and her counsellor Ximenez had been proved right: Spain's strategic frontier was on the southern side of the Mediterranean. It was dangerous to risk the whole Maghreb coast becoming dominated one day by Arab principalities, vassals of the Turks, and corsairs, with French and Ottoman units, allied against him, cruising to the North. If Charles did not intervene quickly, a large Muslim state could be formed in North Africa, which, propped up by the Turks, would always represent an immense danger to Spain. A powerful counter-thrust was required, to push the Muslims into the Eastern Mediterranean, which was now their undisputed domain since the Spanish had not managed to drive them out of the once Christian coasts of the Levant.

Charles V himself led the expedition. He assembled a large squadron at Barcelona: 16 of Doria's galleys, 23 caravels from the King of Portugal, about a 100 Spanish ships, 12 from Genoa, as many from Naples, 4 from the Order of Saint John of Jerusalem and about 280 transport ships. There were 412 ships in all under the command of Doria. At the head of the armies was the Marquis del Vasto, with 10,000 Spaniards, 8,000 Italians, 8,000 Germans and 700 Knights of Saint John under him. Against this enormous force, Barbarossa had only 60 galleys and galleons and a few thousand Turkish and Arab soldiers.

The battles were not very fierce and the skirmishes of no great significance. The Christian emperor had superior forces and some of his units did not even need to take part. Barbarossa had little chance once the forts of La Goulette, the ramparts of Tunis, fell. Charles then gave orders to march on the town, where the 50,000 Christian slaves broke their chains, attacked the Muslims still in the city, and thus tipped the balance. Barbarossa had to flee to Bône, and return to Algiers from there.

Charles tried in vain to spare Tunis and its inhabitants but had to allow his troops three days of pillage; 30,000 people were massacred, 10,000 enslaved. The Spanish were particularly notable for their greed and savagery, destroying buildings and works of art, carrying off anything that looked valuable, and killing all the Muslim slaves who could not come with them. Charles brought this disorder to an end only with the greatest difficulty. He then restored the kingdom to Moulay Hassan, who became the vassal of the Christian emperor and was given a garrison of 1,000 Spanish soldiers and 10 ships. Moulay Hassan also agreed to pay to Spain an annual tribute of 12,000 crowns, to pursue pirates, to permit the Catholic religion on his territory and, above all, to make over to the emperor La Goulette and the other fortifications in his kingdom.

The conquest of Tunis (July 1535) made a considerable stir in Europe. Charles was endowed with extreme courage and all the other warlike virtues. 'Your glorious and incomparable victory at Tunis seems to me, by my faith as a Christian, of a dignity which far surpasses all others of ever-lasting memory,' wrote Paolo Giovio when he sent Charles the section of his *Histoire Universelle* containing an account of the battle. This was an enormous exaggeration of the emperor's merits. Nonetheless, people compared them very favourably with those of the other Christian princes who talked a lot about the Turks but did nothing . . . Francis I was one of them, and he had even been invited by Charles to take part in the expedition to Tunis, although he had preferred to remain neutral, trusting neither the Christian emperor nor Suleiman.

Christendom also wondered what Charles was going to do next. Would he pursue the Infidel into Greece or even to Constantinople, where the setback at Tunis was thought to have provoked extreme discouragement, if not despair, in the sultan? Charles V was not so naive: he knew that the capture of Tunis had decided nothing. The Ottoman forces were intact, Barbarossa remained tireless and supremely bold. In the following autumn, he ravaged the Balearic Isles and the coast of Valencia.

In the Dockyards of the Golden Horn

The main effect of the Spanish counterattack on Tunis was to accelerate Turkish naval preparations. It convinced theTurks that they should put into practice the plan of action discussed at the beginning of the year by Ibrahim and the French ambassador, Jean de La Forest. They would launch a second front at sea. This idea greatly pleased the French king, although he honoured by no means all the undertakings he had made. The fact remains that the co-operation then established between the French and Ottoman fleets radically altered the balance of power in the Mediterranean.

In the dockyards of the Golden Horn, preparations continued for the whole of 1536 under the sultan's personal supervision. 'Twice a day he went to the arsenal and the places where the guns were cast . . . to hasten on and encourage the work,' La Forest noted. Guns and fifty galleys were brought from Alexandria, and much ammunition and provisions were assembled. 'The Italian expedition was so well known,' La Forest also remarked, 'that children went around in the streets saying that it was planned against the emperor.' Terrifying rumours, amplified by distance, went the rounds: the Pope considered leaving Rome, Southern Italy was in 'a marvellous state of fear'. The following spring, 200 ships were launched.

For the Western nations it was a very slow business to build a fleet, which demanded huge sums of money; for the Ottomans, only a few months were needed to lay down and then launch several hundred boats. Not only were the resources of the Ottoman treasury virtually limitless in the great years of Suleiman's reign, but the different countries of the empire could supply everything necessary for building and maintaining ships. The forests of Bithynia and the mountains by the Black Sea supplied abundant reserves of wood, while Crimea and Bulgaria also provided iron. Material needed for sails and tents was woven in Greece, Egypt and certain parts of Anatolia. Hemp and oakum came from the wet regions by the Black Sea, notably from Samsun, where rope was made, from Thrace and from Izmit; tow – to caulk the boats – came from Thrace, Macedonia and Egypt; pitch from Albania, tallow from Bulgaria, Wallachia and Thrace. While their rivals had to import most of the material and equipment their fleets needed – the canvas for Charles's ships came from Flanders – the sultans found everything they required in their own territory.

Another great Ottoman advantage was that decision-making and command were in the hands of a single person. The Habsburgs were constantly involved in discussion and negotiation with their Neapolitan, Spanish and Genoese admirals and the owners of the boats who hired out their services. Doria could choose to serve either Charles V or Francis I in 1528. Charles and Philip II had to take account of their admirals' demands on several occasions. They were also constantly short of money. Suleiman never had to deal with such problems.

Galata, on the East bank of the Golden Horn, was the most important arsenal. In about 1550 it contained more than 120 covered docks, in each of which 2 ships could be laid down or sheltered from the weather. The chief admiral lived at the Galata arsenal. Under his orders were two important officials, the *kethuda* (or deputy) and the *emin* (or administrator). The former was the highest-ranking official, the latter was personally responsible for the employees and workers. Many were Greeks from Istanbul or the islands, renegade Christians or foreigners attracted by the sultan's rates of pay.

Boats were also constructed in the shipyard at the entrance to the Dardanelles, at Gallipoli, Bayezid I's old arsenal, which had been enlarged and strongly fortified by Mehmed II. Suleiman had renovated it and made it the second most important in the empire, before Izmit, near the forests of Bithynia, and Sinop, on the Black Sea. When it was necessary, such as before a major naval expedition, boats could also be launched from various other places in the empire since the construction of galleys did not require major installations.

Within a few months, the Ottomans managed to put together a considerable fleet. They had assembled 100 boats for the campaign against Rhodes, 135 against Castelnuovo in 1539, 200 (including 130 combat galleys) for the Malta campaign of 1566, and 200 (150 constructed at Galata in a single winter) after Lepanto. It was then that the chief admiral *kapudan pasha*, the famous Kiliç Ali, having observed that it would be difficult to obtain at once equipment and sails for so many ships, was told by the Grand Vizier Sokullu that: 'The power and resources of the Sublime Porte are so infinite that, if the order was given, it would be possible to obtain ropes of silk and sails of satin . . .' It was about the same time that Cyprus, a Venetian possession until then, fell into the hands of the Ottomans, and Sokullu stated to the *bailo* of the Republic: 'There is a great difference between our loss and yours. In capturing a kingdom, we have cut off one of your arms. In defeating our fleet, you have only cut our beard. An arm which has been cut off never grows back, but a beard which has been shaved grows back all the thicker' (see Appendix 8).

Venice Expelled from the Aegean

On 17 May 1537, the sultan left Constantinople with his sons, Princes Mehmed and Selim, for Valona on the Albanian coast, one of the places in his empire closest to Italy. The fleet was under the command of Lutfi Pasha, the sultan's brother-in-law, and Barbarossa. La Forest accompanied Suleiman, clear evidence of the French and Ottoman agreement concerning the war. The ambassador was deeply impressed by the Turkish camp: 'I went to the Great Lord's camp and he arrived in his pavilion, built like a huge castle and beautifully enriched with hangings, embroidery and cloths in figured gold inside. And afterwards he led me to a high place where he could show me the great expanse of the country, covered by the marvellous and infinite number of their pavilions.'

The aim of the expedition was first to capture Brindisi, which controlled the road to Puglia, and then Naples and Rome;[3] meanwhile, Francis I was meant to march on Genoa and Milan. But the plan failed because Francis, once again, changed his mind. Probably acting on the advice of the Duke of Montmorency, he waged war in Picardy and Flanders although he had agreed with the sultan to fight in Italy. The French fleet, which was supposed to meet up with Barbarossa, was still at Marseilles when Suleiman had already reached Valona. Suleiman therefore ordered the units which had disembarked at the end of the peninsula to get back on to their boats. It was Corfu – that is to say, the Venetians – that they were going to attack.

The prosperity of Venice, 'a shippers' aristocracy', was totally dependent on its maritime trade in imported and manufactured goods. The former were spices, silk and oils coming from distant countries for sale in Europe, while the latter – textiles, glassware, paper – were sold overseas. The Venetians would have starved to death without wheat from Egypt, the Balkans, Thessaly, Sicily and Turkey. The republic could never go to war for long for fear of running down supplies, and it possessed a powerful combat fleet specializing in lightning raids. When the market for wheat was in crisis, they even seized foreign cargo ships, mainly Ragusan, which were carrying cereals.[4]

There was one condition for this maritime trafficking without which the Serene Republic – like Great Britain in the 19th century – would have suffocated: freedom of the seas. For a long time, Venice and its possessions had only been seriously threatened by a single danger: the Ottoman Empire. One underlying principle therefore formed the basis of their foreign policy: to accommodate the Turks as much as possible; to manoeuvre between them and the other powers; to do everything to preserve good relations with the Porte while taking account of the different factions in Istanbul, the often unpredictable about-turns in Ottoman policy and the savage customs of an age in which it was common to take prisoner all the crew and passengers, Christian and Muslim, of a boat and sell them into slavery. In the course of time, the Venetian Empire unravelled and it slowly lost its dominating influence in the Cycladic archipelago, on the Dalmatian coast and later in Cyprus.

For the most part, relations between the Venetians and Turks were kept up. The Doge was the first and often the only sovereign to receive letters of victory from the sultan. He was also the only one to be invited to the great festivities at the palace, where the *bailo* was for a long time the sole ambassador accredited to the sultan. Since the peace of 1502 which the Republic had been forced to sign with Bayezid II after several set-backs, no major incident had come between the two countries – although this did not prevent the Venetians from fortifying as strongly as possible all their points of resistance, from maintaining a powerful fleet and from organizing their defences in minute detail all the way along their thin maritime empire. The Venetian arsenal was a model of its kind, which always took advantage of all the latest technical innovations, while their soldiers and sailors were without rival in their skills. They would all fight side by side from Friuli to Cyprus, trying to retain control of their long and narrow string of territories. With each crisis, one or more was absorbed by the Ottoman ogre; the diplomats who took over could not always limit the damage which had been done.

Suleiman had for a long time followed the policy of peace with Venice laid down by Bayezid and continued by Selim. The Grand Vizier Ibrahim, linked by ties of friendship to Gritti,[6] was a firm supporter of such a policy, and Ayas Pasha, who replaced him at the head of government, felt the same. But it was now Barbarossa who had influence at the palace and he naturally favoured war against the Turks' great maritime rival. Since he was still at heart a corsair, naval campaigns were far more profitable to him than expeditions to the Danube and Azerbaijan.

Venice had by no means welcomed the *rapprochement* between the Ottoman Empire and France which had put an end to its own dominance in the waters of the Levant. All Christians – except the Venetians – who wanted to trade in the Eastern Mediterranean had, by virtue of a treaty[6] of 1536, to put themselves under the protection of the French flag. It was easy to predict that French political and economic influence were going to increase at the expense of the Venetians. For them, it meant the end of an era.

Did this feeling of discontent exert an influence on the Venetian senate when Francis I asked them to join with him and the Turks in league against Charles V? Far from joining the Franco-Turkish coalition, the Venetians threw themselves into the emperor's arms. This decision annoyed the sultan, but he was even more angry when he learnt – La Forest spread the rumour – that Charles had undertaken the expedition against Tunis at the instigation of the Venetians. He told the *bailo* at Constantinople that he 'knew well what they were doing openly and in secret for his mortal enemy the emperor, and he ordered them to abandon the agreements they had made with him or he would declare himself their enemy and was determined to make war against them the following year with fire and blood'.[7] A little later – probably at the instigation of Francis – he sent his chief interpreter, Yunis Bey, to the Venetian senate and solemnly advised them 'to declare themselves friends of his friends and enemies of his enemies. Otherwise he would make war against them with all his power.' The threat was clear, but it had no effect.

The pretext for war was an attack by Venetian galleys on a Turkish vessel carrying an Ottoman diplomatic mission. This was not the first time Venetians had attacked the sultan's boats, but Ayas Pasha had always smoothed over the problems. This time, the sultan wanted war: his anger at such law-breaking was fierce and, before the Venetian government even had time to punish those who were responsible, he ordered his fleet to leave Otranto and sail for Corfu.

The Turks disembarked 25,000 men and 50 cannons on the island, and then another 25,000 men, who immediately ravaged the nearby villages. Corfu had been in Venetian hands for 150 years and they had fortified it very strongly. But although the Turks knew it would not be easy to snatch the island, they met with resistance far fiercer than they had expected. They put an enormous cannon in action, which fired 19 cannon-balls in 5 days; only 5 of them hit the target while the rest flew over the town and landed in the sea. Suleiman called upon the garrison to surrender, promising he would spare their lives and property. The Venetian commander replied by rounds of cannon fire, all of which hit their targets: two Ottoman galleys were sunk and four soldiers killed with a single shot. This 'unprecedented' event convinced the sultan to raise the siege. It was then that he uttered his famous saying: the capture of a thousand fortresses cannot pay for the loss of a single Muslim life.

In reality, Francis's volte-face probably had more influence on Suleiman's decision to put an end to fighting in Italy than the loss of four of his men. His plan to invade the peninsula from both North and South had collapsed. Back in Constantinople, he ordered Barbarossa to put an end, once and for all, to Venetian domination in the Aegean.

The Serene Republic had until then managed to retain control of these isolated and defenceless islands. Most of them had long been dominated by leading Venetian families, who extracted large profits from them. Some were used as places of refuge or repair by Christian corsairs. The Ottomans had every reason to try and snatch them.

For Barbarossa and 70 galleys, it was child's play. Almost all the islands surrendered without resistance: Siros, Patmos and Ios, the property of the Pisani; Astipalaia, which belonged to the Quirini; Aegina, where Barbarossa took 6,000 inhabitants into slavery; Paros and Antiparos, where the Veniers ruled. Naxos was also plundered, even though Duke Giovanni Crispi promised to pay an annual tribute of 5,000 ducats. Andros, Serifos, Skiathos and Skiros were captured in turn during a second campaign. Twenty-five Venetian islands in all were subdued and devastated, and thousands of young Christians, men, women and children, were carried off. The siege of Napoli de Romania (Nauplia) lasted longer. Strongly protected by high cliffs and excellent fortifications, Nauplia had held out against Mehmed the Conqueror and then against Bayezid II. Suleiman entrusted Kasim Pasha, the Governor of Morea, with the difficult task of conquering it. Kasim used the normal Ottoman tactic of setting up a huge gun which threw missiles weighing 300 pounds, but even this did not prove sufficient. The siege lasted 18 months, until the treaty in which the Venetians gave up their maritime possessions.

The Long Series of Christian Disasters

Europe was stunned by Barbarossa's campaign in waters which had until then been Christian. After his daring raids on the Venetian fortresses and islands, the countries closest to the danger – and, most of all, the

Venetians themselves – were seized with fear. What would happen if the Turks decided to move North, towards the Republic's Dalmatian territory, towards Venice itself? The powers in the peninsula determined to unite, with the Pope, who feared for Rome, taking the initiative. With Venice, Genoa and Charles of Spain, he formed the Holy League. It was agreed to hire 200 galleys and about 100 other boats and to arm 50,000 soldiers: 20,000 Germans and the rest Spanish and Italians. Joint command was given to Doria, the patriarch of Aquila, and a Venetian called Capello. As always, desperation was followed by extreme optimism, and they decided between them how they would share out the Ottoman Empire: Charles would take possession of the ancient Byzantine Empire, Venice would get back all its possessions and gain Valona, Castelnuovo and the mouth of the Cattaro, and the Knights would be able to return to Rhodes. In the event, things turned out rather differently.

The plan might indeed have worked if all the powers involved had had a genuine desire to defeat the enemy. But while the Pope certainly felt such a desire, the Venetians were restrained by prudence and Charles did not have his heart in it at all. Distrustful, preoccupied with the German Reformers and the worries of his enormous and dispersed empire, and afraid of being outmanoeuvred by his enemies, Charles wished neither to reinforce the power of Venice, his rival in Italy, nor that the Pope should gain a major advantage from the campaign.[8] He thought he had found the ideal solution of buying off Barbarossa. The old corsair demanded the whole of the African coast; Charles offered him merely Bône, Bougie and Tripoli – if he gave up his whole fleet and destroyed the Ottomans'. These negotiations went on for several years. Nobody trusted anybody else. Was Barbarossa sincere or was he trying to cheat Charles? The bargaining eventually broke down, but it may partly explain the strange behaviour of Doria and Barbarossa at Preveza.

It was there, just off the Ipirean coast of Greece, on 28 September 1538, that the strategists had chosen as the place to launch the attack – exactly where, in AD 31, Octavian had defeated the fleets of Antony and Cleopatra: Actium. Since Doria delayed, the patriarch of Aquila took charge of operations by ordering the attack on the castle at Preveza. This achieved very little but alerted Barbarossa, who arrived immediately with 22 boats. Doria took his time to join them but brought 81 Venetian ships, 36 of the Pope's galleys and 50 Spanish galleys. Not at all keen to open battle, he agreed to do so after a council of war with the Venetian and papal commanders, who had been given strict instructions by their governments. The battle should have been decisive; in fact, it ended in uncertainty.

Because of the immense difference in numbers, the Turkish fleet should have been utterly destroyed, but in fact it left the battle almost intact. The Ottoman commanders had manoeuvred brilliantly, Barbarossa in the centre, the corsairs Turgut on the right wing and Salih Reis on the left. Two Venetian ships were blown up, and two Spanish ships, one Venetian and one of the Pope's, were all captured. But Christian losses were nonetheless fairly light and Doria could easily have continued fighting. At dusk, however, he disappeared into the night; several days later, he again refused to attack the Ottoman fleet, and nothing could make him change his mind. Was he obeying the orders of Charles V, who knew the Turks could not be decisively defeated but wanted to have the Venetians at his mercy? More likely, the emperor wanted to keep his fleet intact to defend the Western Mediterranean against corsairs and an always possible threat to Spain. It had become very clear, once again, that the emperor and the Venetian had quite different interests. Charles looked West, to his kingdom, while the Serene Republic had always to think about the Eastern Mediterranean because of its trade and its few remaining possessions in the Levant.

Preveza was a disaster for Christendom, even greater than Lepanto would prove, thirty-three years later, for the Turks, who made up their losses in less than a year. It was not only a question of the loss of prestige. Venice left the League and was then quite unable to face the Turkish fleet on its own, especially when reinforced by the King of France's galleys. The Serene Republic, supported by Francis I, then sued for a separate peace. Suleiman accepted this suggestion, while making it clear that this was an act of pure generosity on his part.

Negotiations were held. Tomaso Contarini, an old man of 88, led the Venetian delegation. When he received an audience with the sultan, who immediately showed his irritation, Contarini asked for all the fortresses and islands captured by the Turks to be returned. The reply was to demand instead the immediate surrender of Nauplia and Monemvasia (which had not yet fallen). A few months later, Senator Luigi Badoero arrived, authorized to offer 300,000 ducats without requiring the return of the captured territories. Negotiations continued for three months. Finally, on 20 October 1540, cut off from its lines of communication and deprived of its vital supply of cereals, Venice had to yield completely.[9] It paid 300,000 ducats as a war indemnity and gave up Nauplia,

Monemvasia and all the islands Barbarossa had captured in the Aegean. Malta and Sicily were now also at risk from a Muslim thrust which had almost reached the Atlantic.

From now on, even in Seville the corsairs were feared: the sultan's galleys went everywhere, thanks to bases spread all the way along the coast – including Algiers, the most powerful, which Charles would soon try in vain to capture. 'The game was almost lost for Christendom . . . because of its internal divisions . . . it was an enormously important event.'[10]

Suleiman, who had beaten a coalition consisting of the emperor, the Pope and Venice, controlled the Mediterranean. A few weeks after Preveza, Christian forces avenged their defeat by seizing the fortified town and citadel of Castelnuovo, near the mouth of the river Cattaro. The Turkish squadron had fled without Doria attacking it: it was now too late for operations at sea, he had said. But the Turkish forces in fact returned a few months later, expelled the Christians after furious battles and recaptured Castelnuovo. Spanish, Venetian and papal troops had all proved unable to stand up to the Ottomans. Christendom was more than ever on the defensive. 'What limit could be assigned to the greatness of Islam, when heaven made its support so obvious! Land and sea now obeyed the sultan. Venice returned to obscurity, ceded the towns of Napoli de Malvoisia and Napoli de Romania and faithfully paid the tribute for Cyprus. France, always searching out the emperor's enemies, made a secret offer of armed assistance to the Sublime Porte. The Ottoman flag was flying over Buda.'[11]

The Europeans were well aware of the danger. But what could they do against Barbarossa and the Turkish fleet, against a power with limitless resources, which could, in a single arsenal over one winter, lay down more than 150 ships? A power whose galleys and sailing boats were in the Balearic islands, at Cadiz, in Italy, and even on the Danube, where Barbarossa had penetrated in the summer of 1541, bringing fire and the sword to both banks?

What could be done except protect themselves by land, to prevent the Turks from disembarking, raiding, bringing war on to Christian territory? First of all, they strengthened the defence of strategically significant positions. Malta, with its knights, in the middle of the Mediterranean and Messina in the middle of its strait received new fortifications, protected ports and strong garrisons. Naples and Southern

Italy – Reggio, Otranto, Trani, Barletta – bristled with fortresses, several hundred in all. The South and East coasts of Sicily, which were even more exposed to Turkish attack, also organized their defence: fortresses full of troops, hundreds of watch towers all along the shore to give the alert. These works lasted for the whole 16th century and beyond, but they proved effective in the end.

Even Spain made constant efforts to improve its defences on its Levantine coast. In Valencia, an elaborate system of coastal defence was established, and the same was done in the South, where the presence of a large population of Moors, as in North Africa, who had not forgotten that the land had until recently been theirs made the problems even more difficult. In the Mediterranean, the Ottoman fleet seemed to be everywhere at once. Almost every season, rumours flew around Europe that the Turks were planning a landing in Spain to take part in a revolt of the Moors. Some years, it was about to take place – or so it was believed. Salih Reis, the Ottoman Governor of Algiers, marched with his troops to Fez and stayed there four months. Not long afterwards, Piyale Pasha, one of the greatest Turkish admirals, took a fleet of 150 boats to Minorca and destroyed and plundered towns and villages. In five years, in one year, maybe even tomorrow, the heir of Ferdinand the Catholic, who had expelled the Infidels from Spain, might face a new war of reconquest in the peninsula.

Early on, the emperor considered landing in Turkey and attacking in Hungary at the same time. But he soon realized that he would need the help of all Europe for such a plan and that there was no point in envisaging it. To restore the freedom of the seas in the Mediterranean and break the Ottoman stranglehold would already be a great achievement. He had to strike – and strike fast – at Algiers. In the autumn of 1540, Charles V was sure Suleiman was planning rapidly to follow up his successes at sea by launching a major expedition to the West. Where? Nobody knew that, but everybody trembled in anticipation.

The Master of the Mediterranean

Charles hastened to assemble troops and ships. He would have liked his expedition against the sultan to unite Christendom against Islam. An attack on Constantinople was impossible, so they would seize Algiers instead! Hardly two years after Preveza, at a time when the King of France was on the best of terms with Suleiman, how could Charles possibly realize his dream? He was given neither financial assistance nor soldiers. The Pope celebrated a solemn mass at Lucca, but the emperor departed, as the Archbishop of Pamplona remarked, 'weighed down with more benedictions than money'.

Paul III (Alexander Farnese) did, however, give some good advice with his benedictions, which the emperor was foolish enough to neglect. It was a mistake to undertake an African expedition in October, the Pope had suggested; Charles should certainly wait for the spring. Doria was of the same opinion. Ferdinand kept repeating to his brother that the real Turkish threat was to Hungary and Vienna, but to no avail; Charles was determined on his expedition. The crusade would only take forty or fifty days, he guessed, and the time was ripe because the Ottomans never set out for war during the winter.

At the end of August 1541, he therefore set out for Palma de Majorca, where his ships were to assemble. There were 200 from Portovenere with German and Italian troops in them, 150 which brought Spanish troops from Sicily and Naples, and 200 from Spain carrying guns, ammunition, equipment, and 1,000 troops, both foot soldiers and horsemen. Nearly 500 boats in all transported 24,000 soldiers and 12,000 sailors. Doria commanded the Spanish fleet and the Duke of Alba, the army, with Prince Colonna at the head of 5,000 Italians and Giorgio Frontispero leading into battle 6,000 Germans. The most famous Spaniards of the day also took part: men like Hernán Cortés, the conqueror of Mexico, who provided money and his two sons for a galley. The Spanish princes and dukes, however, who looked upon him as an adventurer and an upstart, refused to consult him about operations even at the most critical moments of the expedition.

In Algiers, meanwhile, were 800 Turkish soldiers and 5,000 Moors under the command of Hassan Ağa, the son of Barbarossa. The enormous difference in effective strength should have made the Christian expedition a mere promenade; in fact, it turned out to be a disaster.

The Christians had not considered very carefully where to land. While there was an ideal sheltered beach, situated at a fair distance to the East of the town, they chose instead a place much closer to the town but exposed to the winds off the sea. A storm compelled them to delay their landing, and then the lie of the land – 'the hills and swellings' – proved unexpectedly difficult and slowed down their progress. On 25 October, the army arrived in three columns before the city, which was prepared for the assault within the walls. Torrential rain started to fall that night, and the storm which was unleashed tore out the anchors, broke the cables and smashed the boats against each other. The sailing ships sank first, the galleys survived slightly longer, but the slaves soon ran out of strength to go on rowing. Panic seized the troops and crews, whose diverse origins prevented most of them from being able to communicate with each other. The Italians fell back, the Germans fled without fighting.

Two days later, they were missing 160 boats and 1,200 men. Charles V, solely responsible for the disaster, turned to prayer. Doria was furious: 'I feel humiliated by the lack of consideration the emperor gives to my advice,' he told him. 'I have, however, had enough experience at sea for my concerns to be taken into account.'[12] Cortés thought they should continue to fight because the garrison at Algiers was so small, and the Governor of Oran agreed with him. Their advice fell on deaf ears.

Harried by the Turks and Arabs who rushed out of their fortresses with cries of '*Allahu akbar*' (Allah is great), the Christian soldiers tried in vain to disembark. It took them five days to reach Matifou and their ships – or what remained of them. Another storm sank several ships and left many more at the mercy of winds and currents. The emperor and his troops took refuge in Bougie, where they had so few provisions that they were reduced to eating 'dogs, cats and grass'. Some ships landed in Spain, others in Italy and Sardinia. Losses of men, weapons and *matériel* were enormous. 'Never in his life had such losses taken place as had happened now, when all the artillery, amunition and horses which were in his company had all been lost; so many men and sailors were dead that no one knew how many . . . and it is estimated that the total loss reached more than four million in gold.'[13]

The disaster had a considerable impact. The emperor had almost been taken prisoner, and news of his death had even reached Venice, where it had 'astonished and frightened the Lords [of the Republic] not because of his [Charles's] personal loss but because, if it was true that he had come to mischief and they could no longer appeal for his help, whenever the Great Lord wished to compel them to do things that were not pleasing to them, they would be exposed to all the appetites of the said Great Lord.'[14]

The Great Lord Suleiman was more than ever the master of the Mediterranean. Charles's 'personal loss' meant little to the other Christian sovereigns, but he also represented a line of defence – and by no means the least – against the 'appetites' of the Turk.

Hungary: A New Turkish Province

While his ships were flying the Turkish flag all the way from the Barbary coast to the Red Sea, Suleiman continued his unceasing conflict with the Habsburgs.

For Charles and Ferdinand, Suleiman was the permanent enemy of Christendom who threatened the security of the countries they had inherited, freedom of navigation in the Mediterranean, and perhaps even Spain itself. Their long-term goal was always, and now more than ever, to expel from Europe the 'pagan', the tool of Satan. But it was first necessary to force Suleiman to leave Hungary, which Ferdinand wanted for himself alone. The sultan's aims were the exact opposite. Conquest was his army's *raison d'être*, his duty was to extend the frontiers of Islam, and the security of his empire demanded a constant struggle against enemies always ready, as he well knew, to seize on the slightest weakness on his part to strike a deadly blow against him. He used every means – war, of course, but also diplomacy – to maintain the disunity of Christian Europe and weaken the Habsburgs.

This combat continued until Suleiman's death. Sometimes mere skirmishes broke out between the *Grenzer* (Christian frontier posts established by Ferdinand) and the garrisons in the little forts organized for defence in depth, on one side, and the irregular troops of the Turks and the Porte's vassals, on the other. On other occasions, major pitched battles brought into conflict armies led by the chiefs of state in person. Later, the Turkish advance stopped and proper frontiers were established. Not long afterwards, the flowing back began.

Yet at the end of the 1530s, nobody could know anything of that. A little earlier, in a simple policing operation for the sultan, the *beys* of the frontiers had inflicted a severe defeat on the army of 25,000 men assembled by Ferdinand at Eszek on the river Drava expressly to put an end to Ottoman raids. The Turks had cut to pieces the German, Austrian and Bohemian troops, forcing them to retreat in snowstorms which very few survived. The heads of the Christian commanders were sent to Istanbul, and that put an end to the conflict. For a few months, all was quiet along the river Drava.

In 1538, when Suleiman himself led an expedition, a more significant episode occurred. Moldavia had been a Turkish protectorate since 1516. The voivode, Peter Rares, had appeared before Suleiman to signal his country's submission to the Ottomans. In return for their semi-independence, the boyars had to make over to the sultan each year 4,000 ducats, 40 mares and 24 colts. Rares himself had taken the tribute to Istanbul the first time. He had then received a sable caftan (a privilege normally reserved for the viziers), two horse tails (like a provincial governor) and a janissary captain's bonnet. Relations remained cordial for a time, until Suleiman learnt that Rares had been plotting against one of his allies, Sigismund of Poland. He also suspected him of being involved in the murder of Gritti, Zapolyai's counsellor. Suleiman therefore took to the field to teach him a lesson. At Jassy, the khan of Crimea arrived 'in magnificent deployment' with his son and 8,000 knights. Rares's palace was burnt down and knights pursued him into Transylvania, where the capital, Suceava, surrendered without resistance. The voivode's treasury further enriched Suleiman's. Rares was deposed and his brother Etienne installed in his place. In the future, his successors had to be approved by the Porte before being elected by the boyars. The whole southern region of Bessarabia was annexed by the empire and made into a new *sancak*. Ottoman troops were put into the fortresses of Akkerman (Cetatea Alba) and Kiliya. The Ottoman Empire controlled territory on the river Dniester – and would continue to do so until 1812.

Suleiman returned to Constantinople, where his successes were celebrated at the same time as Barbarossa's victories in the Mediterranean. The citizens joined in the great festivities to celebrate the triumphs of the Ottoman army. The Grand Vizier Ayas Pasha died in an epidemic of the plague and Lutfi Pasha, of Albanian origin and married to the sultan's sister, was appointed in his place. He occupied the post for only two years and was dismissed after a dispute with his wife in which he, although in every other respect one of the most distinguished talents of his day, behaved with such brutality that he almost killed her.[15]

The expedition against Rares, it was very clear, had only been a prelude. Despite the 'peace for several centuries' the Porte had agreed with Ferdinand, relations between the Porte and the emperor's brother remained bad. Ferdinand, who had had to renounce the Hungarian crown and only governed the provinces in the North-West, a third of the country, now more than ever laid claim to the kingdom which Suleiman considered his by right of conquest. John Zapolyai was the sovereign, but, as the sultan pointed out to the Austrian ambassadors, 'I can take it back, for the country and its inhabitants are mine to dispose of.' The peace was only a truce. Both sides knew and wanted it that way.

The crisis erupted with the death of Zapolyai in July 1540, which revealed a stratagem he and Ferdinand had employed against Suleiman.

According to a secret treaty they had signed in 1538, each of them could rule in peace over their own region of Hungary, but with the death of Zapolyai (who was a bachelor at the time) Ferdinand would receive the whole kingdom. A year later, Zapolyai had married Isabella of Poland, the daughter of King Sigismund, who soon bore him a son called John-Sigismund. Thus the future of Hungary was again in doubt, especially since a group of nobles led by Martinuzzi, the Bishop of Nagyvarad, viewed with disquiet the possibility of Habsburg domination of Hungary. Then Zapolyai died, a fortnight after the birth of his son, which made a tricky situation yet more difficult.

Ferdinand claimed at once that the child was not Isabella's and occupied Buda. At the same time, he sent an embassy to Istanbul to demand that Isabella's kingdom be made over to him. It was obviously quite out of the question for the Porte to accept such a Habsburg territorial expansion. Suleiman, annoyed that the treaty between Ferdinand and Zapolyai had not been brought to his attention, first sent a palace dignitary to establish the existence of the son of Zapolyai and Isabella. To show that the baby was hers, 'the queen took her infant in her arms and presented it to the Turkish ambassador as an orphan, with no support except the protection of the Great Lord; then, with a completely maternal grace, she bared her breast of alabaster and nursed the baby in the presence of the Turk, who kneeled, kissed the feet of the new-born and, putting his hand on the chest of the Porte's poor little protégé, swore that the son of King John, to the exclusion of all others, should rule over Hungary.'[16]

Almost as soon as the ambassador had left, Ferdinand laid siege to Buda, and Isabella and the baby fled the town and sent a message asking for Suleiman's help. The sultan recognized John-Sigismund as King of Hungary, vassal of the Porte, and decided on war. Ferdinand's envoy had not only obtained nothing but he had almost had his nose and ears cut off because of the sultan's fury. He was spared, however, because of the falcons he had brought, 'which had greatly pleased the emperor'.

Suleiman was now determined to annex Hungary. John-Sigismund would remain a minor for too long and his mother was incapable of imposing her authority on the quarrelsome and turbulent feudal lords of Hungary. Besides, Ferdinand had opened hostilities and seized several Hungarian towns.

Yet again, the sultan set out for the Danube territories at the head of an army. The campaign turned out to be more like a promenade. The sultan's troops did not even have to fight. Turkish units from Bosnia and Serbia joined up with Isabella to fight against Ferdinand's troops commanded by Roggendorf, while the Turkish flotilla which sailed up the Danube entered Buda, which had already been abandoned by the German soldiers. Soon the *padishah* and his son, Prince Bayezid, were encamped before the capital. He sent gifts to the queen. Suleiman informed her that Ottoman law did not allow him to present himself to her, but he asked her to send her son to him. Isabella was terrified, hesitated for a whole night and finally accepted. Accompanied by his nurse, two old women and six of the queen's chief counsellors, the little prince was brought to the sultan's camp in a golden carriage. The sultan looked at him for a few moments and then informed Isabella's counsellors that he had decided to incorporate Hungary into the Ottoman Empire and was going to take possession of Buda.

On 2 September 1541, he made his solemn entrance into the town. As always, he went immediately to say his prayers in a church which had been transformed into a mosque. The former Governor of Baghdad, Suleiman Pasha, was appointed commander-in-chief of the troops. Exceptional powers and his rank of vizier allowed him to take decisions in response to Habsburg attacks without referring the matter to the Porte. A leading dignitary, two days later, took a diploma to the queen 'written in characters of gold and azure' in which Suleiman promised 'by the Prophet, his sabre and his ancestors' to give up the kingdom to John-Sigismund as soon as he had reached the age of majority. Meanwhile, the prince and his mother had to leave Buda for Transylvania, where he would rule as vassal of the Porte.

While the sultan was at Buda, Ferdinand, who absolutely never gave up hope, tried yet again to obtain the kingdom of Hungary. His ambassadors, it is hardly necessary to mention, met with a complete refusal, and Rustem Pasha, the all-powerful second vizier (and Suleiman's son-in-law), demanded the return of the towns captured by Ferdinand in his last campaign and the payment of an annual tribute for the Hungarian territory under his control. A magnificent present – an astronomical clock which fascinated Suleiman – made not a jot of difference to the sultan's attitude. The Austrian ambassadors were taken to the camp, so they could see for themselves the formidable strength of the Ottoman army. They were given sugar, wine and meat for their journey, and they left for Vienna without any sort of agreement. Hungary was under

Turkish control – and would remain so for more than 150 years, until the Treaty of Carlowitz, in 1699.

3,137 Stone Cannonballs

Ferdinand, for all that, had not disarmed. Despite the promises he had made to the Hungarian nobility, the main victims of the Turkish occupation, he had been quite unable to prevent it. His diplomatic efforts had been in vain and his troops had been beaten. The Hungarians trusted him less and less. But since he had improved relations with the German Protestants, thanks to concessions, he thought the time was ripe for a union of Christian Europe against the Infidel. Before setting out on campaign, he tried a new opening at Istanbul: his ambassador still asked for the return of Hungary but offered an annual tribute of 100,000 ducats in return. He did not even obtain an audience with the sultan, who had heard from the King of France of Ferdinand's military plans. One of the viziers threatened Ferdinand with a 'tragic fate' and Rustem Pasha said: 'Ibrahim only touched Vienna with a finger; I will grab it with both hands . . . If you are not admitted to kiss the *padishah*'s hand, it is because your unworthy proposals have deprived you of that honour.' The ambassador feared for his life for a moment but was finally allowed to leave Istanbul. He had obviously obtained nothing. For 100,000 ducats, or even for much more, Suleiman was not going to give up one of the cornerstones of his policy: weakening the Habsburgs!

Suleiman responded in powerful and impressive fashion to the new Habsburg crusade. It was the eighth campaign he had commanded in person. Preparations were rushed ahead even faster than usual. Supplies of food alone required 371 transport boats sailing up the Danube. Other boats brought cannons and ammunition up the river, while long lines of camels carried the rest of the equipment and provisions overland. On 23 April 1543, Suleiman left Istanbul by the Adrianople gate with the usual ceremonial (see Appendix 9).

Hostilities broke out in Slavonia and Hungary. The fortresses of Ferdinand's allies and feudal lords soon started to fall. Valpovo, on the right bank of the Danube not far from Eszek, held out for longer but then succumbed to bombardment by the *beylerbey* of Rumelia, Ahmed Pasha, who is said by chroniclers to have rained down on to it 3,137 stone cannonballs. The bulletin telling Suleiman of the victory was confirmed by the sending of 70 noses and pairs of ears! The siege of Siklos lasted eight days. Pecs fell, and then most of the fortresses in the hands of the

Habsburg feudal lords. Suleiman continued up the Danube without resistance.

On 23 July, Suleiman made a ceremonial entry into Buda, where the victorious army chiefs were rewarded. Then, as autumn was approaching, Suleiman ordered his army without further loss of time to make for Gran (Esztergom), the spiritual capital of Hungary: 40 large cannons and 400 smaller ones were transported up the Danube on boats and then the siege commenced. The resistance of the garrison (1,300 Germans, Italians and Spanish) was short-lived. When a cannonball hit the gold cross on the top of the cathedral, Suleiman cried out: 'Gran is ours!' Two days later, the cathedral had become a mosque, where Suleiman said his prayers.

Shortly afterwards, Szekesfehervar fell in turn. Suleiman attached a symbolic significance to this, since all the Kings of Hungary were buried there. He then sent letters to the King of France, to Venice, to Ragusa and to the Governors of the Ottoman Empire announcing his capture of these Hungarian fortresses. By the end of September, the sultan was on his way back to Istanbul. He had triumphed over his enemies, extended the territory of his empire, and strengthened his European frontiers. The crusade of Christian, largely German, knights – no French had taken part – had once again failed completely.

The Humiliation of Charles V

Ferdinand understood that nothing could weaken the power of the Ottomans and that any further efforts would be in vain, disastrously expensive and probably dangerous. To defeat the Turkish giant, a huge army and a great deal of money were needed. All the European countries would have to take part. But any such plan was far from realization: the powers which were most well-disposed – Charles V and the German princes – could bring help only in symbolic form, and it is better not to mention the others! They therefore had to cease hostilities and make peace. Charles V shared this view: like Suleiman, he needed peace. The sultan might have been able to consolidate his position in Hungary and the Danube region and make a further attack on Vienna. But he had learnt the lesson of 1529: Vienna was too far from Constantinople and autumn was coming on. Even more important, he had again turned his attention towards Persia, where relations with the shah were rapidly deteriorating and there were more and more incidents between the frontier *beys*. War was inevitable in the area.

Peace negotiations with Ferdinand were long-drawn-out: a treaty took four years to agree. The first Austrian plenipotentiary, Jérôme Adorno, died the day before discussions commenced. A second envoy, Nicholas Sicco, was at once sent out – he travelled so fast that ten horses died of exhaustion *en route*. He immediately offered an agreement based on the *status quo* in Hungary, with an annual tribute of 10,000 ducats payable to the sultan, 3,000 to the Grand Vizier, and 1,000 to the other three viziers. The Turks refused; Veltwick, who represented Charles, was also opposed to such a settlement, but an eighteen-month truce was agreed nonetheless. The next year, Veltwick came as the representative of Charles as well as Ferdinand, but the sultan and then Veltwick both fell ill. When they had recovered, the ambassador presented the sultan with gold and silver vases and then, after a speech, proposed an annual payment of 10,000 ducats for the part of Hungary under Ferdinand's control – which implied recognition of the Ottoman claim to sovereignty over the whole of Hungary. Negotiations began again and lasted for six months. The Turks' demand for further territories was naturally rejected by the Austrians. Eventually a sum of 30,000 ducats was agreed for the territory (the West and part of the North of Hungary) which Ferdinand would retain.

On 13 June 1547, a peace treaty replaced the truce of 1545. Suleiman had not given up his intention of defeating 'the King of Spain' on the battlefield, but much had changed since the Hungarian campaign. The peace of Crespy between Francis and Charles had disappointed him, and it had been followed by the death of Francis: the sultan could no longer count on France. He also needed to prepare for his Persian campaign.

Charles V was included in the treaty and for the first time put his signature next to the sultan's on such a document. It was the first treaty 'which obliged Austria to make an annual cash payment which is described by Ottoman historians as a tribute'.[17]

Europe judged Charles V very severely. The sultan was the enemy of Christendom, the Beast of the Apocalypse who had to be annihilated. In negotiating with him, the Catholic emperor had treated him as an equal, and no one forgave him for it. The Hungarians, who had suffered the most from Ottoman conquests, were particularly furious. The emperor had abandoned them and could no longer be counted on to help them regain their kingdom: the Habsburgs were certainly incapable of ruling Hungary. Charles V, who had already been greatly humiliated, soon learnt of their views, although his ambassador did not dare to report back the invective against the emperor which had been heard at the Hungarian Diet.

The Treaty of Constantinople – also signed by France, the Pope and Venice – did not put an end to the hostility between the Habsburgs and the sultan. The man who considered himself the leading Christian monarch still experienced exactly the same feelings of horror towards the chief of the Infidels. But Charles, like Suleiman, was unable to fight on two fronts: against the Lutherans in Germany and the Ottomans.

It is impossible to overestimate the extent to which the Turkish presence in Europe changed the history of the continent, and the countries between the Rhine and the Danube especially, at the time of the Reformation. The Protestants were the principal beneficiaries of Charles and Ferdinand's conflict with the Infidels. 'Without the Turks, the Reformation would easily have suffered the same fate as the Albigensian revolt.'[18] It was Ottoman pressure on Hungary and Central Europe, and Charles's consequent need for the help of the German Protestants in order to resist it, which prevented him settling the religious problem by force in 1526 and dissolving the Diet of Speyer; which compelled him to sign the peace of Nuremberg with the Protestant princes in 1532; which made him accept the Treaty of Passau; and which, finally, constrained him in 1555 to sign the peace of Augsburg, officially recognizing the existence of Protestantism in Germany.

The Protestant leaders, who detested the Turks just as much as Charles did, showed great skill in making use of every opportunity offered by the almost permanent struggle the Habsburgs had to keep up against the Ottomans. Meanwhile, they never, or hardly ever, brought Charles and Ferdinand the help they asked for and never formed the alliance with Suleiman he more than once proposed, notably in a letter he sent to the Protestant princes in 1552. He later offered his help to the Lutheran princes of the Low Countries. Melanchthon maintained relations with the Orthodox patriarch of Constantinople, who acted as an intermediary with the Porte.

The Turkish menace was one of the principal causes of the expansion and consolidation of Protestantism in Europe and sometimes made direct efforts to achieve this (as in the North of Hungary and Transylvania, where Calvinism, or 'Calvino-Turkism', became the dominant religion; Transylvania took great pride in being the first country to proclaim liberty of conscience).

Although the Habsburgs were embarrassed and often paralysed in their combat with the Reformers by the Turkish threat, the reverse was also true: Charles and Ferdinand could not put all their efforts into their struggle against the Infidel because of their unceasing conflict with the Protestants. Charles's resources of men and money were both limited and he was never able to give his brother the kind of help which would have enabled him to achieve a decisive victory over the enemy of Christendom. Incapable of carrying through both his major objectives – bringing the Protestants back into the bosom of the church and expelling the Turks from Europe – it was the struggle against the Turks which was sacrificed.

The Ottomans knew this very well and favoured the Protestant cause wherever they could.[19] There was also a kind of sympathy among the Ottomans for the Protestants because they were equally opposed to the worship of idols. By dividing the Habsburg forces, the Turks and the Protestants in the 16th century probably assured each other's survival.

5
Francis I and Suleiman

In February 1525, when Francis I surrendered before Pavia to Lannoy, Charles V's lieutenant-general on Milanese territory, the kingdom of France was in mortal danger: the Spanish to the South, the English to the North, the Constable of Bourbon trying to seize Provence, Paris threatened, Francis a sick captive in Madrid. If it had not been for the energetic actions of the queen mother, Louise of Savoy, and the chancellor Duprat, there would have been good reason to fear the worst. Intense diplomatic efforts persuaded Henry VIII, the Pope, Venice and Florence that the real danger came from the emperor and his dreams of a universal monarchy rather than from the French king, who only wanted to bar the route through the Duchy of Burgundy to Charles. All of them were well aware of this: 'If we do not unite against the Imperial forces, they will submit us all to their domination,' wrote Guicciardini.[1] Although this formula was no longer current, it expressed an idea that was: 'the policy of balance'. It received practical expression with the formation of the League of Cognac in 1526, which Henry VIII encouraged but did not join.

For the queen mother, however, who knew how changeable the policies of the European sovereigns could be, the League of Cognac and the alliances she and Duprat tried to put together were not sufficient. With Charles and Ferdinand, both keen to dominate Europe, as adversaries, France needed stronger forces. To prevent the Habsburgs attacking the Very Christian King, a powerful enemy to their East was needed.

This idea – an important motif throughout French history – was not new, even in the aftermath of Pavia. For many years exchanges of views had been held between the King of France and the sovereigns of Eastern Europe about Francis's candidature for the title of Holy Roman Emperor and, shortly afterwards, in an attempt to detach Poland and Hungary from the House of Austria. It was Rinçon, whose role in Franco-Turkish discussions will be described below, who led the negotiations. He laid out to Sigismund the danger to which he and his nephew, King Lewis II of Hungary, were exposed by the ambitions of the Habsburgs and asked him to 'favour in every way' the King of France. In return, he would bring them 'help and favour' against the Turks if need arose. Rinçon achieved complete success. A marriage between one of Sigismund's daughters and a French prince was planned. Equal success greeted a mission to the voivode of Transylvania, John Zapolyai. 'The House of Austria would ruin me if it could,' he told Rinçon, 'and since I'm sure of that, I will willingly do everything I can to fight them.' Jerome Laski, Sigismund's ambassador, came to Paris and the marriage of the Duke of Orleans to Sigismund's eldest daughter was agreed in principle. The King of Poland, however, was prudent enough to make few commitments to Francis; Lewis II, the brother-in-law of Charles and Ferdinand, did even less. At this point the disaster at Pavia and Francis's capture ensued. They had to look further, find an even more powerful means of support. Louise of Savoy and the French court did not hesitate: they would have to appeal to Suleiman.

The Accomplice of the Great Turk

Neither the departure date nor the name of the man who led the first diplomatic mission are known to us. The decision was certainly taken by the queen mother herself very shortly after news of the defeat at Pavia had arrived. The ambassador left France with very valuable gifts: a magnificent ruby, a golden belt, four gold chandeliers. Neither he nor the twelve men who accompanied him reached their destination; the pasha of Bosnia assassinated them all while they were *en route* so he could seize the riches they were carrying. The French court immediately sent another embassy, led by a Croatian noble in the service of France, John

Frangipani, who bore a letter from the regent and another one from Francis, which the king had hidden in the sole of his boots. Francis had also written to Ibrahim, whose immense influence he was well aware of. He instructed Frangipani to demand compensation for the assassination of his previous ambassador, which was granted at once. The pasha was called to Istanbul, offered his excuses to Frangipani and gave back to the Porte the precious objects he had seized. It was thus that Ibrahim acquired the huge ruby which he wore for many years on his finger and which the King of France is said to have worn in jail.

In his letter to the sultan, Francis asked Suleiman to attack the King of Hungary while he attacked Charles V. Frangipani spoke even more clearly to the sultan about a mission 'to release the king'; otherwise, he said, there was a real danger of the emperor becoming 'the ruler of the world'. The Porte agreed to everything. There might even have been the possibility of a naval attack on Spain by the Turks and Venetians at the same time as a Turkish campaign in Italy or along the Danube. It was extremely important for the sultan to have a powerful ally against the House of Austria, his major enemy in Europe. His response to Francis, splendid in form and elevated in thought, deserves citing in full:

> He [God] is the exalted, rich and generous one who succours us.
>
> By the grace of him whose power is glorified and whose words are extolled; by the sacred miracles of Mohammed (may God grant him his benediction and salvation), sun of the heaven of prophecy, star of the apostolic constellation, leader of the company of prophets, guide of the cohort of the elect; with the consent of the saintly spirits of the four friends, Abu Bakr, Omar, Osman and Ali (may God's gratification be with them all), as well as all the favourites of God – I who am the Sultan of Sultans, Sovereign of Sovereigns, Distributor of Crowns to Monarchs over the whole Surface of the Globe, God's Shadow on Earth, Sultan and *Padishah* of the White Sea and the Black Sea, of Rumelia and Anatolia, of Karaman and the countries of Rum, Zulcadir, Diyarbekir, Kurdistan, Azerbaijan, Persia, Damascus, Aleppo, Cairo, Mecca and Medina, Jerusalem and all Arabia, Yemen and many other lands that my noble forebears and illustrious ancestors (may God illumine their tombs) conquered by force of arms and that my August Majesty has also conquered with my blazing sword and victorious sabre, sultan Suleiman-Khan, son of Sultan Selim-Khan, son of Sultan Bayezid-Khan.

You, Francis, King of the land of France, who have sent a letter to my Porte, the asylum of sovereigns, through your faithful agent Frankipan [Frangipani], you have also given him verbal messages to bring to me, you have made me understand that the enemy has seized your country and that you are now in prison and ask here for help and succour to bring about your release. All that you say was expounded to me from the foot of my throne, where the world seeks refuge, and my imperial understanding has taken in every detail and I have gained complete comprehension of it all.

It is not surprising that emperors are defeated and taken prisoner. Take courage then and do not let yourself be overcome. Our glorious forebears and illustrious ancestors (may God illumine their tomb) have warred unceasingly to drive back the enemy and conquer territory. We also have followed in their footsteps. We have at all time conquered provinces and strong citadels difficult of access. Day and night our horse is saddled and our sword is girded.

May the most-high God bring about what is best! May whatever he wishes be accomplished! As for the rest, you will be informed when you question your above-mentioned agent about politics and news here. Thus you will know it.

Written at new moon of *rebiul-akhir* 932 [1526] at the residence in the empire's capital, well-defended Constantinople.[2]

Bearing this beautiful letter and the promises of the sultan, Frangipani quickly left Istanbul. At Brescia he met up with Francis I, who had just signed the Treaty of Madrid which accepted all Charles's demands: he renounced his claims to Burgundy and Italy (including Genoa), to his suzerainty over Flanders and Artois, and undertook to fight against the Turks. But the king had sworn in the presence of a lawyer that commitments made under duress had no validity. He was free – that was the essential thing, even though his children had been kept as hostages. He sent Frangipani back to Istanbul to thank Suleiman for his 'remarkable generosity of heart' and the promises he had made. For the moment, he had no need of them; Suleiman had in any case decided to take up arms against Hungary. We know what that led to: the Battle of Mohacs, the defeat and death of King Lewis II.

Must Francis I be held responsible for that 'Christian disaster'? Almost all Turkish historians affirm that the King of France had urged the sultan to attack Lewis and that Suleiman had consented 'out of pity for the misfortune of that fallen prince full of bitterness'.[3] In fact, the sultan had other reasons to attack the King of Hungary, as we know, and France's encouragement counted for nothing in the Hungarian disaster. That tragic event, however, could not fail to please him. The Turkish presence in Central Europe compelled the emperor to keep a strong contingent of troops there, which was exactly what Francis wanted. Furthermore, Lewis was the brother-in-law of Ferdinand and Charles – his defeat was also their defeat.

No one in Europe was deceived as a general outcry broke out. The Very Christian King, the accomplice of the Great Turk, was responsible for the death of the young king! The Austrians unleashed a flood of propaganda, while Charles and Ferdinand conveniently forgot, or at least pretended to forget, that Francis had not been the first to go for help to the Muslim princes. Pope Innocent VIII had shown no scruples about keeping Prince Cem, brother of Bayezid, as a hostage in return for the sum of 40,000 ducats. And if one believes Guicciardini, Alexander VI, one of the Borgia popes, was not entirely innocent of the death of that unfortunate son of Mehmed the Conqueror. The same pope encouraged Alfonso of Naples to form an alliance with the Great Turk against Charles VIII of France. Ludovic Le More had sought the sultan's help in the Italian Wars. The Christian princes periodically asked for the help of the Shah of Persia against the sultan. In the very year of Pavia Charles V had written to Shah Tahmasp, and he did the same four years later. In 1548, Portugal, an intensely Catholic country, sent 20 pieces of artillery to Shah Tahmasp to fight Suleiman.

When political necessity required, 'the tool of Satan' was not always an enemy. For although Francis was very careful to keep intact his image of devoted servant of the church, his main duty was to guard the frontiers of his own country, and he was often to take part in (or even initiate) plans for a crusade shortly after – and sometimes at the same time as – assuring the Great Lord of his eternal devotion and discussing projects for campaigns against Charles V with him. He was a past master of such balancing acts, which he had started to use very early. At the beginning of his reign, when he was negotiating with the Habsburgs about plans to conquer England and Italy, he instructed his ambassador to allay 'the suspicions of Christendom' by asking the Pope and 'other princes to enter into a treaty against the Infidels so as to lull them and stop them thinking further about the matter'!

That is more or less what he did after Mohacs. Although he did not have open relations with the Turks, he pursued such contacts in secret and, above all, used immense skill to put together a network of alliances against Charles and Ferdinand in countries to the East of the Habsburg possessions. He supported Zapolyai when he became King of Hungary and offered an alliance to Sigismund, King of Poland. When Zapolyai was expelled from Buda, it was probably Francis who advised him to seek Suleiman's help. A treaty was even signed between Francis and Zapolyai, in which the latter agreed to fight Ferdinand until all the children of France held by Charles had been released. He later had to give his personal help in Italy. Zapolyai also agreed to nominate as his successor the Duke of Orleans if he did not have any heirs of his own.

When he came under attack throughout Europe, the Very Christian King made great efforts to show that his ties with the Infidel, whatever people said, were aimed solely to benefit Christianity and the Christians. His negotiations with the Porte in 1527–8 were settled rapidly and Suleiman granted him everything that he wished, although he refused to restore a church in Jerusalem which had been turned into a mosque – because, as he put it in a very friendly letter, Islam did not permit a mosque to change its function. But the sultan added: 'The places other than the mosque will remain in Christian hands. No one will molest those who remain there during our just reign. They will live in tranquillity under the wing of our protection . . . they can retain in complete security all the oratories and other buildings they occupy at present without anyone being able to oppress them or torment them in any way.'[4]

Suleiman also agreed to extend and renew the guarantees accorded to the French and Catalan residents of Egypt in the Mamluk era: freedom to move about and to pursue their livelihoods, the French consuls' right of jurisdiction over French nationals, the right to maintain churches. These privileges were the forerunners of the 'capitulations', which were to play such a major role in the relations between France and the Ottoman Empire.

Despite his success in obtaining such advantages for the Christians of the Orient, Francis's enemies continued to accuse him of being 'the executioner' of Christendom. His propagandists, led by du Bellay, hailed Francis's role as the defender of Christianity without being able to silence criticism, especially when the sultan again marched on Buda and then Vienna. The Habsburgs and their pamphleteers naturally did not fail to stress the connection: Frangipani's mission had been followed by Mohacs, Rinçon's mission in Central Europe by the expedition against Vienna – it was the King of France each time who egged on the Turks to attack Christians! Such propaganda campaigns made an impact, especially among the Protestant princes of Germany whom Francis needed in his anti-Habsburg struggle. And Suleiman was said to be planning another assault in the Danube region!

Francis understood that the whole of Europe was going to rise up against him and that he had at least to pretend to remain the Very Christian King, the adversary of all enemies of the true God. In fact, everybody wanted peace. The war raging in Italy had ended only in the sack of Rome by the German soldiery of Charles V, the invasion of the Milanese territories and the kingdom of Naples – which brought nothing but misery and disaster. The queen mother in France, Louise of Savoy, was keen to free her grandchildren, who were still prisoners of the emperor. Margaret of Austria was able to use the general mood of lassitude to sign a comprehensive peace treaty with her. The peace of Cambrai, 'The Ladies' Peace', was agreed in 1529. Charles gave up his inheritance, his beloved Burgundy, and with it his dream of lying in state one day at the Champmol monastery by the side of John the Fearless and Philip the Bold. Francis abandoned Italy, and turned his back on all his allies, on Venice and on the sultan.

The King of France spared no effort to convince the other Europeans of his sincerity. He spoke to the German princes of his 'horror' that people believed he had incited 'the barbarians' to invade Hungary. To the Bishop of Auxerre, he wrote that if any ambassador said in his presence that he had encouraged the Turks in such an enterprise 'you can tell him that he is lying through his teeth because my predecessors and I have too long maintained the honourable reputation of the name we bear for us to change now'. Du Bellay also spoke of the king's sincerity on every possible occasion.

Did people believe du Bellay and, indeed, Francis himself? To think the king was going to completely alter his policies would have been a major error. If Charles had now given up – no doubt sincerely, although under constraint – his plans for Burgundy, Francis remained attached to the Valois dream of ruling Italy. He wished to take control of the Milanese territories and Genoa, which he could only achieve with the help of the Turks, who had the means to create a diversion to the East and disembark in Italy at the same time. What he needed was a real alliance – and he was willing to do anything to get one.

The First Embassy

Suleiman had hardly been delighted by the sudden *volte-face* of the French king, one day his faithful friend and the next making unrestrained speeches against him and his 'barbarians'. Francis had therefore to reassure him first of all, to persuade him that the words he uttered in public had no significance and that his feelings of sincere friendship were unchanged. Rinçon, who represented Francis at the Hungarian court and heartily detested the Habsburgs, was put in charge of the mission. He explained that his master had signed the peace of Cambrai only to secure the release of his children and that it was otherwise utterly unimportant.

The second objective the king had assigned to his ambassador was to make sure that Suleiman attacked Charles V in Italy rather than Central Europe, where the Turkish danger would only unite the German princes around the emperor. It was in the interests of France to divide the Germans. The ambassador left France in March 1532 – very secretly, because the imperial forces had threatened to torture him if they caught him – but was held up by illness in Ragusa and only reached Belgrade, where he met the sultan, in the following year. He was met with illuminations and gun salvos. 'The Turks', he wrote to the king, 'all had torches on the end of their lances, and, since there were over 400,000 of them, you can well believe that compared to all those flames, the bonfires of Rome and the Saint Angelo castle put together would be like a village beside Paris.'[5]

Suleiman had shown his friendship for Francis by receiving his ambassador in such style, but he did not grant him what he wished. Embroiled in his campaign in Central Europe – the expedition against Güns, which turned out rather badly – the sultan could not make an about-turn and attack Italy. But although he made this clear to Rinçon, he did offer the help of Barbarossa and his fleet in Italy. Francis, however, turned the offer down: his reputation as a traitor to the Christians was still on the increase and he needed public opinion to cool off. He signed with Henry VIII the Treaty of Boulogne, which proclaimed that they would 'resist the damned efforts and acts of violence of the said Turk, our common enemy and adversary'. The French king did not believe a word of it – and nor did the King of England, who merely wanted to coax the Pope into granting his divorce from Catherine of Aragon. Such restrictive clauses were introduced into the accord as to make it quite inoperable. France's excellent relations with the Ottoman Empire, in any case, were not at all affected. Soon they were to become even stronger.

On both sides of Europe, the problem had not changed: to avoid the threat posed by Charles's ambitions of conquest. How could anyone weaken his immense power? There was only one possible response, as on every occasion Europe was menaced by a great empire: uniting against the principal enemy. Francis expressed it very clearly on one occasion to the Venetian ambassador: 'I cannot deny that I wish to see the Turk all-powerful and ready for war, not for himself – for he is an infidel and we are all Christians – but to weaken the power of the emperor, to compel him to make major expenses and to reassure all the other governments who are opposed to such a formidable enemy.'[6]

The sultan saw things in exactly the same way. His enemy in Central Europe was Ferdinand, King of Austria and Bohemia, who controlled part of Hungary and wanted all of it. But the real power was Charles, the emperor. It was he whom they had to strike against by land and sea, who threatened the Ottoman Empire with all his forces, those of a European coalition. Suleiman was not mistaken: there were no more crusades because the European sovereigns, now that great monarchies had been formed, were primarily concerned with their own political and, more and more, economic interests. There was much talk of religion, but it played only a minor role. The *idea* of a crusade, however, continued to exist: plans were drawn up, the Pope was promised men and money by everybody and Charles still dreamt of entering Constantinople at the head of an army. But nothing was done: the countries of Europe were too concerned with tearing each other up, snatching provinces and towns. The sultan of Turkey knew that he was the enemy, the only real enemy, and that if, by a miracle, the princes of the West managed to still their internal quarrels, they would fall on him with one accord. Though he was a great conqueror, of course, Suleiman was also constantly on the defensive against a Christian world which was united in wanting to destroy him; he therefore needed to have at his disposal an ally to the West. His alliance with the King of France was created because it was 'in the nature of things'.

The two governments worked on it for almost four years. They had to act in secret so as not to give Francis's enemies further occasion for protests which would have compelled him to back down or, at least, temporize even more. The negotiations opened by Rinçon in Belgrade were continued in Venice the following winter (1532–3), where he was detained by illness for several months. His discussions were with Yunis Bey, the Porte's chief interpreter (and, like Ibrahim, of Greek origin), in whom Suleiman had complete confidence. A little later – or perhaps at the same time; we do not know exactly – Francis sent his representative in Hungary, an Italian called Camillo Orsini, to Istanbul. Despite all precautions, Ferdinand and Charles soon learnt that something was afoot. At that period, as at many other times, everybody was betraying everybody else, and their ambassadors learnt from an important personage, none other than Luigi Gritti, that 'Francis, who wants Genoa and is determined to have it, has sent an embassy to the Great Turk to find out what he can hope for from Barbarossa and his fleet'. This information was completely reliable: it was through the former corsair turned *kapudan pasha* of the Ottoman fleet that relations between France and Turkey were, in the first instance, to develop.

During the summer of 1533, while Francis was on his way to a meeting with Pope Clement VII in Marseilles, an envoy from Barbarossa came to see him at Puy-en-Velay. He brought with him a number of French prisoners, still chained up – whom, to the king's 'very great pleasure', he released there and then – and some magnificent gifts, including a lion. Shortly afterwards, an ambassador from Suleiman also arrived in France to ask the king not to make peace with the emperor 'because the sultan was going to force him to give back everything he had taken during the king's imprisonment; furthermore, if Francis wanted to become emperor himself, the sultan would help him by sending a strong enough army'. That was going a bit too fast – Francis had certainly not asked for as much – but Franco-Turkish relations remained very amicable. Ibrahim claimed: 'The King of France is on terms of peace and concord with us, like a brother to the emperor of the Turks.' Indeed, Francis is said to have told the Pope that he not only would not oppose the Turkish invasion of the Christian world but would contribute to it as much as he could – to regain what belonged to him 'and had been usurped by the emperor'.

After this visit to France by the Turkish envoys, negotiations got under way. Rinçon went first to see Barbarossa in Africa, then to Rhodes and finally to Aleppo, where he met up with Ibrahim. They concluded an agreement by which the sultan promised soon to send Barbarossa to the coasts of Naples and Africa. Suleiman ratified the decision and sent the huge sum of 600,000 ducats to Barbarossa, who left at once for Italy. It was then that he ravaged the coasts of Calabria and Campania and tried to capture the beautiful Giulia di Gonzaga. Shortly afterwards, he seized Tunis.[7] This represented a great triumph for the French: the whole of the Eastern and Central Mediterranean escaped from Spanish domination;

Charles's lines of communication were threatened. Suleiman at once sent a mission to France to announce the good news.

The Ottomans disembarked at Marseilles in October 1534. It was the first time the French had seen Turkish warships and they were frightened by foreigners in strange costumes who spoke an incomprehensible language and refused to drink wine. Yet no unfortunate incidents occurred during the stay of these Muslim visitors, and the embassy reached Châtellerault, to meet up with the King of France, and accompanied him to Paris. The Turks were received with great solemnity although the clergy and other Catholics, outraged by the honours shown to infidels, displayed a good deal of reserve. Francis, however, was hardly affected by this.

Europe was fascinated – and disturbed – as it followed carefully the developments of French policy and guessed that the Very Christian King was preparing an alliance with the Scourge of God. They were even more convinced of this when they learnt that Francis I had sent an ambassador to Istanbul who for the first time was permitted to reside permanently in Turkey.

For this delicate mission, Francis I chose Jean de La Forest, a noble from Auvergne with an excellent reputation. An apostolic pronotary, abbot of Saint-Pierre-le-Vif-de-Sens and knight of Saint John of Jerusalem, La Forest could by no means be accused of collusion with the followers of Mohammed. He had studied in Italy with a Greek scholar called Lascaris and knew Italian as well as ancient and modern Greek. His broad culture gave an intellectual stamp to the mission. With him went Guillaume Postel,[8] one of the leading humanists of the day, who had been asked by the royal library to investigate Oriental manuscripts. Nobody, however, was deceived by these stratagems: La Forest's mission was not scientific but political. It quite clearly went beyond a simple discussion of commercial accords – the 'trading truce' – that Francis had claimed in advance, as on previous occasions, would be to the advantage of all Christians.

The instructions La Forest received before his departure were clear. He had first of all to go and see Barbarossa, let him know of the French plan to attack Genoa by land and ask him to do the same at sea. The submission of Genoa and Corsica, said Francis I, could only prove helpful to the sultan's plans. La Forest also had to thank Suleiman for his letters to the King of France, 'full of such goodwill, esteem, great affection, humanity and generosity', and to propose that he should proclaim 'a universal peace', on condition that Charles gave back to France Genoa, Milan and Flanders and agreed to let Zapolyai rule in Hungary. If the emperor refused, they would make war on him. Suleiman would either give France a subsidy of 'a million in gold' or take part himself and Barbarossa would attack Sicily and Sardinia and establish a vassal there who would pay tribute to the sultan. La Forest was also to try and dissuade the sultan from attacking on the Danube wing, because that could only lead the German princes to rally round the emperor, which was very much against the interests of the French king. It was a defensive and offensive alliance, the first of its kind to be made with the *padishah* by a major European power. France introduced Turkey into the European concert of powers.

La Forest left Paris in February 1535 in company with Barbarossa's ambassadors and their entourage, about a dozen men in all. With them were Postel and Charles de Marillac, a lawyer in the *parlement*, who acted as his secretary. La Forest went first to see Barbarossa in Tunis and then, in June 1535, was taken to Istanbul in the *kapudan pasha*'s galleys. Suleiman was then in Persia, on the way back from his Baghdad campaign. The ambassador did not, contrary to what some people have said, go to see him in person. The French envoy received in Azerbaijan, and who has been confused with La Forest, was probably an official agent sent by Francis to let the sultan know of the imminent arrival of a permanent ambassador. Suleiman, however, did not return to his capital until the beginning of the following year – which meant that none of Francis's plans could be put into effect.

The relationship between Francis and the Porte was unaffected, but Charles V had been able to profit from the sultan's absence to strike a major blow destined to establish freedom of navigation in the Mediterranean again. He also, and above all, aimed to demonstrate to the Europeans that he, rather than the French ally of the Infidel, was the true defender of Europe. It was then that he took La Goulette and Tunis, and a rumour went round that he was planning to take his army into Greece and even as far as Constantinople. Furthermore, he managed to cast a chill over the relations between Suleiman and Francis, who had remained neutral at the time of Tunis. On that occasion the sultan must have said to the French ambassador: 'How can I trust your king when he always claims to be the defender of the Christian faith and always promises more than he can deliver?'[9]

The Alliance

Once again, the King of France's position was by no means easy. Yet his skill, and that of La Forest, nonetheless managed to inspire Suleiman with fresh confidence. They started again to formulate a plan of campaign in Italy, and La Forest obtained a signature on the famous treaty which was the origin of the 'capitulations' which enabled France to retain for several centuries its political and religious protectorate in the Levant.

That accord (the first and only true agreement, since the others were merely concessions granted as favours) established as a precedent the idea of the permanent presence of French – and then other – diplomats in the empire. It led to ambassadors in Istanbul and consuls in all the large towns representing their nationals to the Turkish administration. They protected all such people and their property and made sure they enjoyed the privileges granted in the same treaty: exemption from the taxes imposed on Muslims and minorities; freedom to bequeath their goods to whoever they wished; the presence of a French official in any court case involving a French subject; the right of the consul to resolve all disputes, civil or religious, between nationals; a ban on enslaving subjects of either nation; a ban on imposing any kind of forced labour; freedom of movement by land or sea and freedom to trade anywhere in the empire. The French had also the right to practise their religion without interference from the Turkish authorities and could not be forcibly converted to Islam.

The treaty gave France 'the flag right' – merchants from any other European nation, except Venice, who wanted to trade with the Porte had to sail 'under the banner and protection' of France. When Turkish and French ships met at sea, they had to hoist their sovereigns' flags and greet each other with salvoes.

At the beginning of the 17th century, France obtained the right to protect Christian pilgrims going to Jerusalem, which gave them a *de facto* and then *de jure* protectorate over the Catholics, persons and property, of the countries ruled by the sultan, particularly the sacred sites. From that day dates the tradition, which every French regime has kept up, of defending the cause of the Oriental Christians.

The treaty was open to the other Christian nations. Some, such as England and Holland, obtained 'capitulations' at the end of the 16th and beginning of the 17th centuries which gave them the same advantages. This soon meant that no nation was specially privileged, but in 1581, when the capitulations were renewed, an article laid down that the ambassador of the King of France had pre-eminence over those of all the other sovereigns of Europe.

The commercial treaty dealt solely with persons and property, but it was certainly intended to form part of something much greater: an alliance of the two sovereigns against Charles V. Although no document has come down to us and none may ever have existed, there is no doubt that the two sovereigns promised each other military assistance. The plan of campaign was based on a double offensive: Suleiman would attack the kingdom of Naples by land and sea, and the King of France would attack the North of Italy; the fleets of the two countries would co-operate. On the Turkish side, elaborate preparations, directed by Barbarossa and Suleiman in person, were made. There was feverish activity in Istanbul and Edirne, with the sultan 'making great haste to put his land and sea forces in order'.

Yet, because of faults on both sides, the results were meagre. Francis was always impeded by the accusations of complicity with the Infidel thrown at him and Suleiman gave priority to his own interests. When Francis arrived to fight in Italy, he started campaigning in Artois and Picardy – which was contrary to the accords. He tried to use diplomatic means to help Suleiman by detaching the Pope and Venice from the emperor's side. Paul III refused. Yunis Bey, sent to the Serene Republic to ask the Venetians to declare themselves 'friends of his friends and enemies of his enemies', failed in the task – particularly since the Venetians, by sinking several Turkish boats, unleashed Suleiman's anger and gave him the pretext he sought for seizing Corfu. Francis's decision to fight the emperor in Flanders (when he was supposed to have attacked in Milanese territory) was not going to distract him from his objective – although it was an objective he never attained. After a six-day siege, Suleiman decided to give up his attack on Corfu and return to Constantinople.[10]

The operations had been very badly coordinated, to put it mildly. Both of them missed the mark, and the King of France was torn between the interests of his kingdom, which told him to co-operate with the Turk, and the reproaches dictated by his Christian conscience. The Pope managed to persuade him to join the League of Nice, which he had just formed with the emperor and the Venetians.

A cooling-off period naturally ensued, made even worse by the meeting of Francis and Charles at Aigues-Mortes. Francis even promised to break with the Turks. And the emperor, received in Paris with great splendour, started off the rumour that he had offered Francis the imperial crown of Byzantium! People spoke of a definitive rupture of the Franco-Turkish alliance and new possibilities of a crusade, yet this showed poor understanding of Francis and ignored Rinçon, the tireless Spaniard who had succeeded Jean de La Forest as the French ambassador to Istanbul.

Rinçon was a man whose excessive stoutness prevented him from being a soldier, yet he had long enjoyed great credit with the Porte.[11] He knew whom to bribe and was on this occasion particularly generous. His account books tell of expenses such as the following: 'To Lutfi, the chief pasha, to win his affection and favour towards the king's plans and calm his suspicions about the emperor's visit to France: gifts of different kinds of gowns, as much gold brocade as silk, to the value of 300 ecus of gold . . .' To Mohammed, the third pasha, and to Rustem Pasha, he gave gowns worth 150 ecus. Indeed, 150 different people, from the leading figures down to guards and messengers, were 'softened' in this way by the ambassador.

His success was complete. The sultan forgot about the sumptuous reception Charles had been given in Paris and Francis's undertaking to take on the Infidel. Indeed, he wrote to him of 'the affectionate feelings of brotherhood there have been between us up to now' and sent Yunis Bey to invite Francis to the festivities to celebrate his sons' circumcision and the marriage of his daughter to Rustem Pasha. Not long afterwards, when Francis had realized that Charles was planning to dupe him, he instructed Rinçon to renew his alliance with the Porte in view of his forthcoming war with the emperor. Suleiman accepted at once and begged Rinçon to go to France to ask the king to join battle as soon as possible. Since he was preparing the Hungarian campaign which immediately followed the death of John Zapolyai and had to stop Charles's forces from joining up with his brother Ferdinand's, it was very much in his interest that Francis should also attack the emperor. Before the departure of Rinçon, he was accorded an exceptionally long and friendly audience with the sultan. It lasted two or three hours, which, the ambassador wrote proudly, was 'an honour he had granted no one else, either Christian or of his own religion'.

The unfortunate man was never again to see either the sultan or Turkey. He was received in Paris as a hero and showered with honours by the king, but Charles conceived a hatred for him in line with the major role he had played in bringing about war against him.[12] On 8 May 1541, he left the French court to return to Istanbul in the company of a Genoese captain called Cesare Fregoso. They had both been warned of the dangers they faced in Italy, but decided to gain time by embarking on the Po rather than taking the safer route over the Alps. On the following day, men in the service of the Marquis del Vasto, who governed the Milanese territories in the emperor's name, captured their boat and killed them both. News of their death did not come out for two months, when it created an immense scandal. Nobody was in any doubt that Charles was the instigator. Suleiman, in a fury, wanted to impale the Austrian ambassadors, and everybody in Europe, including the Pope, condemned an act of extreme cruelty.

The Turks in Provence

The behaviour of Charles, the emperor and Catholic King, had been ignoble, but it also proved pointless because Francis soon found another ambassador as energetic and skilful as Rinçon. Captain Polin de la Garde, appointed on the recommendation of Guillaume du Bellay, possessed the same talents as his predecessor and rapidly made a name for himself.[13] As soon as he had been given his instructions by the king – the same as he had given to Rinçon – Polin left to meet up with Suleiman in Hungary. The sultan had just completed his conquest of the kingdom, which he had made into a *pashalik*[14] of the empire, by defeating Ferdinand's army. At exactly the same time, Charles had suffered disaster at Algiers. Suleiman had reached the very pinnacle of his glory. Polin accompanied him to Istanbul and immediately revealed his skills as a diplomat. 'He came and went, trotting, treating and monopolizing,' said Brantôme, 'and did it so well and so effectively won over the captain of the Porte janissaries that he talked to the Great Lord as he wished, had many interviews with him and made himself so agreeable that he obtained everything he wanted in the end.'

Polin left for France and then returned to Turkey. His speed of movement astounded his contemporaries: it took him three weeks to get from Istanbul to Fontainebleau. Aretino wrote to congratulate him. At last the plan of campaign was ready: Francis would fight the imperial forces in Flanders; part of his fleet would attack Spain and the rest would support Suleiman's in the Mediterranean. The Turkish fleet was to attack the emperor by sea while his army took on Ferdinand in Central Europe. Suleiman wrote another letter to Francis which has become famous: 'Most glorious of the princes of the religion of Jesus,' he said, 'you must know that, at the entreaty of your minister Paulin [Polin], I have granted to him my powerful fleet equipped with everything necessary. I have ordered Khair ad-Din, my *kapudan pasha*, to take account of your plans and draw up a strategy to destroy your enemies . . . Be careful that your enemy does not again deceive you: only when he understands that you will always be determined to war against him will he be willing to make peace. May God bless those who appreciate my friendship and are protected by my victorious arms.'[15]

Immediately afterwards, at the beginning of April 1543, 150 Turkish boats – including 110 galleys – cleared the Dardanelles in the direction of Italy, while Suleiman once again set off towards the Danube territories with 'an army like the water in the sea'.

For two months, Barbarossa's men ravaged the coasts of Calabria, Sardinia, Corsica and Naples. At Gaeta, aged almost 80, he was married to the very beautiful 18-year-old daughter of the governor, Don Diego Gaetano. Doña Maria, who converted to Islam, was the great love of his last years: his passion for her is said to have hastened on his death.

The inhabitants of Rome were terrified and prepared for departure,[16] but Polin reassured them by telling them that the Great Turk had ordered Barbarossa to spare the papal domains. Nice was also spared for the time being and Barbarossa made for Marseilles.

When he landed in France for the first time, he was given a magnificent reception. François de Bourbon, the Duke of Enghien and lieutenant-general of the forces in the seas of the Levant, was waiting there in the name of the king with 50 ships. Barbarossa and his entourage were sparkling with gold and precious stones. The young duke – he was 23 – made over to the Turkish admiral-in-chief a sword of honour and gifts of silver. He received in return, as presents for the King of France, several magnificent Arab horses with very valuable saddles and cloths. A huge crowd from Marseilles was fascinated to watch the sultan's boats come into port. Many court gentlemen and their wives had made the long journey to see at close range the former corsair who had become king of the Mediterranean. Indeed, so many courtiers made the journey that Francis was obliged, after a few days, to stop them departing – for fear that he would be left completely alone.

The great festivities held to celebrate the meeting of the French and Turkish fleets almost ended very badly. Delighted with the honours bestowed on him, the *kapudan pasha* recalled nonetheless that he had not come to France just to take part in banquets and parades. He soon realized that Francis's plans were on a quite different scale from the undertakings he had made and, even more, from the considerable war machine the Turks had put into action. The French fleet was poorly equipped and extremely undisciplined. If the King of France had prepared everything to welcome the Turkish admiral in splendid style, the provisioning of his crews had been totally neglected. Barbarossa became violently angry. 'He became red with rage,' said Sandoval, 'tore at his beard, furious to have made such a long voyage with such a large fleet and to be condemned to inaction in advance.'[17] Francis gave orders to equip the Turkish fleet with what was needed. But, once again, the agreed plan of action was thrown in doubt. Barbarossa had wanted to attack Charles V in Spain, where Doria's fleet was to be found. Francis recoiled from the reproaches of Christendom. As usual, he was not able to follow his decisions through to the bitter end; as usual, he adopted a half-way solution which achieved nothing yet managed to irritate his allies.

Polin was dismayed and rushed to the king. It was agreed that, instead of a direct assault on Charles V, they should attack his ally, Charles of Savoy, and the town of Nice.[18] Since the Duke of Enghien had only 18 galleys, he embarked 12,000 of his soldiers on other boats. A company of Tuscans was placed under the orders of Leone Strozzi with a few companies of Provençal volunteers under Polin, who, at least in theory, directed operations.

The Turco-French fleet reached Villefranche on 5 August and Polin called on the citizens of Nice to submit to Francis I. He received two parliamentarians to explain to them why Nice was well advised to ally itself with the powerful King of France rather than remaining under the domination of the weak Duke of Savoy. But although the garrison consisted of only 6 companies of archers and 300 soldiers who guarded the ramparts, they refused. On the next day, the Turks launched their attack, without great success. Polin again appealed for the men of Nice to surrender and sent an ultimatum. Not only was it rejected but Jean-Benoist Grimaldi, the man who brought it, was arrested, whipped and hanged. The town was surrounded. Three main redoubts were established: one on the Cimiez hill with large-bore cannons, one on the side of mount Boron, where an immense gun was trained on the castle, and one on the slope of Mont-Gros, close to the road from Villefranche.

Up until 15 August, assaults and bombardments followed in quick succession without a decisive result. Then Barbarossa's 120 galleys arrived from Villefranche and, with an infernal noise, all opened fire together. A breach was opened in the walls near the Pairolière gate. The Turks, Tuscans and French poured in and a Turkish standard-bearer was about to plant his flag on the summit of the ramparts when a woman of the people, a washerwoman whose name has been handed down – Catherine Ségurane – flew at him, beater in hand, seized the flag and led the retreating men in a counter-attack. The assault was beaten back: the Turks and French left 300 dead behind them as well as many wounded.

Further bombardments and assaults took place over the following days. Finally, the people of Nice, unable to continue their resistance, decided to surrender if they were allowed to go free and keep their property. This was not at all what the Turks had in mind, since they were far more interested in pillaging the town than in the advantage their actions had brought to Francis in his conflict with Charles.

Discussions between Polin and the Duke of Enghien turned sour. To finish the matter off, the Turks attacked the citadel, which had still not surrendered. The French prepared to do the same and then suddenly discovered, to the disgust of their allies, that they had no more gunpowder. 'They would have preferred to fill their boats with wine at Marseilles', said Barbarossa, 'than with the equipment needed for war . . .' The *kapudan pasha* was even preparing to put the French leaders in irons when a message was intercepted to the commander of the citadel. The Duke of Savoy urged him to hold out for a few more days, the time for reinforcements to arrive. The Turks were beginning to tire of a pointless campaign and the French were tired of trying to collaborate with an ally who was so different from them. If the campaign continued, they said, they would end up coming to blows, so they agreed to call a halt at that point.

Francis I suggested that the Ottoman fleet should spend the winter in Toulon. But when the boats were about to set sail, an event occurred which seemed to confirm the view of those who believed Barbarossa and Doria were in cahoots and had come to an agreement to spare each other's fleets. Polin learnt that Doria was coming to Villefranche and let Barbarossa know. The emperor's fleet is at your mercy, he said. The Turkish admiral gave orders to weigh anchor and then, when he reached Antibes, suddenly stopped. I will go no further, he said, because I do not wish to forget Doria's good conduct at Preveza and Bône. This led Brantôme to say: 'The glory of one was also the other's glory. Their masters would not otherwise have valued them . . . Their slaves said that the crow never puts out the other crow's eyes. . .'

Before the Turks' arrival in Toulon, the town had emptied of inhabitants 'because it was not fitting for the ordinary people and inhabitants of Toulon to stay behind and entertain the Turkish nation.' Barbarossa behaved as if he were in a conquered country, but law and order reigned supreme. 'Seeing Toulon,' an eyewitness reported, 'one would have thought one was in Constantinople, with good order and justice prevailing and everybody working at his job and producing Turkish merchandise.' An iron discipline was imposed on the troops. Polin, who sometimes had difficulties with his ally, said: 'Never did an army live more strictly or in better order than that army.' Turkish and French officers gave each other gifts, despite the poor relations between their leaders. Virgilio Orsini, the commander of the French galleys, received a box made of ivory and ebony with pictures of the eleven Ottoman sultans painted on it. Polin offered to the Turkish admiral-in-chief, as a gift from his king, some objects in silver gilt and a clock in the form of a globe.

The Turks did not only receive clocks and gilded table-services. Francis I paid a sum of 30,000 ducats a month to Barbarossa. The Ottoman troops lived off the land. Barbarossa's table was supplied in abundance with chicken, kid, rabbit and fruit.[19] All this cost the French treasury very dear. Provence and the area around it also had to pay. Lyons was compelled to lend 6,000 francs and the Comtat Venaissin region paid 600 ecus, with which the janissaries 'bought fresh bread'. The Count of Grignan, the Governor of Provence, was ordered to tax the salt storehouses of the province. Private individuals like Count Strozzi lent money. Attempts were made to hasten the departure of the burdensome friend who was taking his time: the longer Barbarossa stayed, the greater the payments he received. And the Provençal coast delighted the Turks. Sinan Çavuş, who wrote an account of Barbarossa's expedition, was enthusiastic. 'Countless trees bear bitter oranges and lemons,' he wrote, 'and countless are the flowers on each tree. When its rose garden is full of roses, the nightingale's laments fill the ears. Without a peer in the whole country of the Francs, the region bewitches whoever sees it . . .'[20]

But despite the pleasant climate, relations between Francis and the Turks became more and more strained. Plans to attack Genoa were made and then abandoned. The same went for the towns of the Spanish shoreline: despite his disapproval, Francis could not prevent Salih Reis from ravaging Cadaques, Rosas, Palamos and other towns and villages.

In Europe, anger against the King of France kept on increasing. When Cardinal du Bellay was sent to the Diet of Speyer to defend his master, he was not even allowed into Germany. The Diet also made it known to him that it considered the French king 'as much an enemy of the aforesaid Christian world as the Turk himself'. Francis was the outcast of Europe and there was even discussion of taking away from him his title of Very Christian King and excommunicating him, although the Pope was opposed to this. Strange rumours started circulating again about Barbarossa's relations with Doria: at one point it was thought that the *kapudan pasha* was ready to sell Toulon to the imperial forces. It was high time that the Turks left, especially since the Duke of Enghien had just won a brilliant victory against the Spanish at Ceresole (April 1544) and it was impossible for the French to negotiate with the emperor while the Infidels remained on their soil.

Finally, Barbarossa, who had left Turkey over a year earlier, announced that he was going to depart. He received 800,000 golden ducats, which 34 men piled up for 3 days and nights in white and scarlet sheets. The French freed 400 Muslims who rowed in their galleys and the Turkish boats raised anchor. Polin, appointed 'captain and commander-in-chief of the Army of the Levant', was aboard one of the 5 boats in his squadron 'to give an account to the Great Turk of how things had turned out'. He witnessed the devastation unleashed on Procida and Ischia, Pozzuoli, Policastro, Lipari – 'believed to be impregnable, and which had one of the greatest batteries ever seen' – Port'Ercole and Talamona. Many villages in Puglia and Southern Italy were raided and the inhabitants enslaved. Jérôme Maurand, Polin's chaplain, who was aboard the *Reale*, left striking and horrifying descriptions of these events.[21]

When they had passed the straits of Messina, Polin managed to convince Barbarossa to let him go ahead to Istanbul. He wished to give his version of events to Suleiman before the chief admiral presented his own. Fêted by the sultan and his viziers, Polin prudently managed to leave the Bosphorus before Barbarossa arrived. The chief admiral feared his master's anger since his expedition had met with no success, but Suleiman was too shrewd to feel resentful with him for a setback for which he knew Barbarossa was not responsible. The blame lay fairly and squarely with Francis, who had not known how – or had not been able – to make use of the enormous trump card Suleiman had given him in putting his fleet at his disposition.

As for Francis, he came out of the operation fairly well. The Ottoman presence in Western Europe had frightened Charles and inhibited the movement of his troops. His victory at Ceresole allowed Francis to negotiate without embarrassment with Charles. It led to the peace of Crépy-en-Laonnois (Crespy), which contained, as one of its principal articles, plans for the marriage of Charles, Duke of Orleans, one of Francis's sons, with either the emperor's daughter (who would bring the Low Countries as a dowry) or with his niece, Ferdinand's daughter (who would bring the Milanese territories). Francis gave up his suzerainty over Flanders and Artois and renounced all claims to Savoy; Charles reaffirmed that he no longer sought Burgundy. As usual, a clause laid down that Francis would support the emperor in his struggle against the Turks; as usual, it meant nothing. Yet when he learned of the contents of the treaty, Suleiman once more flew into a violent rage. He criticized Francis for not having used against Charles the powerful fleet he had put at his disposition. The French resident in Istanbul, Gabriel d'Aramon, only just escaped being impaled. Later the sultan calmed down when he was told that Francis only wished to deceive public opinion by undertaking to fight at Charles's side against Suleiman. Such an explanation was, indeed, nothing but the truth.

'Friendship and Fidelity'

To retain his friendship with the sultan, Francis I, however, had to do more than just offer a stream of fair words – which were not totally believed in Istanbul. He therefore used one of his normal methods by offering to act as intermediary in peace negotiations between his old friend, the sultan, and his new Habsburg allies. Suleiman, who was preparing a new Persian campaign, wished for peace to the West. Ferdinand had just suffered two severe defeats. The loss of Buda had discouraged and terrified him: he and Charles wondered if the rest of Hungary under Ferdinand's control was going to fall in turn under the Turkish yoke and if even the German countries were not in danger of sharing the same fate. They entrusted Francis with the task of obtaining a truce – times had changed! The Turks took a lot of coaxing. Polin was charged with sounding out Suleiman's intentions and then Jean de Monluc was sent to Istanbul to negotiate. He was not well received. The peace of Crespy was criticized: Francis had signed it 'without telling his friends'.

A skilful diplomat, de Monluc replied that his master had proposed a universal peace in Europe so that his ally would have 'greater desire and leisure to enjoy the victories God had granted him'. He made long speeches to the effect that Suleiman had obtained the greater advantage from the peace than Charles V, who had now lost his domination over the Christians of Germany and had to submit to the humiliation of 'coming to him to sue for peace'.

Did Suleiman believe it? At all events, peace was in his interest. Finally, de Monluc agreed on a truce for a year at the very moment when news of the Duke of Orleans's death arrived. Francis's hope of obtaining the Low Countries or the Milanese territories evaporated. He no longer needed a truce! In the spring of 1547, he sent his ambassador Gabriel d'Aramon to Constantinople with a large and sumptuous entourage and splendid gifts including 'a large clock made in Lyons with a fountain which would work for twelve hours when water was poured in – a masterpiece of great value'.[22] D'Aramon's mission was to persuade Suleiman to attack Charles at once in Hungary and launch an expedition by sea in North Africa.

But Suleiman was preparing a campaign in Persia and had no wish to fight on two fronts at the same time. He was in favour of peace, and it was agreed on 13 June in the form of a five-year truce.[23] In a very cordial letter to Francis, 'restorer of the Christian world', Suleiman excused himself for not responding to his wishes, 'the season being too advanced'. He announced, however, that he was sending an army of thirty or forty thousand men to Croatia and the imminent departure of a fleet 'to protect our friends and fight our enemies, as befits my imperial dignity'. He finished by evoking their 'friendship and fidelity which we shall preserve with the same constancy as in the past'. The King of France learnt of neither the truce of Adrianople nor this letter. By the time it arrived, he was dead.[24]

6
The Tragic Period

Freed, at least temporarily, from all worries to his West, Suleiman was able to turn his attention to the question of Persia. Since the campaign of 1535–6, there had never been peace on the eastern frontier of the empire. The allegiance of the feudal lords, Muslim as well as Georgian, was always doubtful. All transferred their support from the shah to the sultan, and back again, according to the interests of the moment. Under cover of Shiism, Safavid propaganda continued in the East of Anatolia, where Shah Tahmasp's emissaries tried to win over the population. The energetic measures taken by Selim I had no more solved the problem than the victory at Chaldiran. There was still a real danger of seeing the Porte's authority disintegrate in these provinces. A quarrel in the bosom of the Safavid imperial family provided Suleiman with the opportunity he had been waiting for to strengthen Ottoman power by war.

The shah's brother, Elkaz Mirza, was in dispute with the shah and took refuge at the sultan's court. Suleiman perceived at once that he could use him as a rival against Tahmasp and received the prince with exceptional consideration and ceremonial. He is even said to have been given, along with other presents, shirts sewn with Roxelane's own hand. 'The wind which was blowing for a war against the Persians came from the Harem' and if that opportunity had not presented itself, another would have been found.

Everybody wanted to take on the heretics. Roxelane hoped that her son Selim would be appointed *kaymakam* (governor) during the sultan's expedition, which would allow her to prepare the way in the capital for the day when the succession was in question. Mihrimah, the sultan's daughter, and her husband Rustem Pasha thought the campaign would give Bayezid, their candidate for the throne, the chance to perform glorious deeds. Besides, a war against the heretics was always popular at Istanbul: had not the unfortunate Ibrahim Pasha been greatly reproached for appearing too friendly towards Persia?

In the spring of 1548, Suleiman again led his army on campaign in person. Elkaz Mirza was already in Azerbaijan, trying to stir up a revolt against the shah. The sultan reached Erzurum by way of Konya and Sivas. Elkaz Mirza came to meet him and asked him to launch an immediate assault on Tabriz, the capital, which his brother had abandoned. He suggested they should massacre all the inhabitants or at least expel them. Suleiman refused and preferred to lay siege to Van, the main fortress in the region, which he had conquered in 1534 and the shah had recaptured. It did not hold out for more than a week. It was already the end of August and, since winter comes early in Eastern Anatolia, the sultan made straight for Aleppo (by way of Diyarbekir) for the cold season. Meanwhile, his generals expelled the Safavids and occupied the fortresses in the region of Lake Van. Alongside, Elkaz Mirza ravaged Western Iran, Qom and Isfahan, whence he sent lavish gifts to his Ottoman protector from the immense treasure he had accumulated at his brother's expense. But while he concentrated on raiding, he did not notice the trap that his other brother, Sohrab, was laying for him. When he was captured, Tahmasp spared his life but shut him up in the fortress at Alamut. He was assassinated shortly afterwards.

At the end of winter, Suleiman left Syria to go to Erzurum. From there he sent out his second vizier, Ahmed Pasha, to clean out the Safavid *beys* from the area between Kars and Artvin. He achieved the most striking successes of the campaign by occupying about 20 fortresses and placing the whole region under the control of the Ottoman forces. The sultan returned to Istanbul and sent letters to all the European sovereigns, announcing his victory, with the capture of 31 towns, the destruction of 14 fortresses and the construction of 28 others. The campaign, which had lasted about 20 months, had consolidated the Porte's authority in

Eastern Anatolia. But Suleiman had failed to achieve his main objective: to meet the shah in a great battle, crush him and be finished with the Safavids once and for all.

A few years later, war against the shah again got under way. But the campaign, planned for the summer of 1552, was interrupted when it had hardly begun by the gravest crisis the empire was to face in the 16th century – the crisis which ended only with the execution of Prince Mustafa, the brilliant heir to the throne, by his father.

In the Name of *Raison d'Etat*

Suleiman's two wives had borne him eight sons, four of whom were still alive at the beginning of the 1550s: Mustafa, Selim, Bayezid and Cihangir. Only the first of these was not Roxelane's son. His mother was Gulbahar, the woman who accompanied Suleiman when he was Governor of Manisa and whom Roxelane had managed to supplant in the *padishah*'s heart after a long struggle and countless intrigues. From that day, 'the Russian woman' had reigned in the palace as absolute mistress. Suleiman, however, was getting older – he was 56 in 1550 – and she was well aware that if Mustafa ever took the throne, he would assure it for himself by strangling his brothers, who were also her sons. As for herself, even if her life were spared, she would have no choice but to live in the sinister Old Seraglio, where the wives in disgrace and the mothers of former sultans were sent. Roxelane had no choice: Mustafa had to be defeated – or he would do away with her and all her male descendants.

The threat to Roxelane and her sons was all the more serious because Mustafa was indeed a man of great talent. All those around him were unanimous: he would be a sultan worthy of his father. Europe knew and was afraid. 'Suleiman has among his children', Postel wrote in 1537, 'a son called Mustafa, marvellously well educated and prudent and of an age to rule, since he is 24 or 25 years old; may God never allow a Barbary of such strength to come so near us.' Busbecq spoke of his 'remarkable natural gifts'.

Selim, on the other hand, had long possessed the reputation which earned him his nickname of 'the Sot' (*sarhoş*). Nothing was said about Bayezid because there was nothing to say. Cihangir, hump-backed and deformed, although apparently rather a wit, was not in the running. Of the four, only Mustafa was truly popular. Many people – the discontented *timariotes*; the old aristocracy who saw themselves deprived of their privileges by the Islamicized Christians (the *devşirme*); the victims of the

European economic and financial crisis which had slowly but surely reached the Ottoman Empire; and all those who thought that Suleiman, after a thirty-year reign, ought to hand over power to his most capable son – began to look to Mustafa.

Was there a plot to dethrone Suleiman in favour of his son? We will never know for certain, but it is clear that Mustafa knew of the plans of Roxelane and her sons. Should one of them become sultan, his fate was sealed: the deaf mutes of the Seraglio would put a noose around his neck. It is not unlikely that at 37, well aware of his abilities and personal popularity, and seeing the destiny of the empire in hands enfeebled by age, Mustafa should have decided to try and take power for himself rather than wait for a succession crisis with all the immense dangers that would mean for him.

In the fight to the death which ensued, the man who first engaged the other in combat would prove the winner. Mustafa had on his side much of the army, but Roxelane and her two sons could make use of the first lady's immense personal influence, the weight of the administration and the court and – still more important in these circumstances – the total support of Rustem Pasha, the crafty Grand Vizier who had become the son-in-law of Suleiman and Roxelane.

This first minister of more than humble origin (said to have been a swineherd in his childhood) who became the sultan's son-in-law and was at the very pinnacle of the administration for fifteen years was a most peculiar person. Born in a small village near Szeged and, like all the dignitaries of the civil administration and army, a Christian by background, he detested everything which reminded him of his former religion. According to Bernardo Navagero, the Venetian *bailo*, 'he took account of those Christians who gave him most'. Although his appearance was almost repulsive and he was both gloomy and greedy, 'one could make him do what one wanted with money'. Busbecq, who knew him well, claims that he sold 'even the roses and violets which grow in the sultan's gardens and that he made his servants put on one side, so he could sell them, the cap, breastplate and horse of each prisoner'. Small in height and with a complexion so dark he seemed purple-faced, he was hardly good-looking, but his qualities as a statesman and administrator made up for his physique. A glutton for work and the possessor of a remarkable memory, 'proud and short-tempered, he was of limitless ambition and his greatest pleasure was to hear it said that the Ottoman sovereigns had never had a wiser and more prudent man in their service'. Nobody could match him in his ability to fill up the coffers of the state – and his own. When he died, he left a fantastic fortune 'unexampled before him'.[1] It had allowed him to build many mosques and other religious foundations in Istanbul and several other towns in the empire.

The campaign against Persia opened in 1552. Suleiman appointed Rustem Pasha *serasker* (commander-in-chief) and the expedition made for the Anatolian plateau. The troops took up their winter quarters in Karaman, in the South of Turkey. It was there that the intrigue against Mustafa was carried out.

Rustem sent Şemsi – the *ağa* of the *sipahi*, and one of the men Suleiman trusted most – to the sultan to tell him that since he was not at the head of his army, the soldiers thought that his strength was failing him and that it was time to put a younger prince on the throne. He also let it be understood that Mustafa, to his certain knowledge, did not spurn such proposals and had even established relations with the Safavids of Persia so they could help him realize his plans. The sultan's presence at the head of his army, he added, was indispensable. When Suleiman received Rustem's envoy, he was thrown into a towering rage. 'God protect us', he said, 'from Mustafa daring to take such infamy upon himself during my lifetime.' He therefore put off the war against Persia and summoned Rustem back to Istanbul.

The following summer, Suleiman himself led his army on campaign and summoned Mustafa to appear before him. It is easy to suppose that Roxelane and her coterie had made good use of the winter months in the palace at Istanbul to turn Suleiman even more against his eldest son. In any case, he was determined and clearly convinced by the proofs of Mustafa's treachery when he wrote to tell him to appear immediately at his camp, which was established at Eregli in Karamania.[2] In his letter he said that Mustafa would be able 'to clear himself of the crimes he was accused of and would have nothing to fear if he came'. Mustafa was faced with a difficult choice: to go and see his father and risk his life, or to refuse and implicitly admit that he had intended to betray him. He eventually made the courageous decision, whether because he was sure of his innocence or because he thought nothing could happen to him amongst the army.

Busbecq, who received his account from eyewitnesses, tells the story in the following terms: 'Mustafa entered, the drama commenced, and he was seized on every side. But the prince, in the moment he believed would be his last, regained his strength and was animated with heroic courage. He knew that if he triumphed, he would gain the throne; he imagined the disorder, where the heat of battle would arouse pity in the janissaries; he saw them already armed to defend him against Suleiman's barbarity; he believed he could hear himself proclaimed emperor by the whole army. This was indeed exactly what Suleiman had feared, and he had taken the precaution of hanging up curtains behind his tent, where this tragedy took place, so that nobody could see anything or even suspect anything and no noise could be heard. Yet Mustafa's ardent desire to live and reign made him invincible, although alone against them all; the result of the combat was still uncertain, but Suleiman, on the other side, impatient for success, raised his head above the hanging and saw that his mutes were ready to succumb; his fears were greatly increased and he looked menacingly at them, his eyes full of anger, and filled with cruelty at their lack of courage. What was the effect of this look on the mutes? I cannot describe it: the fury he excited in them was without parallel. They instantly threw themselves on Mustafa for a second time, knocked him straight down and snatched his life from him; they immediately exposed the body of the unfortunate prince on a carpet in front of Suleiman's tent so that the janissaries should understand his power and authority from the fate which had just been inflicted on the man they wanted to have as emperor.'

This murder had an enormous effect on the troops. Busbecq was no doubt right when he said that if the janissaries had had someone to lead them, nothing could have stood in their way. Suleiman would probably have been overthrown. Without a leader, 'they could only bear with patience what they could not prevent'. They turned their anger on Suleiman, whom they insulted and treated as a crazy old man, and then on Roxelane and Rustem, who had extinguished 'the most brilliant sun whose brightness would have increased the glory of the imperial house'. To calm them, Suleiman sacrificed Rustem. They were given to believe that the sultan had discovered that the Grand Vizier had instigated the murder, and his seal was taken away from him. His disgrace did not last long: two years later, Rustem resumed the responsibilities of his post.

With Mustafa dead, his son Murad remained. He too was an enemy for Roxelane, who wanted all trace of Mustafa and his line to be extinguished. She is said to have persuaded the sultan that the young man was going to incite the janissaries to rebel and that he was acclaimed as the future sultan whenever he appeared in public. Once again, Suleiman gave way. He sent a dignitary to Bursa, where his grandson lived, with an order of execution. 'The emperor wants you dead at once,' he said to Murad. The reply was simple: 'I am willing to die in obedience not to the emperor's orders but to God's.'

Not long afterwards, Cihangir, Suleiman's favourite son, also died – apparently of grief at Mustafa's brutal end.

This series of deaths one after the other made a great impact within the empire and beyond it. Some saw the assassination of the heir to the throne as a further sign of the influence exercised by the Porte slaves, the Islamicized Christians who now occupied all the responsible posts and had ended up as masters of the empire. Public opinion was very critical of Suleiman and, even more, of Roxelane and Rustem Pasha. Writers and artists, whom the young prince had protected,[3] bewailed his loss. Poets wrote elegies full of regrets about the loss in such abominable circumstances of one of the most brilliant hopes of the House of Osman. A poem by Yahya, one of the most famous poets, particularly displeased Rustem Pasha, who asked the sultan to have executed a man who was so reckless as to rebel against one of the *padishah*'s judgements. Suleiman did not dare: too much blood had already been spilt.

Europe, meanwhile, breathed a sign of relief. It was known that the heir to the throne had been intelligent, courageous and ambitious. After Suleiman's conquests, what limits could there be to the expansion of the empire under a sultan with such talents? Rumours about Suleiman's health had long been current, and disaster was feared as soon as Mustafa came to the throne. His disappearance did not totally dissipate all anxieties because next to nothing was known about the other sons of Suleiman. The most dangerous one, however, was no longer among the living.

Peace with the Safavid Ruler

When these horrendous executions had been carried out, Suleiman led his army to Aleppo to spend the winter. It was there that the English traveller, Anthony Jenkinson, took part in Suleiman's entry into the town in all his glory. At the head of the procession, he said, were 6,000 light horsemen, the *sipahi*, all dressed in scarlet. After them came 10,000 tributaries of the Great Turk, in yellow velvet and head-dresses of the same colour, in Tartar fashion, and with bows in their hands. They were followed by 4 captains dressed in crimson velvet, each with 12,000 men under his command, with helmets on their heads and scimitars in hand. Next, 16,000 janissaries, dressed in violet, each armed with an harquebus and wearing on their heads head-dresses of white velvet decorated with jewels and precious stones and surmounted with feathers. Behind them were 1,000 pages of honour, all dressed in gold-coloured cloth, half of them armed with harquebuses and the rest with bows; then three men in leopard skins and helmets on their heads, carrying a pole with a red horse tail, their standard, at the end of it, followed by seven pages of honour dressed in costumes silver in colour and mounted on white horses decked out in silver, with precious stones, diamonds, emeralds and rubies. Six further pages of honour, likewise dressed in gold-coloured cloth, went before the Great Turk himself, 'marvellously majestic', with only two pages in golden costumes on each side and, at the same time, a white courser covered in golden material embroidered with the most precious stones; on his head was a turban of the finest white cloth surmounted with white ostrich feathers. Six young women followed behind, mounted on palfreys covered with cloths silver in colour embroidered with pearls and precious stones; their head-dresses were also of great value, and they were each escorted by two eunuchs armed with small bows. The Grand Vizier was behind them, wearing a crimson jacket and escorted by 15 janissaries on foot, all wearing velvet of the same colour. Then came the other pashas with their slaves, about 3,000 in all; 4,000 armed horsemen brought up the rear. According to Jenkinson, Suleiman's army, including the regiments who were encamped at several days' march from Aleppo, made up about 300,000 men all together.

Operations started in spring. Before putting his army in battle order, Suleiman held a meeting of his senior officers at Diyarbekir. He spoke of the enemies of the faith who had raised their heads once again, of the dangers they posed to Islam. We ought to eliminate them, he said, by taking war into their country. All of them cried out: 'We will march joyfully under the *padishah*'s orders not only as far as India and China but even to mount Kas' (a legendary country in Muslim folklore). The sultan had once again taken his men in hand: the tragedy of Mustafa was forgotten.

Once more, the army set out towards Persia along the valley of the Euphrates and Erzurum. Prince Selim was at the head of the army, on the right wing with the Anatolian troops, and those of Rumelia were on the left under the command of *beylerbey* Sokullu Mehmed, the future Grand Vizier. From Kars, Suleiman sent Shah Tahmasp an insulting letter of the kind the Ottoman sultans always used as a prelude to hostilities with the Shiite heretics. 'If you are not willing to return to the bosom of orthodoxy, you will be exterminated. As the Koran says, we have drawn our sword to show our anger . . .' Operations could commence. The Turks ravaged the whole region of Yerevan. In the town itself, the shah's palace was razed to the ground. In Nakhichevan, not a single stone was left standing.

Shah Tahmasp's response then reached Suleiman. It was no less insulting. It called the Turks cowards for showing no spirit of nobility in their use of arms. 'Your strength is not in the sword and spear. You rely on guns and cannons and show your valour by pillage and arson.' The exchange of insults between the viziers of the two emperors went on. 'We can see clearly where the earth has quaked,' the Ottoman wrote back. 'Now that we have retreated from Nakhichevan, the jackal bravely takes to the forest. The lands of Persia are still darkened by the Ottoman standards. If the Persian people dared to appear in the open country to fight, we would be ready to drive them back without guns or cannons but simply by using the sword and spear.' The Safavid leader responded to this as if Suleiman had been asking for peace. 'Not at all,' retorted Suleiman's vizier, calling the shah an 'unbeliever', although he added that if he desired peace, 'the blessed Porte is always open to friends and enemies'. At one point, the Turks thought they would be able to join battle with the Safavids. At the news that they had captured several fortresses, Suleiman immediately sent the Grand Vizier with 4,000 janissaries and all the Rumelian and Anatolian troops. But, as usual, the shah and his army had retraced their steps: the Turks merely found a ravaged area which all the inhabitants had left.

The war could have continued indefinitely without achieving anything more than piling destruction on destruction. Tahmasp saw that whole regions of his country had been ruined and was ready to make peace. He achieved a few military successes, for the sake of honour, and then sent an ambassador – the captain of his bodyguards – with full powers to negotiate, to the sultan's headquarters, which were then at Erzurum. The ambassador asked for an armistice, which was immediately granted. Suleiman too was tired of the war. Hostilities came to an end and the sultan left to take up winter quarters in Amasya.

It was there that several months of negotiations opened between the shah's grand master of ceremonies and the Grand Vizier. The Persian plenipotentiary arrived with splendid gifts and a letter full of praise for God, his Prophet and Ali as well as protestations of peace. The shah asked for Shiite pilgrims to be allowed to visit undisturbed the Holy Places of

Islam. Suleiman agreed. Peace would be maintained as long as the Persians did nothing to violate it, he told the shah; he also observed that Ali was not the only companion of the Prophet, who had said: 'My companions are like the stars; in following one of them, you are taking the right direction.'

Signed in May 1555, the peace of Amasya put an end, provisionally, to the long combat which had for so long covered in blood the eastern border lands. The shah recognized the limits of the Ottoman Empire established by Suleiman's recent annexations. He also undertook – at least in words – to put an end to the raiding and Shiite propaganda of his partisans in Anatolia. The Persian and Ottoman emirs had to act in such a way that peace should not be disturbed on the frontiers. Although he was not totally satisfied with these provisions, Suleiman gave orders that these clauses should be followed strictly. For a certain time, he was also to make efforts to maintain good relations with the khan of Uzbekistan, who ruled the territories beyond the Oxus, in order that he should bring sufficient pressure to bear to stop Tahmasp from attacking the Ottomans. The sultan wanted to have his hands free: a political storm of the first magnitude was about to break over the empire.

A 'Communist' Rebellion

Suleiman was now 60. For a man of his age – in the 16th century – he carried his years very nimbly. His beard was now grey, his silhouette plumper, his long and slender neck had sunk down into his shoulders, yet his appearance was still dignified and majestic. 'Although his face was sad, his severe look nonetheless possessed great majesty,' wrote Busbecq, who met him at his camp in Amasya. His health was good, 'if his poor colour was not a sign of some hidden illness. But he knew as well as women how to repair the injuries of time. He put on rouge and was particularly careful to do so on the days he bid farewell to an ambassador, so that he should notice the plumpness and good health that the colour in his cheeks seemed to indicate that he enjoyed.' He had been sober all his life and was still more so as he grew old. He knew nothing of drunkenness and the other vices to which his son Selim II and several of his other successors succumbed. Even his severest critics, Busbecq tells us, could find nothing to complain of beyond his excessive submission to his wife.

Deeply committed to his religious duties, Suleiman on the threshold of old age did not yet go so far as to prescribe a return to the simplicity of the first sultans. It was only later, a few years before his death, that the silverware in the Seraglio was replaced with clay plates.

The Seraglio at Constantinople always possessed a splendour which left foreign travellers dumbfounded; they described the trappings of the sultan's horse, 'decked all over with fine Oriental pearls', his scimitar encrusted with emeralds, rubies and diamonds 'and other exquisite materials, which is the richest thing one could possibly imagine', the clothes of the empire's dignitaries, 'some dressed in gold cloth, others in velvet, red, white and blue satin, beautifully decorated with ribbons and water silk and threaded with gold and silver of the finest quality'. 'Look', said Busbecq, 'at that sea of turbaned heads, each circled in folds of the whitest silk . . . Look at those magnificent robes of every kind and every colour . . . Everything sparkles with gold, silver, purple, silk, velvet . . . Words are lacking to give an idea of that strange and astonishing spectacle. It is the most beautiful I have ever seen.'[4]

Hurrem Sultan (Roxelane) was still alive and possessed considerable influence. She played a major role in Suleiman's decisions, and her tools occupied most of the highest positions in the state up to the rank of Grand Vizier (Rustem Pasha). But the mistakes and crimes of the aging sultan should not be laid at her account. Suleiman remained the man he had always been, energetic and pitiless, until his last years, especially when he felt the fate of the empire, or his own, was at stake. Even if he was influenced by his entourage, he alone bears responsibility for the death of Mustafa and, shortly afterwards, for that of Bayezid. Completely lucid and level-headed, it was he who took the decisions. To his dying day, he held on to the reins of power.

That power certainly remained solid. The empire was still the empire, powerful and rich, and the emperor's authority was still intact. Difficult times had not yet come, but there were already some worrying signs.[5] The economy was shaky, money was beginning to lose its value, and the enormous expenses of the army and the court brought with them a heavier burden of taxes. To suppress discontent and maintain order, janissaries were sent into the provinces. The only result was that they confiscated land and often property, which increased the dissatisfaction of the population. The elite army's *esprit de corps* and discipline also suffered.

Mustafa's dramatic end had not settled anything. He was mourned by large sections of the population, and legends about him were retailed and embellished from the day of his death onwards. As often happens in such circumstances, a man suddenly appeared from nowhere claiming to be the prince, who had somehow managed to escape the noose in the Seraglio. He formed a government with viziers and the pretence of an administration in Eregli, in North-West Anatolia. Hundreds and then thousands of rebels took his side. He then entered European Turkey, where most of Thrace, Macedonia and Dobrogea soon recognized him as sultan. He failed to seize Edirne, however, which he had wanted to make his capital. He preached a sort of communism which attracted to him tens of thousands of malcontents, to whom he handed out riches taken from the propertied classes and the state. The movement extended its influence until the day when Prince Bayezid seized the self-proclaimed Mustafa and hanged him. The rebellion was crushed but is nonetheless revealing of a spirit of revolt always to be found beneath the surface of the Ottoman Empire. The execution of thousands of the pretender's followers settled nothing. This was made very clear when, immediately afterwards, Bayezid's own revolt erupted, the last major 'business' of Suleiman's reign.

This rebellion, one of the most serious the Ottoman Empire had ever known, would not have been on such a large scale if tensions between the ruling classes and the discontent of much of the population in the country, particularly in Anatolia, had not reached the point they had in the years which followed Mustafa's execution. That event had had a considerable impact and had been followed by the business of the 'false Mustafa'; together, they had greatly aggravated the general discontent and made clear to what extent the peasants were dissatisfied with the deterioration of their conditions of existence resulting from inflation and a heavier burden of taxation.

The pressures of larger populations, while the area of land under cultivation was increasing only slowly, made the situation even worse.[6] So did the diffusion of firearms among the inhabitants of the countryside, the recruitment of volunteers to replace the *timariotes* as these declined (see Chapter 12) and the coming monetary crisis, brought on by the 'price revolution' and the influx of cheap silver from Europe into the Ottoman Empire. Everything was coming together to produce serious troubles. They would explode later, towards the end of the century, in the Celali insurrections.

Another Dynastic Tragedy

At the period we have now reached, the main effect of the discontent and sense of irritation some people felt was to bring to Bayezid, when he revolted against his father, the troops he needed to carry on a conflict which ended only with his death. After Mustafa's disappearance, the struggle for the throne narrowed down to two princes, Selim and Bayezid, of more or less the same age – around 35.

Roxelane worried little about the future of the dynasty, but she had enough influence over her two sons to prevent them coming to blows, even if her preference seemed to be with Bayezid, who was intelligent and without any known vices, while Selim's reputation for rudeness, idleness and heavy drinking[7] was already firmly established. Roxelane died in March 1558 and her sons immediately set on each other.

They had both recruited supporters. The discontented *timariotes* and peasants took Bayezid's side, while the janissaries were for Selim. It was Rustem Pasha, a past master of bloody ploys, who set in motion the complex intrigue which opened the conflict.

The Grand Vizier loathed the second court equerry, Lala Mustafa, because he had been the protégé of his predecessor Ahmed Pasha. Knowing that he was completely devoted to Bayezid, he appointed him grand master of Selim's court in the hope of ruining him once and for all. But Lala Mustafa, who was not conspicuous for his loyalty, instead used his new position to try and obtain further promotion, perhaps even to the post of Grand Vizier. He therefore proposed to Selim that he should lead Bayezid on to make errors which would ruin him. Selim agreed and approved of Lala Mustafa's plan to send Bayezid, who would have no suspicions because of their long-standing friendship, a letter offering help in getting rid of his brother. Bayezid, who desired nothing else, readily agreed – he had been caught in the trap. When Selim was shown his reply, he exploded with rage. But when, a few weeks later, he received a letter from his brother – written in fact by Lala Mustafa – full of outrageous proposals and accompanied by the gifts of a skirt, a woman's bonnet and a distaff, he became still more furious. Selim therefore informed his father, who sent Bayezid a letter full of strong criticisms which never arrived. Lala Mustafa – who had himself arrested and killed the messengers – made Suleiman believe that Bayezid had assassinated them. The sultan indignantly deprived Bayezid of his governorship of Konya and appointed him to Amasya, further away from Istanbul. Selim, meanwhile, was sent to Kutahya.

The two brothers continued their preparations for war without Suleiman being able to calm them. Bayezid refused to leave Konya, and assembled the troops, about 20,000 in number, who had come there to join him. It was open rebellion. Suleiman sent janissaries, *sipahi* and guns to Selim under the command of Sokullu Mehmed Pasha, the third vizier and the most capable man in the government. The battle took place near Konya. Bayezid's army, less well armed and made up mainly of Turkomans and *timariotes*, was defeated. Bayezid fled to Amasya, where he decided to put an end to a dispute which served no purpose in his father's lifetime. He sent a letter to Suleiman asking to be pardoned. Once again, it was intercepted by Lala Mustafa.

Bayezid could only take flight. As a rebel son defeated by the sultan's army, his fate was clearly laid down: if he fell into the hands of his father's soldiers, he would be handed over to the mutes and suffer the same fate as his brother Mustafa. He assembled an army of about 10,000 men and left for Persia with his four sons. The horsemen sent by Selim did not manage to catch up with him. In the autumn of 1559, the prince reached Yerevan, where the governor received him with the greatest respect. A little later, Shah Tahmasp, delighted to have such a hostage in his hands, went to Tabriz to welcome him. The shah held magnificent festivities in his honour. Thirty heaped plates of gold, of silver, of pearls and precious stones, 'were poured on the prince's head'. He was offered nine horses, magnificently harnessed. Bayezid gave as good as he got. 'On the shah's route were spread out satin, damask, silk and rich cloths, and he was given fifty horses with silver trappings.'[8]

But behind these showy displays, some sordid bargains were being hammered out: what would Suleiman give in return for Bayezid? Exchanges of letters and diplomatic missions commenced. Suleiman presented his son as a rebel who deserved the severest punishments and then pretended he wanted to be reconciled. Selim sent the Persians dozens of letters full of insults about his brother. Tahmasp admitted that the death of Bayezid and his sons would be just, according to the precepts of the Koran: 'Kill idolators and rebels.' But, in return for freeing them, he asked quite simply for the governorship of Baghdad for himself or his sons.

Suleiman, who naturally had not the least intention of letting the Safavids back into Baghdad, responded evasively. He was not only determined not to give Tahmasp anything for Bayezid; he wanted to use force to compel Tahmasp to give up his rebellious son. He asked the khan of Uzbekistan and the Caucasian tribes to attack the Safavid ruler, 'who has received my criminal son and thus violated the peace between us with the baseness whose sign is engraved on his brow . . .' But they were all distinctly cool at the prospect of taking on Tahmasp and his formidable army. They replied that if Suleiman were to come with his admirable troops, they would join up with him at once. Suleiman, who knew that his soldiers were not at all disposed to set off again into such inhospitable terrain, therefore decided to temporize.

Months went by in inconclusive negotiations. If Bayezid were set free, he would stir up further agitation and perhaps organize an alternative centre of power in Anatolia. Both the sultan and the shah knew this. The latter wished to obtain as much as possible in return for the prince, the former to give as little. During this time, Bayezid had become a prisoner. Under various pretexts, his soldiers had been taken away from him: he was completely powerless, yet still the shah's guest of honour. Finally, Tahmasp wrote to Suleiman that Bayezid's stay had proved very expensive and that he had to take that into account. Suleiman understood: what the shah wanted was money. He promised to compensate him handsomely and to make him a gift 'in proportion to the importance of the event'.

All that remained was to find an opportunity to arrest the prince and hand him over. This occurred in September 1561 during festivities in which Bayezid took part at the shah's side. One of Bayezid's chamberlains, a certain Mahmud Pasha, came up to the shah and said in his ear: 'Be careful of a son who has betrayed his father and could take away your life . . .' Terrified, the shah got up and left. Bayezid immediately had Mahmud's head cut off, but two of Mahmud's accomplices declared that the prince had tried to incite them to assassinate Tahmasp. The populace learnt of this and assembled, crying out against Bayezid. The shah therefore gave orders for him to be arrested 'for his own protection' and at the same time put a thousand of Bayezid's soldiers to death – all those in his entourage. Then, since he had promised never to hand him over to Suleiman, he delivered Bayezid to Selim's envoy.

The unlucky man was strangled with his four sons. A little later, his fifth son, 3 years old, was also put to death in Bursa by a eunuch that Suleiman had sent with a janissary. The latter, who was supposed to act as executioner, fainted when he saw the child coming forward to kiss him. As soon as Suleiman learnt of his son's death, he sent the shah a vizier with 300,000 pieces of gold and 100,000 more from Selim – now the sole surviving heir of the House of Osman.

Nobody knows what the old sultan thought about the death of Bayezid, which had come several years after Mustafa's decease and meant that the throne would go to a man whose mediocrity he was well aware of. The Venetian ambassador, Marcantonio Donini, however, reports the sentiments attributed to Suleiman at the time: 'I thank God that I have lived long enough to see the Muslims free of war between my sons. I will therefore be able to live out the rest of my days in peace. If the opposite had occurred, I would have lived and died in despair.'[9] Anything was better than a shattered empire.[10]

7
The Twilight of the Empire

Around the year 1550, the Turks, with the help of the corsairs, were in effect the masters of the Mediterranean. The Spanish, on the defensive almost everywhere, were only successful in a few surprise attacks; their major expeditions failed completely. In the years which followed the disaster at Algiers, the Ottomans came close to completely overwhelming their defences.

Barbarossa's expedition to the Italian coast had been a mere promenade: if he had attacked Doria while he was at Villefranche, he would certainly have inflicted a setback on the Spanish fleet from which it would never have recovered. The death of the great sailor in 1546 did not weaken the Muslim fleet because he left behind him captains of equal ability: Piyale Pasha, a Croat of Christian origin, who married Suleiman's granddaughter; Turgut Reis, the most famous of the corsairs and also from a Christian background; Salih Reis; Kiliç Ali Pasha, usually known to history by the name of Uç Ali, also a Christian and born in Calabria.

The Pirates of the Sea

Turgut, Barbarossa's direct heir, had been taken prisoner by Doria in the course of a surprise attack on Corsica, and then released in return for a huge ransom paid by Barbarossa. As soon as he was free of his chains, he put together a fleet, ravaged the African coast and went to Italy. Pozzuoli and Castellammare were literally emptied of inhabitants, who were either released for ransom or taken into slavery. On his return from Africa, he took Sousse and Monastir, before laying siege to Mahdia, then under the nominal suzerainty of the *bey* of Tunis. The town was said to be impregnable, but gold coins were skilfully employed to persuade the inhabitants to open the gates – without a shot being fired!

The capture of Mahdia, although of very minor importance in itself, induced one of the periodic shudders of terror among the Christians which Muslim successes sometimes brought on. Without even asking Charles V for his view, the viceroy of Naples, Alvares de Toledo, Doria, Cosimo de' Medici and Pope Julius III decided to try and recapture 'the new Algiers'. They assembled about 50 galleys and for two months put down a siege before the town, whose walls finally gave way and let the attackers in, thanks to a war machine called the *sambuca*.[1] But Turgut had already left the town: victory without capturing him was a very incomplete triumph. The corsair had retreated to Jerba, where the Christians believed it would be very easy to capture him. Turgut then made use of a stratagem which had already been successfully used – by Mehmed the Conqueror, among others. Since he knew where the enemy were going to attack the island, he made a road out of planks and rubbed grease into them; his ships could then be pulled on rollers from the port of Alcantara to the other end of the island. Battery fire, meanwhile, was used to deceive the imperial fleet, which was stuck in the port. Doria did not understand the tactic which had been used against him until he saw Turgut capture, almost under his eyes, the ship which was coming to his aid. The result was total defeat.

No sooner had he escaped from Jerba than Turgut tried to attack Malta. The island had been controlled by the Knights of Saint John ever since Suleiman had driven them out of Rhodes. Malta put up a strong resistance and the corsair only managed to disembark at Gozo, the neighbouring island, where he led away into captivity almost all the inhabitants, 5–6,000 people in all. His boats then set out for Tripoli at a rapid pace.

That town, whose strategic position was as important as that of Tunis or Malta, had been given to the Knights of Malta by Charles V. Everybody knew that the garrison consisted of only a few knights and some Italian and Moorish soldiers, commanded by Fra Gaspar de Vallier,

Marshal of the Langue d'Auvergne. The Turkish artillery opened hostilities in their usual fashion by pounding the ramparts, which soon gave way. The garrison quickly became tired and parleys were held in the presence of Gabriel d'Aramon, France's ambassador to Suleiman, whose good offices had been asked for by the Grand Master of the Order, Jean d'Olmedes. An agreement was reached that the garrison and the inhabitants would be allowed to go free. But as soon as the Turkish admiral, Koca Sinan, had entered the town, he had them all arrested. If he had not kept his word, he said, it was because the knights had not: Suleiman had given them their liberty, after the capture of Rhodes, on condition that they give up piracy, which they had completely failed to do. D'Aramon nonetheless managed to negotiate the release of the French knights; the rest were enchained and taken to Istanbul. The Ottoman flag now flew over Tripoli, and Turgut was appointed governor; the town soon regained the prosperity it had lost while it had been under the rather lazy control of the Order.

The Ottomans continued to pose problems in the Mediterranean. The Maltese were terrified of the possibility of a new attack. The Spanish wondered if the Ottomans were going to disembark on the Andalusian coast or the Levant. But Suleiman, who was preparing for war against the Safavids, was too tied up with his internal problems to launch any major initiatives to the West. The corsairs continued to raid and enslave. Salih Reis, the Governor of Algiers, made surprise attacks on the Spanish coast and seized Portuguese galleys, but nothing decisive occurred. Then, in the summer of 1553, Turgut came to the aid of Sampiero Corso's Corsican exiles and French troops (commanded by Polin de la Garde) when they disembarked on Corsica and took over the whole island, then under Genoese control. This, however, could not last long – the island occupied a position too strategically important for the imperial forces to be able to accept its loss – and the Genoese soon regained control.

Soon after this, the *kapudan pasha* Sinan was replaced by Piyale Pasha. The new admiral set about reorganizing the Great Lord's fleet and co-operating even more closely with the corsairs. Every spring, the Turkish boats left the Bosphorus to meet up with those of Turgut. They ravaged the Calabrian coast, captured Reggio and took the inhabitants into slavery. In North Africa, Piyale seized Oran in 1556 and Bizerta in the following year. For his part, Salih Reis left his lair in Algiers, carried out a lightning raid on Morocco as far as Fez, and snatched the *peñon* at Velez and then Bougie, where the governor gave himself up. He was executed 'for his cowardice' a year later at Valladolid. In the very same year, 1558, Piyale Pasha took to the sea and, with 150 galleys, was able to devastate Sorrento, Massa and, soon afterwards, Minorca. It was quite impossible to stop these 'pirates of the sea', whose galleys, with 25 to 30 banks of oars, were light and manageable and well able to escape the Christian boats every time, although they too, when the occasion arose, were by no means averse to 'piracy'.

The Capture of Jerba

Raiding towns and enslaving inhabitants – these were mere inconveniences for the major countries of the Mediterranean, and Spain most of all, compared to the corsair tactic of harassing Christian shipping in a huge area including Sicily, Sardinia and the Atlantic coast of Cadiz. In some years, Catalonia and the Levant were threatened with famine. The problem had to be resolved once and for all.

Philip II, recently crowned King of Spain, had just signed the peace of Cateau-Cambrésis with the King of France. He believed the occasion was propitious for striking a major blow against the corsairs and the Turks. The sultan had aged, was deeply worried by the disputes between his sons, and desired only to live out his last years in peace. He could rely no longer on the support of the French fleet. In 1559, therefore, Philip agreed to an operation against Tripoli which would destroy a nest of corsairs, free Italy from a permanent danger and weaken the Turks. Both the Duke of Medina Celi, viceroy of Sicily, and the Grand Master of the Order of Malta, Jean de La Valette, had long favoured this plan, the former for his personal glory and the latter because he hoped that Tripoli, recaptured, might be given back to the Order. Destiny was not to grant them such successes.

Preparations took a long time: six months was required to gather the troops – Italian, Spanish and German – at Genoa and Naples with about a hundred ships, including 53 galleys. The disaster at Algiers in 1541 should have taught Philip II and the Duke of Medina Celi, the commander-in-chief, about the dangers of undertaking an expedition in the Mediterranean in the winter season. Five times in a row the fleet put to sea; five times unfavourable winds brought them back to port. The ships spent six weeks in Malta in this way, losing 2,000 men to illness. Philip II's 'surprise attack' had evidently failed. The Turks were alerted by the corsair Kiliç Ali and knew of every detail of the operation which was under way. News arrived one day of a large fleet (250 ships) which had been equipped. Should they proceed nonetheless to attack Tripoli at once? Medina Celi preferred to establish himself at Jerba instead and use it as a base of operations to give them the best chances for a later assault.

At the beginning of March, the island was in the hands of Christians who were starting on the construction of a fortress in the hope of receiving reinforcements from Sicily. Suddenly Piyale Pasha's galleys turned up. Expected in June, he had broken all records for speed and taken 20 days from Istanbul to reach Jerba in mid-May. What should the Christian commanders do? Scipion Doria suggested they should rely on the battery along the shore and join battle. The other Doria, Giovanni Andrea, and Orsini, the commander of the papal contingent, advised them instead to raise anchor and take flight. This policy was agreed upon. Suddenly, panic seized the men who were disembarking in rowing boats, and their commanders were quite unable to restrain them. The galleys set out in complete disorder and the sailing boats were thrown back on to the coast by a rising wind. Piyale Pasha had only to reap the fruits of the errors made by the Christian commanders: 20 galleys and 27 transport ships were sunk, and 18,000 soldiers were drowned or killed by Turks who charged on them, sword in hand. Orsini fell into Piyale's hands and was beheaded. The disaster was total.

As for the garrison at Jerba, 2,000 men had remained in the new fortress which was bombarded unceasingly by 14,000 Turks. The Christians wanted at first to come to their aid, assembled troops and prepared provisions. Then Philip II changed his mind and decided it was better to attempt a diversion. But when it was discovered that the Duke of Medina Celi, believed to have been captured or killed, was in fact safe and sound, no one gave any further thought to the garrison at Jerba. When the Turks captured the well which served the fort, the garrison surrendered.

Piyale made a triumphal return to Istanbul. A huge crowd came to welcome him on the banks of the Golden Horn and the Bosphorus. From a stand which overlooked the entrance to the harbour, Suleiman took part in the procession of galleys with the admiral's ship at the head and the leading Christian prisoners at the rear: Alvaro de Sandi, the commander of Jerba, and the Sicilian and Neapolitan admirals, Sancho de Leyva and Berenguer de Requenses. They were shown to the populace with the other prisoners in the streets of Istanbul over the following days. The Turkish galleys, painted in red, sailed past and then the captured Christian ships, without masts or rudders, were towed along like miserable carcasses. Thousands of people acclaimed the victorious crews;

only the sultan remained unmoved. According to Busbecq, who was then at Constantinople, Suleiman had such a severe and sad expression on his face 'that one would have thought the victory did not concern him and that nothing new or unexpected had occurred'.

The Great Lord had seen so many things, won so many victories and also undergone so many trials that, in the evening of his life, nothing mattered to him any more. The empire was threatened with a major succession crisis; the *padishah*'s sadness was not without reason.

Nonetheless, what a great success the Turks had just achieved! Now they dominated the Central as well as the Eastern Mediterranean. Suleiman was master of the bolt-hole at Tripoli, and his vassals, the corsairs, were at Algiers, Bougie and all along the coast. It was said that the Spanish might abandon Oran. Despite the winter, Tuscany was laid waste; Italy and Spain were in a state of fear. It was more obvious then than at any other time: in 1560, the Turks were masters of the sea. Rumours were rife that the sultan's armada was going to return, this time to La Goulette or even to Oran. Such news, although often false, did the rounds from Istanbul to Ragusa, Naples, Vienna and especially Venice, the main European centre for intelligence gathering. Everywhere people thought they saw 'the Turkish fleet'. As soon as a few galleys left the Sea of Marmara, rumours reached as far as Brussels that the van of the sultan's fleet was approaching. This is what happened in 1561, when about 50 Ottoman ships advanced to the entrance of the Adriatic, and then made a sudden about-turn, perhaps because of the conflict between Bayezid and Selim or because of the death of the Grand Vizier Rustem. Europe got used to living with these rumours, some of which were true – if the Porte had an excellent system of spies, the Christian states also possessed similar advantages.

Setback at Malta

The years went by, however, without any of the Christian fears being confirmed. The Turks hardly showed themselves at all. If small fleets here and there carried out surprise attacks, the time did not lend itself, in Turkey, to major expeditions by sea. Both sides harassed each other on occasion, but nothing more. A few times, though, operations on a larger scale were carried out. In the autumn of 1562, for example, the Spanish lost 25 of their 28 galleys in the bay of Heredura and had to abandon to their deaths several thousands of their men. A few months later, Oran was attacked, the Spanish stronghold in North Africa, but the fortress of

Mers el-Kebir stood up to the bombardments of the Algerians, who were forced to turn back.

Was the tide going to turn? The Christian success made a major impact in Europe. It crowned Philip II's policy of ship-building and re-armament: his fleet increased in size from around 50 galleys in 1564 to almost a hundred a few years later. In the autumn of 1564, a fleet under Garcia de Toledo (appointed chief admiral by Philip II) consisting of 150 ships and 16,000 men at last managed to seize the *peñon* of Velez, planted like a splinter right opposite the coast of Andalusia. Good use had been made of the subsidies provided by the Pope and credits voted by the Cortes of Castile. Suleiman soon received news of these events.[2]

The loss of the *peñon* of Velez was all the more keenly felt in Istanbul because the Spanish, spurred on by Castilian pride, made every effort to inform the whole of Europe about it. Some even exaggerated the importance of the fortress and concluded, rather prematurely, that the Great Lord's influence at sea was now in decline.

Suleiman, pushed on by his entourage, took up the challenge. The Grand Vizier himself, Turgut and Kiliç Ali made every effort to persuade Suleiman of the danger to the coasts of Tunis and Algiers posed by abandoning fortresses like La Goulette and the *peñon*. Princess Mihrimah, Suleiman's daughter, was greatly angered by the exactions imposed by the Knights of Malta on Muslim pilgrims travelling to Mecca by sea. Anger reached a peak in the palace when it was discovered that a boat bringing goods destined for the Harem had been seized by the knights off the Ionian islands and taken to Malta. The arsenal on the Golden Horn was set to work day and night.

At the beginning of the year 1565, preparations for the huge Turkish armada – 200 boats including 150 combat galleys – came to an end. The news reached Ragusa and Venice. Philip II also knew about it. Everybody was sure that the Turks, with the help of the corsairs, were going to launch a formidable expedition – but in what direction? While people were speculating about this, it was learnt at the beginning of April that the sultan's fleet had left Marmara. On board were 9,000 *sipahi*, 5,000 janissaries, 15–16,000 *azab* and a powerful artillery. Mustafa Pasha was appointed commander-in-chief, a member of the Isfendiyaroğlu family which had once ruled over part of Anatolia and claimed to be descended from the Prophet's standard-bearer. The choice of this 70-year-old man for such heavy responsibilities was not, perhaps, an obvious one, especially since he did not get on at all well with the commander of the fleet, Piyale Pasha, and hardly better with Turgut Reis.

As usual, the Turkish fleet proceeded at top speed – but was it towards La Goulette or Malta? the Christian chiefs of staff asked themselves. By mid-May, there was no longer any doubt: Malta was the target. Philip II learned from the viceroy of Sicily that the sultan's squadrons had rounded Cape Passero in Southern Sicily. The early arrival of the Turks, expected in mid-summer, caused great surprise in Malta. Preparations were not totally finished, although the Grand Master, expecting to be attacked, had long since reinforced the walls, called all the knights home and engaged auxiliaries. He could count on about 8,500 men, including 700 exceptionally valiant knights, to defend the Order and the Christian faith. Foreigners had responded to La Valette's appeal, starting with Garcia de Toledo, the viceroy of Naples. After making sure that Naples and La Goulette would be able to resist assault, he went to Malta to examine the fortifications. These he found to be in good repair, although he regretted the fact that there were not more soldiers to defend them. He therefore sent provisions to the Grand Master and promised him men, while Philip II merely assembled 4,000 men in Corsica and authorized de Toledo to send wheat and money from Spain.

On 19 May, the Turks arrived alongside the South-West of the island. The anchorage was excellent and Mustafa ordered the disembarcation of 20,000 men and 5 cannons, although this was against the advice of Piyale, who would have preferred to wait for Turgut. The whole island was soon in Turkish hands, except for the Saint-Elmo fortress, which protected the two ports, and the Saint-Angelo and Saint-Michael fortresses. When Kiliç Ali and then Turgut arrived, the bombardment of the Saint-Elmo fortress had already started and it was impossible to change tactics; it was this which led to the Turkish setback.

As always, the Turkish artillery had been planned with care and proved formidable. For more than three weeks, the batteries bombarded the fortress, which eventually gave way. All the defenders (130 horsemen and 300 soldiers) died. But the Ottomans had meanwhile lost three weeks, during which the garrison of the island had had time to prepare itself and to receive 600 soldiers from de Toledo – accepted by La Valette with a joy one can well imagine – and during which the Turks had lost their most valorous and experienced fighter, Turgut Reis, who was hit in the head by a fragment of stone. La Valette soon received further major reinforcements: more than 11,000 men on 40 transport ships with 90 galleys sent by the commander of the galleys of Seville, Alvaro de Bazan, by the Pope and by Philip II, who had finally agreed to allow the *tercio* to leave Lombardy.

Seeing that the Saint-Elmo fort had cost them such effort and that progress was so slow, Mustafa Pasha, who had already lost 5,000 men, became violently angry and – it is not known why – nailed the corpses of the defenders of the fort to planks which he ordered to be thrown under the ramparts of the town. As his only response, the Grand Master ordered all the captured Turks to be killed and their heads fired like cannon-balls into the enemy camp. Then, when Mustafa called on La Valette to surrender, the latter pointed out the ditches in the ramparts and said to him: 'There is the only ground I am willing to yield to your master – he can come and fill it with the corpses of his janissaries.' The bombardment started up again.

Mustafa then decided on an all-out attack against the two other forts, Saint-Angelo and Saint-Michael, with his forces and the supporting troops which had been brought to him by Hassan, the *beylerbey* of Tunis. On 15 July, in overpowering heat, Hassan launched an attack at the head of 6,000 troops against the Saint-Michael fort, while Kandelisa, a corsair of Greek origin, attacked the port. All their efforts were in vain: Saint-Michael did not give way and the Turkish losses were enormous, with only 500 survivors. The expedition had paid dear for the death of Turgut and the incompetence of its commander-in-chief.

On the Christian side too, the corpses piled up, although this in no way diminished the Grand Master's resistance. He even led a cavalry charge which threw disorder into the Turkish ranks.

At the beginning of September, Christian reinforcements sent from Sicily arrived: 9,600 men who had managed to leave Messina despite a tempest the like of which they had never seen. Piyale Pasha considered attacking the Christian fleet, but what would happen to the land forces if he lost his galleys? He therefore gave up the idea and launched a final attack on the Christian forces, who had now been reinforced by a strong contingent of fresh troops. Several thousand Turkish soldiers were killed; totally demoralized, some of them preferred to lie down on the ground rather than fight. The game was over. On 12 September, Piyale Pasha's fleet raised anchor. The Knights of Malta could proclaim loud and clear that it was they and they alone who had pushed back the Infidel. The Pope, who felt no great love for the Spanish, echoed their boast far and wide.

At the very beginning of October, Istanbul learnt of the defeat. The failed expedition had cost the Turks at least 20,000 men, and perhaps as many as 35,000.[3] The effect was disastrous and Christians were molested in the streets of Istanbul. It was the first time one of the Great Lords had lost in a major naval expedition. But the Ottoman fleet was intact. The day after Malta, the Turkish threat in the Mediterranean remained the same. Nothing could prevent the Ottomans, if they so wished, from putting an end to all Christian trade. Opposed to states whose finances were constantly in poor repair and which, like Spain, had to crush their whole population with taxes for each new campaign, the Ottoman Empire had means which enabled it to build an immense fleet very rapidly and to equip for war as many men as it needed.

At the end of 1565, spies and renegades put the rumour around that the Ottoman fleet was preparing to return to Malta in the following spring. A battle had been lost, but the long war by land and sea between Turks and Christians was far from reaching its end. Almost every year, Turks and corsairs ravaged the Mediterranean coasts. Cyprus was soon captured from the Venetians, and then there was Lepanto (17 October 1571), which should have brought the Ottoman Empire to its knees, yet three years later the Christians lost Tunis once and for all. It was only at the end of the century that Turkish naval power weakened and then ceased to exist at just about the same time as the Spanish, in the aftermath of the Portuguese War, turned away from the Mediterranean and towards the Atlantic.

War in Hungary

After the Treaty of Constantinople in 1547, the problems of Central Europe became a secondary concern. Ottomans and Habsburgs both had other preoccupations than stirring up war again. The tragic deaths of Mustafa and Bayezid, wars against Persia – such things kept Suleiman too busy to try and snatch more territory along the Danube. He merely strengthened his fortified positions.

Many things had also changed in Europe. Charles V had abdicated in 1556 soon after signing the peace of Augsburg in 1555. His attempts to eliminate Protestantism in Germany had failed and he shared out his possessions between his son Philip II and his brother Ferdinand, who had become emperor. But it was Philip, with his gold from America, who was rich. The new emperor never had the means to undertake a long and costly campaign. He did, however, build a line of defence in depth in

Central Europe, made up of small wooden fortresses occupied by Spanish, Italian and German contingents. Although these defences were fairly light, in accordance with the emperor's finances, they still proved effective: the *limes* were strong enough to discourage the Turkish *beys* at certain points.

Ferdinand made an attempt, at the beginning of the 1550s, to take control of Transylvania – where Isabella and her son John-Sigismund ruled under the suzerainty of the Porte – but this ended in complete failure. Ferdinand made use of a monk called George, soon to be Cardinal Martinuzzi, who was an ambitious intriguer and one of Isabella's counsellors, to persuade her to give up her throne in his favour. In return, she received possessions in Silesia. Suleiman was furious and arrested Malvezzi, Ferdinand's ambassador in Istanbul, and locked him up in the Castle of the Seven Towers (he had to remain there for two years and died shortly after his release). At the same time, he ordered the *beylerbey* of Rumelia, Sokullu Mehmed Pasha,[4] to take the offensive in the region of Banat. Temesvar, Veszprem and Szolnok were occupied in turn. Then came Lippa, where the Turks were besieged by Italian troops and had to spend the winter. Once again, there was discord in the imperial ranks: the Germans complained of the cold and the bad food, while Martinuzzi was suspected of secret relations with the Porte. Ferdinand had him killed (or, at least, gave tacit approval to his murderers), although this achieved nothing and only discredited further the Habsburg cause in Central Europe.

Both sides, however, were tired of a war which led nowhere. When Ferdinand asked Rustem Pasha to open negotiations and release Malvezzi, therefore, the Porte accepted: Suleiman was once again looking towards Persia, where the Safavids had just inflicted a defeat on the *beylerbey* of Erzurum. A truce of six months was agreed and Ferdinand's envoys to the Porte, Anthony Verantius, Bishop of Pecs, and François Zey, commander of the Danube flotilla, left for Constantinople. They were instructed to offer a tribute of 150,000 ducats for Hungary itself, and 40,000 more for Upper Hungary and Transylvania. The Porte refused, the ambassadors left to receive fresh instructions and Malvezzi fell ill in Vienna. It was then that Ghiselin de Busbecq was sent to replace him in Constantinople, which he reached in January 1555. He left at once for Amasya, where Suleiman then was, but although he promised to pay a large sum of money, he only managed to prolong the armistice for six months.

Proposals for treaties (Ferdinand sent four of them to Constantinople) and renewals of the armistice succeeded each other without putting an end to the military operations: the fortress of Tata, near Komarom, was occupied by the *sancakbey* of Esztergom; Suleiman wanted Szeged to be given up to him. Busbecq, who faced the French ambassador de La Vigne and representatives of John-Sigismund, all of them completely opposed to the Habsburgs, had to use his supreme diplomatic skill – and the money at his disposal – to persuade the Porte to agree to a treaty which was at least honourable, if not advantageous, to his master, for it was very evident that Suleiman was not going to give up his conquests in Central Europe nor his suzerainty over Transylvania. One proposal presented by the unfortunate ambassador so irritated Suleiman that he was put under house arrest, although this was admittedly in his own residence.

Finally, the death of Rustem Pasha, in July 1561, brought Ali to power, who immediately revealed himself as far easier to negotiate with. A treaty was concluded in June 1562: peace was confirmed for eight years; Ferdinand had to continue to pay a tribute of 30,000 ducats a year for the Hungarian territories he retained as well as the arrears he owed; differences of opinion, notably on the question of frontiers, were to be sorted out by arbiters in the most equitable fashion; the Turks imprisoned by Suleiman were released without ransom, etc . . . Nothing had changed: Transylvania remained a vassal of the Porte and Central Hungary, including Buda, continued to belong to Suleiman.

Two years later, the death of Ferdinand again put everything in doubt. Maximilian, his son and successor, almost immediately reopened the question of Transylvania. Was it not his first duty to combat the enemy of Christendom? He knew that Suleiman was old and ill and thought that the subsidies he had received from the German Diet, from the Pope and from Philip II would enable him to inflict on the old man of Constantinople the victory Europe had so long been waiting for. The mediocrity of his army – 40,000 men in all, if we are to believe Busbecq – should have made him more cautious.

'Our soldiers are by no means courageous,' Busbecq wrote at the time, 'but are all disobedient and have little love for either work or the exercise of arms. What are our generals like? Most of them are dominated by greed of the most sordid kind. Others are reckless and despise discipline; many give themselves up to the most outrageous excesses of debauchery . . . After all that, can we have any doubt of our future fate?'

In Europe, many shared these views. Vienna was again under threat and even the English Protestants prayed for the success of the Catholic emperor. But he believed, with reason, that the enormous distances the sultan had to cover to reach Central Europe would prevent him from mounting any major operations before autumn.

Leading his army in person, Maximilian attacked John-Sigismund – Isabella had died in 1559 – and harried the Turks all along the frontier. He snatched Tokaj and Szerencs, but the Turkish response was rapid: Mustafa Sokullu, the Grand Vizier's nephew, seized several towns in Croatia. Then both demanded that the other return what he had taken.

Suleiman imprisoned Maximilian's envoy in Istanbul. He sent units, under the command of the second vizier Pertev Pasha, to Transylvania and then ordered John-Sigismund and the Crimean khan, Devlet Giray, to march on the two towns held by Maximilian. Finally, he himself took to the field at the head of a huge army: 300,000 men and an immense artillery.[5] War in Hungary started up again.

The Last Campaign

Suleiman had not led an expedition in person for more than ten years. The Muslims reproached him for this: the first duty of the *gazi*, the successor of the caliphs, was to combat the Infidels. This was, no doubt, what his pious daughter Mihrimah and the *şeyh* and religious leaders of his entourage said to him. The information they had received made it clear that the defences constructed by the imperial forces were weak. The sultan would not have to fight, the Governor of Buda said – as soon as he appeared, towns would surrender to him. Above all, Suleiman wanted to efface the memory of the defeat at Malta by a rapid and crushing victory over the Christians.

The departure ceremonies were even more sumptuous, even more dazzling, than usual. 'The display he put on surpassed everything we had seen at the time of earlier expeditions.' Before the procession had even moved off, 'poets sang in advance of the triumphs of the great *padishah* of the world'.

The sultan who left Istanbul on 1 May 1566, never to see it again, had become an old man. A picture[6] shows him with sunken cheeks and a sparse white beard. Another portrait[7] represents him as stooping and thin, looking older than the 70 years he had just attained. He no longer had the strength to ride a horse and he was driven in a carriage on the long journey which took him from the Bosphorus to Belgrade in forty-nine days. The roads were so bumpy that the Grand Vizier, who travelled a day in advance, had to repair them as best he could. Suleiman suffered so much from gout that he stayed in his carriage even to receive his viziers.

The army's progress was once again delayed by bad weather. Torrents of rain swelled rivers and ruined roads. Bridges were swept away as soon as built. The sultan suffered from the continual jolts, but he stoically refused to stop. Hardly a day's rest was taken at Sofia, two at Niš and three at Belgrade. Further on, the difficulties increased. Many of the camels that carried the baggage were drowned. The sultan even had to sleep once in the Grand Vizier's tent, because his own could not be pitched.

At last, they crossed the Danube and entered Zemun, on the right bank, in solemn state, and the sultan reviewed his troops. He welcomed John-Sigismund, accompanied by forty Transylvanian nobles, with great ceremonial. Preceded by the grand chamberlain, the grand marshal of the court and three masters of ceremonies, four pages wearing gold cloth carried the young prince's stirrups. Ahead of him walked 100 janissaries carrying presents he offered to the sultan, including twelve richly decorated vases and a ruby worth 50,000 ducats. The four viziers stood around a throne sparkling with gold and precious stones. The sultan was invited to sit down – although on a throne without support for his back – and then Suleiman offered John-Sigismund his hand to kiss, called him 'his beloved son' and promised to come to his aid and supply him with whatever he wished. John-Sigismund then asked that the band of territories between the river Tisza and Transylvania be ceded to him, a request which was immediately granted. In bidding him farewell, Suleiman twice got up to kiss him and then gave him daggers and sabres incrusted with jewels, a saddle decorated with precious stones and a magnificent charger 'sumptuously fitted out'. At Zemun, Suleiman also received Grantrie de Grandchamp, the French ambassador, come to present the best wishes of his master Charles IX.

Suleiman's plan was to reduce the town of Erlau, which controlled the narrow corridor leading to Transylvania, before seizing Komarom and Gyor. But when he learnt that Count Nicholas Zriny, the lord of Szeged, had killed a Porte dignitary and carried off much booty, he resolved to march immediately on Szeged. Once again, bad weather slowed down the progress of the army in the plain between the Danube and Tisza. Although it was the middle of summer, the rivers were extraordinarily swollen. Crossing the Danube, the Sava and the Drava, each time on rapidly constructed bridges, proved difficult. The heavy artillery, pulled by oxen, got stuck in the bogs, the army stumbled in the mud. Finally, on

5 August, Suleiman reached Szeged where 90,000 men and 300 cannons were waiting for him. Before the town walls, he at last regained the strength to mount his horse and ordered the siege to commence.

Zriny had hung up red cloths on his fortress and the central tower sparkled with metal plaques, placed there 'to honour so great a monarch'. Cannon fire from the fortress indicated the start of battle. Almost at once, the old town went up in flames. Zriny had set it alight so as to put batteries of cannons on the ruins. Attack followed attack, and bombardment succeeded bombardment. From his sick bed Suleiman in turn threatened and tried to win over Zriny with promises. Almost a month went by, until the day when the exterior bastions had all been taken by the Turks and only the central tower was in the hands of the besieged forces. Zriny then decided to die a hero's death. A chain of gold about his neck, a black hat studded with a diamond on his head and 'the sword of his youth' in his hand, he led out his 600 remaining men and launched an attack on the enemy while repeating three times the cry of 'Jesus!' Wounded and taken prisoner, he was decapitated by putting his head just in front of the mouth of a cannon – a punishment he had recently inflicted on a Turkish *ağa*.

Not long afterwards, the citadel was blown up, burying 3,000 men in the ruins. But Suleiman never knew that the fortress had fallen or that Gyula had been captured by his vizier Pertev Pasha. He had died on the night of 5–6 September in his tent. Only his doctors and the Grand Vizier Sokullu Mehmed Pasha had been present at the time.

No succession crisis occurred because Selim was now the sole heir to the throne (see Appendix 4). But the army was on campaign and if the troops had learnt of their sovereign's death, operations would have stopped. The chiefs would have been unable to maintain discipline. The janissaries would at once have demanded the accession gifts they received every time there was a change of sovereign.

Sokullu Mehmed Pasha took all these things into account. He immediately sent a messenger to Selim, who was acting as governor in Kutahya, and while he waited for his arrival, kept the sultan's death a complete secret. He only told Feridun Bey, his absolutely reliable secretary, and the sultan's chief standard-bearer, Cafer Ağa, probably because of his talent for imitating Suleiman's handwriting to perfection. Using the sultan's illness (which had prevented the *padishah* from moving for the last few weeks) as a pretext, he barred the sultan's tent even to the viziers. Sokullu even did away with the doctor who knew too much.

Operations continued as if directed by Suleiman himself, who gave written orders – actually forged by Cafer – to his army chiefs.

On 8 September, the *Divan* met and sent out signed letters of victory to the provincial governors, the khan of Crimea, the Shah of Persia and the major European sovereigns[8] (see Appendix 12). Gratuities were handed out. In the name of his master, Sokullu sent the head of Zriny to the Governor of Buda for him to send on to the Emperor Maximilian. He declared that the sultan wanted the fortifications at Szeged to be rapidly repaired and the construction of a mosque there actively pushed ahead. Suleiman wished to visit it, he added, when the swelling on his foot had gone down, so he could thank God for his victory. The soldiers had other concerns and suspected nothing – discipline was maintained with no difficulty.

Forty-three days went by like this, then Sokullu gave the order for departure. The sultan was still believed to be travelling in a closed litter. 'From time to time,' the chronicler Peçevi points out, 'Sokullu approached the throne, pretending to make a report to the sultan. He also gave the impression of discussing the report with him after he had read it out. The *silahdar* Cafer Ağa, who later became the Grand Vizier's son-in-law, was at the dead man's side and wrote a reply to the report . . . Many rumours were going around, but the Grand Vizier's skilful tactics managed to dissipate all suspicions. No one knew for certain if the *padishah* was dead or alive . . .' A miniature, which illustrates the chronicle of the Szeged campaign by Feridun, shows us the sultan's four-wheeled carriage drawn by two horses and, riding alongside, the Grand Vizier followed by the army chiefs.

Meanwhile, Selim had left Kutahya and, without stopping in Constantinople, tried to head off the funeral cortège. He met up with it near Belgrade. Sokullu then leaked the news of the sultan's death to the dignitaries and called the readers of the Koran and ordered them to begin the prayer for the dead before the imperial tent. 'When from the right this song arose: "All earthly domination passes away, all men have their last hour" and the other side replied: "The Eternal One alone is not touched by time or mastered by death," the whole army exploded in a tremendous lament . . . The next morning, before sunrise, the funeral ceremony started.' The ministers and leading personages wore black headbands, the sultan's private guard put aside their headgear and donned blue aprons. The whole army wept in silence. When the sun rose, Selim appeared, dressed completely in black. He advanced towards the carriage and raised his hands to invoke heaven. His tutor and the master of ceremonies supported him under the arms. The viziers stood to the right, the leading personages to the left, and the muezzin intoned the prayer for the dead. When it was finished, the new sultan again raised his hands to heaven and then retreated into his tent.

It was then that the army began to protest. The soldiers cried out: 'The sultan said nothing about our gifts! . . . We shall come back for you, sultan!' Two days later, gratuities were distributed, and although the soldiers considered them insufficient, it was possible to calm them down and the cortège continued on its way. In *The History of Suleiman*, by Loqman the miniaturist, the long coffin is shown surrounded by dignitaries on horseback, preceded by janissaries in thick ranks; behind the funeral carriage come the squadrons of *sipahi*, lances in hand.

The day Selim made his entry into the capital, serious incidents occurred. The previous night had been spent in meetings around barrels of wine and, when the cortège moved off, the janissaries, many of them drunk, closed ranks so as to completely block its passage. Tumult ensued as the *kapudan pasha* and the second vizier, Pertev Pasha, were dragged from their horses and attacked. Sokullu escaped by throwing coins to the rioters. When the mutineers reached the Seraglio, they seized the viziers and dragged them before the sultan, who was obliged to give way and increase their pay. As the troubles continued, the Grand Vizier had several people beheaded: order was soon restored. Among the immediate decisions taken by Selim, people noticed that he sacked the two *kazasker* (army judges) who had presented to him as 'a very humble remonstrance' their wish to maintain the ban on the drinking of wine announced by Suleiman several years earlier.

Suleiman's embalmed corpse was buried in the tomb which the great architect Sinan had built near the Suleimaniye mosque several years earlier. As is customary in Islamic countries, the ceremony was very simple, and history has preserved no record of it. The tomb of a believer, however powerful he was, is only a provisional dwelling which contains his mortal remains. The mausoleum itself is of ample proportions without being monumental. The alley which leads there is not on the direct route to the immense and sumptuous neighbouring mosque, so visitors are often unaware that they are only a few steps away from the resting place of the sultan of sultans. Nearby, and slightly set back, is the mausoleum of Hurrem Sultan, Roxelane. All around these two monuments, funeral sculptures, bent by time and battered by the weather, some of them surmounted with immense stone turbans – evidence of the important positions occupied by these men – stand in silent guard.

Baki, the great poet, wrote an elegy on the death of Suleiman which has become famous:

> O you who are taken in the nets of ambition and glory, until when will you nurse your passion for the things of this world, your passion which knows no respite? . . .
>
> The Hungarian unbelievers bowed their heads before his flashing sword! The Franks knew well the cutting edge of his sabre!
>
> The sun has come up; will the king of the world not awake from his sleep? Will he not leave his tent like the sky? Our eyes scan the road: no sign comes from the throne, the sanctuary of glory! The colour in his cheeks is faded, he lies with lips dried out, like a pressed rose without sap . . .

Part Two
The Empire of Empires

8
The Orient at the Time of Suleiman

Did Suleiman plan to conquer the Indies? His father, Selim I, and probably also the great Mehmed II after the capture of Constantinople both dreamed, like so many others, of following in the footsteps of Alexander. Suleiman had the means to do so: a powerful army, flourishing finances. The name of the sultan of Constantinople was known and respected everywhere.[1] Conquest would have been relatively easy. And yet neither Suleiman nor his father or grandson ever achieved it. Selim I died too soon, Suleiman had too much to do in Europe, by land and sea, against the Habsburgs. His only attempt, as we shall see, failed through the fault of one of his admirals.[2]

It is pointless to rewrite history, but one can always dream: the Ottomans installed in India, the Portuguese expelled from the peninsula and the positions they held on the Cape route. A few decades later, the route to the Far East closed to the English and Dutch . . . What a difference it would have made in Europe and the Orient! This fantasy is less extravagant than it seems. The fight for control of the spice routes in the 16th century between the Turks and the Portuguese lasted a long time and on several occasions the result hung in the balance: events could have turned out quite otherwise than they in fact did.

Until the arrival of the Portuguese in the Indian Ocean, almost all trade between Europe and the Far East and South-East Asia was in Muslim hands. Ships weighed down with spices and products worth a great deal even in small quantities (aromatics, ivory, amber, tortoiseshell, pearls, precious stones, gold, tin) either took the route through the Straits of Hormuz and the Persian Gulf to Basra (where the merchandise was taken in caravans to Baghdad, Aleppo and Damascus) or instead passed by way of the Red Sea and the Gulf of Suez, near Alexandria and Cairo. It was the taxes imposed and the profits of merchants, caravaneers and intermediaries of every kind which brought prosperity to the transit countries. The luxury and beauty of Cairo excited the admiration of foreign travellers. Two hundred of her traders were said to have fortunes of over a million ducats, and another two thousand possessed more than 100,000 ducats each.[3]

All this changed in 1497 when Vasco da Gama discovered the eastern passage and sailed round the Cape of Good Hope. Portuguese penetration into the area was not the result of chance and da Gama's long journey was not intended only to discover new lands or spread the Christian faith – as the Muslims soon learnt. Friendly at first, he soon proved demanding and brutal. The sovereign of Mozambique was obliged to pay tribute to him, followed by the ruler of Zanzibar and then all the others. Less than ten years after the discovery of the Cape of Good Hope, the whole coast of East Africa belonged to the Portuguese, who started to build forts on the Indian coast as well: at Cochin, Diu, Calicut and Goa.

In 1502, da Gama closed the Red Sea and the Persian Gulf to Muslim shipping. Albuquerque seized the island of Socotra, at the entrance to the Red Sea. The ports of the little kingdom of Hormuz, at the entrance of the Persian Gulf and under Iranian suzerainty, were captured and burnt, the population massacred, the women and children mutilated. Muslim commerce between India and the Mediterranean had been dealt a death blow, with consequences one can easily imagine for the economy and states of the region.

The Mamluks of Egypt were affected most of all. The Sultan Kansuh al-Ghouri wrote to the Pope to appeal to him to intervene with the King of Portugal. The only response of Manuel the Fortunate, then at the height of his prosperity, was to build up his fleet even more. The Muslims could do nothing but take up arms, but the Mamluks were horsemen and not sailors: they had no experience of naval warfare and their fleet was not capable of taking on the Portuguese. Their light boats were ideal for the Mediterranean but quite unsuited to the surging seas of the Indian Ocean. Their whole fleet had to be built from scratch. They had no forests and had to import wood; they had to bring engineers and workmen from abroad, cast cannons and even forge the nails. Bayezid, the Ottoman sultan, provided Kansuh with wood, masts, oars and 300 cannons, but the Knights of Rhodes seized the wood *en route*.

The Mamluks lived through difficult days. The Portuguese threatened to land on the coast of Hijaz and go to Medina and carry off the Prophet's body. Albuquerque and his troops behaved with unheard-of cruelty, burning towns and villages and massacring whole populations. Kansuh formed an alliance with the sultan of Gujarat, Mahmud Begara, and the Prince of Calicut. The Portuguese fleet was forced back and put to flight near Bombay, but the Mamluks were defeated soon afterwards. They then decided to take over Yemen, probably to use it as a base against the Portuguese and also, certainly, to have a retreat in case an Ottoman invasion, which all the signs indicated was imminent, forced them to leave Egypt. Kansuh's campaign in Yemen, however, ended in failure.[4]

The entry of the Ottomans on the scene was to change everything. They had already taken an indirect part in the contest between the Muslims and the Portuguese. The defeated Mamluk sultan had called on their help. The Ottomans had then sent him captains, galleys, 2,000 bowmen and guns. One of their admirals in the service of Kansuh, Selman Reis, had constructed a fleet of galleys. It was he who had commanded the fleet which was given the task of defending the Red Sea ports and who had compelled the Portuguese admiral, Lopo Soares, to take flight before Jedda. But Turkish involvement in the struggle against the Infidel who threatened the Holy Places had gone no further.

When Egypt had been conquered, the Ottomans were directly under threat. As successor of the caliphs and guardian of the Holy Places, it was the Ottoman emperor who received the gold of Ethiopia, the products of the Nile valley and the considerable sums represented by the taxes and duties levied in the country. Since payments on transported goods made up a large part of these taxes, the Ottomans had a direct interest in the maintenance of freedom of navigation in the Red Sea and the defence of the routes which led there. For the first time in history, the conquerors who came from the depths of Asia extended their influence into Southern Arabia.

For the first time, too, a land-based empire, agricultural and pastoral, came into contact with one of the maritime states, born of the 'sea-faring revolution', whose prosperity and even existence depended on trade. The conflicts between them would prove to be more or less permanent all along the 'frontier line' that their socio-economic power and maritime technology laid down: light Mediterranean galleys, easy to manoeuvre for defending the coastline, faced far heavier sailing ships built for the great oceans and for the defence of trading posts where products piled up and changed hands. The Red Sea and Persian Gulf were the domain of the Turkish galleys, the Indian Ocean belonged to the Portuguese sailing ships – each side crossed the 'frontier' only very rarely.

Selim I wished to be the successor of Alexander, the 'emperor of the world'. It seems clear that he had completed the conquest of Egypt as a step towards the conquest of India. Plans for the empire to expand eastwards were frequently discussed in powerful circles in Istanbul, where memories of the Ottomans' Asiatic origins were strong. In his *Hitayname*, Ali Akbar Hitaki spent twenty chapters describing the Middle Empire to Selim and inviting him to conquer it. The corsair Piri Reis had, in 1517, brought him a 'map of the world' inspired by sources including Christopher Columbus. Only the western section of the map survives, in the Istanbul Museum – Selim is believed to have kept the eastern half to prepare for his Asian campaign. All the evidence makes clear that he had set his sights far more to the East than towards Europe. It was his unexpected death at the age of 50 which turned Turkish ambitions in a quite different direction.

Suleiman looked towards Europe, although more from necessity than personal taste. His enemy was 'the King of Spain', Charles V. The danger came from the North rather than the South or East. As a 'fighter for the faith' – *gazi* – he wanted to extend the frontiers of Islam into the Christian countries.

The Ottomans were in fact less interested in maritime commerce than the conquest of fresh territories where they could extract revenues from taxes on the produce of the earth and the exchange of merchandise. Operations in the Balkans and Central Europe brought them greater profits than major naval expeditions into warm seas could have done. We must never forget that the sultan of Constantinople could not carry out two major military operations at the same time: an expedition towards the Indian Ocean, certain to be long and difficult, and the war in Europe his Christian enemies would have unleashed if they had seen him tied up in a far-away campaign. Besides, his army and fleet of galleys were not equipped, his soldiers poorly trained, for such a campaign.

Suleiman nonetheless hesitated and seemed for a while to keep two irons in the fire. His campaign to Belgrade (1521) towards the Danube territories was followed two years later by the capture of Rhodes, which opened the route to the South. No final decision had been taken even in 1525.

The Grand Vizier Ibrahim Pasha had brought back from Cairo a new version of Piri Reis's *Book of Maritime Knowledge*. Apart from descriptions of voyages into the Indian Ocean and information about Portuguese naval technique and commerce, the book contained an appeal to Suleiman to expand the Ottoman Empire by sea and combat the Infidels who dared to come near the Holy Places. For his part, the admiral Selman Reis pointed out to the sultan that the Portuguese were taking over more and more of the trade between Europe and the Indies. He advised him to strike to the South by attacking the fortresses that the Portuguese had built along the whole coast of India and Persia. Much was known in Istanbul about the Christian voyages of discovery and the danger they represented for the Muslims. At one point, it seems, Suleiman was preparing a campaign towards the Red Sea and Indian Ocean: he ordered the Egyptian fleet to be reinforced. Finally the plan to make war near the Danube tipped the balance, leading to Mohacs and the march on Vienna.

In the same year, 1529, Suleiman nonetheless had a canal built between the Nile and the Red Sea. In fact, as Suleiman turned his attention to Europe, the Ottoman fleet, for several years, only conducted routine operations. But then it became known in Istanbul that India had been invaded from the North by Babur, a Turkish descendant of Tamerlane, who became the first of the Great Moghuls. The kingdom of the Lodi, in Delhi, collapsed. The whole peninsula was in anarchy. The kingdom of Gujarat, on the West coast, remained the only island of stability amid disorder, but the sovereign, Bahadur Shah, knew this could not last as Babur and his son Homayun made no secret of their desire for conquest. At one point, he considered asking the Portuguese for help, but, since that cure was worse than the disease, he had to turn to the other great power: the Ottoman Empire. Bahadur's ambassador met a reception in Istanbul which was all the more friendly because of the valuable gifts and large sum of gold he brought. For their part, the Lodi, who had been expelled from their kingdom by Babur, also called on the *padishah* for help. Their envoy promised Suleiman that the Portuguese governor would be sent to him 'in a cage of iron'.

These appeals from the Muslim princes of India would certainly not have been enough on their own to convince Suleiman to intervene if the circumstances created by the occupation of Baghdad and then Basra had not in a sense invited him to do so. The Ottoman Empire was in contact with the two routes – by way of the Red Sea and the Persian Gulf – taken by all the trade from the Indian Ocean towards the Mediterranean. It was also in contact with Portugal, which clearly intended to dominate the Indian Ocean and reap the rewards of all the trade, particularly the spice trade, with Europe. If the sultan ever planned, during the whole of his long reign, to extend his power towards South-East Asia, it was then.

In 1538, 60 boats, including 24 galleys, were laid down. The Ottomans used wood brought by sea from Antioch to Alexandria and Damietta, thence to Cairo and on camels to Suez. A Genoese architect had to draw up the plans. Since the Serene Republic was then at war with the Porte, a dozen Venetian ships, seized in Alexandria, joined the expedition. In all, 78 vessels put to sea with 20,000 men including 7,000 janissaries on board, as well as a large artillery and every kind of equipment. Such a force left little doubt that the Turks planned to land in India.

The fleet was put under the orders of Hadim Suleiman Pasha, the *beylerbey* of Egypt, a eunuch of Greek origin aged over 80 and so fat it took four men to lift him from his seat. Cruel and unscrupulous, he was probably not the ideal choice. He certainly brought about the failure of the expedition. When he passed Jedda, he extorted a large sum of money from the governor by threatening him with torture. He then made rapidly for Aden, where he invited the sovereign, Omar Ibn Daoud, to a banquet on board his ship, seized him and hanged him from the main mast. Shortly afterwards, his men seized the town. This act of treachery had a disastrous effect in the Arab countries and was to have serious consequences. Suleiman, who had never ordered the capture of Aden, was violently angry – although he did not give back the town, one of the best placed and most easily defended on the Red Sea.

Hadim Suleiman Pasha left a garrison of 500 men in Aden, which he established as a *sancak*. He then made for Diu, the large fortress on the West coast of India. The town, powerfully fortified by the Portuguese, was besieged on the land side by the Indians of Gujarat, the Turks' allies. As soon as they had arrived, the Ottomans looted the town, which hardly made a good impression on the Indians. Then, since bad weather seemed imminent, the Ottoman admiral took his ships into shelter. On the way, four vessels were shipwrecked, and their cargo spilt on the beach. Among the objects scattered on the sands, the Indians found saddles for many horsemen – a clear sign to the sultan of Gujarat that the Ottomans had come not to help him get rid of his enemies but to occupy his country.

The Turkish fleet, however, had returned to Diu, where the siege commenced. For a whole month, nine huge cannons bombarded the fortress without a pause, but to no effect. The largest cannon-balls only scratched the walls and every assault failed. The Portuguese had almost run out of provisions and ammunition when they were astonished to see the Turkish fleet raise anchor and set out for the high seas. Suleiman Pasha had retreated, probably because of rumours about the imminent arrival of a powerful fleet which had been spread by the local rulers to frighten him off. He paid the price there for his conduct in Aden: the Indians no longer trusted Turkish promises and only wanted to get rid of the Turks as soon as possible. They were now convinced of the superiority of the Portuguese, although this was far from certain.

This was the first and last Ottoman campaign in South-East Asia, the only serious attempt to conquer territories beyond the Red Sea. All the signs are that Suleiman intended to undertake a campaign by land in India. A Muslim historian confirms this: 'At that time, the Sultan Suleiman, the son of the Sultan Selim, showed his intention of expelling the *frengi* [foreigners or Europeans] from Indian ports and himself taking control of that region.'[5] Responsibility for the failure of the expedition rests largely on the shoulders of Suleiman Pasha. A man who had revealed great ability as a chief and administrator in Egypt committed mistake after mistake before Diu, not least in alienating his Gujarati allies by his brutality. The old man, however, compensated for these errors by opening up a new province – Yemen – to Ottoman domination.

After his setback, Suleiman Pasha stopped off in Aden. From there he made for Tihamah, the plain alongside the Red Sea, in the region of Zabid and Mocha, where several hundred Mamluks were stationed, the remnant of those troops who had disembarked during Kansuh's campaign. Always quick to get rid of those who annoyed him, Suleiman Pasha ordered the execution of their chiefs and installed an Ottoman administration. A *sancak* was established at Zabid, to which he added, on the way home, the region of Jizan (further North). A few years later, in 1547, San'a and Ta'izz were conquered by Uveys Pasha and Ozdemir Pasha, later the first *beylerbey* of Abyssinia. The Ottomans dominated Yemen, although with some difficulty, up to 1635, and then from 1849 to the First World War.

Suleiman Pasha was promoted to the post of vizier on his return to Constantinople and became Grand Vizier in 1541, when he was nearly 90.

Suleiman gave him the task of preparing a major expedition into Hungary – his plans for expansion towards the southern seas had been abandoned once and for all.

The Portuguese remained masters of the Arabian Sea route, which meant that fewer exotic products were offered for sale in the markets of the Mediterranean. They did not, however, disappear completely. Sometimes the Venetians were compelled to buy pepper – Portuguese pepper – in Anvers, but the trading posts of the Levant almost always had a supply, although it varied in quantity, of the precious commodity. The Muslims managed to keep the sea route relatively free. They would, indeed, have liked the Ottomans to assume responsibility for this and constantly asked, although without success, for the sultan to take the initiative.

Suleiman Pasha's disastrous expedition had left bad memories. Limited operations were carried out, although they did not achieve very much. They did, however, allow Muslim vessels to pass through the Portuguese net.

In 1551, however, since Aden had been taken by the Portuguese, a fleet of 30 ships was sent South under the orders of Piri Reis, the famous cartographer, who commanded the Egyptian fleet. Aden was recaptured without difficulty, Muscat was taken and the Portuguese governor, John of Lisbon, imprisoned. Then, however, against the sultan's orders, Piri Reis laid siege to Hormuz. The fortress, as at Diu, was quite impregnable and the Turks, after a month's siege, turned back to Basra. His enemies spread the rumour that Piri Reis had been given 'valuable gifts' as the price for his departure. His expedition ended in disaster when several of his ships were sunk in a confrontation with the Portuguese and the rest had to take refuge in the Shatt al-Arab, at the entrance to the Persian Gulf. Of the three which had survived, another was shipwrecked off Bahrain – Piri returned to Cairo with only two ships. Even the sumptuous gifts he brought the sultan could not soften Suleiman's heart, and he was executed when he reached home.

Another admiral was sent to Basra with orders to bring back the ships abandoned by Piri, but he also failed. Finally the task was entrusted to Sidi Ali Reis, a marvellous sailor who had fought at Preveza under Barbarossa's orders: he had to get the 15 galleys out of the trap in which they had been caught. Another battle led to another defeat. Pursued by the Portuguese, he eventually reached Gujarat, where the sovereign was willing to welcome him but sank his ships, as he did not want to upset the Portuguese. Suleiman's admiral had to return to Turkey by the land route

– it took him almost four years to reach Constantinople by way of Sind, the Punjab, Afghanistan, Transoxania, Khorasan and Iran. The narrative of this journey handed down to us by Ali Reis, who was also a geographer, a mathematician and a poet, is one of the liveliest and most informative accounts of the countries of the Orient at that time.

Ali Reis's expedition was to be the last major attempt by the Ottomans to fight the Portuguese. During the following decades, the sultan's ships sometimes penetrated the Persian Gulf with some difficulty, but the Red Sea always remained open to them. In order to prevent the Portuguese from snatching control of that area, they had to occupy part of the Eritrean coast (Suakin and Massawa), from where they sometimes, without great success, launched raids into the interior of Abyssinia. Their territory was later limited to the coastal band which they turned into a *beylerbeylik*. But they could not maintain this position for long: keeping up a powerful fleet in the Red Sea would have cost them far more than the advantages they gained from the possession of that inhospitable coastline.[6]

In spite of difficulties and occasional setbacks, trade between India and the Near East was never interrupted. In 1561, for example, Lisbon found itself as short of spices as the Egyptian ports had been at the beginning of the century. Around the year 1564, Alexandria received almost as much spice as Lisbon, and Aleppo was once again a major transit centre. The Portuguese never achieved a complete blockade, but the Turks, for their part, never managed to cross 'the frontier line' between the two empires.

And yet, with the enormous resources it had at its disposal, the allies it could always have acquired in the Islamic world and the Indies, the Ottoman Empire at the time of Suleiman was certainly capable of clearing the Portuguese out of the southern seas and greatly expanding its own power in the direction of South-East Asia and even the Far East. Were the light Ottoman galleys inferior to the powerful, heavy Portuguese sailing ships 'built for the ocean, which were superior to [his] boats propelled by oars'?[7] There is little evidence for this. In certain circumstances, as when they had to carry out a disembarcation, the oar-powered boats were more manoeuvrable and reliable than the huge Portuguese sailing boats, although the latter certainly had the advantage in sea battles. They were better adapted to sailing and fighting on the oceans than the Turkish boats, manned by Levantine crews and built for the Mediterranean. But the Turks could without doubt have rapidly built in their boatyards and put to sea a huge Red Sea fleet under the command of corsairs – a fleet expressly intended to launch an attack on the Portuguese squadrons. It was the will that was missing.

Suleiman was always under an obligation to fight with his perpetual enemies, the 'soldiers of the Cross' to the North, while all the people in his entourage capable of influencing him came from the interior of the empire, particularly the Balkans. Such Serbs, Albanians and even Greeks did not set their sights on distant horizons; even if they were well informed of the major events which shook the world, there was nothing to inspire them with the idea that the empire should intervene in countries and seas which were so unfamiliar to them.

Always preoccupied with Europe and his dreams of crushing his only worthy rival, 'the King of Spain', Suleiman would undoubtedly have struck towards the South if the Portuguese conquests had seriously threatened the empire and its economy and finances. This never occurred: Portuguese expansion towards the Orient was never a danger to the Ottomans. Traders far more than conquerors, the Kings of Portugal only snatched the coastal bases they needed for commerce. The sultans, on the other hand, occupied vast inhabited territories to extract fiscal and material resources. Their interests were so diverse and concerned such different areas that neither side ever felt it had to make the immense effort needed for a major campaign. Paying little attention to what happened in the Indian Ocean and on far-away islands, but surrounded by 'Europeans' and deeply involved in his European policy, Suleiman began to lose interest in Asia.

In his entourage, the more far-sighted regretted this. Nearer our own day, one of the great Orientalists of the 19th century, Arminius Vambery, agreed: 'If Suleiman, instead of flooding Hungary and Austria with his janissaries, had included the conquest of India among his plans, his efforts would have been crowned with a success far greater and more durable than those which awaited him on the Danube. He had a powerful, and always victorious, fleet while the descendants of Babur had none. His prestige was great – indeed unparalleled – in Arabia, Egypt and the whole Islamic world, and the gang of adventurers from Central Asia were very capable of achieving victory over the worshippers of Vishnu – it would have been child's play for the valiant, disciplined and well-armed janissaries. As masters of India, the Ottoman sovereigns would have played an infinitely more important role in history than their conquering ancestors. Who knows what the destiny of Asia would then have been?'[8]

9
The Greatest City of East and West

The capital of the Byzantine Empire for fifteen centuries, Constantinople – Istanbul[1] – naturally became the Ottomans' capital as soon as they had conquered it. Once the city had been built up again from the ruins, not to mention the devastation caused by the Franks of the Fourth Crusade and long periods of decadence and misery, Mehmed II established himself there. Bursa and then Edirne (Adrianople) had never been more than provisional capitals for the first sultans. From the beginning of the Hegira (the Muslim era which was established when Mohammed fled from Mecca to Medina in AD 622), the ultimate aim had always been Constantinople. Had the Prophet not promised immortal glory to whoever should take possession of it? And what place could possibly make a worthier seat for the greatest empire of the Orient?

For a start, its geographical situation is one of the most beautiful in the Mediterranean. Seven hills – as in Rome – look down on a sea which opens up and then cuts into the land in the West to form the Golden Horn; to the North, a deep and narrow strait, the Bosphorus, forms the juncture between the Black Sea and the Mediterranean, the North and South, the Slav lands and the Islamic countries of the Orient. From the terraces of Topkapi Saray the eye can take in the last slopes of the Balkans and the first slopes of the Asian plateau, the waters of the Sea of Marmara and the entrance to the Black Sea.

For millennia, the promontory had been one of the great meeting points, since it offered exceptional facilities for important military or maritime as well as political undertakings. A thousand years before Christ, populations who no doubt came from Europe had founded a village at the bottom of the Golden Horn and then at the tip of the promontory where the Seraglio stands. In 657–8 BC, Byzas, a sailor from Megara, established the city which would preserve his name. The Delphic Oracle had even described as 'blind' all the other Megarans who had established themselves in Chalcedonia on the Asian shore and did not realize what a magnificent port the Golden Horn, protected from tempests from the North and South, offered – the only safe spot, apart from Salonica, between Piraeus and the Black Sea. None of the great conquerors of history made the same mistake. Philip of Macedon, the Avars, the Persians, the Bulgars, the Arabs – all of them tried in vain to take control of it. Bayezid I laid siege to the city in 1391, Murad II in 1422. It was Mehmed II who achieved immense glory by conquering it, on the morning of 29 May 1453.

Nothing, or almost nothing, then remained of the city of the *Basileus*. It had withstood so many attacks that no major buildings were left standing. The imperial palaces, said to have surpassed in splendour those of the Sassanid emperors and Abbasid caliphs, were no more than ruins. Those of the Blachernae and Constantine Porphyrogenitus had fared little better. Of the 700,000 inhabitants the town had once contained, only 30,000 or 40,000 were left. Their number diminished still further when Mehmed II ordered some of them to take up residence in the provincial towns. This left large amounts of empty space and they were therefore replaced by thousands of Turks, Jews, Armenians and Greeks brought in from the Balkans and Anatolia. An appeal was made all over the empire for artisans to help repair the houses and construct public buildings. A large palace – which later acquired the name of the Old Seraglio – was soon built on the site of Theodosius's forum, on the top of the third hill. Mehmed installed himself there in 1457 and then gave orders for another palace to be built on the rocky spur which looks down on the Golden Horn, the Bosphorus and the Sea of Marmara. This was Topkapi Saray, as we call it today. Life soon returned to the town.

Twenty-five years after the conquest, there were already 70,000 inhabitants in the town. There were 400,000 at the start of Suleiman's reign, 500,000 around 1550 and probably 700,000 by the end of the century. Istanbul was then a very large town, the most populous in the known world, swollen all the time by a constant influx of new people, some of whom came voluntarily while others were brought by the Turkish sovereigns; wherever they went, they would select the best workmen and artisans they found to come and reconstruct and beautify their town. Thus, after his victories in Persia and Egypt, Selim I had sent back to Istanbul a thousand Iranian artists and workmen, who played a major role in the rise of Turkish ceramics, and at least as many Syrian and Egyptian artisans. In the same way, after the Belgrade campaign, Suleiman brought Serbs to Istanbul who were housed near the Castle of the Seven Towers.

A Capital Open to the Whole World

This constant influx of men and women gave the 16th-century capital the cosmopolitan flavour it always retained. At the time of Suleiman, the Ottoman Empire, monolithic and highly centralized, was the only truly international empire; Charles V's was a fragile dynastic construction held together by nothing but its sovereign.

Istanbul was also the only capital at the time which was truly open to the world. The most diverse populations came to take refuge there, to live and work: Jews expelled from Spain, Greek traders and sailors, Arabs, Sudanese and even Catholics eager for adventure or compelled to leave their countries of origin. Everyone lived there, prospered or came to grief under the protection of the *pax Ottomanica*; provided they did not make trouble and paid their taxes, they were left in peace.

All formed groups according to their ethnic or religious background. The Catholics (the 'Franks') lived at Pera and Galata, the Armenians near Marmara and at Sulu Monastir and Samatya, the Greeks at Fener and Galata on the Bosphorus, the Jews along the Golden Horn. The large Armenian colony had a sort of monopoly on the Iranian transit trade with the West. Step by step, they had taken up positions on the route from Persia to Istanbul and now came to reside in the capital, where they began to play an important role in finance. The Greeks, who had been more or less eliminated in the aftermath of the conquest, had come back in force and made up an even larger community. Working as small traders and shopkeepers or looking to the sea for their livelihood, they dominated trade in the Eastern Mediterranean. Some were very rich and occupied important positions in Suleiman's time. Yunis Bey, his interpreter, had the rank of an ambassador and acted as one on several occasions. The Jews mainly worked in commerce and banking as money-changers, intermediaries and brokers. In the 16th century, they formed the 'minority' which was most favourably regarded at the palace. As well as these three major categories of non-Muslim immigrants – *dhimmis* – other peoples came to the capital from all sides: Albanians (who worked as itinerant salesmen and pavers), some of whom gained major positions in the empire in the following century (two became Grand Viziers); Tziganes (who made iron utensils and exhibited bears); Iranians, who carried on the silk trade with their country of origin; Egyptians and Syrians (masons and ceramicists); Moldavians, Wallachians and Serbs, who made cheeses or *pastirma* (dried and flavoured meat).

There was no hostility among the Ottomans towards Infidels. Pogroms were unknown in the Turkey of the sultans, a model of tolerance at a time when this was a rare virtue in Christian countries. Incidents between Turks and minorities were caused by isolated individuals or unscrupulous officials, never by hostile or xenophobic crowds and still less by the authorities. The immense majority of Muslims, Christians and Jews shared the same modest life style and confronted the same difficulties, grouped around their own church, mosque or synagogue.

The non-Muslims – who represented 40% of the population of the town – were mainly Christians: Greek Orthodox, Armenians and, in very small numbers, Catholics. The two major communities represented nearly 30% of the total population, while the Jews made up 10%. They were grouped into *millets* (nations), each administered by a religious chief officially recognized by the sultan and responsible for his co-religionists to the Ottoman government. The leading community, the Greek Orthodox – *Rum milleti* (meaning 'Roman', that is to say Byzantine) – were led by the patriarch, an important personage with the rank of 'a pasha with three tails' whose tribunal had jurisdiction over all the Greek Orthodox of the empire. The Jews also formed a *millet* under the authority of the *Haham Başi*, or chief rabbi, who enjoyed the same privileges as the patriarch. The same applied to the Gregorian Armenians, whose *catholicos*, strangely enough, was granted authority over all the sultan's subjects who did not belong to any of the major communities: the Catholics, the Nestorians and the Jacobites. One of the main functions of the community leaders was to raise the poll tax or *ciziye* which all Infidels (except those with official posts like the palace doctors) had to pay to the sultan. Each *millet* owed an agreed sum which the patriarch, chief rabbi and *catholicos* were responsible for collecting and making over to the treasury. Only adult males able to provide for their own needs were liable.

Next to the *dhimmis*, the Turks were the most numerous. It was they who gave the capital the atmosphere of a major Muslim town. They had arrived at the same time as the minorities, mostly from Anatolia, in the decades which followed the conquest and, in the 16th century, they had continued to fill up the empty spaces and those one-storey wooden houses on stone foundations or wooden structures filled with *pisé* which have hardly changed over the centuries and were still, not twenty years ago, so characteristic of old Istanbul.

After the conquest, only the cisterns, aqueducts and drains of the old Byzantine town remained, and the Turks could have built a splendid new capital. However, they did not. Was this the result of habits inherited from a long nomad past? An expression of Muslim disdain for the things of this ephemeral world? Whatever the reason, they built houses to last a single lifetime – only those meant for God were planned, like him, to be eternal.

Palaces, Hovels and Mosques

There were three major inhabited areas: *Istanbul*, the former Greek city, surrounded by walls, where Turks now formed the majority; *Galata*, full of taverns, traffickers and warehouses, which had been a Genoese town and a landing post for the ships from the West – above were the vineyards of Pera, where the great powers, starting with the French, opened their embassies in turn. Opposite, on the other side of the Bosphorus, on the Asian coast, was *Uskudar*, known to the Europeans as Scutari (the point of departure for the caravan routes towards the countries of Asia), with its *han*, the intense commercial activity which almost made it a town apart, and its princely residences by the sea.

Less populous districts extended these three major built-up areas: one was on the Stambouli shore of the Golden Horn, towards the sanctuary of Eyup, where the Prophet's companion, Eyup Ensari, lies; another was along the shores of the Bosphorus, where the rich would later build their summer residences or *yali*; and the third was in the vicinity of the Castle of the Seven Towers, near the Sea of Marmara.

In Istanbul itself, houses mushroomed at random, especially after the end of the 16th century. The authorities tried in vain to stop them actually encroaching on the roads, but everyone built their houses more or less as

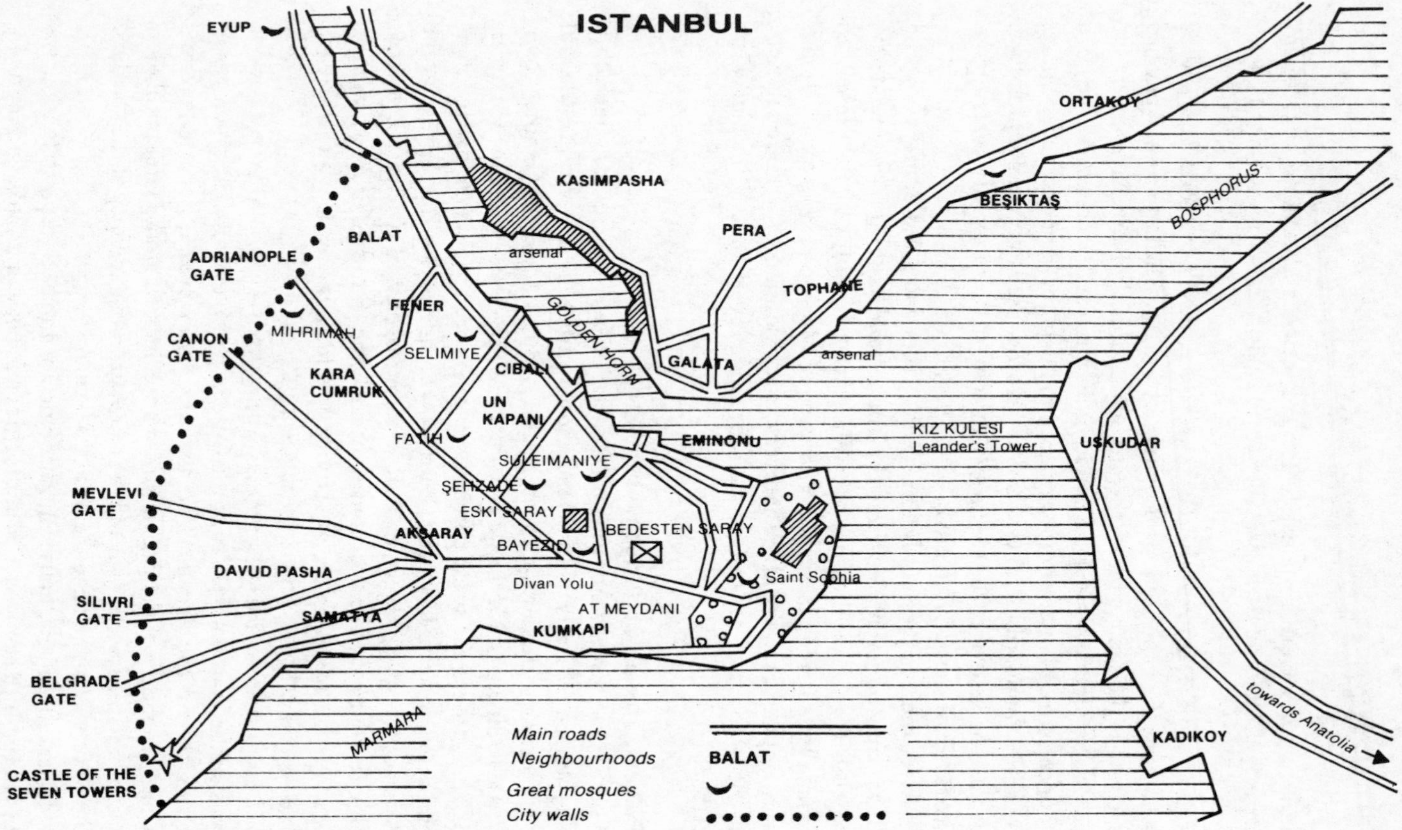

Map II. Istanbul at the Time of Suleiman

they wished. Sometimes whole districts were ravaged by fires – 750 houses on a single occasion in 1564 – and then rebuilt according to people's personal needs. Large green spaces separated the blocks of houses: private gardens, vineyards, vague plots of land which gave the town a slightly rustic atmosphere which the Turks, who love nature, easily adapted to.

The capital retained the general plan of the Byzantine city. The impressive walls which protected the new Rome for more than a thousand years were repaired and reinforced in the years which followed the conquest. The main artery was still that which linked the Augustaeum with the forum of Constantine, the ancient *Mese* or *Divan Yolu*. As the only large flat avenue running through the town, it was the route taken by Suleiman when he set out for Edirne (Adrianople) to bring war to the Danube territories. In all the others, traffic was slow: since the roads were narrow, tortuous and mostly at a slope, people got stuck in mud in winter and covered in dust in summer. There were few carriages – men (usually Armenians) transported almost everything on their backs. Tombs were situated beside fountains, the residence of a rich businessman just next to cabins of mud and wood where whole families lived on top of each other.

The district next to Saint-Sophia and the Hippodrome, and those next to Bayezid's mosque and the Suleimaniye, attracted the palace dignitaries and the leading members of the bourgeoisie, although they could not be called 'residential areas' since more modest dwellings were also to be found there. Every district was named after the principal activity which took place there: Tophane (the cannon foundry), Kagithane (paper-making), Sali pazar (the Tuesday market). These names have survived to this day.

The residences of the important persons of the state – the viziers, leading functionaries and army chiefs – were real palaces, like the sultan's Seraglio, with several buildings set among flowery, shady gardens. The high walls surrounding them hid from view the luxury within. Built first in wood and then, from the beginning of the 16th century, in stone, these *konak* had one or two storeys of thirty or forty rooms, divided into two wings which separated out completely and were sometimes, in very large residences, linked up again by a covered passage at the level of the first floor: the *haremlik*, where the wife, young children and other females lived; and the *selamlik*, with the bedroom of the head of the family, the men and the adult male children as well as the reception rooms, more or less luxuriously decorated with faience, panelling and carpets, depending on the owner's wealth, but simply furnished with divans and sofas along the walls. The separation of the sexes was the same in the dwellings of mud and wood which housed the rest of the population. A simple partition made of planks or a felt curtain always screened off a part of the house, however humble, as belonging to the women. Unlike Arab houses which often open on to an interior court, the Turkish ones almost always faced the street. *Moushrabieh* on the lower part of the window allowed one to look out without being seen.

Mosques, schools and charitable institutions, together with fountains, took up a large part of the town. On all sides the graceful Ottoman minarets, slender as arrows, stretched up to the sky. They looked down on the immense domes, themselves supported on semi-cupolas, among the cypresses which shaded gardens and cemeteries. Just after the conquest, many churches had been transformed into mosques, Saint-Sophia first of all, which the victors had kept intact, although they buttressed the walls and covered some of the mosaics with plaster. Later, it was surrounded with four minarets, although there were still only two at the time of Suleiman.

The outline of the town buildings was much the same as today. The great mosques had almost all already been built. Each of the sultans, to glorify God and make his own name immortal, had built his own. Mehmed the Conqueror did this on the ruins of the church of the Holy Apostles (the pantheon of the Byzantine emperors); Bayezid II built the one that bears his name near the Grand Bazaar; Selim I ruled only eight years and did not have time to build his mosque, and his son Suleiman ordered its construction on the fifth hill. A few years later, the mosque which would bear his name, the Suleimaniye, the largest and most beautiful of all the imperial mosques, rose up on the slopes of the third hill, surrounded by hospitals, *medrese*, hospices and charitable institutions. Suleiman also had built the Şehzade *cami* – the princes' mosque – in memory of his sons Mehmed and Cihangir, and his daughter Mihrimah built another one, which bears her name, near the Adrianople gate.

In the 16th century, other mosques, large and small, often sumptuous, were put up by important personages – Grand Viziers, admirals and leading dignitaries. Some, in truth, were just local oratories, where people went to make their devotions and exchange news. Around 1550, according to Pierre d'Alby, who visited Istanbul at the time, there were 300 mosques in the town. In the following century, the traveller Evliya

Çelebi counted 15,714 places of worship, but the French traveller Grelot put the number at 5,000 – which seems rather more likely and would include the 300 mosques.

Maintenance of the mosques and the charitable institutions which depended on them was assured by foundations which received revenues from lands, villages, gifts, etc. They never lacked resources – charity is one of the essential duties of every good Muslim.

The Seraglio

Some way apart from the town and at the centre of the three built-up areas was the empire's seat of government and the *padishah*'s personal residence: the imperial palace or Seraglio. This collection of single-storey buildings with pavilions scattered among the gardens was in broad outline little different in the 16th century from what it is like today. As in all Oriental palaces, three courts separated from each other the external services, the official palace and the sovereign's private apartments, including the Harem; the whole complex was surrounded by high, severe walls protected by powerfully armed towers. The site, chosen by Mehmed II in person, was ideal: the only place in the city which looked down on the Sea of Marmara and the Princes Isles, the Bosphorus and the Golden Horn, the heights of the European shore and those on the Asiatic coast. 'We see there the leading example of the genius of the Turkish race for choosing the best sites for building.'

No authorization was needed, at the time of the sultans, to go into the first court. Anybody, man or woman, Jew or Christian, rich or poor, could go through the Imperial Gate (*Bab-i-Humayun*), the huge portal in black and white marble. Once inside, one had to keep a respectful silence. Although the courtyard, when the sultan held an audience, was full of men and horses, there was no noise, but 'two or three thousand janissaries,' as the Emperor Ferdinand's ambassador said, 'who seemed to have been painted or sculpted in marble, and as many horsemen; although they were numbered in thousands altogether, we were utterly amazed to never hear a cry or a single word . . .' Another traveller relates that even the horses seemed to make less noise with their shoes than elsewhere!

To the right of the entrance were beautiful trees and the orangery. To the left, the church of Saint Irene (which is still there), whose construction dated back to the earliest centuries of the Byzantine Empire, protected the armoury. Then there were administrative buildings, artists' and jewellers' studios, the Mint, the sultan's bakery and a little mosque for his personnel. Finally, at the back of the court, near the central or Salutation Gate (*Bab-es-Selam*) which led to the second court, were two raised stones which people turned their eyes away from as they passed. The heads of leading dignitaries whom the sovereign considered unworthy to go on living were displayed there after their execution. Nearby was the fountain where the executioner – who, oddly enough, was also the palace gardener – and his assistants would wash their hands when they had completed their grisly duty. These 'Exemplary Stones' were destroyed in 1839 at the time of the *Tanzimat* reforms, and the fountain was put away in a shed. How many heads of leading persons were cut off here? Nobody knows, but it has been remarked that the crueler a sultan was, the more candidates for important posts there were, under Selim I among others, whose viziers always carried around with them their last will and testament. 'May you become the Sultan Selim's vizier' remained a common curse in Istanbul for a long time!

The Divan *Court*

Four centuries ago, as today, one entered the *Divan* court through the Central Gate (*Orta Kapi*), a thick medieval-looking construction which was fortified and flanked by two octagonal towers. As the threshold of his sovereign majesty, the place where the *padishah* lived and governed, everyone approached it with respect. They had reached the heart of the empire, the source of all power.

The place was enchanting: fountains surrounded by trees of rare species, with flowers, gazelles and ostriches moving freely and only the murmur of waters on the lawn to break the silence. A portico went all the way round the courtyard and opened on to various official buildings: the palace treasury (*hazine*), secretaries' offices, guest rooms and, finally, the *Divan* room, where the Grand Vizier and leading dignitaries met four times a week in Suleiman's day, although less often under his successors. There were two rooms of modest size, linked by a wide arcade and each surmounted by a dome. One of them was the true *Divan* room, the other the chancellery. Next to it, a little room was used as the Grand Vizier's office.

The *Divan* room, which was refurnished at the beginning of Suleiman's reign, was of an unheard-of luxury. Panelled half-way up the walls, the upper half of the room was decorated with arabesques encrusted with gold and precious stones. The mantlepiece was in silver gilt, just next to a fountain made of crystal. The inside of the dome was covered with gold.

The whole room glittered with gold and jewels. From a little grilled window set in the top of the wall facing the door, the sultan could watch the proceedings whenever he wished.

The sultan received the visiting ambassadors in the *arz odasi*, at the entrance of the Third Court. The splendour of such receptions depended on the importance the Porte wished to give the sovereigns they represented, but there were always fabulous amounts of gold, jewels, precious cloths and shining arms. The meal was sometimes served on a simple service, sometimes on plates of silver or even of celadon – the shade of green was said to change when poisoned food was put on them! The master of ceremonies always presented 'robes of honour' to the ambassador and those who accompanied him. The quality and number of such robes depended on the consideration the sultan wished to show for the king or emperor they were sent to. Those he wanted to single out most of all received robes woven in gold, or gold and silver, thread, and some were even bordered in sable. The least distinguished were made of white camel hair. Such handing over of robes often led to long discussions if the ambassador considered they did not befit the rank of his sovereign.

Several travellers have left accounts of the reception of ambassadors by Suleiman the Magnificent. That by Jérôme Maurand, a priest from Antibes, who accompanied the Turkish fleet to Constantinople in 1544 after its stay in Provence, is particularly colourful. He was received at the palace in Captain Polin's entourage.

'On this side and on that, as my most illustrious lord passed by on his way to the second gate of the palace, were the *sipahi*'s horses, some of them mounted and very richly decked out. Every horse we saw had reins of gold and silver, and armour as well; most had on their forehead a strip of gold or silver in the shape of a rose, in which a ruby, a hyacinth or a turquoise was mounted; they had bridals in the Turkish style, embroidered with gold or crimson silk and enriched with turquoises. Each of the horses had a chain under its chin made of gold or silver and worth about 500 ducats, depending on the amount of gold or silver in it. They wore small Turkish saddles, completely golden; on the croop, three palms of gold brocade or velvet embroidered with gold, with rows of buttons hanging from each side and made of gold thread or crimson silk. The horses were very beautiful Turkish or Barbary horses, with coats of black or brown, chestnut, grey, blotched, dappled or white, and worth at least 200 ducats. I was told that the Great Lord usually keeps 6,000 mounted *sipahi* in his palace.

'When my illustrious lord had passed with his suite between these horses, which was a beautiful thing to see, we arrived at the large second gate of the said palace, which is guarded by janissaries. Those who guard it are 12,000 in number . . . and wear a huge array of feathers as a crest upon their heads. As soon as my very illustrious lord had gone through that second gate, the janissaries stationed in good order round the cloister all got up, bowed down as my illustrious lord went by, and paid homage to him. In the middle of that cloister, which is covered like a monk's cloister, there is an open space with a wide variety of trees, especially cypresses, and where many kinds of animals like stags and roe-deer, ostriches, Indian goats and other animals wander freely among the trees . . . To return to my most illustrious lord, who had reached the place where the lords Bassas usually held their audiences and was received there with the greatest politeness by the four lords Bassas who presented him to the Great Lord. When he had explained the purpose of his mission and the Great Lord's dragoman had given him his reply, accompanied by the lords Bassas, he kissed the Great Lord's hand, followed by the other members of his mission.

'The Great Lord, in the third room, was seated on a brocaded cushion, dressed in white satin and a rather small turban; on the top of his turban we could see a mere three fingers of crimson velvet, which was formed into folds. On the front of his turban there was a sort of golden rose and, in the middle of this rose, a very brilliant round ruby, half the size of a hazel-nut; on his right ear he had a pearl hanging down in the shape of a pear, the size of a hazel-nut and very beautifully made; under his chin, at the opening of his cassock, which was of white moire, he had ten or twelve beautiful pearls instead of buttons, the size of large chickpeas. After Monsieur the Ambassador had kissed the hand of the Great Lord, the lords Bassas led him into the audience room, all decorated with carpets and with little seats a palm and a half in height covered in carpets. It was there that my illustrious lord the Ambassador ate with the four lords Bassas, Monseigneur the Prior of Capua and the others who had kissed the Great Lord's hand. They were served in Turkish style.

'The other gentlemen who had not entered to kiss the Great Lord's hand were given places to eat within the cloister of the Porte, or palace of the Great Lord, where the janissaries of the palace guard also sat.'

At the other side of the court, twenty cupolas sheltered kitchens where food was prepared for everyone who lived in the palace: the sultan himself, the women of the Harem, the pages and the staff of the school for pages and the slaves, making up 800 people in all at the time of Suleiman. Two meals were served in winter, one at 10 in the morning and the other at 4 or 5 o'clock in the evening; in summer, there was also another meal after evening prayers.

Although the produce was excellent, food was frugal: bread, salad, jam and fruit in the morning; meat (mutton, lamb, poultry and, for the sultan, a couple of pigeons), soup made of cereals or fine herbs and dessert (*baklava, mahallebi*), with flavoured water sprinkled over everything, formed the evening meal. Wine was never drunk, at least in public. At the end of his life, Suleiman banned it altogether. Fresh vegetables came from the Seraglio garden, olive oil from the Peloponnese, dried vegetables, sugar, syrups and spices from Alexandria. The Venetian ambassador provided Italian cheeses. Caravans of camels brought huge quantities of frozen snow from Mysian Mount Olympus overlooking Bursa, which was used in summer to make the sorbets the women of the Harem adored.

Service at the sultan's table was very quick. A witness, Baron Wenceslas Wratislaw, who once took a meal there, says that he observed from a distance the 200 servants arrive, all dressed in red robes and wearing bonnets embroidered with gold. They formed a line from the kitchen to the sultan's apartments, bowed their heads in respect and then became quite still, 'like statues'. The steward brought out a dish of porcelain, and then another, which he handed to the first servant, who handed it to the second, who handed it to the third, and so on up to the *maître d'hôtel*, who stood at the entrance to the private apartments. He passed on the dishes in turn to another *maître d'hôtel*, who did the same, and so on. The last man put them in front of the sultan.

The School for Pages

The third gate in the palace was the Gate of Felicity (*Bab-i-Saadet*), which opened on to the private section or *enderun* of the palace, an almost sacred place where only members of the sultan's household, slaves and a few people like doctors who had been authorized by the chief of the white eunuchs, the *kapi ağasi*, were allowed to enter. People kissed the threshold of the *Bab-i-Saadet* before crossing it and then kept silent. Twenty-five white eunuchs kept guard. To the left and right of the gate was a double entrance, flanked with marble columns, to the school of pages, where the elite of the young Islamicized Christians were trained for the leading civil and military positions in the empire.

The palace pages (*içoğlanlari*) were divided between a Large Chamber (*buyuk oda*) and a Small Chamber (*kuçuk oda*) to the right and left of the Gate of Happiness. The pages were given instruction and an education which made them into Oriental 'men of honour' and warriors (rather like the training for the Samurai in Japan, some have said). They learnt Turkish first of all, for many of them could only speak it badly, then the Islamic 'humanities' and Arabic – the language of the Koran – and Persian (the language of the court and chivalry). Later, they learnt about the grammar and literature of these three languages, the Koran and the commentaries on the Koran. Then came study of Islamic theology and law, history, mathematics. Part of the day was given over to physical training, considered just as important as intellectual matters. The sultan's servants had to possess physical endurance just as much as intellectual vigour. Jousts and contests were organized on holidays. The sultan took part and rewarded the winners. Wrestling, the supreme Turkish sport, and horsemanship were particularly encouraged.

The *içoğlanlari* underwent an extremely strict discipline and had no contact with the outside world. 'White eunuchs', who were responsible for their conduct, oversaw them day and night, and they were kept totally apart from women. Loyalty and complete self-mastery, refined politeness and as wide a culture as possible – all these talents were needed by the future dignitaries of the empire, as well as the personal abilities to make a good impression in the eyes of the supreme sovereign. Suleiman attached the first importance to the training of his pages: he took part in the selection examinations, followed their progress in their studies, asked them questions and tried to spot the most promising.

The education of the *içoğlanlari* in the Large and Small Chambers usually lasted four years. A further selection process then took place, and the best were taken into the administration of the interior palace, or *enderun*, where the sultan carried on his private life. Others became part of one of the Porte's cavalry regiments or *sipahi*.

The *enderun* college in the 16th century was divided into three divisions (*oda*). The private section, or *has oda*, had 40 members who were in charge of the sultan's arms, his clothes and his security at night. The elite of the elite, they also had to look after the room where the relics of the Prophet were kept. Their leader, the *has oda başi*, never left the sultan. Ibrahim was promoted directly from that post to the post of Grand Vizier. One of the three state seals was granted to him and he occupied a position of considerable power, only surpassed by the *kapi ağasi*, whose power in the palace was almost absolute. An intimate of the sultan, he gave advice on every subject, including affairs of state. When he left the post, he was usually appointed *beylerbey*, sometimes Governor of Egypt.

The sixty treasury pages (*hazine oda*) guarded the sultan's valuables, while the thirty office pages (*kiler oda*) dealt with all aspects of meals. Promotions and redeployments, which occurred every two to five years and whenever a new sultan came to the throne, allowed some pages to move up a rank from the third to the second *oda*, or from the second to the first, which was also the most sought after. Such changes were based on age, except when, as often happened, young men distinguished themselves by particular merit. In that case, advancement could be very rapid. When a young man attained the rank of *eski* (or ancient) of the first chamber, he could then be appointed a provincial governor, superior officer of the janissaries or chief of one of the subdivisions of the *birun* which dealt with the 'exterior services' of the palace: ushers, gardeners, standard bearers, stewards, doctors, tailors, artisans, falconers or bodyguards, including the 'noble guard' (*muteferrika*), whose members came from the school for pages or were the sons of dignitaries.

Including the 8,000 janissaries and the 15,000 Porte *sipahi*, the *birun* in 1527 was made up of about 25,000 people in all, while the *enderun* had a mere 700. Promotion in the *birun*, as in the *enderun*, was based on both seniority and merit.

In an empire without a hereditary nobility, the *kullar* (plural of *kul*, slave) formed the only true aristocracy, those who had the immense honour of approaching the sultan to serve him. It was a privilege they alone, and never their children, possessed: every man was his own ancestor and descendant. Neither office nor wealth, which the sultan could confiscate whenever he wished, was ever inherited. The often immense fortunes of the leading dignitaries were taken into the sultan's coffers without anybody having the right to object. Wealth, like nobility, lasted only for a lifetime. The men who exercised power in the *padishah*'s name were 'employees', taken on for life to perform specific tasks, who could be dismissed at any time up to their death and with no rights they could oppose to the sultan's sovereign will.

Yet what advantages counterbalanced such total submission! What possibilities there were for young men who had been admitted to the school for pages! An intellectual and moral training, an unparalleled education of body and soul. 'They were instructed in letters and arms as if they were the sultan's children,' wrote Paolo Giovio in 1538. And Busbecq made a similar point: 'The Turks are overjoyed when they discover an exceptional man, as if they have found a precious object, and they spare neither work nor effort to develop his talents, especially if they see that he has an aptitude for the arts of war. We are quite different: if we find a dog, a falcon or a horse, we are very happy and spare no trouble to perfect their talents. But if a man happens to possess extraordinary natural ability, we don't take the same trouble to perfect his talents. No more do we think to concern ourselves with his education. We take great satisfaction in well-trained horses, falcons and dogs and are well served by them, but the Turks get much more satisfaction from a man who has been perfectly educated insofar as the nature of a man is far more worthy of admiration than that of other animals.'

Whatever his origins, a brilliant subject was sure of reaching the highest positions in the state. Honour and wealth, which were indeed inseparable at the time, were promised him, yet they could be instantly taken away again if he failed to fulfil the hopes which had been placed in him or if he excited the suspicions of the sultan or Grand Vizier. Nothing was acquired for all time; constant effort could never be relaxed. Nowhere was the Tarpeian Rock closer to the Capitol. And yet how splendidly and rapidly a successful man could advance!

A historian has retraced the career of Ali, one of Suleiman's Grand Viziers.[2] Born in Dalmatia, he was taken away as part of the *devşirme* system. He came to the palace when Ibrahim was in charge of the chamber of pages. He was soon promoted to the post of Porte guard and then Suleiman's 'chief taster'. He then left the palace to take up positions outside. He became general of the *gureba*, the fourth division of the Porte cavalry, was promoted to general of the *sipahi* – the first division – the sultan's second and then first squire, then general of the janissaries and finally *beylerbey* of Rumelia. As a reward for his services during the Persian campaign of 1548–9, Ali was appointed pasha of Egypt and then vizier. When he returned to Constantinople in 1553, he became third vizier and then, on Rustem Pasha's death, Grand Vizier. He was certainly the son of a shepherd or a very humble peasant.

There are countless eyewitness accounts of the *devşirme*. As a general rule, it seems not to have been resented by the empire's Christian subjects as an outrageous imposition. Most of them accepted willingly the opportunities it gave their sons, poor little peasant boys, of attaining, perhaps, the fabulous positions of Grand Vizier, *ağa* of the janissaries, or one of the leading dignitaries whose fame even reached the hovels in Serbian or Albanian hamlets.[3]

Slavery in the Orient – as European travellers often stressed – did not carry the same badge of shame as in Europe. It was considered, rather, as the surest route to honours and fortune. It was also frequently transitory, since manumission was very common, although often against the wishes of the individual involved, who usually preferred the security of his present state to an uncertain future.[4]

The Selamlik *and the Harem*

It was in the pavilions of the third courtyard – the *selamlik* or men's quarter – that the sultan lived, worked and slept. Like every good Muslim, he performed his ritual prayers in his private mosque, but on Fridays he went in great ceremony to Saint-Sophia, Istanbul's main mosque since the conquest. None of the buildings was more than one storey high and, although they were solidly built, they looked more like a nomads' camp than the palace of a powerful sovereign. Yet the interiors were sumptuous; everywhere, there was marble and gilding, exquisite cloths, little pieces of furniture of the most delicate workmanship, the most beautiful carpets ever woven. The walls were covered with faience from Iznik, shimmering with colour, which had just been enriched by the famous tomato red with its flower and leaf motifs which brought a reflection of nature – to which all Turks are sensitive – into Ottoman art.

The sultan's private apartments were surrounded by rooms for the pages and white enuchs. They communicated with Roxelane's bedroom through a secret door. Nearby was the room for the holy relics which contained the Prophet's cloak, staff, sabre and seal as well as hairs from his beard. These sacred objects had been brought from Cairo by Selim I. The conqueror of Egypt, as pious as he was cruel, had this sumptuous pavilion built just next to the imperial apartments so he could venerate the relics at any time. The sultan sometimes spent the night on a rest bed near the chamber of relics, where four imams took turns, day and night, to read the Koran. There were also pages in the sultan's private service, as we have seen, who were in charge of guarding the sacred treasure and organizing the ceremonies which took place on certain religious festivals. The cloak and seal were then taken out of their display cases, and the sultan, his pages and the members of his household with the highest rank took them to receive the veneration of the crowd.

Next to the chamber of relics and the private apartments was the Harem where the sultan's wives and concubines lived. In the middle of the 16th century, it was far from being the vast tangle of buildings it became a century later and which we still see today. Nothing remains of the buildings Suleiman constructed for Roxelane's entourage when she moved into the Seraglio, except, it seems, for the 'interior throne room' where concerts and performances were for a long time put on for the women of the Harem. They were later engulfed in the other buildings and totally transformed in the course of the successive enlargements of the palace which resulted from the considerable increase in the number of people who lived there.

Roxelane had occupied it at first with only her personal entourage. Selim II, Suleiman's son, took Nur Şultan – his favourite concubine and later the mother of his eldest son – to live in Topkapi with her woman servants, and later installed the whole Harem there. The Old Palace built by Mehmed II on the third hill became no more than a place to which the favourites and concubines of dead sultans retired, along with their unmarried sisters and women who had to leave the Harem simply because their time had gone and they had been replaced by younger women. Only the queen mothers (*valide sultan*) or those who had managed to find a husband ever left. This 'palace of tears', as it was called, for more than three centuries would see hundreds, no doubt thousands, of wretched women within its high walls – women who fell into despair and disappeared without leaving a trace.

The Harem was then to become a state within a state which sometimes had greater influence than the *padishah* and his ministers. For 150 years, power was in the hands of women and the black eunuchs, who had such influence that leading dignitaries and the ambassadors of major countries had to go through them to obtain what they wanted.

How many women were there in the Harem? About 300 in Suleiman's day and over 1,000 by the end of the century. In such numbers, we must count many domestic servants, including the black women who did the hardest work. The others, the *ikbal*, were only a few dozen in the 16th century, although they reached two or three hundred in the 17th. All were non-Muslim, which meant Christian, because Muslims could not be enslaved. Many were Circassians, famous for their beauty, but others were Greeks, Serbs or Italians. A Venetian woman called Baffa, Murad III's favourite, would rule the empire at the end of the 16th century, instigate the murder of Mehmed III's nineteen brothers – and end up strangled in her bed. They were bought at slave markets or given by pashas keen to win the sultan's good graces and have an ally in the palace who could one day prove useful.

Most of these young women were very happy to have been admitted into this almost divine place, about which such extraordinary tales were told, and where they had a chance to lead a life of luxury and pleasure and perhaps even become a favourite one day. Their families had often used money to attract the attention of a leading functionary in favour of their daughter, just as the Christians used every means to get their sons enlisted among the emperor's future pages.

Like the boys taken up by the *devşirme* system, the girls who entered the Harem received a complete education: sewing, embroidery, cooking . . . Those with particular talents were encouraged to develop them. Each girl became part of an *oda* (chamber) under the direction of a woman of a higher rank who, like a tutor, organized her future career for her. She received clothing, food and money. The Harem was ruled with a firm hand and organized like an army corps, and each woman was given responsibilities as Guardian of the Jewels, Mistress of the Robes, Directress of the Table, Guardian of the Baths, and so on. Thus they slowly attained higher and higher rank and gained more and more wealth.

To be noticed by the sultan was the supreme ambition of every girl who entered the Harem. When he paid a visit to the *valide sultan*, he might make a remark about one of them which would be immediately noted down and understood, or he might notice one of them during festivities in the throne room. She would then leave the anonymous crowd and be given an apartment and slaves. She was massaged, depilated, scented and dressed. Then she had to wait . . . Perhaps she would never be called for and would return to live among the other aging women before being sent to the 'palace of tears'. If she was lucky, the sultan might marry her off to a *sipahi* or a palace functionary. But perhaps she might learn instead that she was going to share, that very night, the bed of him to whom, after Allah, the whole world belonged.

It sometimes happened that the sultan, preceded by his black eunuchs, visited the chosen woman's bedroom, but more often it was she who was taken to the imperial apartment in the greatest secrecy. All the doors and windows were kept closed as the little procession went by. Only the eunuchs in the guard were told what was happening. A torch was blazing at the door and another in the room. His Imperial Majesty was already there. The young woman approached his bed respectfully. She raised the coverlet to her forehead and then to her lips. She crawled up to the sultan from the foot of the bed, using her elbows and knees to help her. This custom, which was in common usage in certain Oriental courts, notably in China, also had to be observed, it is said, by any man who married an Ottoman princess.

In the morning, the sultan would leave his bed-partner with the clothes he had worn the day before and the money and jewels they contained. He would also send her a present, large or small according to the pleasure he had received. Then she was taken back to her apartment with the same discretion as had been shown the previous night. She might never again see her lover of a few hours and would return, after a short while, to the ranks of the anonymous odalisques and lose her short-lived privileges. Perhaps, though, he would call for her again once, twice or even more often, especially if she had won the *valide sultan* over to her side. Then she could hope for anything, especially if she had borne him a child, a boy, and if it was the eldest. She would then become a legal wife in all but name (*baş kadin*) and would have reached, or nearly reached, the summit of honours. She would indeed have everything: riches, slaves, precedence, influence. If, further, her son actually came to the throne, she would become the *valide sultan*, the second most powerful position in the empire. She was the first lady of the palace, and not the chief *kadin*, whose influence she disputed fiercely. The *kadin* rarely achieved victory in their disputes with the *valide sultan*. As in all Muslim societies, contrary to widespread opinion, it is the woman and especially the mother who directs the household – in this case, Suleiman's 'household', the Harem.

The chief of the white eunuchs, the *kizlar ağasi* (literally 'the girls' general'), helped the *valide sultan* and not the chief *kadin*. He was a slave from Nubia and acted as her 'executive power', her intermediary with the outside world and the representatives of other governments. His powers were immense and his wealth considerable. As the administrator of the Holy Cities, he ranked in the hierarchy immediately below the Grand Vizier and *şeyhulislam* and above the chief of the white eunuchs. He was often more powerful than them all and was also responsible for the education of the young princes who lived in the Harem until the age of 12 or 13, when they were sent out into the different provinces as governors.

Suleiman's Harem, even before Roxelane's arrival, was not a source of much gossip. In the following century, things were very different. Ibrahim I had a deranged imagination and went in for orgies with the women of his Harem. He not only covered his beard with pearls and precious stones and drenched himself in perfumes; in a mad obsession with furs, he covered the sofas, the walls and even the floors of his apartments with sable.

Society

All through the year, Turkish Muslims had their waking hours divided up by the *muezzin*'s call to prayer five times a day. Not everyone said them all, but it was usual to recite the morning and evening prayers at home and the midday prayer at one's place of work. Lighting was very expensive and therefore unusual, so all activities took place during the day. Everybody stayed at home in the evenings unless they went to the mosque for the last prayer. Apart from that, it was not permitted to go about at night. As soon as day dawned, however, the town was swarming with men who had washed rapidly and were on the way to work. They went to the baths to clean themselves properly at least once a week.

Men and Women

Men wore baggy trousers, a shirt and a *dolman* (jacket). A belt, in which money and sometimes a pen-box and a handkerchief could be put, was tied around the waist. A long caftan kept them warm during the winter. They wore leather slippers on their feet, yellow for Muslims and any colour for Infidels. According to their wealth, they would wear a more or less luxurious ensemble: linen, silk or fine wool for the jacket and for the caftan, which was sometimes lined with ordinary fur or with a more luxurous material like sable.

As for headgear, the Muslims wore turbans and the Infidels (non-Turks and foreigners), plain skullcaps. The turban was made of a single piece of cloth, several metres long, of more or less fine quality, rolled around a cap (usually of felt). Suleiman laid down rules which regulated the exact shape and height of the turbans which men could wear, according to their position; punishments were also laid down for those who contravened these regulations. The sultan and leading dignitaries put sprays of diamonds in their turbans. One can get an idea of all this on the tomb-stones in the main cemeteries of Istanbul, where hundreds and hundreds of turbans, almost all different, can be seen in rows under the great cypress trees. The men of the people simply knotted a piece of cloth around their shaved heads. The intellectuals and men of religion generally wore beards, which added to their dignity.

Women could only reveal how elegant they were in their own houses or when they paid visits to women friends or relatives, yet, like women everywhere, they loved to deck themselves out and those who had the means dressed luxuriously. Lady Mary Wortley Montagu described thus the costume worn by the women of the Harem or high society: 'A pair of drawers, very full, [that] reach to my shoes and conceal the legs more modestly than your petticoats. They are of a thin, rose-colour damask brocaded with silver flowers, my shoes of white kid leather embroidered with gold. Over this hangs my smock of a fine white silk gauze edged with embroidery. This smock has wide sleeves hanging half-way down the arm and is closed at the neck with a diamond button, but the shape and colour of the bosom very well to be distinguished through it. The *antery* is a waistcoat made close to the shape, of white and gold damask, with very long sleeves falling back and fringed with deep gold fringe, and should have diamond or pearl buttons. My caftan of the same stuff with my drawers is a robe exactly fitted to my shape and reaching to my feet, with very long straight falling sleeves. Over this is a girdle of about four fingers broad, which all that can afford have entirely of diamonds or other precious stones. Those that will not be at that expense have it of exquisite embroidery on satin, but it must be fastened before with a clasp of diamonds . . . The head-dress is composed of a cap called a *talpack*, which is in winter of fine velvet embroidered with pearls or diamonds and in summer of a light, shining silver stuff.'[5]

Thomas Dallam, an English organ-maker who had gone to Constantinople to show the organs which Elizabeth I had offered to Mehmed III, managed to catch a glimpse of the young women of the Harem playing ball through a grille, thanks to the help of a dignitary of the Seraglio. They were wearing on their heads little bonnets made of golden yellow material, with necklaces of pearls, ear-rings and jewels on their dresses. They wore tunics, which were either red or blue. Their breeches reached the middle of their legs and were made of cotton so fine 'I could see the skin of their thighs'. Some wore elegant closed shoes made of rope, others had naked legs decorated with a gold ring, or a kind of velvet buskin four to five inches high.

Not all Turkish women, of course, were dressed like that, but their costumes always included the same items: long trousers (or *şalvar*), a bodice, a vest (or tunic), a caftan, shoes and slippers for indoors, a bonnet or a skull-cap. Finally there was the *yaşmak*, the veil which all Muslim women wore when they were outside and which differed in shape and material according to the country.

These women, stylish or simply dressed, and married to rich traders, leading functionaries or humble artisans, were – contrary to the general belief in the West – almost all the only wives of the husbands their families had chosen for them. Polygamy, up to a maximum of four wives, was permitted by Koranic law but rarely practised by the Ottomans. Lady Mary Wortley Montagu testifies to this: ''Tis true their law permits them four wives, but there is no instance of a man of quality that makes use of this liberty, or of a woman of rank who would suffer it.' The same applied to the poorer classes. To provide for several wives would have been beyond the husbands' means. Those who could afford it did not make use of the privilege, often because they wanted to avoid domestic problems. And besides, it was something that was 'not done'.

On the other hand, and again contrary to received opinion, the single wife, provided she had produced children for her husband, ruled her house exactly as she saw fit (even if she was theoretically under the authority of the head of the family) within fairly wide limits; the *kadi* could even make an appeal to the husband if the wife so wished. The whole household – son, daughter-in-law and servants, whatever their age – owed her obedience. She chose her daughter's husband and her son's wife – or, rather, her husband took the decision under her direction. The daughters, of course, were completely under her control until their marriage – when their mother-in-law took over – and the sons, especially if they lived under their parents' roof, which often happened, were also subject to her during their father's lifetime. When he died, the wife of the eldest son 'took power'. The fact that the family home was divided into two parts, the *haremlik* and the *selamlik*, in no way diminished the mother's authority over the whole household, which she ruled, according to temperament, gently or with a firm hand.

Is the difference between such women and Western women at that time – or at any time – so great? 'Upon the whole, I look upon the Turkish women as the only free people in the empire,' wrote Lady Mary.

The Corporations

Apart from soldiers and those who worked in the service of the state, the inhabitants of Constantinople and the provincial towns lived on the work of their hands or commerce. All, or almost all, were members of corporations which gave the economy a sort of extreme rigidity which remained more or less intact until the middle of the 19th century.

The Ottoman corporations, which were similar in general terms to those of the Graeco-Roman world and the Middle Ages in the West, originated in the *ahi* organizations which grouped together many inhabitants of towns in the 13th and 14th centuries.[6] They were inspired by the *futuvva* (semi-religious fraternities which had become fellowships) which dated far back into the Oriental and Abbasid past. Extremely powerful and independent under the Seljuks of Rum and in the Anatolian principalities, the centralized and authoritarian Ottoman state established its control over them, partly to keep groupings in check which could easily have become forces for opposition, and partly to protect the people against speculators and fraudulent traders, as it had every right to do. The regulations about commercial transactions (*ihtisab*), derived from religious law, were issued for this reason. The organizations of *ahi* thus became simple corporations of artisans and traders (apart from the largest traders, who had dealings with foreign countries and were not subject to the *ihtisab*).

In the 16th century, there were a thousand corporations in Istanbul, formed into about fifty 'groups' in which the masters, workers and apprentices were separated. Since the number of shops and studios was limited, and it was difficult to start a new business, the masters formed a sort of social class which guarded its privileges very carefully. Each corporation (*esnaf* or *tayfe*) was under the authority of a *kethuda*, the real chief of the corporation, assisted by a committee of 'Ancients' (the 'Six'), who were all elected and included a *şeyh* and a *duaci* (who directed the prayers). Religious in origin, the corporations remained deeply marked by Islam. Each had one or two 'patrons' who were believed to have invented the profession: David for the gunsmiths, Joseph for clockmakers, Jonah for the fishermen, etc. The *şeyh* took the place of honour in ceremonies to welcome new recruits and in the traditional processions, which were always preceded by prayers.

Even thieves, beggars, prostitutes and clowns had to join corporations. Isolated individuals did not exist in the Ottoman Empire. Since there were no political groupings or organizations representing national or local interests, the only theatre of communal life was that of the separate professions. Everyone received help and protection both in their working lives and in difficult circumstances. The professions, with the agreement of the authorities, controlled prices, competition, efforts to stamp out cheating, and the distribution of raw materials. They tried to prevent illicit trading and, in general, anything which could encroach on their privileges. As soon as an infringement of the regulations was discovered, they called on the authorities to intervene, the *kadi* passed judgement and the police carried out the punishment, which could be anything from a mere beating to imprisonment or a ban on the practice of one's profession.

The corporation thus drew on the principles of solidarity which were so powerful in the Muslim world. Genuine 'mutual aid societies', they received contributions from their members proportional to their resources. They also received gifts from masters whose apprentices were promoted to a higher rank and from the sultan when the members passed in procession before him on the occasion of certain festivals. The sums were handled by the corporation's committee of directors and were used to help members who were ill or temporarily out of work, for charitable works (notably distribution of food to the poor) and for religious ceremonies. Masters who wished to expand their businesses were allowed to borrow money at the symbolic rate of 1%. A sort of social security was thus in operation, controlled by the interested parties. The state merely made sure that the corporations remained within their professional and economic domain and that they exercised over their members the controls laid down by the regulations in force.

The members met up several times a year in ceremonies like the one which accompanied the promotion of an apprentice to the rank of companion. These either took place at the corporation's headquarters or, in the summer, as part of an excursion into the country, one of the Turks' favourite diversions. The event would open with a prayer, and then the *şeyh* abjured the apprentice kneeling down before him always to remain a good Muslim and observe the rules of the corporation. He would put a sort of apron around him and murmur a few sentences in his ear: the corporation's secrets. Fifes and drums would ring out, and the ceremony would come to its conclusion with an auction of samples of the apprentice's work – he could use the proceeds to help establish himself in business.

From the Turkish Baths to the Bazaar

In every district there were Turkish baths which permitted the population to carry out the demands of Islam. The Prophet's religion demanded that all the faithful be in a state of purity for the Friday midday prayer and that they go for a complete ablution when they became defiled, notably after sexual relations. 'They have the belief', wrote Spandugino, 'that washing their body all over will take away all the sins they might have on their soul . . .' Thus, there were public baths to be found more or less everywhere in the town, distinguished by the domes which surmounted them. They varied greatly in luxury and size and, on separate days, were visited by both men and women. The women were lazier and sometimes spent afternoons or whole days there with friends to be massaged, depilated and made up. News was exchanged, along with gossip and more or less innocent games. Every bath included a room where one undressed, basins of warm water, and a series of other rooms with hot and cold water. The public baths were maintained by money provided by a charitable foundation (*vakf*). Coffee was introduced at the end of Suleiman's reign, and soon each bath had its *kahveci*, employed to prepare the drink, which rapidly became popular, over a brazier (see Appendix 13).

In the commercial districts of the town, near the Grand Bazaar, at Eminonu and at Uskudar, the *han* – some of which have survived to this day – sheltered travellers and merchandise. On the ground floor, in vaulted rooms, were stables and warehouses. Dormitories and bedrooms were situated on the floors above. Some of the *han* specialized in a particular kind of merchandise and others in the produce of a particular country. Some sold the merchandise in large quantities and to individuals while others packed it up for sale to retailers. Their solid walls and heavy doors meant that even valuable objects like jewels, gold and furs could be kept safe. They too were usually maintained by religious foundations.

Although people could buy their supplies in any district of Istanbul, the commercial centre of the city was *Buyuk Çarşi* or the Grand Bazaar, known today as *Kapali Çarşi*. Its *bedesten* and the many shops which surrounded it made it without doubt the most important economic unit in the Eastern Mediterranean.

The *bedesten* and *çarşi* were covered markets on one floor surmounted by small domes and illuminated by openings in the walls and ceiling. Solidly built of stone and brick, and with windows protected by thick iron grilles, the *bedesten* was the market for materials and other precious goods. It was also used as a depot and a safe by the rich Stamboulites who came to put their valuables there. That was where the major business transactions took place, and the huge transfers of capital required by large-scale domestic and international trading.

The market in the true sense of the word was the *çarşi*. Dozens of little shops, lined up along the narrow streets, offered for sale all the commodities needed by the inhabitants of a major city. As today, the shops were grouped according to their speciality. In one alley, leather goods would be for sale, in another, cloth, in a third, bronze work, and so on. The famous 'Egyptian market' (*Misir Çarşi*), even 400 years ago, gave off a thousand different smells from bags bursting with spices.

There were several other permanent markets: the horse market, the poultry market, and even the slave market. The latter was held near the burnt column on the *Divan Yolu* (the main artery through the city). One could buy male slaves or black women for domestic work. Young girls brought from Georgia, Circassia or Russia were kept in the *han* and treated very well until they were sold to rich merchants or leading dignitaries. The most beautiful ended up in the palace. Thus 20,000 slaves, men and women, were sold each year in the market in Istanbul.

In the Ottoman Empire, and especially in Istanbul, the supply of foodstuffs and raw materials, and the fixing and control of their prices, took on a major importance. In no circumstances was the customer to suffer. The Grand Vizier, representative of the sultan and responsible to him, was in charge of applying the law. Every Wednesday, the *Divan* held in the Seraglio discussed the affairs of the capital, including the food supply. The distribution and selling prices of such produce were decided on and communicated to the leaders of the corporations. The *kadi* or judges made sure that such decisions were carried out and punished offenders. For this, they often employed the services of the *muhtesib*, their deputies in all matters concerned with the corporations and overseeing the markets.

Every Wednesday, the Grand Vizier made his inspection of the market, which was by no means a symbolic walk-about. The first person in the state after the sultan spoke with the shopkeepers and their clients and, if necessary, meted out punishments on the spot. He stopped in the fruit market, the cereal market, the vegetable market and the abattoirs. Nothing must escape his notice. The authorities even checked the quality of the merchandise. A shopkeeper had to obtain a stamp of approval and pay a tax (*damga resmi*) which guaranteed the quality of the product or metal before he could put anything made of bronze, gold or silver, or even more horseshoes, on sale. Instruments used for weighing or measuring produce also had to be stamped before they could be used. In Istanbul as in the provinces, traders had to pay special taxes on their shops, for their right to a place in the market, and so on.

The sultan's most constant concern, in the economic sphere, was to protect the population from profiteering.[7] This was why the authorities intervened all the time to prevent unjustified price rises. A maximum price (*narh*) for each product was laid down from above after consultation with the corporations; no shopkeeper was allowed to deviate from it. Such prices were usually fixed for a long period, unless there were important changes in production costs, and they enabled traders to make a reasonable living (the profit permitted was in the range of 10 to 15%) and the people to get all they needed in good condition and at a fair price. People selling the same product were all in the same souk – as is still true in many Oriental towns – so there was practically no competition and profit margins were never sufficient to allow significant price reductions.

Let us not, however, make the mistake of painting an idyllic picture of 16th-century Turkey as a society which functioned like a well-oiled machine, where everybody received a just reward for their work and saw all their needs easily satisfied. There, like everywhere else, fate favoured some people more than others. Immense riches were to be found alongside extreme poverty – just because the sultan organized the supply and prices of food did not mean that the housewife's basket overflowed with tasty items.

Suleiman's Turkey achieved a level of social justice no higher than Francis I's France or Henry VIII's England. But it remains true that the Ottoman public authorities showed more concern for the fate and needs of the population than was ever shown in the countries of Christian Europe.

10
A *Dirigiste* and Authoritarian Economy

'An ocean of men and beautiful women such as one can find nowhere else,'[1] Constantinople formed a huge conurbation which absorbed products of every sort, and most of all food, in enormous quantities. Almost everything had to be imported from far away because the region around the city produced little: vegetables, a few cereals, wood, mutton, game and plenty of fish. The rest came from the countries of the Black Sea (Bulgaria and Romania), which provided meat, cereals, wood, wool, honey and metals in abundance, from Anatolia and Thrace (cereals, fruit, horses), and from Egypt, which gave the capital its total supply of rice, sugar and cotton as well as large quantities of wheat. Coffee, spices and horses came from the Arab countries, silk and carpets from Persia. Manufactured goods, which were more and more in demand, arrived from Europe, along with gold and silver coins; pearls, precious stones, spices and silk fabrics were imported from South-East Asia and the Far East.

All of these imports – a large majority of which came from the countries of the empire – were organized by a 'meticulous, authoritarian and *dirigiste*'[2] government. The whole system was aimed at stopping the kind of profiteering which would particularly disadvantage the humbler sectors of the community. In economic matters, protection of the consumer was the government's primary concern.

The major importers of meat and wheat, the staple diet of the Turks, were closely watched. Some were merchants who disposed of large sums of money, while others (apparently the majority) merely acted as a cover for capitalists, notably the leading dignitaries of the palace. Nothing would have been easier than for them to come to an agreement to bring about artificial price increases – if the state had not kept a constant eye on them. The same applied to traders in leather and to those specializing in luxury goods who needed a great deal of money for their imports from Europe. The government made use of an army of inspectors, controllers and agents of every kind, who prevented large as well as small traders from evading the agreed prices and the regulations in force. In addition, the control exercised by the corporations reduced still further the margin left for trickery and profiteering, especially in the 16th century, after Suleiman, with his extreme concern with justice, had reinforced the battery of regulations laid down by his predecessors.

Artisans and small traders who sold the products they had themselves made also carried on their professions within limits laid down by the state. They could not raise or lower their prices, but they were also prevented from changing their methods of work, increasing the size of their operations, or adding new products to those they made or sold. In Istanbul, there were tens of thousands of them, quite apart from the innumerable pedlars who sold vegetables, fruit, yoghurt and used goods, etc. These were often recent arrivals in the city who had fled from the poverty of their native villages, just like those who, even today, make the streets of old Istanbul resound every morning with their cries.

Such a rigid system of economic control, based on traditions dating back a long way into the Oriental and Byzantine past, effectively protected both traders and consumers. Everyone was satisfied, so there was no reason for change. Their fathers had acted in the same way, corporations assured reasonable profits to the traders and artisans: the wisest course was to continue with the system as it was. Few were the people who feared that, in a world shaken by new discoveries, rigid and outdated traditions could endanger the Turkish economy and even the empire itself.

Minorities and Foreigners

All the sultan's subjects, minorities and Turks, were equal in the exercise of their profession. Because non-Turks preferred or Muslims disdained a particular profession, different groups might be more or less well represented in different professions, but no careers were actually closed to the minorities. The Jews above all sold wine, *raki*, slaves, perfume, gold jewellery and pearls. They were also to be found in finance as money-changers, bankers and intermediaries of every kind. Like the Greeks, they also acted as tax farmers. In the 15th and 16th centuries, the sultans encouraged the immigration of Jews, who were considered a rich and energetic sector of the population. At the end of the 16th century, there were estimated to be about 160,000 of them in Constantinople and Salonica. As almost everywhere in Europe at the time, they played a major role in Turkish economic development, not only in the capital and surrounding regions but in the whole empire: Aleppo, Cairo, Alexandria, Tripoli (Syria), Rhodes and North Africa. Some achieved very important positions: Joseph Nasi, a Portuguese Marrano, was to be appointed Duke of Naxos by Selim II (see Appendix 14).

Greeks were prominent in all trades connected with shipping, from the humble boatmen on the Golden Horn to the major traders in wheat, who continued to deal on the black market with the countries to the West, starting with the Aegean islands, when exports of cereals were not permitted. Many sailors were Greek, as were most of the fur traders. The Armenians, still few in number in the 16th century, began to look towards international trade, particularly with Asia.

Foreigners – in other words, Europeans – were involved exclusively in trade with their countries of origin, apart from the religious who ministered to the churches.

The Venetians always took first place, although they slowly but surely lost their privileged position. After the capitulations were agreed with France, the Venetians were not the only people to possess the 'flag right'.[3] The capture of Constantinople had turned the Black Sea into a 'Turkish sea' and deprived them of all trade with the countries in the region. As the Serene Republic's relations with Suleiman deteriorated still further, it lost most of its possessions in the Aegean. Nonetheless, trade between Venice and the Ottoman Empire, both Istanbul and the commercial ports of the Levant, remained important throughout the 16th century: luxury products and manufactured goods were transported to the Turkish ports, while raw materials and spices came in the other direction.

Ragusa (present-day Dubrovnik), whose commercial significance was to decline in the following century, was still an important staging post between Italy and Turkey. Whenever relations between the Porte and the Venetians were soured, it benefited from the interruption in trade. It was thus, at the Italians' expense, that Ragusa carved out for itself the important position in the spice trade between Europe and the Levant which it long retained.

The Genoese too had lost all their positions in the Black Sea, including their important storage centre in Caffa. They had also had to suffer the consequences of the help they had brought the last Emperor of Byzantium in 1453. Mehmed II had their fortifications at Galata razed in reprisal. After that, their role in Turkish trade continued to diminish. They did, however, maintain a presence at Galata and Pera, and their ships often came into Turkish ports either on their own account or in the service of other traders. Apart from all this, Genoa was always, and long remained, the major banking centre where everyone, Ottomans included, came to make deals.

Florence, which had obtained capitulations from Mehmed II, was still fairly active in the Levant. The Jewish traders of Livorno, who were under Tuscan protection, were actively involved in trade with the Jews of Istanbul.

There were also new arrivals to take on these long-established colonies of foreigners. The French, who had just begun to trade in large numbers with the Orient, were the most important, although they came far behind the Venetians. Commercial exchanges developed from the time of Francis's alliance with Suleiman and from that day until the end of the Ottoman Empire, the French benefited from the privileged regime offered by the capitulations. Since France and the sultan were not at war during the 16th and 17th centuries, the French were spared many of the difficulties encountered by the citizens of other nations. This is not to say that life was always easy: the ambassador often had to intervene in Constantinople, like the consuls in the provinces, to support or defend his subjects. When relations between the two countries were good, everyday difficulties could be resolved fairly easily, although greedy functionaries and local authorities were always a menace. But when the sultan was annoyed with the king, when there was a particularly xenophobic Grand Vizier or when incidents had broken out at sea or elsewhere between the Turks and the French, then more and more complications would arise and discussions would go on forever. Traders would be required to pay damages for insult, which were sometimes heavy.

The King of France's subjects were still few in number in Constantinople. For a long time they could be counted on the fingers of one hand. Later there would be far more of them, such as in Smyrna (Izmir) in the 17th century. They also became established in Aleppo, Sidon, Cairo, Tripoli and Damascus. A century later, there were more French than any other foreigners in the Ottoman Empire.

At the time of Suleiman, the other foreign communities were even smaller. An English presence, mostly in Smyrna and Aleppo, was only established after the capitulations obtained in 1580. The Dutch also arrived there, a century later. The almost constant state of war between the sultan and Charles V and his successor Philip II prevented any trade between Spain and the countries of Central Europe, which received Levantine produce only by very roundabout routes.

Trade between the Eastern Mediterranean and Poland was on a significant scale, especially in the second half of the 16th century, when an increase in agricultural prices had brought a huge influx of money to Poles, who could therefore afford foreign products. Circulation of goods was made much easier by the peace the Turks had now established to the North of the Black Sea after they had occupied the Crimea. The Turkish market offered the Poles spices, rice, textiles, silk fabrics from Bursa, dye-stuffs and horses, not to mention Greek wine. Some of these goods were then re-exported to Germany, the Baltic countries and Russia. The Turks bought metals, which the Ottoman Empire was in constant need of, as well as cloth from England, Holland and Germany, skins and amber, and furs.

All these products had long also been part of the major trade with Russia. At the sultan's palace, there was an immense need for furs. Ermine and sable were used as borders for the robes of the princes and leading dignitaries. Expensive furs were offered as gifts to honour important people. Those who could afford it decorated their cloaks with fur, or used it to make bonnets, great-coats, and so on. One of the sultan's officials was given as his personal duty the purchase of goods from the Russian traders. The Greek furriers in the capital worked the large quantities which arrived there. No Russian traders lived in Istanbul or any of the other towns. They operated especially from Azov, since it had fallen under Turkish domination, Caffa and the Crimean ports. It was there that the Turkish, Iranian and other traders went to sell their silk fabrics, pearls, textiles and valuable weapons, which were later sent on to Moscow.

An Open Market

The economy certainly had an important place in the sultans' political decision-making, although we must never think that it was one of the essential motive forces behind it. It was partly to establish Istanbul as an international market for spices and to re-open the trade routes towards Central Asia that Suleiman and Ibrahim, at the start of his reign, fought the Persians and wanted to shatter Portuguese dominance in the Indian Ocean. Similar motives lay behind the policy of friendship with the Uzbeks (aimed against the Safavids of Iran) and the later plan to construct a canal between the Don and the Volga (to combat the nascent imperialism of Moscow). The same, it is even clearer, applies to the granting of capitulations to certain foreign countries – concessions offered either to gain their political goodwill or to support the economic and financial interests of the empire (see Appendix 15).

Following the age-old traditions of the Orient, men in the Ottoman Empire and the wealth they produced were all considered to be in the service of the sovereign. Institutions and economic activities were just instruments of his power, and he used the organs of the state to retain absolute control over them. Everything was based on the old principle formulated in *The Book of Maxims for the Prince*: 'No power without soldiers, no soldiers without money, no money without the well-being of one's subjects, no subjects without justice.' Rights and duties balanced out: the sovereign had absolute authority over his subjects and their possessions, but he also had a duty to administer them justly and to see to their well-being.

The Ottoman economy, therefore, was not a market economy – or, to be more exact, it was a market economy of a particular type which was quite different from the capitalist system which had just come into existence in Western Europe and which was based on the pursuit of profit by men who buy and sell goods to increase the yield of their capital without any outside state intervention. In the 16th-century Ottoman Empire, the economy had two main aims: to supply resources to the state, and to keep the population satisfied by providing them with everyday and luxury consumer goods. The state was thus led to control both production and distribution, on which its own resources as well as its subjects' well-being depended. The economy was not regulated by the laws of the market but 'was a function of the state at the same time as it functioned to maintain it'.[4]

In these conditions, there were no problems with the balance of payments. To import goods which supplied the market and provided money for the treasury in the form of duties was the principal, indeed the only, concern of the state in economic matters. The granting of capitulations to the European powers was aimed, above all, to encourage them to import the products they needed from the empire, which meant they had to pay customs duties. The Ottomans never, or only too late, understood the advantages of encouraging exports which brought in gold and silver. At a time when the pursuit of profit and monetary expansion in Western Europe were ushering in the age of capital, the Ottoman Empire remained stuck in out-dated traditions and principles. The resources from various duties and taxes as well as the tributes paid by the countries they had subdued were more than enough to supply resources for the state and provisions for the people. They never looked any further than that.

Turkey was thus an open market, first of all to France, then to England, Holland and finally to all the European countries. In the 16th century, the main export of French and (from 1580) English merchants was linen. There were few Turkish manufacturers to be harmed by this trade, but in the following century the Europeans offered silk and woollen goods for sale, and then everything that the nascent Turkish industry could have produced. The revolution in prices caused partly by the influx of gold and silver from the New World into the countries of Western Europe gave them the means of production which enabled them to conquer new markets. They were compelled to find further openings for their industry and went to buy raw materials in the Orient. They were able to do so because of their large supplies of precious coin and the inflation these had brought about and maintained. There were two important consequences: commerce with the Ottoman Empire took the form of a 'colonial' trade; and Turkish industry remained forever at the level of craft production and never became truly capitalist.

From Silk to Pepper

Particularly after 1550, these problems began to be taken seriously, although no one could guess the dimensions they would assume a century or two later. For the moment, the Ottomans experienced the first shocks of the 'price revolution' and the inflation and erosion in the value of money that went with it. Not long afterwards, the *akçe* would be devalued, yet difficulties of this kind seldom disturbed the sleep of the sultan or his Grand Viziers during Suleiman's reign.

Traders continued to bring in the expensive luxury products that the Ottomans had long imported from Europe: cloth, paper, sugar, (French) hardware, glasses, panes of glass, rare spices and metals like tin and lead. As for export, Anatolia, Thrace and the Balkan countries sent the produce of their agriculture and animal husbandry, especially leather and wool, through Istanbul. Other ports dealt in cotton, silk, wax and alum. There was a huge trade in wheat, particularly with Italy, which always had to make up the domestic deficit with imported wheat and which suffered a grave crisis in providing food for its citizens around the middle of the century. In 1551, 500,000 hundredweight of wheat left Turkish ports for the Italian peninsula on Venetian, Genoese and Ragusan ships. Prices doubled between 1551 and 1559. But the shortage of cereals in Turkey, together with epidemics, led the authorities in 1555 to prohibit all exports. When smugglers tried to replace legal trading, incidents occurred between European ships and the Turkish galleys used for surveillance.[5]

In the Ottoman Empire, silk was traded on a very large scale. Most of it came from Gilan and Mazandaran, the areas of Iran by the Caspian Sea which produced the finest quality silk, as well as Khorasan. Caravans carried it across Anatolia to Bursa, which had long been the major trading centre. It was bought by Italians, Florentines and Venetians, who could make enormous profits, sometimes as much as 70–80 ducats a *fardello* (150 kg). Since the conquest of Syria, the Ottomans also controlled Aleppo, the other major commercial centre for silk, where Armenian and Tartar traders arrived from Persia by way of the Euphrates valley or Diyarbekir. Turco-Iranian wars interfered with the trade throughout the century and cut it off altogether on several occasions, but the increasing taste in Europe for brocade, satin, taffetas and tussore silk, and the continuous development of the luxury textile industry in Europe, meant that the trade of the Turkish 'silk towns' grew larger and larger all the time.[6]

In parallel with this trade, the silk manufacturing industry took off in several Turkish towns, notably at Bursa, where a thousand looms were working at the start of the century for both the domestic market and export. Turkish Muslims were almost always the bosses. In Aleppo, around the year 1560, there were 5,000 weavers at work.[7]

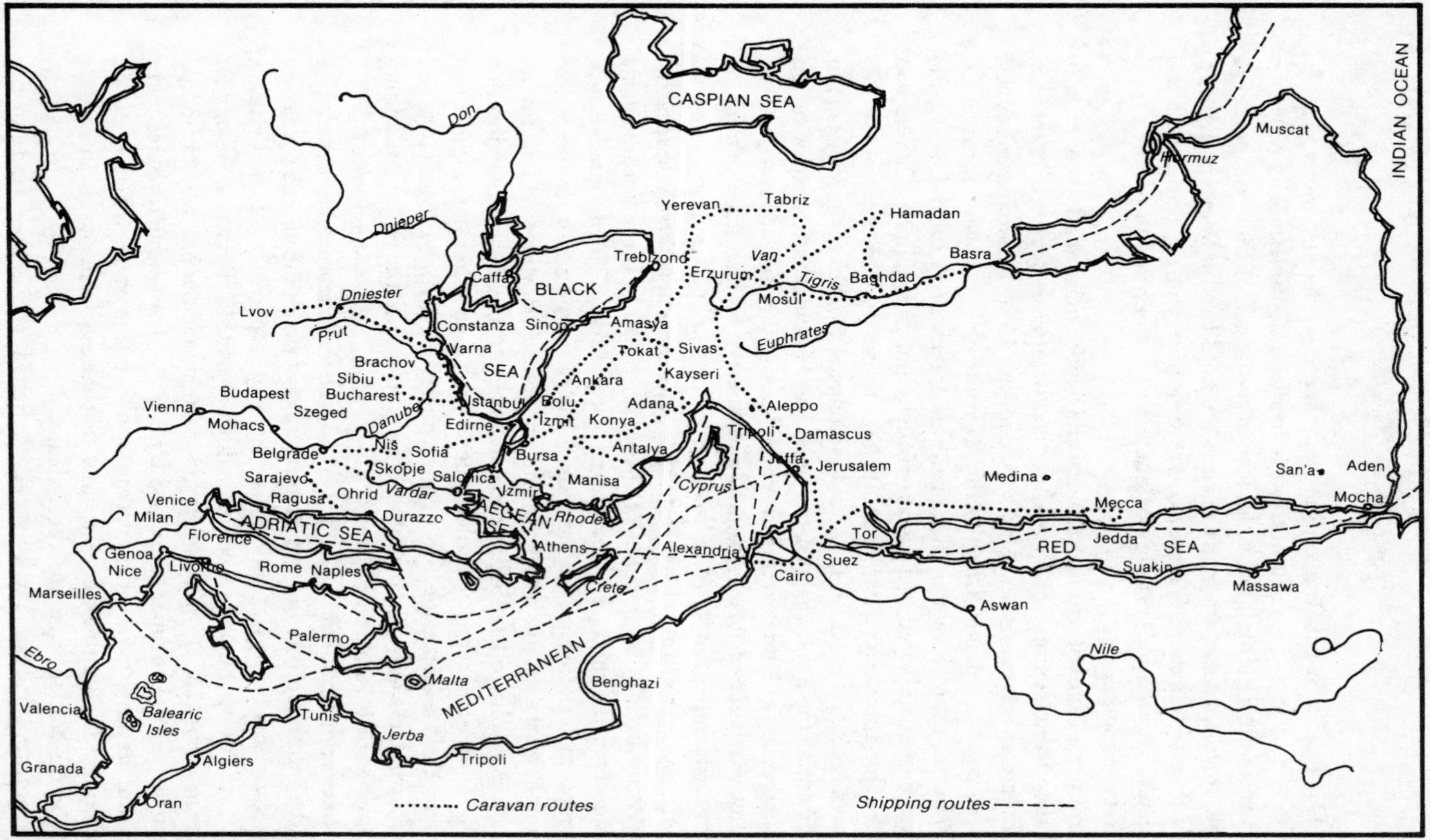

Map III. Caravan Routes

The traffic in silk was nothing compared to the enormous trade in spices, 'the first of the international trades . . . the essential object of Levantine commerce'. From the 12th until the end of the 17th century, a mad craze for aromatic spices had taken hold first in Western Europe, and then in Northern Europe, where still more was used. In Russia and Poland, people used 'prodigious quantities', which led to protests from Western travellers.

A large proportion of these spices, and pepper most of all, went by way of the Ottoman Empire, even after the Portuguese fleets had started to compete by carrying pepper directly to the West. From ancient times, spices had been taken either by the sea route or in caravans across Asia. This latter route, however, had been almost completely abandoned in the 15th century in favour of a passage from Indonesia and India (Calicut was the major commercial centre on the South coast) to the ports of the Red Sea and the Persian Gulf. Boats of low tonnage went as far as Suez port or El Tur, on the Sinai coast, if the winds were favourable. Larger vessels disembarked at Jedda or, if they set out later to take full advantage of the monsoons, stopped at Aden or the South coast of Arabia. Each year, at the time of the monsoon, 10 to 15 boats raised anchor in Calicut with cargoes which brought profits of 100% or more to their owners. From these ports, caravans took the merchandise to Mecca, which had for centuries been a major transit centre, and thence to Alexandria, Cairo, Damascus or Aleppo, where foreign buyers took delivery. Large quantities were also brought by sea to Istanbul or the other ports of Asia Minor, or by caravan across Anatolia to Istanbul and, particularly, to Bursa, where Florentine and Venetian merchants would come to exchange material for spices and where the traders came for supplies to sell in Crimea, Moldavia and Wallachia, the most important intermediaries with the major consuming countries of Russia and Poland.[8]

At every point of passage, the price of the merchandise increased. The traders took their profit and the Ottoman state its duties. The treasury made large amounts of money in this way, especially when the taxes collected in Egypt and Syria weie added after 1517. Between the port of embarcation and sale in the Eastern Mediterranean, it has been estimated that the price of pepper increased by 2,000%. Enormous fortunes were built up in the great Muslim towns thanks to this trade, which could be carried on in complete security now that the *pax turcica* could impose its law in the Middle East and the Balkans.

Contrary to what has long been believed, the pepper trade in the

Mediterranean was not greatly affected by the Portuguese discovery of the Cape route. Neither the spice route nor the Indian and Indonesian ports facing the Mediterranean were totally cut off except for brief periods. Early in the century, the Draconian surveillance by the Portuguese in the Indian Ocean had severely limited trade, but by the mid-century it had almost returned to its former level. The Portuguese could not be everywhere at once, and the maintenance of a tight system of policing would have cost too much. Around 1550, 40,000 hundredweight of spice passed each year through Alexandria alone. The Venetians bought 12,000 hundredweight, as much as in the best years at the beginning of the century. The finances of the sultan of Constantinople were on a very firm footing.

The Trade Routes

Between the Ottoman Empire and Europe, commercial exchanges usually took place by sea. Only a few kinds of merchandise, especially those coming from Venice or going there, were transported by the land route from Ragusa or Spalato (Split). All the others went by way of the Mediterranean, round Sicily, landed at Modon or Koron, in the southern Peloponnese, or Crete, where boats set out for Constantinople or the Dardanelles or the commercial centres of the Levant (Smyrna, Alexandria, Beirut, Tripoli). Crossings varied greatly in time, and one could never tell when merchandise would arrive. From Marseilles or Venice to Constantinople, in good weather and with a favourable wind, took at least a month and more often 60 to 80 days. From Constantinople to Alexandria took a fortnight including stops at the Levantine commercial centres; from Messina to Tripoli in Syria, 20 days. In exceptional cases, the journey from Livorno to Tunis could be done in 6 days, but it sometimes took as many as 20. It was only towards the end of the century that these times were cut down little by little, whatever kind of boat was used.

In the Mediterranean (or, to be more exact, in the Eastern Mediterranean), Berber or Christian corsairs always presented a mortal danger. Convoys escorted by warships were sometimes used to guard against them, but this method required large vessels and could only be used once or twice a year. It was never attempted in Suleiman's day. Ships defended themselves as well as they could, usually fairly ineffectually, since they were at best poorly armed. Flight was usually the only answer, for the boat and its merchandise would otherwise be captured and the crew and passengers would have a good chance of ending their days on a Berber galley or in a harem in Tunis or Algiers.

The hazards of commerce by sea were considerable at the time, quite apart from the dangers represented by sudden storms and unforeseen winds for anybody who crossed the Mediterranean or Aegean. In 1604, J. de Gontaut-Biron, Baron de Salignac and Henry IV's ambassador to the sultan, took two and a half months to reach Constantinople. He left Venice on 1 November and only arrived on 19 January after escaping corsairs, weathering several storms, and coming to grief at the entrance of the Dardanelles in snow and icy rain. This, of course, was a voyage by an important personage, on a good ship and with a first-rate crew. One can imagine what crossings on overloaded small or medium-sized boats, often in the hands of sailors of fortune, were like.

Overland journeys were neither faster nor safer. There were three principal routes linking Istanbul with Europe. One led to Belgrade by way of Edirne, the Maritsa and Morava valleys, Plovdiv, Sofia and Niš. This was the route taken by the army convoys for the northern garrisons or by the sultan when he set out for war against his Christian enemies. Another more or less followed the direction of the ancient *via Egnatia* and took the route from Salonica towards Monastir, Ohrid, Ragusa and the Adriatic ports. Finally there was the road which linked Istanbul and the valley of the lower Danube, also by way of Edirne.

These roads – or, rather, tracks – were covered with gravel and sometimes paved. Villagers were obliged to maintain them. The Ottoman communication routes were among the best of their time. Several bridges built in the 14th, 15th and 16th centuries are still in use. It took five days from Istanbul to Edirne, between ten and twelve to Sofia and at least twenty to Belgrade.

In the Balkans, travelling was perhaps even less safe than in Asia. Bands of brigands, unemployed mercenaries and soldiers on the loose would all attack travellers and assassinate or ransom them. One could never be too well armed. When Suleiman crossed the Balkan countries on his last campaign in 1566, brigands attracted by the passing troops were so numerous that 'several were executed at each stopping place'.

In Asia, distances were greater and voyages even more difficult because of the climate. 'In Asia we saw whole regions which were uncultivated and depopulated,' wrote a Frenchman called Tavernier. 'There are vast deserts to cross, and the passage is dangerous for lack of water and Arab raiders.'[9] From Constantinople the caravan routes made first for Izmit (ancient Nicomedia) and then towards Sapança, where they crossed others, which were used more often, coming from Bursa, Bolu, Amasya and Tokat, a place of passage for travellers from Smyrna. From Tokat, some went towards Erzurum, Yerevan and Tabriz, in Iran, and others to Diyarbekir by way of Sivas or to Aleppo, the centre of the network where roads left for Syria and the Red Sea. The routes from Baghdad and Mosul and those from Tabriz (by way of Deir ez Zor) also ended in Aleppo. Certain caravans left Istanbul or arrived there on fixed dates: the one from Smyrna every week, the one from Aleppo three or four times a year, the one from Persia six or eight times a year. The journey to Smyrna took ten to twenty days, whereas two or three months were needed to reach Persia.

It was in Turkish territory, however, that journeys were least difficult and also least dangerous.[10] The roads were relatively – very relatively – good. There were caravanserai on the major routes, especially in the Asian sector, 30–40 kilometres – a day's journey – apart. Many had been built by the Seljuks of Rum in the 13th century. The Ottomans enlarged them and constructed others. They were usually maintained by religious foundations, like the *han* (or inns) in the larger towns. Pierre Belon, who accompanied the French ambassador, Gabriel d'Aramon, to Turkey in 1547, described the one at Kavala, 'a large edifice' which Ibrahim Pasha had had built, where he and his companions found food and lodging for three days: 'When the soup is cooked, anyone who wants some must bring his wooden dish. Meat and bread were also served . . . to everyone regardless of religion or race, and without payment.' The few caravanserai which still exist (like Sultan Han, built in 1236, on the route from Kayseri to Sivas, with its thick walls, huge domed rooms set around a large courtyard with a little mosque at the centre) give some idea of what these large stopping-off posts, where hundreds of men and animals ate and took shelter, must have been like.

Except for short distances or on the plains, where carts were sometimes used, transport was always by means of beasts of burden: camels, donkeys and horses, and mules towards the end of the 16th century. Wagons were only used with any frequency in the 18th century in Europe, and even later in Asia.[11]

11
Town and Country

Istanbul was very far from being the whole of Turkey. If the lives of people from the countryside and the distant towns were not substantially different from those of the inhabitants of the capital, the same was by no means true of those who inhabited Anatolia and the Balkans, the vassal states and the far-away provinces. Apart from a well-born and rich minority, life was hard for everyone. But was it much harder, on the whole, than the lives of the people who lived in Central and Eastern, not to mention Western, Europe?

In many areas, Ottoman occupation had improved the lot of people hitherto subject to Christian feudal lords. First in Anatolia and then in Europe and the Orient, it replaced the often anarchic despotism of the Muslim principalities and Christian states by the centralized authority of an empire which was administered as firmly and justly as men and circumstances permitted.

The Peasants

The Turkish peasant or *reaya* was a free man who could be neither bought nor sold. He was allowed to change his residence, although he was then obliged to pay a tax. In certain cases, the *sipahi* (who received the revenues from the land) could compel a peasant to return to his holding, but, to do so, he had to make an appeal to a *kadi* and wait for his sentence. There were many exceptions to these rules, which varied according to the area and circumstances: sometimes the *reaya* could immediately have his residence in town legally ratified, but other *Kanunname* demanded a delay of twenty years. In any case, his fate was quite different from that of the serfs of Western Europe in the Middle Ages or in Eastern Europe at the dawn of the modern age. He was subject to the judgements of the *kadi* alone, who had to decide the case on the basis of the regulations of the *Şeriat* and the *kanun* laid down by the sultans. The *sipahi* carried out the sentence and received damages but – quite unlike the European lord of the manor with whom he has often been compared – had no powers of jurisdiction. The separation of powers was total.

The peasant's holding could not be taken away from him, although all land in the Ottoman Empire was considered to belong to the sultan (apart from foundations – *vakf* – or the *mulk* lands which were in private hands), and the peasant was therefore only a long-term occupant. His children or widow could succeed him, but the regulations again varied from area to area. The *reaya* was allowed to sell his land, with the permission of a representative of the state.[1] The system was sufficiently supple to guarantee the state that the land would be constantly cultivated and that the *sipahi*, the soldier who owed his service to the state, would have a constant income. As for the *reaya*, he was certain of being able to live on a plot of land sufficient to provide a living for himself and his family.

The land tax payable by the peasant was proportional to the size of his holding. It was called a *resmi-i-çift* when the farmer was a Muslim and an *ispence* if he was a Christian. The amount varied greatly from province to province, depending on the tax systems which preceded the Ottoman era in each principality or state. It also depended on the personal status of the contributor. All such details were set out in the registers (*tahrir*), published every thirty years, where the name of every adult was listed, together with the size of his holding and the tax he was liable to pay. Although the amount was calculated in monetary terms, it was paid in kind (that is to say, in cereals). Taxes were also levied sometimes on particular produce (mutton, pork) as well as on windmills and in the event of marriages, registration of property, etc. These were included in the category of so-called *orf* duties, which derived from the secular authorities. There were also 'religious' taxes based on the *Şeriat*. The land taxes were paid directly to the *timariote*; the others were farmed out and paid to the *sancakbey*.

Was the *reaya* oppressed by the long list of taxes and rent payments? Once they had been paid, did he live in misery or reasonably decently? It seems that in this respect as well, the fate of the peasant in the Ottoman Empire was better than that of country dwellers in Europe. Many rustics from Christian countries bore witness to this when they set fire to their houses and fields – to avenge themselves on oppressive feudal lords – and fled to Islamic lands. The welcome the sultan's troops received from such populations is also clear evidence. The potential oppressor of the peasants – the *timariote* – had no right to dominate them or pass judgement but a policing role pure and simple, subject to the control of the *kadi*. No coercion could be exercised except as a result of a decision by the *kadi*; the *timariote*'s other duty, tax collection, was limited by a set of rules and a precise scale of payments. The authority of the centralized state was organized tier by tier down to the most distant *reaya* in the country, who had the right – which no one could refuse him – of appealing to the sultan himself to obtain justice.

This system continued to function, if we ignore a few inevitable slip-ups, until the last years of the great Lawgiver's reign. Then, here as elsewhere, everything started to go wrong, as we shall see. The burden of taxes increased with the extension of tax farming and authority began to break down. The peasants fled from their lands, which no longer provided enough to feed them. This led to oppression by a 'new class', based on the possession of large real estate, which little by little replaced the *timariote* system.

How and where did these Anatolian and Rumelian peasants live out their lives, which cannot have been very happy but were not completely wretched either? Mainly in small towns to tiny villages. The population, which had greatly increased in the Ottoman Empire at the same time as throughout the Mediterranean, was widely spread out. Some of the villages consisted of only a few houses; any which contained more than 400 dwellings counted as a 'town' (although some of the administrative centres were, in fact, smaller). The inhabitants of the villages, as of the towns, cultivated the land.

Despite the difficulties of communication, there were contacts between villages and between villages and towns. The main gap was rather between Christians and Muslims, although it was far less wide than one might imagine. Hostilities broke out only rarely; on both sides, the Turks' natural tolerance won the day.

In the European part of the empire, Rumelia, there was often a Muslim majority in the plains and towns. The large Turkish private estates were established in low-lying territory like Thessaly. The Christians retreated into the mountains, which enabled them to retain their distinctive religious and ethnic identity and greatly facilitated their national renaissance.

In Anatolia, Muslims and Christians (very largely Greek Orthodox) were far more closely intermingled. On the plateau, in the valleys and on the flatlands by the inland rivers, a large non-Muslim population continued to live side by side with the Turks until the population exchanges of 1923. Everyone lived in his own way, near his mosque, sometimes a *zaviye* (community of dervishes), or his church, without feeling any kind of racial or religious hatred for others. The places of worship – or rather of superstition – were often the same: a Christian saint was venerated by Muslims and, in return, a tree might be considered sacred by Christians as well as Muslims. Muslim pilgrims come to visit the tomb of a saint might sometimes spend the night in a church. The Turks never compelled other people to convert with the important exception, of course, of the men who entered the sultan's service. Apart from anything else, the Ottoman state had no wish to lose its revenue from the taxes on Christians, who had to pay at a special rate.

Most of these populations, especially those from isolated regions, lived within closed economies. Self-sufficiency was the general rule. Women carded, spun and wove the wool from the family herd of sheep, men prepared the skins, made leather goods and the tools, mostly of wood, which were used on the farm. Felt, built up from layer after layer of wool or hair, also took a long time to prepare. It was used for many purposes on the cold plains of Anatolia and in the Balkans: carpets and canvas for tents, blankets, shepherds' cloaks and bonnets. It was also used to make things needed by the army.

All the food came from the garden cattle-shed and the kitchen-garden. Much of the food was based on milk: cheese and especially yoghurt – eaten in large quantities at each meal with onions, bread, salt, cucumbers, dried or fresh fruit. On feast days, rice (*pilav*) was eaten with mutton and sweet sauces based on milk, honey, hazel-nuts and almonds. People drank water or *boza* (fermented barley or millet). Anatolian sheep's tails were used to provide fat both for cooking and for making candles (some of the tails weighed as much as five or six kilos). In the fields the kind of little wheelbarrows in use were smeared with the fat to protect them from stones and brambles.

Each family owned a herd, large or small, without which they would have found it difficult to keep alive: one or two cows, two oxen, or buffalo, sometimes a horse but usually a donkey, goats and some poultry which scratched about for food in the neighbouring fields. A kitchen-garden provided the vegetables needed for daily consumption.

These herds differed greatly from region to region: there were more goats and sheep on the plateaux than the plains; camels were common in the South, horses in Rumelia. Similarly, olive oil replaced sheep fat around the Mediterranean, and linseed or sunflower oil elsewhere. Honey was widely used to make sweet sauces or to sweeten food, and bee-keeping was extremely common. Some areas, such as that around Trabzon, supplied honey to places as far away as Istanbul. Turks have no great love for fish, which seldom found a place on the menu even in coastal regions. It was more often eaten dried.

The staple food, of course, in these areas, just as in almost the whole of Europe at the time, consisted of cereals. On the Anatolian plateaux, wheat was by far the most important. With barley, it was easily the main crop, and the same applies to the Danube plains and Thessaly. The yield was rarely more than 4:1 – less than the average of 6:1 then usual in Western Europe – and was often less; this was hardly enough to provide the essential 1,500 kg necessary to form a subsistence diet for a family of five Turks. Yields were slightly better in the Balkan countries, but we must never forget that taxes of one-seventh, and often more, were deducted from the food the farmer had produced for himself and his family.

Rice was a luxury food, only available to those who had the means to buy it. It was cultivated in the West of Anatolia, in Cilicia, in the Balkans and in the parts of Egypt where irrigation was possible. Sugar cane was produced in Egypt and Cyprus, wine in Greece, Trabzon and the Danube territories.[2]

The houses were extremely rudimentary: walls of beaten earth mixed with straw, a roof made of branches matted together and mixed with earth, on which large stones were placed to stop it blowing away (this could prove dangerous when there were earthquakes). Sometimes dwellings were hollowed in the side of a hill instead, with walls made of dug-out earth. On the ground were *kilim*, carpets of goat hair or felt. At the back, separated off by a hanging, was a section reserved for the women; at the front was the main room. A cauldron was attached above a fire where bricks made of straw and cow manure were burning. Women made these during the good weather and left them to dry out in the sun. The cow-shed was just next to the main room – the warmth of the animals was much appreciated during the harsh Anatolian and Balkan winters. There was no furniture, no leather bags, and usually no wooden boxes to keep clothes in. Provisions (cereals, fat, meat and dried fruit) were kept in clay jars.

The days went by each year, with their joys and hardships, and they were divided up by religious festivals and other holidays whose origins had been completely lost in the mists of time. There were two *bayram*: the *Şeker Bayram* (or sugar festival), which marked the end of the Ramadan fast, and the *Kurban Bayram* (or festival of the sacrifice), when presents were exchanged and sweets and meat were eaten. At the end of winter, dances and offerings celebrated the lengthening days and the arrival of good weather. The whole village took part in the festivities. Every area had its own dances, although the origins of them had been long forgotten. Men and women both took part, although always separately, sometimes two by two and sometimes in circles or semi-circles, dressed in their festive costumes; the women had gold pieces sown on their bonnets, and the men who possessed arms wore them gleaming on their belts.

Had the dances and songs of these Muslim populations been influenced by Christians? It is now usually believed that it was the Turks who had the deepest influence on the folklore of the Balkans after they had conquered the area. Turkish folklore, in any case, came from the ancient depths of Turkish Central Asia and had then been influenced by Islam, sometimes through the intermediary of the *zaviye*. These communities of dervishes, to be found in many areas, gave the peasants access to the only form of culture available in remote regions: the poet-musicians and travelling story-tellers. Dances and songs were accompanied with music, usually just a drum and a wind instrument like a clarinet, but sometimes a tambourine as well.

In certain towns, fairs were held once a year or more often; people from the countryside all around would come and visit them. They were the occasion for commercial transactions, amusements and meetings. In the 17th and especially the 18th centuries, as commercial agriculture developed, these fairs and markets became more and more frequent. The town markets then took on a major significance at the expense of those in the country, which led to far closer links between urban and peasant communities. This meant that the towns acquired a far greater influence on agriculture, partly because peasants came there to find money-lenders.

The Nomads

Of nomadic origin, the Turks rapidly established themselves in Anatolia during the Seljuk era. The large Oğuz tribes splintered, choosing to take up residence in the basins of the high plateaux, which were closer in climate and vegetation to their native regions of Central Asia, rather than in the warm and wet coasts of the Black Sea and the Mediterranean. The sultans were pleased that they had settled down, since it made it far easier for them to keep a eye on turbulent populations who were always in conflict with the peasants and formed bands of brigands which attacked caravans, ransomed travellers and plundered village communities. Once they were settled, it was also far easier to impose taxes on them.

By no means all the tribes, however, stayed put in one place, since nomadism, although diminishing, has continued until our own day. In the 16th century, many tribes crossed Eastern Anatolia and the South-West – where they were called *yuruk* or 'walkers' – the steppes between Ankara and Eskişehir, the Taurus region. In Rumelia, they were most common in Macedonia and Thrace. Their migrations everywhere took the same form: they spent the summer in the mountains of the coastal chain, the winter in the lower plains where the climate was less harsh; they covered a distance of 100–200 kilometres.

In Rumelia, tribal organization was so weak that the authorities could easily control them and impose military service on them. In Anatolia, on the other hand, the authorities did not trust them: Iran was nearby and Safavid propaganda in favour of the Shiite cause might threaten the security of the empire. Many rebellions, strongly supported by the Persians, compelled the Ottoman administration to intervene throughout the 16th century (and later) against nomadic tribes where heterodox sects had long sown the seeds of dangerous political and social ferment. Such conflicts were continuous. The tribes tried to emigrate to Iran, the Ottomans to stop them. The frontier region was long drenched in blood, quite apart from the wars between the Safavids and the House of Osman which went on almost without interruption throughout the 16th and 17th centuries.

Relations between peasants and nomads were not always good. Conflicts often arose as a result of thieving or when crops were devastated by the nomads' flocks of sheep. The authorities therefore tried to lay down routes for them which were at a distance from areas of cultivated land. They did not allow them to remain in the same spot for more than three days. When the peasants were themselves nomads who had only recently settled down, relations were often better. Friction was sometimes caused by membership of different sects, yet such conflicts seldom ended in violence. There were also commercial relations between the different groups: the nomads sold leather goods, woollens and the metal utensils they made to the farmers.

In many areas, in any case, there was no clear-cut distinction between peasants and nomads. It was by no means rare for people who cultivated the land to be forced to take up a nomadic life again; they would abandon houses and land, set off with their herds and live under canvas – and then would sometimes settle down again at a later date. Others counted as semi-nomads and would spend the winter in huts in the middle of the land they cultivated and then set off into the mountains with tents and herds as soon as the fine weather arrived.

These, however, were in a minority. Most of them lived the whole year round under tents which they took with them whenever they moved. Each family had one or several tents, or a large tent divided in two by a carpet or partition of felt which created a separate section for the women, even though they did not wear the veil. Polygamy was widely practised and each woman had her own occupation: one of them would weave, another would look after the animals, a third would cook. They slept on carpets or *kilim* or a mattress of brush, rolled up in goat-hair or woollen blankets. There was even less furniture than in the peasant households: a few utensils in copper or wood, bags or bottles made of leather, a loom. Nothing else. The food was very frugal: milk products like cheese and yoghurt, little cereal cakes cooked over a fire; this would be heated by wood in forest regions or by bricks made of animal excrement dried in the sun.

Most of the nomads were shepherds. They had troops of sheep and goats and also, in certain areas, horses and camels. They would sometimes hire these out to caravans or, at times when the Great Lord set out to war with tens of thousands of men who required food and provisions, to the army.

In the 16th century, the numerous Kurdish tribes were still largely nomadic. They settled down little by little, although some continue their wanderings in the steppes and mountains of Eastern Turkey to this day.

Descended perhaps from the Medes,[3] they occupied territory which included much of present-day Iran and Iraq from the Black Sea to Mesopotamia, from the Anti-Taurus to the Iranian plateau.

Their daily life was little different from that of the Turkish nomads. They also moved with the seasons from the plains to the mountain pastures, and they lived in low tents made of black bands of goat hair which were fixed to the ground with ropes. The women's room was separated from the reception room (which was also the men's room) by means of a partition made of reeds or felt. The women spun, wove and saw to the housework while the men looked after the herds and sheared the sheep. Their basic food was again cereals and white cheese.

The houses in the Kurdish villages, like those of the Turkish peasants, were made of unfired bricks which were dried in the sun and covered with reeds or branches mixed with earth. There was a single main room with a section reserved for women behind it. The floor was made of beaten earth. In the centre, a hearth (*tandir*) in the form of an amphora buried in the ground was a symbol of family life. There was no furniture, but cushions, felt carpets and, sometimes, a wooden box. In the mountains, some of them lived in grottoes or in houses on several storeys, where the roof of one formed a terrace for the people above.

Although they were similar to the Turks in their everyday way of life and their religion – most were Sunni Muslims – the Kurds were by no means completely incorporated into the sultan's empire by the end of the 16th century. The conquest had only just been completed. Selim I had occupied the country in 1516–17, although he had allowed most of the Kurdish *beys* to retain their autonomy. Suleiman had reinforced his authority over the country during the Two Iraqs Campaign, but large areas were still of uncertain loyalty and would often change their allegiance between the sultan and the shah according to the whims of local chiefs who everywhere remained powerful. The population recognized only these chiefs as their leaders for a long time. The disturbances continued until the Safavid dynasty became weaker and finally disappeared, leaving the Ottomans as sole masters of Eastern Anatolia.

The Christians

Scattered throughout the empire, the Christians were far from being a negligible quantity. In Rumelia, a large majority were Orthodox – Serbs, Bulgarians, Greeks and others. In Anatolia, they were Armenians. For the Christians of Eastern Anatolia, Ottoman occupation hardly changed their everyday lives; for those of Europe, it improved them.

The Ottomans demanded only that taxes be paid and that peace be maintained. Religious liberty was complete, and life and property were protected. Habits and customs continued as in the past. Religion and superstition were combined: semi-Christian and semi-pagan festivals divided the year with rest days and joyful family occasions. Easter was the most important holiday, drawing on traditions which dated back a long way into the pagan past: a candle was brought in flame back to the house, and eggs were dyed red – some were kept as a charm against illnesses. On the feast of Saint George, the arrival of spring was celebrated just as it was by Muslims. These feast days were also similar in their combination of meals, singing and dancing, some of which recalled Islamic dances. Births, marriages and, above all, funerals were noisily celebrated. Screams and groans accompanied the body to the cemetery, until the moment when cooked wheat and dried fruit were eaten in the person's memory.

Each village had its priest, as poor as and hardly better educated than his flock, as well as an old woman who would avert the evil eye and cure the sick. There was a general fear of the supernatural and never enough formulas, incantations and appeals for help from 'he who knows' to exorcize malevolent spirits. People came from far and wide to places of pilgrimage, tombs of 'saints' and 'sacred' fountains. Since there were no inns, they would sleep in neighbouring churches. Men and women were equally intrepid and sometimes whole villages came to blows in bloody battles between Armenians and Kurds.

Their dwellings differed little from those of the Muslims: a large room built of unfired brick, a stable, a kitchen-garden, fields all around. Many of the Armenians lived in grottoes which were either natural or dug out of the hills, as did some of the Muslims in the same area. In every hearth there was an icon, before which a flame burnt night and day.

They cultivated the land and raised cattle with the same primitive implements and the same methods as the Muslims. The women spun and wove, saw to the housework, while the men performed the rest of the work. Language and religion made very little difference to the life they led. In some areas, rearing animals was dominant, elsewhere agriculture. Here and there, in Greece, in some parts of the Balkans, in Anatolia itself, wine was produced; the resinated wine of Chios is just one example. Along the coast, Greeks dived for sponges or fish to be sold dry, but the principal occupation by far was agriculture, as it has remained until very recently, which provided men with both food to eat and a way of making a living.

The Distant Provinces

Even further from the centres of power, other peoples lived under the *padishah*'s dominance in autonomous or frontier provinces and vassal principalities.

These peoples – it would take too long to describe them all – lived under the Ottoman Empire just as they lived before, and most of them were hardly concerned about the authorities which governed them from a distant capital. Many knew of only their traditional chiefs, the customs and regulations which had always been theirs. The Ottomans turned a blind eye to all this, provided that taxes regularly filled the state coffers and there was no threat to peace. They rarely intervened, although they showed no restraint when they did so. The Turkomans and Druzes were among the most quarrelsome, the Bedouins the greatest thieves. Everyone had weapons of some sort, even though firearms were prohibited. In this domain too, the authorities often preferred not to intervene and often let the tribes themselves take responsibility for maintaining good order – in return for tax exemptions – rather than trying to bring them to heel by force.

The domination of Constantinople often consisted of no more than the presence of a governor, judges, financial agents and, of course, a garrison, and these merely controlled the system of organization which had been in place before the conquest and which the Ottomans never modified. The governors of these provinces received a fixed salary and not the income from a fund (*hass*). The sultan was content merely to receive a fixed tribute, once local expenses had been deducted, and to raise the contingents of an army when he needed to. Egypt, for example, sent the sultan a sum of 400,000–800,000 gold pieces a year in the 16th century, as well as large quantities of goods in kind: sugar, rice, tow, saltpetre, etc. With the exception of a few areas like Iraq and Syria, where the *timar* system had been instituted, all the Arab provinces were treated in the same way. In remote or unattainable parts of the empire – Armenia, Kurdistan, the North of Albania, among certain Turkoman tribes in the centre of Anatolia – tribal chiefs continued to enjoy almost complete autonomy. Elsewhere, existing principalities were attached to the Ottoman state by more or less strong ties of vassalage such as the *beylerbeylik* of Algeria, Tunis and Tripoli, and the Crimean khanate ruled by Genghis Khan's Giray dynasty. The Sharif of Mecca retained his autonomy, as did the Christian states of Eastern Europe: Moldavia, Wallachia, Montenegro and Transylvania.

Urban Life

The towns of the Ottoman Empire had come into existence and developed under the most diverse historical circumstances and were often hundreds of kilometres apart, yet they were all products of the same civilization – Islam – which had in time stamped them with its particular character and made them quite different from the cities of Western Europe or the non-Muslim cities of South-East Asia or the Far East.

In the Great Turk's empire as in other Islamic states, the different districts of the town were organized to a standard plan. In the centre was the great mosque, a sacred and privileged place, and the focus of the spiritual and intellectual life of the town. Round about were streets full of shops, the bazaar, the *han* and the baths, followed, in a hierarchical order which was observed fairly strictly, by the noblest forms of trade: bookshops, sellers of incense, perfumes, silk goods, and then shops for leather craftsmen, carpets, jewels, material, etc. Finally, at the very edge of the circle, were the most despised and foul-smelling occupations: curriers, dyers, etc. Every profession was concentrated in a particular district, except, for example, the bakers, who were scattered around the city for obvious reasons of convenience. Further out were the residential districts with their gardens and then the humbler dwellings of people who had recently arrived from the country and were still farmers as much as citizens. Last of all came the cemeteries, which often took up a large area, and sometimes ramparts with gates which were closed for the night.

As in the capital, the population was grouped by ethnic origin and religion. The guilds, the only kind of organization permitted by the authorities, played a role of the first importance. Their leaders were responsible for the taxes of their members, for their conduct, and for making sure they respected the regulations. Even more than in Istanbul, there were strong links between the guilds and orders that individuals belonged to, at least in certain areas. The authorities kept an eye on all this but only intervened when there was a threat to public order. The janissaries formed the police force in large or medium-sized towns, but the *timariotes* were responsible for keeping order in those which were smaller.

Public order and provisioning were both assured, but there was no form of municipal organization. The *muhtesib* was responsible for the markets, and that was all. No officials looked after the state of the roads or encroachments on public land. Everybody did more or less as he wished. The result of this struck the French traveller Thévenot: 'Each person took over all the space he wanted for building, without considering if he blocked a road or not.'[4] In Muslim towns, there was no community spirit. Religion was predominant and sectarian and ethnic loyalties took first place. There was no sense of the city as a whole; commitment to one's 'community' or 'district' was central, which meant that nobody ever tried to beautify the city; still less, if possible, was there any town planning.

The roads were laid down without any preconceived plan. But, until the last years of Suleiman's reign, in provincial towns just as in Istanbul, the great avenues inherited from the Byzantine age had more or less survived. The decadence of urban life had brought with it the decay of buildings and a decline in population. The economic and demographic take-off which followed, especially from the second half of the 16th century, was reflected in further development of towns, yet this proceeded in a disorderly fashion and with an absence of regulations which approached complete anarchy, as can be seen in Turkish towns to this very day. We have to wait until the beginning of the 19th century to see the first systematic attempts at urbanization in the capital, later in most of the provincial towns, and as late as the 1960s and even 1970 in Eastern Anatolia. Even in the modern era, the Turkish provincial towns were a network of alleys, where two people could only just pass. Maintenance was non-existent: cesspools in winter and piles of dust in summer. Westerners, whose cities were hardly salubrious at that time, found the Turkish ones still worse. Tavernier speaks of the quantity of water lying stagnant in Smyrna: 'If care had been taken to let it run away, the plague would not have broken out so often.'[5]

The houses were built almost everywhere, in the provinces as in Istanbul, of light and fragile material: wood and *pisé* in the areas near forests, which meant that the fires which sometimes swept whole districts posed an immense threat; just *pisé* elsewhere. Both kinds had replaced the Byzantine and Mediterranean houses of brick and stone which, unlike Arab buildings, were made of solid materials to last forever (except, of course, in the poor districts). Some houses included a ground floor made of wood, with the upper floors consisting of a wooden frame filled with *pisé* or red brick, as in the Ankara region. Around Konya, on the other hand, houses were made of unfired brick with a flat roof covered with a layer of earth.

Blocks of flats housing several families were very rare except in the overpopulated areas of North Africa and Egypt, in centres of pilgrimage like Mecca – or in Jedda, where buildings no doubt very similar to those of three to four centuries ago still survive. They did not contain an interior courtyard or, if they did, it was very small and opened on to the road either through a bay or through oriel windows decorated with *moushrabieh*. Low houses predominated in the whole Muslim world, although the plan varied according to the demands of the climate, local resources and even pre-Islamic traditions.

In Anatolia, the town houses consisted of a single storey and were divided into two parts: the summer and winter residence, or the men's (*selamlik*) and women's (*haremlik*) quarters. The latter were usually on the ground floor, had narrow windows and faced the interior, where the court, garden and kitchen were to be found. The upper floor, reached by a wooden staircase, faced the road with bay windows (*cumba*), so one could look out without being seen. It was there that the Turkish women had for centuries (and, in many towns, still do) rested, sewed, chatted and watched the passers-by. In cold areas, where the winters were long, the fire meant that the kitchen was treated as the main room (*tandir*). In the southern regions, the coolest rooms which received most air were used instead, while people slept on the terrace during the hottest nights. In the Balkan towns recently conquered by the Ottomans, to whom they owed all their development, the immigrant Turkish population had more or less completely adapted their traditional forms of housing to the demands of the climate and local materials. The native inhabitants of these areas continued their traditional way of life and styles of housing alongside the Turks, although they were also influenced by them in the long run.

The main room (*baş oda*), more decorated than the others, always included a platform along the walls, with a divan, lots of cushions, carpets and *kilim*, where people sat cross-legged. At the height of a man, there were niches, where everyday objects were kept, as well as shelves and cupboards, where the bedclothes and blankets taken out the night before were stored in the morning. A chimney made of plaster was used for making a fire, so that there at least they could dispense with a *mangal* or brazier, the only means of heating the other rooms or those houses without chimneys. It was carried from room to room with the charcoal burning; in winter, so as to lose as little heat as possible, it was covered with a large blanket which everyone would pull up to their chin, if possible, and lie under. It is easy to imagine the dangers of fire and suffocation that this kind of heating posed. In richer households, the main room was often decorated with drawings, mouldings and, later, naive paintings. The doors were inlaid with mother of pearl. The other rooms were simpler, with only cupboards for bedding. There was no furniture, except, sometimes, a few boxes.

Everyday Life

Food was served on trays, usually made of copper, around which people sat with their right knee raised and their left leg flat on the floor, which was usually covered with a carpet. The forearm was naked, and people served themselves by pouring their food into a plate, if it was a soup or a liquid dish,[6] or on to slices of bread which were eaten at the end of the meal; the fingers of the right hand were used for meat which had already been cut up. The inhabitants of the towns, just like the country-dwellers, were frugal.[7] The main meal was in the evening: soup, rice, meat and vegetables were consumed by the 'bourgeoisie', although meat was rare in other households. In the morning: bread, cheese and olives. In the middle of the day, the remains of the previous day's evening meal were eaten.

Dishes full of sugar were greatly appreciated: sorbets (*şerbet*), pastries, jams and sweet things of every kind (many based on milk products and honey). Like fruit, these were served on every occasion, although between meals rather than as a desert. The only drink was water on its own or flavoured with a syrup. Wine was never drunk *en famille*. In theory Muslims were not allowed to drink it, and although they did not totally deprive themselves, wine and *raki* (a kind of anisette liqueur) were only drunk in taverns. This went on a good deal less in the provinces than in Constantinople. Such drinks were made by the minorities or imported from abroad, and Christians throughout Anatolia – even in Erzurum, if we are to believe Tavernier – manufactured them.

Despite minor local or religious differences, life went by at more or less the same rhythm in towns throughout the empire, punctuated by the same festivals and the same joyous and unhappy family events, mainly circumcisions, marriages and funerals. The two major religious festivals, the *Kurban Bayram* and the *Şeker Bayram*, were also universally celebrated.

Circumcision normally took place between the ages of 7 and 12. The surgeon-barber usually performed the operation on several boys in the family at the same time to reduce expenses – friends and relatives would be invited to meals and the traditional festivities. A 'rite of passage' which was not accompanied by any religious ritual, circumcision was nonetheless the major event of a boy's youth. It was then that he became a man, although he remained under the authority of his father, who would take his education in hand and decide when it was time for him to marry.

The father decided, and yet it was the mother who set in motion the sometimes complicated plans which brought to their house the girl who would perpetuate the family name. Usually she had already given some thought to the matter and drawn up a list of potential daughters-in-law in her mind. If the girl was not the daughter of a close friend, a third party always acted as intermediary, and an interview was arranged at the house belonging to the parents of the bride-to-be. If this 'visit' was not followed up, the parents would visit another girl, and then perhaps a third, until they had found the treasure they sought. The parents made the choice and not the young people, who were not required to give their consent or even express an opinion. Gifts were exchanged, the contract signed in the presence of the *imam* and two witnesses, the date for the start of festivities agreed. These lasted a week, with each day marked by celebrations – display of presents, decoration of the houses, processions in the street – which were essentially designed to demonstrate the wealth and good breeding of the families involved. When people from a humbler background got married, festivities were much reduced and the young bride went to live with her in-laws on the day the marriage contract was signed. The second marriages of widows or repudiated wives were celebrated with ceremonies which were a great deal less impressive.

Funerals in Ottoman Turkey, as in all Islamic countries, were always very simple: man is dust, and only God is great. Burial took place on the very day of or morning after a death, with only a brief procession round the court of the mosque when the coffin was placed on a stone table reserved for the purpose. The *imam* or a close relative read a few verses from the Koran and then the corpse was taken to the burial place, preferably near the tomb of a 'saint'. The corpse was placed in the earth without a coffin, propped up on the right side and with the head facing Mecca. Later, a tombstone was set up above the head, often with a sculpted reproduction of the turban worn by the deceased. Tombs were not maintained – it is this which gives the major cemeteries of Turkey, with their headstones leaning over and their sombre cypress trees, an atmosphere of abandon and melancholy which so many writers and artists have found poetic and charming.

In the age of Suleiman as well as before and after, the Ottomans carried on their daily life, in the capital and in the country, without haste. They would get up with the sun and then, after their daily ablutions and breakfast, go to their shops or studios on foot or on a donkey. Work was interrupted, for the Muslims, by the mid-day and afternoon prayers and the frugal lunch they ate on the spot. They returned home at nightfall. They would eat their evening meal and say their prayers before going early to bed. The houses were illuminated by cotton wicks soaked in oil, which gave out a light too feeble to permit work of any kind. They got up again at dawn on the following day.

The only nights of the year which were filled with activity were those of Ramadan. People went to listen to the story-tellers (*meddah*) who recited ancient Turkish legends, miraculous and epic stories, and the singers (*saz şairleri*) who composed and sang poems accompanied by a sort of rudimentary guitar called a *saz*. Best of all, they went to see the shadow puppets which were the first signs of a kind of theatre which would develop into the *karagoz*[8] in the following century. The mosques were lit up and festivities went on late into the night, until the moment at the break of day when a signal announced that the fast had to start again.

When the 28 days of fasting had gone by, life returned to its normal pace, which was more or less monotonous depending on the importance of the town and its distance from the centres of power. When a vizier, and even more the sultan, passed by, it was a considerable, and generally unwelcome, event, since it almost always led to disturbance and expenses (requisitions, duties) which formed an addition to taxes most people could well have done without.

The inhabitants of the towns, like the country-dwellers, naturally paid taxes. In theory, but unfortunately only in theory, the only legally permitted taxes were those sanctioned by holy law, the so-called *şeri* (derived from the *Şeriat*) taxes: the tax on non-Muslims (*ciziye*), one-fifth of the loot obtained during war, the tribute paid by the Christian vassal states, customs duties, tithes, duties paid by mines and salt-works, etc. But these sources of revenue had long ceased to cover all the state expenses, and other taxes were therefore added. These were known as *orfi* (or taxes deriving from the authorities) and sometimes '*Divan* taxes' (*avaridi divaniye*).

These were levied with the consent of the *Divan* whenever they were needed or when the sultan was preparing a major military expedition (like Suleiman before the Mohacs campaign). They then quickly became permanent as the requirements of palace and state increased. Among them were the taxes imposed on 'hearths' or households, divided into three classes (rich, average and poor); those, in particular, for services rendered, which were very numerous; taxes paid for formalities dealt with by the functionaries (which meant that the state did not have to pay them); taxes levied on travellers in certain regions for the care and maintenance of roads and bridges, on ships before they raised anchor, etc.

The traders were not spared. They paid a 'shop tax' (*yevmiyei dukakin*), a 'market duty' (*baçi pazar*) payable on all the merchandise sold in the town markets and a 'stamp duty' (*damga resmi*) guaranteeing the good quality, and the weight or size of manufactured goods.

These taxes were far from being the same throughout the empire. In some regions, pre-Ottoman taxes were retained, elsewhere they were abolished or greatly modified. The duties which were most resented were abolished. Commercial taxes were everywhere payable to the *muhtesib*, a municipal official responsible for overseeing the artisans, traders and corporations as well as for assessment of local taxes on trade and distribution of goods.

There were many duties to pay – to set them all out would make an impressive list – but they seem to have generally been accepted without too much complaint,[9] at least until the time of the economic crisis at the end of the 16th century. In the Ottoman Empire, as everywhere else and in every age, taxes were light while the country was prosperous and became much more of a burden when that prosperity came to an end.

The Asian Towns

The towns of the empire, like the capital, benefited from the upheavals in economic life in the 'golden years' of the century and then from the wealth generated by the development of trade with the interior of the country and foreign countries. Their population, especially in Anatolia, increased. Thus, in the course of the 46 years comprising Suleiman's reign, the South-West region (bordered by the Aegean coast, a line going West to East from Manisa to Kayseri and a line going North to South from there to the sea) saw an increase in the urban population from

115,000 to 300,000. In many of the large and medium-sized towns, the population sometimes even tripled, but it generally increased by only about 50% in the smaller towns.

What were the reasons for this great demographic boom in the towns? The development of the economy was of central importance, of course. The urban centres which expanded most rapidly were those on the important trade routes, especially if they were near major agricultural regions. Such activities had a far more powerful impact on the expansion of towns than the administrative or political role they were called upon to play, even if they were residences of imperial princes before they came to the throne. This applied, for example, to Amasya and Manisa, where Suleiman was governor from 1512 to 1520. Amasya possessed numerous religious foundations, some beautiful mosques and twenty-one *medrese*, yet never attained the status of a large town. At the end of the 16th century, however, the flight of peasants to the towns also contributed to the increase in urban populations.

In the 16th century, Bursa was far and away the most populous town in Anatolia. At the time of Suleiman, the population varied, according to the period, from 50,000 to 70,000 inhabitants. This may be small compared to the population of Istanbul (500,000–700,000) but was rather larger than that of most of the other urban centres. Kayseri, for example, was relatively important, since it had 35,000–40,000 inhabitants at the end of the century. Between 1500 and 1550, it had quadrupled in size and gone a long way past 30,000, although the reasons for this are not absolutely clear (it was probably largely because of its position at the crossroads of East-West and North-South commercial routes and at the centre of a major agricultural region). Huge caravanserai, a large bazaar, a *bedesten*, a market where cereals, cotton, wine, honey and merchandise coming from Istanbul, Iran and India were traded, made Kayseri, at the end of Suleiman's reign, the most important town in the interior of Anatolia.

Ankara (20,000–25,000 inhabitants) came next. This too was an important commercial centre whence goats' wool (angora) was sent great distances, even to Europe. After that, among the medium-sized urban centres (10,000–20,000 inhabitants), came Tokat, an important staging post for caravans described by Tavernier as 'one of the major towns of passage in the Orient . . . and one of the best towns in Turkey',[10] Sivas, Urfa, Ain Tabus, Kastamonu. Most of the others, including the principal towns of their *sancak*, were really large villages which were slowly to become medium-sized towns: Aksaray, Karahisar, Konya,

Manisa, Tire, etc. A few years later, Demirci, Eregli, Niğde, Akşehir, Bor, Karaman, Uluborlu, Seydişehir and Ermenek were added to the list. Some continued to increase in size, others remained sleepy backwaters. Very few suffered a decline.

More than international commerce, which mainly affected the trading centres of the coastal region and the larger caravan staging posts, trading within Turkey kept going a lively pace of economic activity which did not dry up even in the 18th century. If a small town was on a much used route, if people from the neighbouring countryside got into the habit of going there to sell their produce, if crafts were started and developed, and especially if the quality of manufacture created specialities, then the town would soon acquire a name which would attract a much larger population: the inhabitants of less fortunate towns; peasants who left land which hardly provided them with enough to eat; janissaries, who, towards the end of the century, saw their income whittled away by devaluations and were looking for a more lucrative profession. Until the middle of the 19th century, the towns and villages of Anatolia continued to play their particular roles and maintained a system of production which, despite reversals of fortune and differing local conditions, provided a livelihood and, usually, prosperity to their inhabitants despite the economic invasion by Europe.

The prosperity of Bursa, at the foot of Mysian Mount Olympus, and one of the Turkish towns which has retained the most charm, dated back far into the past. In 1431, Bertrandon de la Broquière said: 'That town of Bursa is a very good town and a centre of trading – the best town the Turk has.' In the 16th century, Pierre Belon added: 'Bursa's wealth is derived from silk.' It was indeed true that it was silk from Persia by way of Tabriz, Erzurum and Tokat which had first brought wealth to the town. Then came trade in spices, perfumes, sugar imported from Egypt and Syria, and pepper. All these products were sent to Istanbul or exported to the Balkans and Eastern Europe. The Genoese, Venetians and Florentines obtained silk in return for the woollen material they brought, but much of the silk from Gilan and other parts of Persia near the Caspian Sea was worked in Bursa itself by local industry. There were more than a thousand looms there at the beginning of the 16th century, and they all belonged to Turkish Muslims. The sumptuous brocades, velvets and taffetas were used in the sultan's court or sold to Europe. Brusa, as the Europeans called Bursa, also exported cotton goods made in Anatolia to the Balkans. Traders and manufacturers made huge profits and the state took an equally huge slice in taxes. As the seat of the empire from 1326 to 1402, Bursa was always considered, with Constantinople and Edirne, as one of the three capitals of the empire, and the sultans in the 16th and 17th centuries often stayed in the ancient palace there, which was maintained in style. The decline of Bursa, which had already been affected by the wars between the Safavids and the House of Osman in the 16th century, began in earnest when the countries of Europe started to manufacture silk and, above all, with the rapid expansion of Smyrna in the 17th century.[11]

In the Middle East, Aleppo was the empire's major commercial town. Already in Mamluk days, the collapse of the Genoese trading posts on the Black Sea and, a century earlier, the end of the Armenian kingdom in Cilicia had made it one of the most important points of arrival for the caravans from Persia. The town had subsequently been transformed: populous suburbs all along the caravan routes had soon doubled the surface area of the town; beautiful monuments were built and many Christians (Armenians and Maronites) had come to act as intermediaries and dragomans of foreign traders. Selim I's conquest in 1516–17, which incorporated the whole of Syria into a rich and powerful empire and opened up a market of international importance, increased still further the importance of Aleppo at the same time as it brought almost all trade with Iran under Ottoman control. Shortly afterwards, the capitulations granted to foreign governments attracted foreign traders: the Venetians and French, then the English and Dutch, established commercial outposts there. A little later, the rise of Smyrna as a rival trading centre was a major blow for Aleppo, but it still remained the place where European manufactured products arrived (materials, paper, glass) for re-export to Persia and Eastern Anatolia; cotton and silk goods made by the town's industries as well as the raw materials produced in neighbouring districts were also exported from there. The *han* and souks which were built at the time are among the most beautiful in the Islamic world.

'Aleppo is one of the most famous towns of Turkey as much for its grandeur and beauty as for the goodness of its air, not to mention the abundance of goods of every kind and the quantity of trade with all the nations of the earth which takes place there,' Tavernier wrote a little later. The famous trader and traveller never abated in his eulogies of the city, which possessed, he said, 120 mosques, 40 caravanserai, 50 public baths and a population of 250,000 (a great exaggeration). 'One cannot get bored in such a large and beautiful town,' he added, 'which is surely the most considerable in the Turkish empire after Constantinople and Cairo.'

Next to Aleppo, Damascus seemed like a small town, although it too had increased in size as a result of the capitulations. Many *han* for travellers and their merchandise were built then. But ever since the Ottomans had brought peace to the shores of the Red Sea, Damascus's prosperity depended largely on pilgrims to Mecca, who came from all the northern countries of the empire and assembled in Damascus before setting off across the desert. It was there that they bought provisions for three months, mounts and equipment for the difficult journey. When they returned, they sold what they had brought back from Arabia, mainly coffee and black slaves. Suleiman the Magnificent gave orders for a great mosque to be built to the plans laid down by the architect Sinan. Later, other beautiful monuments were added to those inherited from the Omayyads and Ayyubids, which helped to make Damascus what it still remains, one of the most attractive towns of the Orient.

The towns of Egypt in the middle of the 16th century recovered part – but only part – of the prosperity they had enjoyed at the apogee of the Mamluk Empire, when gold was flowing on the roofs and doors of the great palace. The years which preceded the arrival of the Ottomans were a period of upheaval and decadence which were only aggravated by Portuguese inroads into the Indian Ocean. Selim's conquests of the Nile territory, and then the administrative and judicial reorganization instigated a few years later by the Grand Vizier Ibrahim, brought back peace and good order. The economic crisis gave way to recovery. Soon Cairo and Alexandria became trading centres where pepper, spices, pearls and black and white slaves were brought for export. As in all other countries they occupied, the Ottomans built mosques, fountains and buildings for charitable works. In 1518, Hadim Suleiman Pasha added the splendid Citadel Mosque to those inherited from the Mamluks; a few years later, Iskender Pasha built a second mosque and a monastery for dervishes. Their successors built fountains, *tekke* and *imaret*.

Alexandria, whose almost desolate state struck so many travellers (such as Thénaud in 1511), seemed to be dressed in its splendid ruins as in clothes which were far too big for it. The increase in trade linked to the *pax Ottomanica*, however, was to create a new period of prosperity: in 1560, such quantities of pepper came to Alexandria that Lisbon was left with practically none at all. Yet twenty years later the Portuguese traders regained their edge and were in turn followed by the English and Dutch, always at the expense of the Egyptian intermediaries.

The Towns of Rumelia

In the Balkans and the Danube territories, the Ottoman occupation eliminated the political and economic barriers which had kept states apart and suppressed the privileges of the feudal lords; this almost at once brought to the towns a level of development and prosperity which had been quite unknown until then. From the early years of the 15th century, the population began to increase as much because of the waves of immigrants from Asia Minor as because of the movement of country-dwellers into the towns. Many of the newly arrived Muslims were Yuruk (Anatolian nomads) and Tartars, whom the authorities preferred to install in the stategically important areas in the East of the Balkan peninsula and along the communication routes.

The character of the population was also altered by conversions to Islam and the arrival in certain towns of Jews expelled from Spain and Marranos (converted Jews) escaping persecution in Portugal, the South of France, and Italy. Almost everywhere, the Christians remained in a majority, often a large majority, except where the occupiers had built towns for administrative or political reasons or where Muslims had long been dominant. It would not, however, be correct to say that the local population had been driven out of the plains into the mountains – the non-Muslims never ceased to play an active role in economic life.

In the 15th and 16th centuries, the ancient routes became 'living arteries' where much of the trade not only between Constantinople and the subject provinces but between the Balkan territories themselves, the Danube territories and even Russia took place. Active relations were established between the Bulgarian and Romanian areas, which were only to develop with time. The constantly increasing demands of Istanbul required enormous quantities of products of every kind which were transported across the Black Sea, along the rivers (Maritsa, Struma) and overland, with all the predictable consequences for villages and towns of a constant stream of men and merchandise. The route from Ragusa to Istanbul by way of Novi Pazar and Edirne, for example, acquired an importance all the greater because much of the trade with Italy and the neighbouring areas of Europe used it. In Bosnia-Herzegovina alone, 332 inns, 18 *han*, 32 hotels, 10 *bedesten* and 42 bridges were built during the Ottoman period.[12]

Travellers since the 15th century who passed through these regions of Europe when they were under Ottoman control evoke for us the intense activity in the towns, the buildings in Oriental style to be seen there, and the abundance of craft and agricultural products. According to Contarini, who wrote at the end of the 16th century, the objects and weapons manufactured in Sofia 'would be enough to equip a large army'.

The towns situated on the major strategic routes, as well as those which became important administrative centres, soon became prosperous. Crafts, dominated at first by the newly arrived Turks, were spurred on by the needs of the Ottoman army and administration and therefore developed rapidly. Whole regions saw their activities completely transformed.

In Bulgaria, for example, which occupied a sort of central position in the Ottoman European possessions in the 16th century, commerce and crafts were displaced from the North and North-East of the country towards the South. Economic contacts between towns and villages developed, since the latter had now to provide food for a large population of soldiers and administrators and obtain the raw materials their craftsmen needed.

Buda was transformed in this way by the Ottoman occupation, by the large Turkish garrison which was installed there and, still more, by the presence of numerous Muslims. Almost all were Islamicized Slavs who replaced a local population which, before the arrival of the Ottomans, consisted of fewer than 5,000 people (most of whom emigrated). Buda then took on the appearance of an Oriental town, with the development of Turkish crafts, the building of mosques and *hammam*, and the extension of the Muslim districts.

Many other towns in the European part of the Ottoman Empire, at the time of Suleiman and his immediate successors, deserve to be described. Salonica was one of the most active ports, 'where one saw huge Turkish and foreign ships putting to shore all the time'. The population had increased rapidly with the arrival of Jews and Marranos who had been expelled from Spain and Portugal. At the beginning of the 16th century they were in a majority, with at least 15,000 of them and only 7,000 Muslims and 5,000–6,000 Christians. They made Salonica into one of the major commercial centres of the Eastern Mediterranean. They enjoyed an almost complete monopoly of the wool trade and sold 'Salonica cloth' all over the empire. Since they had large quantities of capital at their disposal, they were able to develop their financial activities and credit facilities. Smederevo had started as a powerful fortress and base for Ottoman operations to the West, but it too later became a major commercial centre. Niš was described by Lady Mary Wortley Montagu as having 'so fruitful a soil that the great plenty is hardly credible'. Athens had more than 12,000 inhabitants from the very beginning of the century, almost all Christian. Then there were several other towns, including Edirne, the greatest in Rumelia and one of the most important communication centres in the empire.

Edirne is on the main route from Asia Minor to the Balkans and the Danube territories, the first major stop after Istanbul and a mobilization centre for the Ottoman armies in Europe. It had taken over from Bursa as the capital of the empire – from 1402 to the capture of Constantinople – and was now, in the 16th century, at the height of its prosperity. As in all the large towns in the Ottoman Empire – and in the whole Islamic world – there was a clear hierarchy of wealth. At the top were the money-changers, jewellers, businessmen (often important officials) who invested in foreign trade; next came the manufacturers and traders in cloth (exporters and importers), owners of large properties who cultivated and sold cereals; and, finally, there were the artisans (tanners, manufacturers of soap and rose-water), who produced mainly for the army and the Balkan countries. There were more than twenty *han* and covered markets in Edirne in the 16th century (several are still in existence). French and English merchants took up residence. Beautiful monuments were built. It was there that the Selimiye, the 'glory of Edirne' and Sinan's masterpiece, was erected in the years following the death of Suleiman. It was also an important religious and intellectual centre with more than 50 *zaviye* and *tekke*; the *medrese* there were famous for their teaching. Many travellers have described their impressions of the beautiful town.

Lady Mary Wortley Montagu described its commercial district at the start of the 18th century in the following terms: 'The exchange . . . is half a mile in length, the roof arched, and kept extremely neat. It holds 365 shops furnished with all sort of rich goods exposed to sale in the same manner as at the New Exchange in London, but the pavement kept much neater . . . Near it is the shershi [*çarşi*], a street of a mile in length, full of shops of all kind of fine merchandise . . . The Bisisten [*bedesten*] near it is another exchange, built upon pillars . . . glittering every where with gold, rich embroidery and jewels, [it] makes a very agreeable shew.'[13] The wife of the English ambassador to the Great Lord wrote this description at a time which hardly counted as one of the most prosperous in Ottoman history.

In Bulgaria, the major centres at the time were Sofia, where there had been a large increase in the number of Muslims and a 100% increase in the population between 1530 and 1580; Filibe was also on the route to Ragusa; Silistra was situated on the way to the lower Danube and Wallachia; Vidin, Ruse and Varna, all ports where the population had tripled, clearly reflected the economic dynamism of the golden years of the century. Nikopol (Nicopolis), Velika Turnovo and Sliven also got bigger; Skopje doubled in size. In all these towns, crafts and commerce expanded rapidly. New industries, notably textiles and felt-making, were created, especially in the new Muslim districts (Bulgaria was one of the regions most rapidly and strongly 'Turkified'). Cereals, rice, wood and mutton were sent in great quantities to Istanbul and the rest of the empire. The peace the sultan had brought to the region – there were no invasions or major uprisings there between 1450 and 1595 – favoured prosperity and dramatic population increases.

During the same period, Bosnia developed its crafts and commerce under the influence of immigrants who had come in large numbers from the Muslim areas of the empire. The second half of the 16th century was a period of rapid expansion favoured by the transit trade with the Italian towns through the intermediary of Ragusa. Agriculture was modernized. Towns like Sarajevo and Banja Luka took on the Oriental appearance they retained for a long time. At the end of the 16th century, Sarajevo was the most populous town; in 50 years the number of inhabitants had quadrupled to reach close to 30,000. Muslims were in the majority, especially since many of the local Christian peasantry converted. The adherence of the feudal lords also favoured Islamicization. Bosnia and Herzegovina were very 'Turkified' and were certainly among the provinces which provided the greatest number of important dignitaries to the empire – the Grand Vizier Sokullu Mehmed was the most famous of them.

Belgrade, the first major conquest achieved by Suleiman, had stagnated for a long while and continued to do so in the early years of Ottoman occupation; it first began to make rapid progress in the middle of the 16th century. At the confluence of the Sava and the Danube on one of the major northward communication routes, it was at that time a trading post of the first importance, an intermediary between the commercial centres of the empire, Central Europe and Northern Europe. The occupation of Buda and then Temesvar led to a further increase in activity. A large proportion of the population – 50,000 Christians and Muslims, with the latter a clear majority – were employed in various crafts. The town was then totally Oriental in appearance: a hundred mosques, as many palaces, numerous *han, hammam, medrese*, although there were also churches and synagogues. A large garrison of janissaries was stationed here. All travellers gave high praise to its geographical situation and commercial activity, and considered that it counted as a city.

All the towns I have mentioned or described in broad terms played their part, for various reasons, in the huge increase in urban areas (in both Western and Central Europe and throughout the Mediterranean) which were so typical of the 'long 16th century'. Although there were periodic set-backs and crises here and there, and epidemics sometimes decimated the population, demographic growth continued and the accumulation of wealth increased. To the reasons behind the general 'urban boom' at that time must be added others relating specifically to the Ottoman Empire: Selim's conquests in Egypt and the Levant and those of Suleiman in Europe and the Mediterranean. Not only did they bring in great riches; they also led to the creation of new markets and new exchanges of ideas which heightened, for the empire and its towns, the effects of the century's new circumstances 'in which all wounds were healed'.[14]

12
The Age of the Magnificent Sultan

Suleiman's reign was the golden age of Ottoman civilization. He himself was a man of broad culture, with a deep knowledge of the Koran and religious thinking. Like his father,[1] who wrote verses in Osmanli Turkish as well as Çagatai (Oriental Turkish), Suleiman left a *divan* in Persian which reveals a certain talent. Under the name of *Muhibi* (or the Gracious One), he wrote *gazel* which were very classical in form and dealt with the usual themes of the genre: love, the passing of time, the vanity of earthly goods. Even if his lyric gifts hardly surpassed those of many versifiers of the age, his poems nonetheless display a dignity, a grandeur of spirit and a humility hardly to be expected from the pen of so great a monarch.

From the beginning of his reign, the 'new Solomon' had the ambition of leaving to future ages monuments to glorify his name and give his times a reputation for greatness which would eclipse all other epochs past or to come. The title of 'Magnificent' given him by the Europeans is a sign of the astonished admiration the capital of the empire and the sultan's court inspired in Westerners who had only just left behind the economic crises and acute poverty of the 15th century.

Suleiman encouraged all forms of creativity. Artists, poets, theologians, jurists, historians and scientists were all welcomed at the court – almost inexhaustible funds were made available to them by the sultan. A distich which he enjoyed would be lavishly rewarded. Baki, the most perfect lyric poet of the classical age, had worked as an apprentice saddler; a *gazel* which he sent to the sultan on his return from the Persian campaign opened up to him the path to great honours. He rose rapidly through the teaching and judicial hierarchy. Suleiman would send his own poetry for the 'sultan of poets' to read. Hayali, another poet of the age, received a *timar* of 150,000 aspers. Sinan, the great architect, was treated with a respect given to few others. About thirty painters, who mainly produced miniatures, worked permanently at the palace. In a few decades, at the sultan's express desire, buildings of every kind sprang up in the towns, along the roads and by the shores: mosques, *medrese, han*, caravanserai, bridges, aqueducts, hospitals and charitable foundations. Damascus, Baghdad, Mecca, Medina and Jerusalem were all embellished. At Konya, he ordered the construction of a new monastery for dervishes and a mosque near the tomb of the great mystic and poet, Celaleddin Rumi. 'A detailed description of all the buildings erected by Suleiman could provide the material for a book like the one Procopius devoted to the edifices for which Justinian was responsible.'[2]

Architecture

The capital was, of course, the centre for the arts. When Suleiman came to the throne, Istanbul was already a large town. It was further embellished by the mosques he had constructed and the buildings which went up on all sides, but we search in vain for any palaces or edifices which do not have a utilitarian or religious function. There was nothing to compare with the palaces the Western sovereigns were starting to build for themselves in the same period (the 16th century). Topkapi is no Fontainebleau or Hampton Court, nor does it recall the palaces of the Byzantine emperors. It was formed of a combination of pavilions,[3] some of them gracious and charming, which would not have been considered worthy of housing a king or emperor in the old Europe. The sultans looked there for peace and tranquillity among the trees, and so the architecture was very simple – what we would call functional – although not without elegance.

The buildings were constructed in a sober style and were used as offices, schools, for the palace and the sultan's personal services, and as residences for officials; further away and set back were the mass of buildings which formed the Harem and which were added on to each other as need dictated and without any kind of overall plan. The placing of the *koshk* (which gives us our word kiosk) was determined by the beauty of the view or reasons of simple convenience. The Council Room, for example, was placed near the sultan's personal apartments so he could get there easily; the same applied to the room containing the holy relics. The constructions Suleiman added to Topkapi were neither more nor less sumptuous than those built by the other sultans. Just like ordinary mortals, the sultan knew that men and women are destined to spend only a brief time on earth. Their dwellings are just as ephemeral, and there was no point in building for eternity – everything would disappear one day. 'All who live on earth are doomed to die,' he read in the Koran.[4]

This belief in transitoriness inspired Turkish civil architecture until the 19th century: there were no real palaces, no buildings which reflected the greatness and power of the empire. There was a total contrast between the simplicity of the buildings and the luxury of the interior decoration and the general life style. But what mosques they built! What *imaret* to heal and feed the poor, what schools and *medrese* to teach religion and useful knowledge to the young, what works of art to enrich people's lives!

Sinan

One man dominated the architecture of the 16th century: Sinan. Without him, Turkish art would be incomplete and Turkey would not be what it is. According to the most usual view, Sinan was Greek in origin. Born near Kayseri (Caesarea in Cappadocia), he was taken up by the *devşirme* system and received at the palace the usual education given to future officials and elite soldiers. Other sources[5] say he was born in Cappadocia to a Turkish family. It hardly matters: he was born in Turkey, brought up and educated in Turkish schools, and everything about him was Turkish regardless of what blood flowed in his veins. He was probably born in 1491 and lived to be almost 100. After studying, he made his career in the army. He took part in the expedition to Rhodes, the Belgrade campaign and the Battle of Mohacs; he was then appointed captain in the infantry, 'commander of the war machines' and, finally, colonel in the sultan's personal guard. He was almost 50 before he became the court architect.

During his military career, he had constructed bridges and barracks, aqueducts and siege works. Campaigns in the Balkans and the Orient had given him the chance to see the work of foreign architects past and present. During the Persian war, he had enabled the army to cross Lake Van by building boats to his own design. This had attracted Suleiman's admiration, and a bridge over the Danube during the Wallachia campaign consolidated his fame. Who had taught him the art of building? Probably Acemi Ali, the Persian architect Suleiman had brought back from Tabriz.

His secular buildings reveal his talent as an architect, but his genius went exclusively into his mosques. It has often been said that Sinan copied Byzantine architecture and that his mosques were merely variations on the theme of Saint-Sophia, which had been built in the 6th century by two Greeks called Anthemius of Tralles and Isidorus of Miletos. The major Byzantine works, and not only Saint-Sophia, certainly exerted an influence on Sinan and the other Turkish builders.[6] The Ottoman mosques built before and after the conquest of Constantinople are not in the same style. From the first mosques in Bursa to the *Uç Şerefeli cami* in Edirne (*cami* means mosque), their earliest attempts all bear witness to the constant efforts of leading Turkish builders to resolve the problems posed by all monumental, and particularly religious, buildings: the 'interior space' and the balance between the interior and exterior surfaces. Saint-Sophia and other Byzantine churches helped them to find solutions, and they assimilated and adapted the Byzantine style, but they did not copy it: before 1453, and even before the Turkish arrival in Asia Minor, there had existed a Turkish style which conformed to national traditions and developed, like all artistic styles, under the influence of the other styles it came into contact with.[7]

The earliest Turkish mosques, in the 12th and 13th centuries (the Seljuk era), were fairly similar to those which had already been built in other countries in the Muslim world, notably in Khorasan (occupied by the Seljuks from the beginning of the 11th century). These were hypostyle (that is to say, colonnaded) mosques, completely lacking in unity or any sense of harmony between the interior and exterior, with a large and lavishly decorated portal. In Konya, the five naves of the Alaeddin mosque were separated by 50 columns; the portal seemed tacked on to a building it could easily have not belonged to. But the cupola above the *mihrab*[8] was the first example in which a circular foundation formed the base for a square structure by means of the *trompe l'oeil* angles which became one of the characteristic features of Seljuk architecture. This kind of cupola was destined to be one of the principal elements in future mosques. At Divriği, the *mihrab*'s cupola increased in importance: the most characteristic part of the building, it was divided into twelve segments by ribs and surmounted by a pyramid resting on an octagonal tambour. On the portal was an extraordinary profusion of leaves, cartouches, discs and cylindrical mouldings. The monument was unique in Turkey and certainly showed traces of exotic, perhaps Indian, influences.

In the following era, the age of the principalities, there was intense artistic and intellectual activity, and the concept of interior space appeared for the first time. It was to be the dominant theme of architectural experimentation in the 16th century. There was a development towards greater unity, greater balance between the interior and exterior: the cupola above the *mihrab* grew larger, the number of columns diminished. There were twelve in the great mosque of Bursa but only four in the *Eski cami* in Edirne. In the middle of the 15th century, the *Uç Şerefeli* mosque in Edirne showed the beginning of a solution. There was a great cupola (24.1 metres in diameter, 28 metres high) and no more than four small cupolas. The great cupola leaned on buttresses and its base rested on columns. This created a higher, broader and more concentrated space. Portals and ornaments using vegetal motifs became less common; the facade became barer and was covered with plain sheets of marble; windows were used to keep a balance between relief and recessed surfaces. There were more minarets (four at Edirne) and the exterior court was incorporated into the mosque. This evolution had almost attained perfection in the classical Ottoman mosque, which appeared with Bayezid's mosque in Istanbul at the start of the 16th century.

At the *Bayezid cami*, a great cupola 18 metres in diameter together with two semi-cupolas covered the whole prayer chamber. It rested on four square pillars. Its base was pierced by 34 semi-circular windows. The court was surrounded by porticoes supporting 24 small cupolas and formed a harmonious unit with the prayer chamber. Balance between the interior and exterior had almost been attained. But the two semi-cupolas, in front of and behind the great cupola, were flat and the East and West facades of the building were bare. The disposal of volumes in the form of a pyramid did not yet exist. But while Saint-Sophia was already starting to exert an influence, the memory of these mosques from the principalities era continued, although rather less strongly, to do the same.

It was at this point that Sinan appeared on the scene. With the building of the *Şehzade* mosque for Suleiman as a memorial to his son Mehmed, 'Sinan had already raised to a higher level the style of primitive Ottoman architecture'[9]. The typical pyramid-shaped mosque was now emerging. At 37 metres above the ground and with a diameter of 19 metres, the cupola was no mere 'covering' for the building; the whole structure of the edifice seemed rather to flow out of it as if it gave birth to the arches and semi-cupolas; indeed, it seemed to be the initial element of the whole structure. In places where supports were needed, Sinan tried to give an impression of balance by embellishing them with stalactites, which seemed to be sculpted in wood, a decorative motif inherited from the Seljuks. Minarets of great delicacy and beautiful proportions were built. A few years later, in the mosque built by Mihrimah, the daughter of Suleiman and Roxelane, Sinan borrowed even more elements from Byzantine architecture while stripping his own style down to the bare bones; it sometimes makes one think, writes U. Vogt-Göknil, of 'a thin shell made of porcelain, giving an impression of lightness and limitless expanse hardly at all like an architectural construction'.

With the *Suleimaniye*, the large and impressive mosque in Istanbul to which Suleiman gave his name, Sinan took another step towards perfection. He chose, oddly enough, a plan very similar to that of Saint-Sophia in order, it is said, to beat the Greek architects on their own ground. He varied plain and spherical surfaces, combining semi-cupolas with tympanums and thus giving the impression of a 'cut diamond', as if the edifice were cut out of a cube. The cupola was 26.5 metres in diameter, nearly 48 metres above the ground, and flanked by only two semi-cupolas – which emphasized the lightness of the construction. At the base of the cupola were 32 semi-circular windows, 13 in each of the semi-cupolas and many others in the walls which flooded the building with light. Columns of porphyry surmounted by capitals with stalactite decorations supported the arcades of the side-aisles, and two levels of galleries bore the weight of the vault from the inside. Stalactites decorated the triangular surfaces. The interior of the monument gave the impression of majesty desired by Suleiman. As one approached it from the town, it appeared even more impressive. Its outline rose up like a pyramid among the group of buildings which surrounded it, the *kulliye*. These included two *medrese*, an infirmary, a caravanserai, a medical school and a Turkish bath, all low and seemingly 'humble', planned by the architect to seem to be doing obeisance to the mosque. The *Suleimaniye*, colossal and powerful, was a symbol of the empire at its apogee.

At the end of his life, Sinan said: 'The *Şehzade* is my apprentice work, the *Suleimaniye* my achievement as a journeyman, and the *Selimiye* my masterwork.' The *Selimiye*, which dominates the town of Edirne and the lovely countryside around it, is indeed considered the masterpiece of the great Turkish builder by all architects. Slightly squat when seen from close up, the *Selimiye* with its four minarets appears light and slender when viewed from the plain. The huge cupola is supported on eight columns, and, on the outside, eight buttresses take the weight of the whole building. The semi-cupolas have been suppressed and replaced by a crown of semi-cupolas and tympanums. The walls built in ashlar of two different colours seem to have been cut in blocks. The interior spaces form a completely harmonious effect. Lots of arched windows cut into the base of the cupola and the apse increase the impression of limpidity. In the middle of the court, surrounded on four sides by a portico covered with nineteen cupolas, was a *şadirvan* (a fountain for ablutions). Octagonal in shape in the centre, this faced the simple and majestic main portal, which was also made of marble and decorated with stalactites. On the inside, on the walls of the *mihrab* and the pediments of the windows, faiences from Iznik, among the most beautiful in the world, were to be seen.

Twenty years were still to go by before the death of the great builder. He filled them with immense creative activity in Istanbul and the rest of the empire. Some of the mosques he built would also be crowned with semi-cupolas like the *Selimiye* (the *Atik Valide cami* in Uskudar, for example) and others (like the *Kiliç Ali cami* at Tophane in Istanbul) were based on the same plan as the *Suleimaniye*. His 'unparalleled facility' enabled him to enjoy the challenge of developing architectural forms of every kind.[10]

He had many pupils, several of whom were to carry the fame of Turkish architecture further afield. Akbar, the Emperor of India, asked one of them, Yusuf, to come and build palaces for him at Agra, Delhi and Lahore. In the following century, Shah Jahan, his grandson, gave to a Turk, Issa Effendi, the commission to build a monument to commemorate his grief at the death of his wife – the Taj Mahal in Agra.

The Perfection of the Ceramist's Art

The exteriors of Ottoman mosques in the 16th and 17th centuries were deliberately deprived of all ornament apart from the stalactites on the portals and, sometimes, a contrast between black and white stone. On the interior, however, they were covered in ceramics which made them look like sparkling jewels. In the *Sokullu Mehmed Pasha*, for example, even the cupola gives the effect of a jewel-case made of ceramics, while the *Sultan Ahmed* looks as if it has been poured into an enormous blue mould.

Turkish ceramics, which adorned Seljuk monuments from the 13th century onwards, reached perfection, like the other arts, in the 16th century. All the mosques, as well as certain rooms in the imperial palace, were decorated with coloured faience squares, largely made in Iznik (ancient Nicaea) by Turkish artists and workers with the help of Persians.

At first, they were made of pieces cut from monochrome sheets and assembled on a field of plaster, just like mosaics; two centuries later, the tiles were painted and glazed. The colours were deep blue (close to that of Sèvres china), turquoise, white and black; later, as techniques evolved, yellow and pistachio green were also used. In the second half of the 16th century, leaf green and the famous tomato red completed the Turkish palate, which gave religious buildings and imperial palaces, until the beginning of the 17th century, a splendour which still dazzles us today and has nowhere been surpassed.

Ceramics, one might say, is the Turkish art *par excellence*. The subjects used, at first lettering and geometric figures – that is to say, in the 13th and 14th centuries – soon included stylized motifs like the leaf (*rumi*), and then the lotus and Chinese cloud. Shortly after that, flowers (tulips, hyacinths, carnations) and leaves appeared. They were to dominate in the 16th century, perhaps under the influence of the Italian Renaissance, not only in ceramics but in carpets, fabrics and miniatures.

Without losing any of its originality or the techniques which it had perfected, Turkish art adapted to its Oriental style motifs introduced from its commercial contacts with Western countries, especially Italy, at the same time as it slowly moved away from the influence of Iran and the older Asian civilizations.[11] Chinese and Timurid motifs were so 'Ottomanized' as to become hardly recognizable (Persia only adopted the naturalistic floral style a century later). Decorative forms based on lettering and geometric figures, which were still prominent in ceramics at the start of Suleiman's reign, soon gave way to a semi-realist, semi-fantastic floral style which became exuberant at the end of the century. Whole rooms – mosques, palace bedrooms – were turned into gardens and fantasy greenhouses: clear expression of the Ottoman taste for nature, their passion for flowers.[12]

One of the most beautiful and famous works of ceramics in this naturalistic period was the left panel in the *Rustem Pasha* mosque in Istanbul. The purple stems of the eglantines blend in perfect harmony with the hyacinths, tulips, narcissi and rose buds. In the prayer room and gallery of the mosque there are even more motifs: red and blue tulips on a white background, carnations, green leaves or *rumi*, large red and blue peonies. On the *mihrab*, large blue and white stylized flowers overflow from vases of the same colours. The panels which surround the entrance to Roxelane's tomb (*turbe*) date from the same period. They show a tree with a dark trunk and branches bearing white eglantines with red centres as well as bluish leaves; at its feet is a field of carnations and tulips.

At the *Atik Valide cami*, a little mosque above Uskudar (Scutari), the pinnacle of the Turkish ceramist's art can certainly be found, although this is less a question of originality of design than quality of workmanship. One enchanting panel shows a coral-red vase on a blue background, from which interlaced stems of carnations and tulips escape. In another, a red vase on a creamy blue background is surrounded by thin interlaced stems and green leaves. White carnations bloom in a sort of shield, blue in colour.

Other examples of ceramic art from the same period, in which technical skill is combined with aesthetic sensitivity, could also be described: the *turbe* of Selim II (one of the panels is in the Louvre); Ramazan Effendi's mosque; Selim II's bath and a corridor in Murad III's apartment, both of which can be seen at Topkapi.

The workshops of Iznik (they never existed in Rhodes) also produced plates, vases, ewers, cups and lamps for the mosques in the 16th century which count among the most beautiful pieces in the history of ceramics. Blending Persian, Chinese and Italian influences with their native tradition, the lotus flower, stylized clouds and *rumi*, the large plates and cups emerging from Iznik at the time were true works of art in which the creators' spirit of fantasy – they were often designed by court miniaturists who provided the potters with cartoons – was given free rein. There was sometimes a certain mannerism, when stylization led to a kind of highly fantastical naturalism, but the quality of colour and design, and the subtlety of detail, are always enchanting. The technique had attained perfection. From 1520 to 1540, blue and turquoise were the dominant colours, but the palette was subsequently enlarged and these ceramics attained their apogee at the same time as the tiles.[13] Freed from foreign influences, they proclaimed their own originality. Animals, birds and, less often, people appeared in the designs of these pieces whose fame extended far and wide in Europe and whose 'insouciant elegance and natural grace' were often praised. Important people bought them up and advised each other on which to buy.[14]

The golden age of these pieces in the form of objects lasted no longer than that of the tiles. By the first half of the 17th century, the quality had deteriorated, the design became confused and the colours lost their vivacity. The volume of production fell. There were 300 potters in Iznik at the beginning of the century and only 9 in 1648; in 1720, the studios closed. The workmen were moved to the Tekfur Saray district of Istanbul, where they produced ceramics of variable quality. Iznik was also replaced by Kutahya as the centre of such pieces; artisans, who were mainly Armenians, continued to produce pottery of various shapes and colours there into the 19th century. Yet although these were pleasant and sometimes amusing, they cannot be compared with those of the great period in Iznik.

Painters and Calligraphers

It will perhaps surprise some readers that I devote a few pages to painting. Islam, it is said, does not allow the representation of animate beings, and the Ottoman pictorial arts hardly enjoy a great reputation among the cultivated public in the West. It certainly existed, however, and the works surviving from the 16th century are definitely worthy of attention.

The interdictions on representing the human form in the visual arts have given rise to countless expositions. Two passages in the Koran which are cited (V. 92–1 and VI. 74–2) clearly refer exclusively to idols – images before which people prostrate themselves. A third passage (LIX. –24) is more explicit: God is the only '*musavvir*' (creator) – the term which is used to mean 'painter' in both Arabic and Turkish; theologians have inferred that no one else is allowed to create other beings. The *hadith*, however, in which the Prophet and his companions often condemn representations of animate beings were not put together until the end of the 8th century (more than 150 years after Mohammed's death), no doubt for reasons which had more to do with the historical circumstances of the time than any theological considerations[15] (see Appendix 16).

It remains true that images, or at least those which were accessible to the public, were early made the subject of a complete ban. In the whole Islamic world they were rigorously excluded from mosques, rooms or places where anyone could see them (although there were numerous exceptions to the rule, particularly among the Seljuk Turks), but this applied far less strongly to the private apartments of sultans and important persons. Many texts describe the palace paintings, and fragments have been discovered in recent decades in Afghanistan (the Ghaznavid dynasty), Egypt (the Fatimids) and Syria (Omayyads). At

Qasr Amrah, figures of naked women, closer in form to Oriental than to Greek or Roman canons of beauty, bear witness to the fact that around 740 (more than a century after the Prophet's death) a Muslim prince of the Omayyad family decorated a room of his palace with human (female) figures. A century later, an Abbasid sovereign had a picture of two dancers, one of them pouring wine, painted on a wall of his residence in Samara; again they are of an extremely Oriental type. Mehmed II covered some of the walls in the Topkapi Palace with paintings, including some which were said to upset even people with very lax moral standards (Bayezid got rid of them as soon as his father was dead and sold the easel paintings in the bazaar). All the remaining Muslim frescos have now disappeared, victims of time or fanatics, and almost the whole of Ottoman pictorial figurative art is to be found in manuscripts.[16]

Realistic Painting

In the 16th century, Turkish painting already had a long history behind it. In pre-Islamic times, artists had assimilated Chinese, Iranian and even Indian elements along with those of the Turco-Mongol civilizations whose dynasties then ruled almost the whole of the Near East. The ideal of beauty to be found in the earliest illustrations and very many ceramics is derived from the Turco-Mongol type (with chubby body and almond eyes). Although it is often confused with Iranian art, Turkish painting possesses neither its emotional content nor its systematic idealization of the human figure. Realistic in spirit, it usually limits itself to offering a documentary description of men and events without idealizing them but with a unique sort of poetic fantasy and colourful lyricism which is instantly recognizable to anyone who has even the slightest familiarity with Oriental painting.

Scenes of love are rare;[17] combats, processions and festivals, which show us the sultan or the humble people filing before him or enjoying themselves, are common subjects. There are none of the languid figures or people in unusual surroundings characteristic of Persian art, but men as they are, fat or thin, attractive or ugly. Even the sultans were not portrayed more flatteringly than in life. It would be hard to imagine less enticing figures than Selim II, clumsy and red-faced, drawing his bow in the picture by Nigari; or his grandson, Mehmed III, bearded and puffy, and almost ridiculous on a horse which seems to sink under his weight! Among the many portraits of Suleiman is the one by Nigari, often reproduced, which shows him in his old age, very thin and with drawn features under a white beard.

As in Iranian art, there are many royal hunts and games of polo, followed by scenes where one sees princes resting in the shade under flowers while servants bring them drinks and sorbets. But here the outlines are heavier, the colours cruder, and, of course, the costumes and hair styles different. From the start of the 16th century, Ottoman pictorial art possesses a certain power and robustness, although it lacks subtlety. It is the overall harmony of the surface which counts, rather than the detail. It is certainly an 'Iranicizing' form of painting, but the Turkish character has added its particular stamp; a little later, after a return to a form of Oriental mannerism, it was influenced by Western models, which were incorporated in turn without overwhelming the native tradition.

The Iranian influence, which long continued, is particularly evident in the miniatures which illustrate the collections of poems (*divan*) on standard Oriental themes. It is far less noticeable in those which embellish military chronicles. Since there was no established native tradition, the Turks began by copying the Persians, but they rapidly diverged to give free rein to their gifts of observation and concern for a realism which is often touched with humour. Scenes of battle show lines of janissaries, horsemen, gunners, all with their uniforms faithfully reproduced, drawing their bows or charging, lance in hand, against the heavy Christian cavalry, who are cased in steel, with helmets and breastplates and horses sinking under the weight of the armour. The fight between Turks and Hungarians is agitated: the dead and wounded lie all about, a horse whose rider has been disarmed limps away as fast as it can. On the other hand, in the famous miniature of *King Lewis Holding Council*, the figures are lighter and some are almost Western-looking. They may indeed have been the work of a Christian painter, which is quite plausible because the illustrations for the great chronicles were not the work of a single artist but of studios of several dozen people. In 1557, the studio at Topkapi had 35 workers: 26 Turks, 7 Persians, a Hungarian and a 'Frank'. The *musavvir* executed the faces, the *nakkash* painted the figures and certain scenes, others scattered golden dots on the leaves or decorated the pictures with flowers, clouds, etc.

Certain artists left work in an individual style or even changed the direction of Turkish painting. Matraki Nasuh was one of them. A mathematician, writer, soldier and painter, man of science and observer of his age, he produced a *Description of Suleiman's Campaign in the Two Iraqs* – an exact illustrated account of one of the most famous Ottoman expeditions – and then a *Suleimanname* and an account of Bayezid II's career. His illustrations contain few people and are 'scientific' in the sense that the details he reproduces – the architecture of monuments and depiction of places – are so accurate that one can easily identify them. His style is semi-topographic and semi-cartographic, with all idealism banished; although this was quite new in Turkish art, it proved highly influential, particularly in illustrations for maps. Matraki had accompanied Suleiman in Iraq and brought back with him 107 miniatures and 25 illustrations. His book forms a genuine journal, recounting in pictures the main events of the expedition, the stops, the towns, the forests, the mountains, the animals: a hare in a lion's mouth, swans swimming round a lake near Antioch, and ducks with yellow and pink wings; a deer browses among the leaves while a rabbit looks on. In the desert around Baghdad he put a tiger, a gazelle and rabbits.

Did he also accompany Barbarossa's fleet to France in 1542? He himself or an artist of his studio left a series of little pictures which represent the ports of Marseilles, Toulon, Nice and Antibes. They are all easy to recognize: Nice is surrounded by walls and overlooked by its castle, the nearby hills, the mouth of the river Paillon; Antibes has its ramparts and towers and, before the port, the fine Turkish galleys with their standards unfurled. Although it is not certain that Matraki produced the illustrations for the *Chronicle of the Campaign in Hungary* (1543), they are very much in his manner: the town of Esztergom, with its castle and the island between two branches of the Danube, surrounded by fields scattered with red flowers; Szekesfehervar, the fortress and the bridges, and the capture of the town which completed the expedition, with Turkish flags flying on the castles and churches. Such pictures are quite unlike the royal hunts across fields and idealized forests typical of Persian miniatures.

This concern for exactitude, even though realistic perspective is sacrificed to the need to obtain striking effects with colour, is also found in the painters of the period just after the death of Suleiman (who can nonetheless be considered as part of the same era), notably those who illustrated the *Surname* (*Book of Delights*) and the *Hunername* (*Chronicle*) by the historian Loqman. The first celebrates the festivities held on the occasion of the circumcision of Şehzade Mehmed, the son of Mehmed III, while the second describes events from the accession to the throne of the first Osmanli ruler down to the end of Suleiman's reign. The illustrations are by Nakkaş Osman, one of the most famous Turkish artists of the day, assisted by other painters. Apart from their artistic qualities, they give us abundant and precise information about Ottoman life in the 16th century: the games, the tournaments, the guild processions, the guests in boxes, the sultan and his family. The people look on. The whole life of Istanbul is there. In the *Hunername*, the shapes have evolved still further and possess even more life and colour. One can see the horses galloping off at top speed; the animals in the hunt scenes are clearly leaping.

Portraiture

Turkey is probably the Oriental country in which portraiture first appeared, both because of its proximity to Europe and because of the contacts the court at Istanbul rapidly established with Italian artists. The famous portrait of Mehmed II by Gentile Bellini is the most impressive evidence of this, although Sinan Bey, who had studied in Venice, was his predecessor. Sinan painted a beautiful portrait of the Conqueror which skilfully blends Italian influences with the strong native tradition of Turkey. Although it was not a part of the Oriental tradition, portraiture went on to enjoy a great vogue at court under Suleiman and his successors.

One of the greatest painters of the day, Nigari, owes his fame to the sultan. As the commander of a ship in the war fleet, and thus given the nickname Haydar Reis (commander Haydar), Nigari was little known as a painter in his early years. The portrait of Barbarossa he has left us is astonishingly lively, despite the white beard and moustache and the squat profile which reveal a great sailor in his declining years. In one hand Barbarossa holds a carnation, a common gesture in Oriental portraits, while his other hand is placed on his sword.

Nigari is also responsible for the well-known full-length portrait of Suleiman in old age, his long profile draped in a coat of blue satin with sleeves lined with white fur. His white beard and the emaciated face under his large white turban enhance the impression of dignity and austerity which the sovereign gives; he walks slowly, followed by two bodyguards, one dressed in green and the other in red. What a contrast with his son, the ungainly Selim II who was also portrayed by Nigari! What life there is in the gesture of the white-bearded sultan's left hand as he follows with his eyes the path of the arrow which has just left his bow! The debauched *padishah*, who was also a poet of considerable delicacy, is dressed in a rich style utterly unlike his father's sober attire: a blue caftan embroidered with gold and multi-coloured flowers, clothes made of golden material, an enormous turban with three heron feathers decorated with precious stones emerging from it. Behind him a page carries a carnation in his right hand, arrows in his left: the sultan's ammunition. The puffy and red-faced Selim reveals himself clearly for what he was – a drunkard who was also 'gluttonous and lazy'.[18] Overall, however, he gives an impression of majesty and Oriental refinement.

All these portraits faithfully reproduce the model's features. The concern to get as near the truth as possible, to produce a 'documentary record', is very evident, even if the depiction of 'God's shadow on earth' is hardly flattering. We see here one of the characteristic original features of Ottoman painting in the 16th century, which results in part from closer and closer contact with the West but also, and perhaps especially, from the deep underlying tendencies of Turkish art.

Calligraphy

In the 16th century, the Turks were also the masters of calligraphy, the Muslim art *par excellence*. It was the era in which Şeyh Hamdullah and his disciples covered the walls and pillars of the mosques with elegant, usually ceramic, inscriptions, of verses from the Koran or the names of Allah and the first caliphs. The most refined of the great calligraphers of the age of Suleiman was without doubt Ahmed Karahisari, who composed numerous inscriptions in the Suleimaniye; an album of his preserved in the Museum of Turkish and Islamic Antiquities in Istanbul bears witness to the variety and extreme elegance of his talent.

Since all representation of human figures was banned, sculpture in the round hardly existed in Islamic countries, but this did not apply to bas-reliefs which, from the beginning of the 16th century, made extensive use of floral motifs. Long before that, tombs, fountains, doors and especially the facades of mosques were all embellished with decorations in the form of written inscriptions, intertwining patterns, and motifs of every kind from the depths of Asia which had been 'Turkified' by Seljuk and Ottoman sculptors. In Suleiman's day, motifs representing vegetable life in all its forms were dominant, just as in ceramics and carpets. As for stained glass, the most beautiful panels were again certainly those of the Suleimaniye by Sarhoş Ibrahim, or those of the *Mihrimah cami* near the Adrianople gate out of Istanbul.

Weavers and Tapestry Makers

The art of tapestry making, like the potter's art, has its origin in the depths of time. It was also the nomads' art, practised by the men of the steppes where the Turkish people had wandered for so long. When they took up permanent residence in Anatolia at the start of our millennium, they already had a long tradition of tapestry making. From that far-off era, almost nothing remains. We know much more about the carpets of the early modern age because examples have been preserved from the 15th and 16th centuries and, even more, because European painters like Holbein and the Venetians represented them in their interiors.

Compared to Persian carpets, Turkish carpets made greater use of 'architectural' than floral or animal motifs. They developed in the opposite direction to ceramics, and the Persian influence almost completely disappeared in Suleiman's century. This resulted in a kind of stylization which left no place for the exuberance of flowers and leaves, so characteristic of Persian carpets, which sometimes give the impression of a luxuriant jungle. On tomato red or sometimes blue or ivory backgrounds, outlines of the prayer niche (*mihrab*), a lamp or candlestick stood out. Stylized flowers were scattered over the surface. The borders were extremely elaborate, with interlacing patterns and lozenges of great delicacy. On others (as on certain textiles and ceramics) there were undulating bands and groups of spots of the same colour. The cloud (or *tchi*), said to be of Chinese origin, appeared on carpets and ceramics at about the same time, around 1530.

If similar characteristics were to be found in Turkish carpets for generations, it was at the end of the 15th and throughout the 16th centuries that the finest results were achieved. They came from the great workshops of Uşak, Istanbul and Gordeş, while those of Anatolia, large and small, and local craftsmen produced the *kilim* and *cicim* which reveal such unerring taste. Important persons and rich Western merchants bought them by the dozen. Cardinal Wolsey appears to have ordered sixty.

Craftsmen in the related fields of brocade, velvet and satin making were producing goods on a similar scale to the cross-stitch weavers. The Topkapi Palace has long exhibited the sultans' clothes, preserved through the centuries and carefully labelled. These give us a glimpse of the skill and taste of the men who wove silk and wool in the Ottoman Empire at the time. One robe belonged to Suleiman the Magnificent: on a cream silk background tulips and pink and yellow carnations stand out on their long brown stems; a pair of trousers (*şalvar*), also of silk, gold and silver and belonging to the same sultan, was decorated with a sun surrounded by crescent moons and stars. From Roxelane's mausoleum comes a tomb covering in red velvet decorated with tulips and leaves; the border is green.

These marvellous garments were woven in the workshops of Damascus, Baghdad, Bursa and particularly Istanbul, the only one in the 16th century which was allowed to use gold or silver thread. Many specialized in gold thread, in satin, in weaving only velvet, etc. Production must have been on a large scale since the sultan and viziers traditionally offered robes of honour to the people to whom they wished to show respect. The fabrics destined for the Seraglio were based on designs supplied by the painters of the imperial workshops. Because of this, there is a greater spirit of fantasy than in the carpets; there is also a fidelity to nature which often recalls the motifs to be found in the miniatures of the same era.

The Literary Arts

After the conquest of Constantinople had brought the Ottomans into contact with the Christian world, one might have expected Helleno-Christian culture to exert an influence on Turkish culture and perhaps modify its course, as had happened so often in similar circumstances. Nothing of the sort occurred. In the 15th and 16th centuries, the Ottomans borrowed from the Christians practical skills in many fields – weapon making and navigation, geography and the sciences – but nothing had a deep impact on their age-old culture, with its specifically Asiatic and Muslim background. The traces of Christian influence one can discern in the Turkish culture of the time are without major significance.

Indeed, it was the Christians who became 'Ottomanized'. The *devşirme* system had an important part in this. It is astonishing how easily the young Christians who had been 'kidnapped' and turned into Muslims became Turkish in every way. Almost without exception, they were transformed, after only a few years, into Turkish Ottomans who had a total fidelity to their new ideals; they readily adopted customs, religion and culture. In the melting-pot of the powerful and constantly victorious empire, everything blended in: the Ottomans took almost nothing from the rich Greek and Christian heritage. Avicenna's Neoplatonism and Averroes's Aristotelianism had long given way to the mysticism of al-Ghazali and Arabic and Persian influences. On this occasion, the vanquished were not able to take a spiritual or intellectual revenge on their conquerors.

Turkish culture became far more unified after the lightning conquests of the princes of the House of Osman. Osmanli culture naturally became dominant. Istanbul, the political and intellectual centre of an ever more powerful empire, compelled the peoples it had subdued, whether they were allies or vassals, to use its language. The poets and writers of Azerbaijan, for example, had to use Osmanli Turkish, just as the sultan's subjects were led to speak and write the language of the soldiers and functionaries of the Porte.

In the 16th century, the superiority of the Osmanli dialect had established itself once and for all.[19] There already existed a Turkish literary consciousness, an inheritance of the Turkish past and Persian and Arabic literature. Persian literature, although decadent, was always an important influence, but it was less important than in the previous century when Sultan Mehmed II commissioned the poet Sehdi to write a *shahname* (or versified epic) in Persian about the Osmanlis; he also protected writers and poets from Khorasan and Iran at his court in Constantinople, although this was much resented by the Turks. But then a reaction had set in, in favour of Turkish literature, partly because of the influence exercised on the Turkish world by the great poet Mir Ali Şir Nevai, who had been born in Khorasan. He wrote his immense corpus, which is still read today in Central Asia, entirely in Turkish. 'He breathed life into the inert body of the Turkish language,' Sultan Husain Baikara wrote of him, whose confidant and friend he was at the court of Herat. His erotico-mystical poetry – in which love is spiritualized even when he touches on profane matters – is similar to the kind which inspired the great Persian poets like Omar Khayyam, Nizami, Sadi and Celaleddin Rumi and later became that of his Ottoman successors. They adapted such themes to the genius of the Turkish language and thus gave it a noble literary tradition.

A Constellation of Poets

Great names dominate Turkish poetry at the time of Suleiman: Fuzuli, Baki and many others. Yet what made the century a golden age was perhaps not so much the glory of the greatest of them as the impressive number of writers. There was a whole constellation of poets around the sultan, the princes and the leading dignitaries who protected them. Not all were in Istanbul. Literary circles flourished to some extent almost everywhere in the empire: in Bursa, an old cultural town; in Baghdad, which had just been conquered; in Diyarbekir and Kastamonu; in Edirne, the former capital where the sultan and his court often took up residence.

As in Istanbul, the poets would meet in the *konak* of the richer among them, in the *tekke* (or convents) of the religious orders which were particularly flourishing then – the heterodox orders such as the Bektaşi and Hurufi produced many poets – or even, after the introduction of coffee, in the *kahvehane*. Popular poets were to be found in very large numbers in the janissaries' barracks and puppet theatres. Wandering minstrels accompanied the poems they had composed with instruments they carried around with them. Their themes were often Iranian or Islamic. Some drew on earlier Turkish traditions, others on everyday life. Poetry, both classical and popular, has always had a large place in the life of Turks at all levels of culture. Famous poets, even in recent times, have often found themselves proposed as candidates for leading positions in administration or diplomacy.

Was Fuzuli or Baki the greatest poet of the 16th century? For E. J. W. Gibb, a historian of Turkish poetry, 'the genius of Fuzuli, one of the most authentic poets to whom the Orient has given birth, would be enough on its own to to make famous forever the century of Suleiman'.[20] Fuad Koprulu, while also believing that Fuzuli is the greatest poet in Turkish literature, and that he surpasses Baki in the expression of sentiment, nonetheless places the latter above him for his melodious charm and the impeccable craftsmanship of his poetry.

Fuzuli was born in Baghdad and probably never left. A Shiite Muslim, he was the 'guardian' of Ali's tomb at Najaf. At first he was the subject of Shah Ismail, but he allied himself with the sultan of Constantinople when his city was captured in 1554. Turkish in origin, he wrote first in the Azeri Turkish of Azerbaijan and then in Osmanli, but he also left poems in Arabic, largely religious in inspiration, as well as Persian writings in both verse and prose. His 300 *gazel*,[21] all in Turkish, belong to the usual erotico-mystical genre. He sang of love and sadness, unhappy passions, the passing of time, the approach of death and the poet's increasing despondency.

The form he uses is extremely elegant and his verbal music incomparable. His flowery language is utterly seductive to the reader, even in translation: 'The celestial vault of blue enamel will become rose-coloured, in the tulip-coloured twilight like a crystal cup which lets the reflections of the wine show through.'

There is often something precious about his verse, as in the following image of love: 'If the whirlwind like a cypress raises its head above the earth of my tomb in the desert of suffering, O mirage of a brook, do not refuse your water to that cypress.' Truer and more sincere is the following lament: 'If you do not strike me at once with the sword of your cruelty, you will end up one day by killing me with your neglect. Desire for your beauty spot like musk (black and perfumed) and your red cheek has drowned my eyes in tears of blood distilled from my heart . . . For a long time Fuzuli, like a shadow, has not left the dust of your feet, in the hope that one day you will tread on him.'

In other *gazel* love is less ethereal and more precisely described: 'In early morning the charming cypress bent down confidently towards the bath; the bath sparkled at his candle-like face. Through his open neck, his body appeared; it was completely revealed to the moonlight when he took off his robe. He draped himself in a bath towel the colour of indigo – you would have thought that a shelled almond had fallen among the violets. The edge of the basin had the honour of kissing his feet; the eye of the [cupola's] stained glass was lit up by his gracious appearance . . . water crashes against his body; jealousy snatches peace from my own.'[22]

Fuzuli's muse was not always inspired by mystical subjects. But it seems as if this unhappy homosexual love which appears in almost all the poets was a literary convention and that in life Fuzuli was cheerful, playful and a lover of both sexes. The lamentations put into the mouths of Persian and Ottoman lovers should certainly not always be taken literally.

Fuzuli's great work was a long poem called *Leyla and Mecnun*; it is this, at least as much as his *gazel* and *kaside*, which won for him such an great reputation in the Turkish world. The legend of the love of the two Arab protagonists, created in about the 8th century, is more famous throughout the Orient than the stories of Tristan and Isolde or Romeo and Juliet in Europe. It was written and re-written dozens of times, notably in versions by Cami and Mir Ali Şir Nevai. But Fuzuli's version is considered the most original and beautiful. A poem of impossible love, the adventures of the two lovers are long and complicated: escapes, combats, madness, magic, prodigies, all succeed one another over the course of 3,000 couplets. At the end, the hero and heroine die, are put in the same tomb and united in the beyond, although they have never known each other carnally. Leyla does, however, employ all her powers of seduction when she offers herself to her lover: 'I am Leyla, the desire of your soul, the aspiration of your ill and weeping heart. Profit from the glory of union with me. Come near me, do not let the occasion slip away. Come, take part in the intimate banquet of union, be my companion for a moment! Honour the narcissus with the tulip, embellish the lily with the tender origanum. Bring the turquoise near the ruby, feed the parrot with pure sugar. I show you my cheek like the sun and you reveal no ardour! I lift up the chalice and offer it to you, and you do not instantly leap to your feet?'[23]

The attraction of human love for divine beauty is always present in this long poem. Literal and allegorical meanings blend in with each other, while an incomparable love song rises up, accompanied by human details which have nothing to do with mystical love. It is especially because of this that the work was, and still remains, so close to the heart of Oriental sensibilities.

More perfect, perhaps, in its formal qualities but also more conventional and less humane, the poetry of Baki is the archetypal example of 16th-century lyric poetry. Much influenced by Mir Ali Şir, Baki takes his place in the line of writers of lyric verse who modelled themselves on the great Persian poets. He kept his distance, however, from Arabic and Persian constructions and vocabulary – and some[24] have even wished to see him and other poets of the day as precursors of the modern nationalist tendencies which ended under Ataturk in the almost complete 'Turkification' of the language. A court poet, he never ceased to gravitate around Suleiman and his princes; even after the death of the Magnificent Sultan, he continued to enjoy the favour of his successors. He died laden with honours and was given a funeral on the grand scale.

Apart from a few religious writings and a certain number of poems in Persian and Arabic, what is essential in Baki's work consists in his *gazel* and *kaside*. Unlike many Oriental poets, he left none of those long verse novels inspired either by legend or history (*Chosroes and Shirin, Leyla and Mecnun, Joseph and Zuleika, Beauty and Heart*), by symbolic couples (*Mars and Venus, The Rose and the Nightingale*) or even invented by the individual poet; every kind of writing flourished in Turkish, Persian and Arabic poetry – but, for Baki, a few faultlessly constructed couplets were enough.

A verbal virtuoso, Baki pushed to the limit the art of playing with words. His prodigious technique could make use of every artifice and subtlety of language. With alliterations and double meanings he packed his verses with significances which those who understand how to read him discover with delighted astonishment. For example, there is a couplet, addressed to a beautiful young boy, which can be interpreted in two senses: 'If I say that your body is as delicious as the sweetest creams, you will start at once to be spoilt – you are so fragile, you are so fresh!' or

'If I say your body is as delicious as cream, you will at once get cross – you are so delicate, you are so fresh!'

Despite such artifices, which must have required immense effort, Baki's poety often remains personal and sincere and frequently draws on everyday language. This explains why it has long been popular, as it still is in Turkey today. 'The pleasures of this world are as fleeting as the season of roses': this theme constantly recurs in poetry which sings of the sweetness of life, the countryside around Istanbul, the beauty of flowers or bird song – all the ephemeral joys granted to man in a world which is only a dream.

People have often doubted the sincerity of Baki's sentiments and he was caught out more than once telling a bare-faced lie: 'A fresh young man with a fine complexion is dearer to me than life; no woman has come near me, except for the daughter of the vine [wine]'; this was obviously not the case, since Baki had a son. But convention required that the poet claim to be homosexual, although he was often nothing of the sort.

Baki also wrote more than one poem in praise of wine, as was traditional among Persian and Turkish poets. And yet he made his career among the *ulema*, which would have been quite impossible if he had been known to drink alcoholic beverages. The question of the sincerity of tone in Baki's poetry becomes even less important when we recall that he made no attempt to hide either his smiling scepticism or the absence of profundity in his poetry. A perfect artist, a genius at putting words together, Baki has been well compared, by a historian of Turkish literature, with the Oriental ceramists: 'The world of flowers plays a large part in Oriental poetic fantasy, but in the plastic art of Baki, it is transformed into delicate arabesques worthy to take their place alongside the stylized floral patterns in Persian and Turkish ceramics, where the motifs are always the same, and yet every piece is different from every other.'[25]

All the Others . . .

Fuzuli and Baki dominate the century of Suleiman, but several of the other numerous versifiers count, even today, among the great poets of the Turkish language.

Zati produced delicately wrought compositions, full of fantasy and drawing on popular phrasing and metaphors. Hayali, born in Macedonia, who lived as a dervish before being admitted to Suleiman's entourage (where he received the title of *bey*), became so famous that he was nicknamed 'the Hafiz of Rum' after the famous Persian lyric poet. His poetry is often mystical in inspiration and hard to understand, but is almost always formally perfect. Hayreti Rumi (of Bursa) and Aşik Çelebi enjoyed a great reputation in their lifetime for their *gazel* and *kaside*. So indeed did Fighani, although he was executed on Ibrahim's orders for having written satirical verses about the statues brought from Buda after the victory at Mohacs and installed in the middle of the Hippodrome in Constantinople. Many others have retained their places in the history of Turkish literature since the 16th century: Dunizade Ulvi of Istanbul, Makali, Ruhi of Baghdad, Cenani of Bursa, Riyazi, etc. Some were authors of *gazel* and *kaside*, others of *rubai*, but all of them – mystics, comic poets, inventors of riddles – were recompensed and received sinecures and titles as soon as an important person, not to mention the sultan himself, recognized their talent.

The 16th century was also the period for the most brilliant examples of *mesnevi*, rhymed chronicles on the standard Oriental themes. The *Gul ve Bulbul* (*The Rose and the Nightingale*) by Fazli, dedicated to the ill-starred Prince Mustafa, was considered one of the finest examples of the genre. Lami wrote seven of them including a *Debate between Spring and Winter* which ends in the triumph of the latter, when spring gives itself up to the peace its rival offers. In the same *mesnevi* genre there were also descriptions of towns – Bursa, whose picturesqueness often inspired facile poetry, Edirne and the banks of the Tunca – saints' lives, mystical works. Anything could be a pretext for rhymed verse.

Popular poets were inspired by the same themes, although they sang to different metres (nearer to the ancient Turkish forms) and in the language used by people from modest backgrounds. They mixed prose and verse and sometimes accompanied themselves on a stringed instrument called a *saz*, which is widely used in Turkey to this day.

Although it is far more ancient in origin, it was in the 16th century that the *karagoz*[26] enjoyed its greatest vogue. This marionette theatre – known as 'Karagoz' after the main protagonist – consisted in a sequence of scenes based on dialogues between Karagoz himself, who was coarse but resourceful and sincere and thus represented the people, and Hacivat, crafty and well brought up, who represented the bourgeoisie. Numerous other characters intervened, according to the play. The same man moved the puppets and played all the roles, changing his voice each time. Despite criticism from religious circles, this form of theatre was tolerated because 'by showing sin it taught virtue' (according to a *fetva* laid down by

Ebusuud). Until the invasion of radios and records, it formed one of the favourite amusements of the lower classes and possessed, on certain occasions, an important social and even political role.

Suleiman's predecessors had long encouraged versifiers to sing of their exploits. A large body of rhymed war poetry tells of the exploits and battles of Murad II, Mehmed the Conqueror and Bayezid II. Suleiman was the first to institutionalize this tradition. He created the post of imperial chronicler (*shahnameci*), whose job was to describe the events of the reign in verse in the manner of Firdousi's *Book of Kings*; he was also expected to go as far back as possible in the history of the House of Osman. The *shahname* was written in Persian until the time of Mehmed III, at the end of the 16th century, who gave orders that it must be written in Turkish. Shortly afterwards, the post was abolished, probably because the conquests and exploits of the sultans no longer deserved to be celebrated in the poems of this genre, which were invariably hundreds of verses long.

The literary merit of these long and boring chronicles is generally minimal. When Fuzuli or Baki wanted to praise the sultan's great deeds, they would write a *kaside*.

Prose Writers

Prose burned with a lower flame than poetry. The characteristic style, inflated and artificial, is only tolerable when used by a writer of the very first class. This is clear, for example, in the numerous historians who found in the sultan's military successes abundant material for epic narrative.

Of all the historical writers who published accounts of the great deeds of the Ottoman armies, Kemalpashazade is certainly the most eminent – or, at any rate, the least tiresome. His description of the Battle of Mohacs is probably the finest example of the typical emphatic prose style full of countless bold images. After him comes Hoca Saduddin Effendi, whose *Tac-al-Tevarih* (*Historians' Crown*) recounts the whole history of the Osman dynasty, and, above all, the learned encyclopedist Mustafa Ali, who wrote a *Universal History* as well as a *History of Ottoman Fine Art*. Taşkopruluzade wrote a monumental work made up of biographies of 600 Muslim sages in a fairly plain Arabic style as well as an encyclopedia of the current state of the exact sciences and religious studies.

Besides these major histories of the whole dynasty or sultan's reign, numerous monographs told of the glorious achievements by land and sea of the astonishing Barbarossa or the Turkish soldiers and sailors.

Particular mention must be made of the great jurist Ebusuud, who drew up most of the laws to which Suleiman owes his name of 'Lawgiver'. Nor must we forget to mention Lutfi Pasha, Suleiman's Grand Vizier and brother-in-law, whose *Asafname*, a sort of *Mirror of Magistrates*, is his most famous work.

The development of Ottoman naval power and the prowess of the corsairs naturally helped to set in motion the study of geography and the related sciences. The most celebrated work of the era was undoubtedly that of Piri Reis. His famous map of the world in two parts (only one of which survives) was inspired by the maps which described the recent Portuguese discoveries or those made in the course of Columbus's third voyage. His *Kitab-i-Bahriye* (*Book of the Sea*) consists of 29 chapters, each illustrated with a map. A kind of nautical manual of the Mediterranean, the book described as accurately as was possible at the time the ports, rivers, deeps, etc. A second edition, dedicated to Suleiman, was preceded by a poetic introduction, 1,200 verses long, about the sea and the sailor's life. Another sailor, Sidi Ali Reis, as we have seen,[27] had been compelled to take the land route when he returned from India to Istanbul; he gave an account of this long adventure in a lively and colourful little book called *Mirat ul Memalik* (*The Mirror of Countries*). He also wrote technical books for sailors and a new nautical manual for those who ventured into the Indian Ocean, *Al Muhit* (*The Ocean*).

The most famous work, particularly because of its illustrations, in this general area is the *Matraki Nasuh* and is concerned with the land rather than the sea; entitled *The Directory of Staging Posts*, it describes each of the places where Suleiman stopped off on the way from Istanbul to Baghdad during his Two Iraqs Campaign. A mathematician and astronomer, Matraki was one of the most learned men of his day in the exact sciences.

The Medrese

The *medrese*,[28] first established in the days of the earliest Seljuks, grew rapidly under Mehmed II. Their numbers increased even more in Suleiman's day, when the sultan greatly encouraged the development of instruction. Around the mosque which bore his name of *Fatih* (the Conqueror), Mehmed II had created eight *medrese* for advanced studies and another eight to prepare students for entry to them. Suleiman founded a good many more in the capital and throughout the empire. The six which formed part of the Suleimaniye, including a medical school, immediately acquired great renown, particularly in the sciences. It was then that Takkiyuddin Mehmed had an observatory built in Tophane, where he set about correcting the astronomical tables which had been established in the previous century by Ulug Bey at Samarkand, and it was then that the mathematician and geometer Ali Ibn Veli carried out research on logarithms several decades before any of the Europeans.

In the 16th century, there were nearly 100 *medrese* of every kind in Istanbul alone. They taught the rudiments of Turkish and Arabic grammar, rhetoric, theology, philosophy, astronomy, mathematics, Koranic law and jurisprudence. Some were founded by sultans, princes, *ulema* or leading dignitaries who established foundations or *vakf* to maintain them. All the large towns had several of their own *medrese* (there were 14 in Edirne in 1529), which turned out theologians and priests, lawyers and teachers. No position in the legal and religious hierarchy was open to those without qualifications from the *medrese*. Studies were arranged in a series of 11 classes from primary school up to the most advanced university courses (a hierarchy established once and for all by Suleiman) and divided into two kinds: 'intellectual' and religious studies. A diploma awarded at the end of each class allowed a student to proceed to the next one. Education was free, and some of the students were also housed and fed.

For several centuries, the *medrese* played a role in the Ottoman Empire similar to that of the universities in the West. All intellectual life was concentrated in these establishments, which disposed of large resources and enjoyed the patronage of the most important persons in the state; their teaching staff comprised the leading lights of Oriental culture.

The Koran and Tradition (*hadith*) were the basis of instruction. Human reasoning was regarded with suspicion, but the dominant school of Sunni thinking, led by al-Ghazali, believed that logic, mathematics and astronomy were permitted because they could only help the mind come to know the divine truth. In the following century, fanaticism won the day. The *ulema* came to prohibit the exact sciences and the books in which they were taught. Under Suleiman, on the other hand, as under Mehmed II, knowledge was encouraged, in so far as it did not go against the teachings of the Prophet. People carried out research, although with a fair degree of caution. Thus the Ottoman contribution to the sciences was rather small, except in astronomy and mathematics, areas which escaped the narrow-minded vigilance of the *ulema*.

In theology, bold speculation was not permitted. Anything new was automatically suspect. Reasoning was not allowed in religious study.

Philosophy and religion, despite Averroes, were incompatible. Molla Kabiz, a theologian who claimed that Jesus ranked above Mohammed, was handed over to justice. When the first tribunal acquitted him, Suleiman insisted that he be tried again; this time, he was condemned and executed. Anyone suspected of heresy was considered a danger to the state, especially when the Kizilbaş sect, in alliance with the Shah of Iran, was trying to stir up the people against the Ottomans. This authoritarian attitude was inspired by reasonable considerations in the 16th century; less than a hundred years later, however, it led to the fanaticism which was to be one of the major causes of the intellectual stagnation and decadence which afflicted the Ottoman Empire.

Three Centuries of Decline and Fall

The grief inspired by Suleiman's death throughout the empire was quite genuine. The Turks had lost their greatest emperor, whose reign surpassed in glory all who had preceded him. Even the fame of Mehmed II, who had seized Constantinople itself, paled beside that of the man who had conquered Rhodes and Belgrade, Buda and Baghdad. At his death, the empire extended from Lake Van and the Persian Gulf to the Carpathians, the Adriatic and the cataracts of the Nile. The Eastern and Central Mediterranean were a Turkish lake: corsairs subject to the sultan from Algiers and Tripoli attacked Christian shipping and laid waste the Spanish and Italian coasts. The war with Granada which convulsed Spain two years later would probably never have taken place but for the encouragement, and perhaps subsidies, coming from Istanbul. The sultan's ships were masters of the Red Sea and came to blows with the Portuguese in the Indian Ocean. Ottoman irregular troops spread terror all the way from Azerbaijan to Semmering.

Europe was on the defensive and expecting the worst – if Suleiman's heir turned out to be worthy of his father. Busbecq compared 'the Turk's limitless amibition, immense riches, and countless seasoned troops' with the contemporary state of Christendom: 'Our softness, our listlessness, the false sense of security we feel, our state on the slippery slope towards ruin . . . To avoid such great catastrophes, arms offer us the sole remedy; we must make haste to assemble them, raise troops and exercise them well.' A good deal of time went by before Europe was reassured to learn that the Magnificent Sultan had been succeeded by the Sot, although even he managed to snatch Cyprus, the last Christian bastion in the Eastern Mediterranean, from the Venetians.

The conquests which made the Ottoman Empire in less than half a century the greatest of its day both in area and in the power of its arms owed everything to Suleiman. Like his great-grandfather Mehmed II, he aimed to establish a universal monarchy. Admittedly, his wars against Ferdinand and Charles V to the North and the Shah of Persia to the East were often inspired by the threatening attitudes of such sovereigns: the former never gave up plans for a crusade against the 'Mohammedan barbarian' in Asia, while the latter constantly spread Shiite and Safavid propaganda into Anatolia and as far as Istanbul. Economic considerations also exerted an influence on acts of war designed to protect the sultan's finances and the Ottoman economy, although these were less significant than has sometimes been believed.

But over and above these political and, one might say, material motives, the sultan's conscience was the dominant factor. As the *padishah*, the instrument of God, he was the man who had to establish the reign of Islam in the territories which were still Infidel. A *gazi* and chief of all the *gazi*, 'God's shadow on earth', the sultan had a duty always to extend further the kingdom of Allah, to purify the world from 'the taint of polytheism' (as Christian belief in the Trinity was considered to be). When he brought fire and sword to the 'accursed nations', he was obeying the divine will. Whenever he appeared to forget, his entourage – the religious authorities and his own family – was there to remind him. His equanimity and majesty of behaviour reflected his certainty that he was the man chosen by God to establish the dominion of the true faith. Since the last of the Abbasids had left the scene, was he not the successor of the Caliphs and 'Exalted Imam', *Hilafet-i-Ulya*?

The End of the Age of Conquests

At the time of Suleiman's death, the Ottoman Empire was not only the most powerful in the world in terms of military might, the extent of the territory it controlled and its sovereign's riches, but in the size of its population. With 30–35 million inhabitants, if we include North Africa and the Arabian peninsula, it came far ahead of England (5 million inhabitants), Spain (6–7 million), Italy (12 million divided between many different states) and even France, which was 'full to the brim' but still only had a population of 16–18 million souls. The whole of Europe was probably quite close to the 80 million mark. The sultan's own states made up a third of this figure and formed a single unit, which was a great advantage if one contrasts the ease of movement in Suleiman's empire with the problems his widely separated possessions caused Charles V. Compared to the 700,000 inhabitants of Istanbul, the two greatest cities of Europe, Naples and Paris, had only half, and hardly a third, of that number respectively. London had a population of 120,000, Seville 100,000. None of them could compare in any way with the gigantic metropolis astride Europe and Asia and at the crossroads of the seas, the prestigious capital of an empire dominated for 46 years by a sovereign without a peer who ruled over a limitless supply of administrators and an army which were probably the finest of his day.

Such was the empire of Suleiman, which so terrified Europe that Busbecq predicted that Christendom would be destroyed: 'As soon as the Turk has made peace with the Persians,' he wrote a few years before the death of Suleiman, 'he will fall on us with all the strength of the Orient. Will we be in any condition to face up to him? In my opinion, it would be sheer folly to believe it . . .' The weight of that immense empire, the momentum of that undefeated army, were such that nothing seemed able to halt the advance of those hard, sober men who had been subjected to an iron discipline. They had been seen pillaging and massacring all the way to the gates of Vienna, and the rumours which went the rounds painted them as even more fearsome than they really were.

And yet, even before the Magnificent Sultan left the stage of history, cracks were beginning to be seen in the impressive edifice. Telltale signs started to worry the more farsighted observers: inflation and financial difficulties, rural depopulation, problems with the *timariote* system which had important social and economic consequences, undue influence of court favourites and women in the affairs of state. All was by no means lost in the Ottoman Empire in the years which saw the first signs of crisis in the European nations – a crisis which was soon going to convulse them all. Three centuries were to go by before the empire collapsed, and it still revealed itself as capable of astonishing achievements: Cyprus was conquered in 1571, Baghdad recaptured by Murad IV 22 years after it was lost in 1617; Crete became an Ottoman possession in 1669 and Vienna was besieged again in 1683. And yet the essential fact remains: the end of Suleiman's long reign, in Turkey as in the rest of Europe, also marked the end of the '*beau seizième siècle*'.

This was obviously more than a coincidence. The specific causes of the upheavals in England, France, Germany and the other European countries may not have been relevant in the Ottoman Empire, but its decadence should certainly not be attributed to 'a mysterious psychological deficiency in the Muslims'[1] that a certain kind of historian has long evoked. The sultans' Turkey failed to enter the modern age because its *raison d'être* – conquest – had suddenly failed, and because it had been unable to adapt to the new economic conditions created by the price revolution and the Western powers' frantic pursuit of profit. It was also because the empire was stuck in its own traditions and a nostalgia for the golden age of centuries past, which made it lag further and further behind its European rivals – rivals that were later to become its conquerors.

The countless successes of the Ottomans for more than three centuries were entirely due to the *gazi* spirit which controlled their behaviour. 'Fighters of the faith', they were men whose first duty was continually to advance the frontiers of Islam and submit Christian neighbours to their laws. Such an army of conquerors was destined for perpetual victory. When a major setback occurred, it disbanded or split up – which happened, as we have seen, after Bayezid's defeat by Tamerlane. When a state of inaction continued for too long, the troops began to complain. Yet it was then that a talented sultan would lead the army out into the field again, and the army would again achieve a string of victories – with new lands subdued, more exciting booty, as a reward. The conquered territories would be organized, the garrisons established there would raid towns and villages on the other side of the frontiers – which were imprecise and constantly changing – and, a few years later, a new campaign to the North would take janissaries, *sipahi*, *azab* and the immense artillery, all usually under the sultan's personal command, towards new infidel lands. Dervishes bringing the teachings of the Prophet went along with the army in this holy war. Thus it was from Orhan to Suleiman. Ten sultans subdued or conquered the Tsars of Bulgaria and Serbia, the Kings of Bosnia and Moldavia, the Emperor of Byzantium and the King of Hungary. Vienna was besieged, Rhodes captured from the Knights, Belgrade, Buda and most of Hungary occupied, the Papacy under threat. And then this stream of successes came to an end. Why?

In the long chronicle of Suleiman's battles, we have often seen the Turkish army, caught up in snowstorms and oceans of mud, compelled to turn back as soon as autumn arrived; on other occasions, the soldiers got bogged down by the spring rains almost as soon as they left Istanbul. When the sultan's army set out from Constantinople on 10 May 1529 for the Vienna campaign, they had great difficulty crossing rivers swollen by the rains. The only bridge over the Maritsa had been swept away and many soldiers drowned. The Morava, Sava and Drava had all been turned into torrents. When the bulk of the troops arrived before Vienna, the equinoctial rains had already begun and, for fear of losing his army's 120,000 men and 20,000 camels on the way home, Suleiman gave the order for departure. It was impossible to seize a town which held out until the bad weather began. The siege of Vienna lasted less than 20 days. In 1541 it was in June that Suleiman set out towards Hungary. He had hardly left Istanbul when torrents of rain halted his advance for three days. The same thing happened almost every time. In an era which saw the signs of the 'little ice age' to come,[2] the immense Turkish army, however well organized and disciplined, was incapable of carrying out a long campaign far from its bases. If Suleiman was always trying, without success, to join battle with Charles V and Ferdinand, it was because he knew that it was the only way to obtain a decisive result; lengthy military operations had to be interrupted every time bad weather arrived and put an intolerable strain on communication routes. In Europe, Ottoman expansion had reached its natural limits.

The same applied on the Persian front, where the difficulties were even greater: the lie of the land was even more intractable and the climate harsher. If they set out at the beginning of spring, the sultan's troops would not reach the shah's territories before June. The journey presented many dangers for men and animals, harried by Safavid horsemen and Kizilbaş and surrounded by hostile populations which had been constantly exposed to Shiite and Safavid propaganda. The campaign could not last more than three or four months – to travel back through snow always led to thousands of casualties. The territory also worked to the advantage of the enemy, who could always retreat into the desert to avoid an engagement. The lesson of Chaldiran (where Selim I crushed Shah Ismail in 1514) had been well learnt: the shah would never again join battle with the sultan; its immense size would be Persia's best defence.[3]

Frontiers also became fixed, particularly on the European wing, because the enemies of the Turks had organized their defences. From

1538, in Croatia and Slavonia, fortresses protected the Austrian territories, and a defence in depth was established. Soon afterwards, a system of forts was put in place on the Hungarian border, which long failed, however, to prevent raids and surprise attacks. Land was granted to Serbs in the region, on condition that they stood guard against the Turks. On the Adriatic, other Serbs known as Uzkok were given the same task, although they soon resorted to piracy. Further to the East, round Moldavia and Wallachia, Tartar incursions were difficult to contain. The time for major Turkish advances had past.

Crisis in the System, Crisis in the Economy

The end of the empire's expansionary years had immense consequences. All the basic structures of Ottoman Turkey – financial, economic, social and institutional – were put in turmoil; the impact was all the greater because the crisis ensued at the very moment when profound changes were taking place in the Western world. There were also important psychological repercussions in an army and a people where traditions of religious expansion were deeply rooted.

It would be easy to say that such a powerful empire contained within it the seeds of its own decadence, yet many setbacks could have been avoided. If they were not, Suleiman and his successors over the following decades must take a large share of the responsibility.

It is obvious that the accumulation of riches and the existence of a large network of dignitaries, administrators, religious and military chiefs, princes – and princesses – could only favour intrigue and corruption. Suleiman's court was very different from his grandfather Bayezid's, and even less like the simple life-style of the first sultans. When the Harem was established in Topkapi, women, eunuchs and court favourites were bought to the very heart of an empire which had previously excluded them. Palace and government were thrown into confusion. Several decades later, Koçi Bey gave a dramatic description of this: 'Women without faith or religion entered the imperial Harem. Order and discipline were ruined, laws and decrees ceased to exist.' He attributed this deplorable situation to the fact that the sultans had stopped concerning themselves with affairs of state, and that the post of Grand Vizier had been degraded into a reward for imperial favour and no longer for genuine ability.

Up to the time of Suleiman, royal princes were given their first taste of power in ruling provinces. Although the others ran the risk of being assassinated when one of their number came to the throne, this cruel system at least assured that a prince who assumed power had some experience of affairs of state. When the Law of Fratricide was suppressed and the princes locked away in the Seraglio *kafes* ('cages'), it was the sultan's mother or *valide sultan* who exercised power through the Grand Vizier or he himself who did so in his own interests and those of his clique (or often his wife's clique, when she was the sister or daughter of the sultan).

In the 17th and 18th centuries, certain remarkable men – Murad IV from 1623 to 1640, the Koprulu dynasty of Grand Viziers – controlled the empire at one time or another, yet they were very much the exception. Such a grave situation was made even more disastrous because there were no brakes or limits on the exercise of power. The *ulema* had themselves been corrupted and become accomplices of the courtiers in an attempt to share their spoils. Sultanas, favourites and dignitaries sold off public offices and the right to raise taxes and played a major role in the smuggling of merchandise it was not permitted to export. They also took over the lands and revenues of the *timar*, which had particularly catastrophic consequences.

The role of the *sipahi* had already diminished because they were only very rarely given firearms. The janissaries were provided with muskets (*tufeng*), while the *timariote* cavalry fought to the end of the century armed only with spears, bows and sabres. When the court prebendaries cut off the *timar* which they lived on, the *sipahi*'s ruin was accomplished. They slowly ceased to exist: there were 200,000 in 1550, not more than 7,000 in 1630. They were employed in secondary tasks, like building roads and fortifications, and their lands became part of the large estates which were then being formed, the *çiftlik* or *malikhane* (which gave the possessors a life-time right to raise taxes).

The primary consequence of this weakening of the *timariote* cavalry was the increased importance of the janissaries, who were paid in good money. In less than a century, their contingents increased from 10,000 to 40,000 men. Both their grip on the state and the amount they had to be paid increased in parallel. Because of the devaluation of the currency, however, even their new level of wages was not enough and they had to be allowed to exercise a profession. This led to the decline of the elite corps and the growth of the *seğban*, landless young men engaged by the government at the same time and equipped with firearms. Later these men formed into bands of brigands which posed major problems for the authorities.

The wars against the Safavids and Habsburgs at the end of the 16th century were like a bottomless pit which sucked in money. Territories which were conquered, far from bringing in revenue, led to expenses without any returns. The state had to get hold of more money, which the treasury, partly because of inflation, simply did not possess. It then used the familiar system of tax farming – selling off to the highest bidder the right to impose taxes – as an immediate source of finance.

In the Ottoman Empire, however, the system was disastrous. The palace and dignitaries appropriated lands and used fraudulent means to get hold of tax returns. Certain estates were thus transformed into *vakf* which were no longer under state control. Tax receipts soon became insufficient. The luxury expenses of the court, which attained dizzying levels, the maintenance and payment of the army (now almost entirely in the hands of the state, since the *timar* system had become enfeebled), created a perpetual deficit. The modernization of weaponry meant a further increase in the resources required by the military. With this went the depreciation in the value of money and its corollary, higher prices – and thus a whole range of important social and political consequences.

On the whole, Suleiman's reign was a period of prosperity and economic stability. The system, which was based on consumption rather than profit, functioned without any major crises or serious shocks apart from those which were inherent in it. It was by no means sheltered from the impact of external events, but the power of the central political authorities could deal with those fairly easily. The sultan could lay down the law almost throughout the Mediterranean. The Black Sea was a Turkish lake. The conquest of Egypt and Syria brought immense resources into the empire in the form of agriculture, commerce and taxes. It was from the West, from Europe and the Americas, that the storms would come – storms which found the *padishah* quite defenceless.

Was the influx of gold and then silver from the New World, brought by the Spanish and Portuguese in the age of the great discoveries, responsible for the price increases which gave a 'revolutionary' stamp to the era? The answer is both yes and no. Yes, because such quantities of precious metals suddenly introduced into the economy inevitably lost value in comparison with other products and therefore increased their prices. There is no doubt of the overlap in time between the arrival of the American gold and silver and the price rises of the 16th century.[4] And yet it is also true that before the precious metals reached Europe in what were, after all, fairly modest quantities, the epoch of low prices in the

15th century had *already* played a major role in the economic take-off which was also favoured by demographic, technological, commercial and political developments to be observed all over Europe. It was a time when the populations of villages tripled or quadrupled, when more and more land was cleared once again, and when the earliest industries were born. The first modern states and monetary economies appeared. Changes in prices were an inevitable consequence, and they had started to occur *before* the discovery of America. 'The European conjuncture determined everything from far away.'[5]

The price revolution did not immediately reach the Ottoman Empire. In the earlier decades of the 16th century, variations in prices were minimal. Calculations[6] based on the expenses of the Istanbul *imaret* reveal that they had increased by about 40% in the period up to the middle of the century, which is strikingly similar to Western Europe. But after 1560, Mexican silver and, to a lesser extent, gold invaded the Turkish market and had a considerable impact. In 1588, the price increase was around 300%. The limit was reached in 1606, when the average increase attained 500%. The asper (*akçe*), the older Turkish currency, lost half its value. Its percentage of silver, which had been maintained at 0.731 grams throughout Suleiman's reign and fell to 0.682 just after his death, later collapsed completely. The 1585 devaluation reduced its weight by about half to 0.384 grams, to be followed by 0.323 at the end of the century and 0.306 at the end of the next. The coins became thinner and thinner, with more and more copper and less and less silver, until they were 'light as the leaves of the almond tree and as worthless as a drop of dew'.

The Ottoman authorities were even less able to counteract the influx of cheap money because the European states exploited the situation. They flooded the Ottoman Empire not only with genuine silver but with more and more coins made of alloys which drove out the good money. An immense traffic in fake coins – 5-sou pieces which were 80% if not totally adulterated as well as coppers – took place between the French South and the Ottoman Empire in the 17th and 18th centuries. Dutch and English, Venetians and especially Genoese, came not far behind. In northern Italy, they made fake *aslani*, fake sequins and fake 5-sou pieces which were sent by the trunk load directly to Istanbul or by way of Greek money changers in the Aegean. The merchandise that traders bought with adulterated money cost them virtually nothing. Purchases from abroad increased the prices and led to accelerating inflation. The Turks were the victims, but their government was powerless. Successive devaluations achieved nothing. In 1620, the Porte created a new currency called the *para*, and towards the end of the century the *kuruş*, but both of these suffered the fate of the *akçe*.

Nothing could prevent the erosion of the value of money. Devaluations produced discontent in every social class. This state of monetary chaos worked to the advantage of only the speculators, dominated by the minority populations, and the dignitaries and court favourites who asked for their services to be paid for in sound foreign currencies. Everybody else suffered. In 1584 the janissaries, furious at being paid in devalued money, attacked the Seraglio and demanded the head of the Rumelian *beylerbey* and the *defterdar* who had treated them thus. A few years later, it was the turn of the Porte *sipahi* to mutiny. The janissaries were ordered to deal with them, with predictable effects on morale and *esprit de corps* in the army. Functionaries and all who lived on salaries looked elsewhere for an income. Corruption spread at the same time as the intellectual level of the elites, functionaries and *ulema* – who had long been the empire's major strength – diminished drastically.

Another factor aggravated and accelerated the deterioration in social and economic conditions: the population of the empire increased considerably in the 16th century. After the devastations of the 13th and 14th centuries, the whole of Europe was slowly repopulated, a development which started around 1450 and continued until the end of the following century. The population probably doubled in the course of the 16th century, a phenomenon which had a deeper influence on the destiny of Europe than any other event in the political or economic sphere. The Ottoman Empire shared in these changes, with 12 million inhabitants in 1520, 18 million in 1580 and perhaps 35 million around 1600.[7] The effects were most noticeable in the towns: Konya increased by 203%, Ankara by 95%, Bursa by 101% and Sarajevo by 317%. In the countryside, the impact was smaller and less evenly spread. In Anatolia, the average level of increase was 42%, yet this covered a range from 129% in the Ankara region to a mere 0.88% at Aydin.

The number of country-dwellers at the time was too large for the amount of cultivated land. In the still recent period when conquest was adding fresh territories to the empire, surplus populations were sent from the old provinces into the Balkans, where there were wide empty spaces to be filled. This process of *surgun* (or deportation) played a major role in the 'Turkification' of Eastern Europe. From the 1550s, however, conquest slowed to a halt. About twenty years later, Cyprus was colonized by

Turks – and that was the end of the story. There was no longer an escape route for the excess populations deprived of a means of subsistence by the dissolution of the *timar* system and the leasing out of lands hitherto in the hands of the *sipahi*. When the *timar* system (which assured that the state's military needs would be met and that there would be no threat to those in power) gave way to 'commercialized' agriculture, it was at the expense of the peasants. They had no choice but to set out for the towns, although they often failed to find work there either.

Here we touch again upon the disadvantages of the inward-looking Ottoman guild system, and the role of the Europeans in the deterioration of economic, social and political conditions in the sultan's empire. The closed world of the guilds prevented all innovation, all personal initiative and all change within a system which had been fixed immutably. In the face of European competition which benefited greatly from the capitulations, local industry remained static. Turkish craftsmanship was excellent, but it consisted in the reproduction, often of the highest quality, of works which had already been made. The guilds and the state itself did nothing to stem the flood of Western manufactured goods which were coming in. In the 17th century, half of French industry was working for the countries of the Ottoman Empire. It was fashionable, even among the middle classes, to dress in European materials: linen and silk. The authorities only considered such imports in terms of the customs receipts they brought in and the satisfaction they gave consumers. Exports consisted almost entirely of raw materials, which deprived the empire of goods which could easily have been refined within the country.

The mercantilism the Europeans practised, under the eyes of the Turks and at their expense, remained alien to them. There was no chance, therefore, that they would achieve an industrial capitalism which could create work and develop new resources. The members of the ruling class invested in large-scale trading, in the credit operations with high interest rates which were so developed in the Ottoman Empire and in major agricultural enterprises, but never in the crafts which could have developed into industrial production, just as they did in the West. Apart from arsenals and the armaments industry, there were no enterprises which could absorb a large workforce. The state took no interest in the areas which could have formed embryo industries.

No openings, therefore, were any longer available for the larger and larger group of people who could not make a living on their land, whether because it had been absorbed into a great estate or confiscated for non-payment of debt, or whether the pressure of taxes had obliged them to take flight. Not only were further taxes levied from 1580 to pay for the long wars against Iran and the Habsburgs; with the development of leasing, tax collectors exploited the *reaya* who had been left completely without protection.

In a 'justice decree' published in 1608, Ahmed I criticized governors and district leaders for farming out taxes at too high a price and letting tax collectors try to extort larger sums than the amounts fixed by law and set out in the registers. Judges were so corrupt, he claimed, that they accepted bribes from litigants, imposed unlawful fines and sold the administrative posts they controlled to the highest bidder. These deputies in turn forced the peasants to pay them and feed them, not to mention their entourage, whenever they entered a village. This meant that the ruined *reaya* had to borrow money from a usurer, who asked for work in return for the loan. The peasant thus became more or less a slave, the sultan concluded.

Such peasants left the countryside and swelled the ranks of the city dwellers who were unemployed or gained an absolute pittance. They invaded the military and religious colleges, which thus became filled with men incapable of taking advantage of their teaching. This led to a sharp fall in the ability of the *ulema* and army officers, and a good deal of discontent among the students. Many of them joined the bands of brigands who appeared in Anatolia in the latter years of Suleiman's reign, after the defeat of Prince Bayezid's rebellion. The prince had recruited an army consisting of men of every kind spurred on by need or attracted by booty: *sipahi* who had lost their *timar*, janissaries on the loose, dignitaries who counted on his success. After his flight and death, these men found themselves without a leader and without work, wandering around Anatolia in search of subsistence. They collected in Istanbul, Rumelia, Syria and even the Crimea. It was the 'great flight' (*buyuk kaçagin*) which made the country prey to such bands of rebels or *celali*. These were often formed around companies of unemployed *seğban*, who were all the more dangerous because many of them possessed firearms they had bought fairly cheaply or had kept hold of since they had been granted a licence.

The diffusion of firearms among the *reaya* at the end of the 16th century was certainly one of the main causes of the disorders which were to shed so much blood in Anatolia, an area which had already been torn apart by anarchy and impoverished by the departure of the wealthier classes. The janissaries and Porte *sipahi* were sent in to restore order, but they merely used the opportunity to seize land, like the traders and bureaucrats, and thus created a new class which dominated the country until the 18th century. Less than 50 years after the end of Suleiman's glorious reign, almost the whole of Anatolia was in a state like that of France after the Hundred Years' War.

Such upheavals went on for a long time. Although they eventually came to an end, they left behind a large and unfortunate legacy. The administrators and local notables who replaced the fief holders had become landowners and used their political power solely for personal enrichment. The commercialization of agriculture helped bring about profound changes in the social fabric and economy of Anatolia and the Balkans. At the same time, the janissaries 'invaded' every area of Turkish life. Less and less a product of the *devşirme* system, they were now mainly Turkish Muslims who had used money or influence to get in; they were no longer warriors devoted body and soul to the sultan but an alternative power base which often laid claim to the supreme power. Allowed to marry and carry on another profession (usually as shopkeepers), the janissaries had ceased to be the elite troops of the empire – the *seğban* were the best soldiers – but used their positions all over the country to terrorize the population. It would take two centuries for a sultan – Mahmud II – to come to the throne and deal with them once and for all by means of a massacre.

Nostalgia for the Golden Age

The sombre picture we have just painted ought, if we were ignorant of what happened in the following centuries, to have ended in apocalyptic disaster. And yet, as is well known, nothing of the sort occurred. 'This so-called decadence is a misnomer,' writes Fernand Braudel. Even in its darkest days, the Ottoman Empire remained an immense power. It is not mere chance that the Turkish 17th century (hardly a very fortunate era, as we have seen) produced intellectuals, writers, poets and artists who were among the greatest of the Islamic period. Even the army of janissaries and undisciplined and corrupt *sipahi* managed to ward off for three centuries the assaults of adversaries who desired nothing more than to get rich at the expense of the Ottomans and to share out their possessions between them.

As soon as a dynamic and skilful sultan took the throne, recovery followed quickly. During the early decades of the 17th century, the empire was in complete anarchy, the capital in the hands of rebellious soldiers and vagabonds, the provinces overrun by bands of *celali* and brigands. In less than 10 years, Murad IV restored the empire. He had 20,000 people killed, the *şeyhulislam*, Grand Vizier and many others strangled or decapitated. And yet order and discipline were re-established in the army, town and country again became safe. Baghdad, which had been lost, was recaptured, the route to the Persian Gulf was reopened, and the Persian menace to the eastern provinces was checked for a while.

A few years later, when the throne was yet again in feeble hands, a farsighted and energetic dynasty of Grand Viziers, the Koprulu family, brought back a youthful vigour to the empire. Their methods were undoubtedly of the utmost brutality (Mehmed Koprulu sent 12,000 decapitated heads to Istanbul on a single day), but they were probably necessary; at all events, they brought an end to disorder and corruption, discipline was re-established and the budget balanced. The conquest of Crete in 1689 was a clear sign that the military abilities of the Turks were still intact. In 1683, the sultan was able to send 200,000 men to lay siege to Vienna.

The Ottoman retreat from Europe, which started with the peace of Carlowitz in 1699, the cession of Hungary and Transylvania to the Habsburgs and Azov to the Russians, took three long centuries to complete. 'The sick man of Europe' we read about in history books carried out his retreat without ceasing to fight. Even at the start of the 19th century, Selim III and Mahmud II managed to recapture the dynamism of their distant ancestors, restore the state's authority and reform abuses. So, what exactly was lacking in the empire of Mehmed the Conqueror and Suleiman the Magnificent? Why did it not remain the great power, the terror of Europe, it had been in the middle of the 16th century?

We know some of the circumstantial causes for the Ottoman decline. The execution of Mustafa, on Suleiman's orders, is one of them. If Mustafa, described by all observers as extremely talented, instead of Selim the Sot, had put on the sword of Osman, many things would have been different. The rule of favourites and females, for which Suleiman must take responsibility, also had important consequences, although it was probably less significant than the replacement of the Law of Fratricide by the *kafes* and the disintegration of the *timar* system.

Did Suleiman lack foresight? Some historians[8] have claimed as much. The sultan should have co-operated with Venice and not France, they suggest, should have seized Morocco and not besieged Vienna, should have predicted the Russian menace or followed a different Mediterranean policy . . . It is easy to rewrite history four centuries after the events. The greatest threat to the Ottoman Empire in the 16th century did not come from the man who would one day arise in the forests and steppes around Moscow but from the only too real enemies who were as obsessed with the idea of a crusade as people had been in the days of Godfrey of Bouillon and Saint Louis (King Louis IX of France). The threat was not from the still-to-be-born Peter the Great but from Charles V and Ferdinand, the Popes at Rome who were always ready to support and finance the anti-Turkish projects of the Christian princes. Europe was trying to carve up the empire and stifle its economy. The great mistake made by Suleiman and his successors was quite different: they failed to understand how much the world was changing around them; no 'return to tradition' would ever have been enough to restore the state.

Everything seemed to happen as if the empire had got stuck in the middle of the 16th century. Twenty years after the death of Suleiman, his reign was regarded as a golden age; fifty years later, even more so. In 1630, Koçi Bey, in his memorandum to Murad IV, evoked the Magnificent Sultan's glorious era with poignant nostalgia: 'In the past, the Sublime Sultan was served by devoted *ulema*, who were well-meaning and worthy, and by slaves obedient and eager . . . Today, all that has changed, and turmoil, sedition and dissension have gone beyond all bounds.' The sultan's counsellor also laid down the remedy – a return to the Law of Mohammed – and concluded: 'And then the enemies of the Faith will see order and stability and will say with fear and envy: "The House of Osman slept, unconcerned, for sixty years, but now it has woken again and started to repair the errors of the past." '

Even the reformers of the 19th century believed that they could renew the empire by returning to traditional ways.

The received wisdom among historians is that the Islamic religion, in essence 'conservative', was the main cause of the sclerosis which weakened the empire at the end of Suleiman's reign. Yet this is to confuse cause and effect. Quite apart from the difficulties of finding criteria to classify religions as 'reactionary' or 'progressive', it is noteworthy that the fervently religious early Islamic centuries were also one of the most fruitful and brilliant periods in the history of learning. In philosophy, the transmission of the Greek heritage to the West, pure and applied science, architecture and the decorative arts, the synthesis of Oriental and

Mediterranean culture made the Muslim golden age one of the most accomplished and original civilizations ever seen. How much did the Muslim religion contribute to this flowering and development? At the very least, it was no obstacle. What remains to be explained is the mysterious underlying causes which later, at a particular moment in Ottoman history, made the religion of Mohammed 'dessicated' and 'obscurantist'.

It is not mere chance that the rise in fanaticism coincided with the end of the Ottoman era of conquest and the increasing corruption of the ruling classes. The Ottoman brand of Islam had been hardened by the struggle against the Kizilbaş movement, which Iran made every effort to support, and by the conviction, since Selim I had made the sultan of Constantinople the *imam* and Protector of the Faith, that his role was to act as guardian of the *Şeriat*. To defend their privileges, the *ulema* put up barriers against any kind of learning which could threaten their positions of superiority. The ban (with a few exceptions) on importing foreign books and printing until the beginning of the 18th century well expressed such fears. With fanaticism and all its dire consequences went the 'price revolution' and the transformation of the *timariote* economy into a commercial economy.

Maintained in a state of economic underdevelopment both by the West and by its own working arrangements – industrial and commercial – ill-adapted to the demands of the modern world, steeped in nostalgia for a golden age and still inextricably bound up in its Oriental past, the Ottoman Empire was in a deplorable state. Yet it was in just such a state that it had to face the challenges of a new age, the age of capitalism and early industry.

Notes

At the Dawn of the Golden Century

1. The Safavid dynasty dated back to Sheikh Safi al-Din, who founded the mystic (Sufi) order of Safavid dervishes in the 14th century. Hence the nickname 'Sophy' given to Safavid sovereigns by Europeans.

2. Shiism is a religious movement based on belief in the imams – descendants of Ali, the cousin and husband of the Prophet's daughter Fatima – as the sole authorities fit to lead the community of believers. The line of imams was broken by the 'eclipse' of the twelfth imam Mohammed, who disappeared without descendants after 873. He is the 'Hidden Imam', the 'Master of Time', who will reappear one day 'to fill with justice a world sunk in iniquity'.

The Ismaili Shiites, for their part, believe that the line of imams came to an end with the seventh imam Ismail, who died prematurely before his father, Jafar as-Sadiq. These Ismaili Shiites are in turn divided into 'Eastern Ismailis' (whose leader is now the Aga Khan) and 'Western Ismailis', who follow the Fatimid imams; the twenty-first and last of these 'disappeared' in 1130 and is also due to 'return'.

3. René Grousset, *L'Empire des Steppes*, Paris, 1939. We do not know the precise reasons why the Turkish tribes left Central Asia and set out to the West. Perhaps because the climate and water supply had changed, perhaps because of tribal warfare or other political factors. Some historians believe that the economic and political evolution of China encouraged the nomadic peoples who wandered over the northern steppes to abandon areas where all possibility of southern expansion was closed off to them. In any event, the westward migration took place in small steps and by a process of infiltration, not in brutal waves of invaders.

4. As shown by Louis Bazin, 'Turcs et Sogdiens', *Mélanges Benveniste* (1975).

5. See A. Bombaci, *Histoire de la Littérature Turque*, Paris, 1968.

6. See Appendix 1.

7. These were established all along the Byzantine frontiers from the 11th century, perhaps in imitation of the Turks and Arabs. The look-out posts faced the enemy at a set distance apart, using optical signals to communicate.

8. Long is the list of daughters of the great Byzantine families (and even the royal house itself) who married Turkish princes. Orhan married a princess of the Cantacuzenus dynasty, and so did his son Khalil. Catherine Comnenus, daughter of the last Emperor of Trabzon, became the wife of Sultan Uzun Hassan of the White Sheep dynasty, Mary Comnenus the wife of Kutulu Bey and another Mary the wife of Çelebi (both from the same house), and so on. 'The inhabitants could hardly distinguish between Greeks and Turks. The Greek princes largely blended into the new political formation by marriage, service or hopes of advancement and were soon completely absorbed' (Nicolas Jorga, *Histoire des États Balkaniques*, Paris, 1925).

9. F. Babinger, *Mahomet II le Conquérant et son Temps*, Paris, 1954.

10. F. Braudel, *La Méditerranée et le Monde Méditerranéen*, Vol. 2, Paris, 1979.

11. F. Grenard, *Grandeur et Décadence de l'Asie*, Paris, 1947.

12. Ogier Ghislain (or Ghiselin) de Busbecq was born in Comines, Flanders, in 1522. After occupying various posts at the courts of Charles V and Philip II, he was sent to Constantinople in 1555 as ambassador for Ferdinand I, Charles V's brother and successor. He remained there until 1562. The four *Letters* he wrote during his long stay in the Ottoman capital are among the best informed and most penetrating accounts of the Ottoman Empire in the 16th century. A man of considerable cultivation and curiosity of mind, it was he who discovered the 'Testament of Augustus' or 'monument of Ancyrus' in Ankara. He was also responsible for introducing the tulip and the lilac into Western Europe. On his return from Constantinople, he was employed as Grand Master to the household of Archduchess Elizabeth (wife of Charles IX) and ambassador of Rudolph II to the court of France. He died in Rouen in 1592.

13. Paolo Giovio, *Turcicarum Rerum Commentarius*, Rome, 1531.

14. The term *Porte* (or Threshold) to describe the Ottoman seat of government goes back a long way in Oriental history. It probably takes its origin from the fact that the sovereign received his people's complaints at the door of his palace. At Constantinople, the expression *Bab-i-Ali* (translated as 'Sublime Porte') referred until the 18th century to the royal *Divan* (or council) and then, when the seat of government was transferred to the residence of the Grand Vizier, to the buildings which housed his staff.

15. W.E.D. Allen, *Problems of Turkish Power in the Sixteenth Century*, London, 1963.

16. In 667, the army of the Omayyad caliph laid siege to Constantinople, only to lift the siege the following year. They returned in 674 with a powerful fleet, which cut off the Bosphorus. The Byzantine capital was only saved by the use of 'Greek fire' (an explosive mixture containing petrol) and, in 677, the Arabs retreated and made peace with the Basileus.

17. Many studies of Cem (Zizim) have appeared, dealing with his wanderings through Italy and France, his love affairs, the scandalous attitudes of the Christian princes towards him and his mysterious death. One of the most recent and serious is René Boudard's: 'Le Sultan Zizim vu à travers les Témoignages de quelques Écrivains et Artistes Italiens de la Renaissance', *Turcica* VII, pages 135–56.

18. Split, Durazzo, Zadar and, in the Peloponnese, Koron, Modon and Monemvasia had been under his control for a long time.

19. According to Haci Halifa, the historian of the Turkish naval wars, 300 ships were laid down, including 2 enormous vessels with double bridges and capable of carrying 2,000 sailors and soldiers. They were propelled by 42 oars on either side, each requiring 9 men (*History of the Maritime Wars of the Turks*, London, 1831).

20. The term 'heterodox' would really be more appropriate than 'Shiite', because 15th- and 16th-century Shiism has little in common with that of today (apart from its glorification of Ali and the Shiite martyrs). I have decided to retain the more familiar term, but this proviso should always be kept in mind.

21. The title 'caliph' had completely different meanings in Abbasid and Ottoman times since the Ottoman caliphs were not descended from the Quraysh, the tribe of the Prophet. Since, they claimed, God had made them the most powerful group in the Muslim world, their superiority over other Islamic leaders also gave them the right to bear the title 'caliph'. There is indeed a tradition that Selim I was invested as caliph by al-Mutawakil in Saint-Sophia, but this story is too recent to be taken seriously as historical fact. It arose during the empire's decline, when the sultans revived the classical ideas about the caliphate in order to support their claims to certain privileges as the caliphs of the Muslims (in the Treaty of Kuçukçekmece in 1744, for example, which recognized the independence of the Crimean khanate).

22. 'There is no doubt that Selim's elevation to the position of Leader of the Faithful in 1517 had as great an impact in the Islamic world as the famous election of Charles of Spain to the office of Holy Roman Emperor two years later, in Christendom. That event marked the beginning of the

age of great Ottoman power and also – since every good thing has a price – a tide of religious intolerance. Could Suleiman's great reign have been quite so impressive if it had not been preceded by the conquest of Egypt and Syria?' (Braudel, *op. cit.*).

23. See Chapter 8.

Chapter 1

1. For 'rebelling', according to some sources, although others say – and it seems more likely – that it was carried out in accordance with the Law of Fratricide, laid down by Mehmed II, which allowed a sultan to kill off his brothers when he came to power (see Appendix 4). In that case, Selim would simply have carried this out instead of Suleiman – whom he had certainly chosen as his heir – in order, as an Ottoman historian put it, 'to clear the way for him'. This would have been very much in Selim's style.

2. A scholar who taught the Prophet's law.

3. Şebinkarahisar is a small town in the North of Central Anatolia, about 100 kilometres from the Black Sea. Amasya is a more important town situated considerably further West. Bolu is between Ankara and Istanbul, about 250 kilometres from the latter.

4. Danişmend, in his *Osmanli Tarihi Kronoloji* (II.5), reports the view of the historian Ahmed Tevhid Bey that 'there is a strong presumption that Yavuz [Selim] had three sons, Murad, Mahmud and Abdullah, besides Suleiman, who were all killed on 20 November 1514; if this presumption is correct, Yavuz Sultan Selim would have had his own sons assassinated 18 months and 24 days after the murder of his last brother, thus leaving Prince Suleiman as his sole heir. However, it has also been claimed that these princes were put to death under the reign of the Lawgiver.'

A.D. Alderson, in *The Structure of the Ottoman Dynasty*, seems to have no doubt about the existence and execution of these three princes: 'Selim I was thus compelled to execute three of his own sons.' R. Mantran, in *La Vie quotidienne à Constantinople au temps de Soliman le Magnifique et ses successeurs*, also comes to the same conclusion: 'Selim I had executed, during the first months of his reign, four nephews, two brothers and, a little later, three rebellious sons.'

5. The asper (*akçe*) was a small piece of silver weighing 0.723 grammes at the time of Suleiman. There were 50 aspers to a gold piece (*altun*), a few more to a Venetian ducat. A 'purse' (*kese*) was valued then at 20,000 aspers (in hard currency).

6. Marino Sanuto, *I Diarii*, Venice 1889.

7. There is another striking portrait by Cristofano Dell'Altissimo in the Uffizi in Florence (Collezione Gioviana).

8. In the National Gallery in London.

9. Koran XXI, 79.

10. N. Jorga, *Histoire des Etats balkaniques*, Paris, 1925.

11. Until that time, the danger had not been very great. The appeals of Nicolas V in 1453, Calixtus III in 1455, Pius II in 1460, Paul III in 1466, Innocent VIII in 1484, Alexander VI (who advised Bayezid to capture the Kingdom of Naples) and, finally, Julius II in 1503 all fell on deaf ears.

12. See Chapter 5, page 141.

13. The text of the letter (according to Bâtard de Bourbon) was as follows: 'We order the present fortress to be made over to us, telling you by this our decree that we wish to have this island, because of the great damage and evil actions inflicted on us from here every day. If it is handed over with good grace and including the castle to our imperial majesty, we swear by God who made heaven and earth, by our twenty-six thousand prophets, by the four volumes of holy scripture [sacred to the four Peoples of the Book] descended from heaven, and by our prophet Mohammed, that everybody in the said isle, adult and child, need have no fear of danger or damage from our imperial majesty . . . and if you are not willing to surrender, as is asked, we shall turn the foundations of your castle upside-down and inflict a terrible death on you, as we have done to many others – of that you can be assured.'

14. The Turks had brought to Rhodes 6 cast-iron cannons which shot cannon-balls 6 palms in circumference, 15 iron cannons with cannon-balls of 5–6 palms, 10 mortars firing iron cannon-balls and 12 cast-iron mortars (according to Bâtard de Bourbon). One palm is equivalent to 25 centimetres.

15. The members of the Order were divided into three classes: the Knights, who wore a red habit with a white cross; the priests or chaplains; and the servant brothers. They were also split into eight 'languages' or 'nations' – France, Provence, Auvergne, Italy, England, Germany, Aragon and Castile – each led by a 'bailiff'. The eight bailiffs formed the Chapter presided over by the Grand Master, who was elected by all the Knights. Of the 19 Grand Masters in the period from 1309 to 1522, 14 were of French origin (which corresponds fairly closely to the proportion of French Knights).

16. Quoted by J. von Hammer-Purgstall, *Histoire de l'Empire ottoman depuis son origine jusqu'à nos jours*, Paris, 1835–48.

17. Letter of Villiers de l'Isle Adam to his nephew Fr. de Montmorency in E. Charrière, *Négociations de la France dans le Levant*, Paris, 1840–60.

18. Fontanus, quoted by J. von Hammer-Purgstall, *op. cit.*

19. If the amount was between 20,000 and 100,000 *akçe*, it was called a *zeamet* (normally the endowment of a *subaşi*); above that, it was known as a *has*.

20. *Inventaire de l'Histoire générale des Turcs*, Paris, 1617.

21. Rumelia refers to the whole of European Turkey apart from Bosnia, Hungary, Albania, Morea and the Greek islands.

Chapter 2

1. In J. von Hammer-Purgstall, *op. cit.*

2. In the 9th century, a tribe of Magyar knights had emigrated from the Urals towards the Carpathians, the Danube delta and the Black Sea. According to Arab geographers, these 'Madghari' were Turks. The Hungarians were to take their name from the Onoghours of Bulgar origin, who settled in the region of South-East Carpathia and intermarried with the Magyars. A little later, they moved to Greater Moravia, where for several years their bands of marauders ravaged Northern Italy, Germany, Lorraine and even Burgundy and Provence. When they were crushed by the German king Othon I, their chief, Vaik, converted to Catholicism under the name of Etienne I. The Magyars then became fervent defenders of Christianity against the barbarians, but the indiscipline of the nobility and the system of an elective monarchy made their state one of the weakest in Eastern Europe. John Hunyadi and his son Matthias Corvinus created for a short period (1444–90) an army of mercenaries under central control and weakened the power of the nobility, but the nobles managed to regain their privileges and dissolve these mercenary forces under their successors Ladislas and Lewis.

3. Suleiman's journal, which the functionaries of the imperial chancellery kept up during military campaigns, tells, at each stop, of the main events of the day. For example, the journal of the Turkish campaign of 1526 starts thus: '23 April (11 *receb*): departure from Constantinople; the army stops at Haltali Binar . . . 8 May: the sultan reviews the army. 9 May: rest day; a soldier is beheaded for trampling on the harvest . . . 27 August: the army stops to wait for equipment. 28 August: rest day; the emperor makes it known we will attack tomorrow. A young soldier is beheaded for advancing without being given the order. 29 August: set up camp on the Mohacs plain [battle details] . . .31 August: the emperor,

seated on a golden throne, receives homage from the viziers and *beys*; 2,000 prisoners massacred; the rain falling in torrents . . .' J. von Hammer-Purgstall, in the notes to his monumental *Histoire de l'Empire ottoman*, published lengthy extracts from this journal, although some of it has apparently not yet appeared in print.

4. Kemalpashazade, who performed until his death in 1534 the important duties of *şeyhulislam*, was considered amazingly learned. His style is full of hyperbole and audacious images and ranks among the best prose of a lively and colourful era.

5. Peçevi, a Turkish historian of the sixteenth century.

6. These statues were set up in the Hippodrome, just next to the Aya Sophia mosque and the palace (an engraving by Pieter Coecke Van Aelst of 1553 shows Suleiman crossing the Hippodrome with his entourage; in the background three statues can be seen on high pedestals). This led to a considerable scandal. Matthias Corvinus's library was taken to the Seraglio. Most of the books in it were destroyed in one of the fires which ravaged the palace on several occasions, notably in 1574 and 1665.

7. From ancient times, Ottoman occupation of a country proceeded in two stages. First, the defeated local princes became the sultan's vassals. Sooner or later, they were eliminated and the Turkish state took over direct rule by means of the *timar* system. Osman Gazi used this method with Koşe Mihal, emir of Hermanskaya, and several other rulers. The Karamanids of Konya, the Serbian and Bulgar princes were first vassals and then disappeared completely to make way for Ottoman administration. During this first stage, Christian troops in the Balkans were used as auxiliaries; they were later given the opportunity to become *timariotes*.

8. M. Bandello, *Novelle*, London, 1791–3.

9. He had obtained the throne of Bohemia as well, where Lewis was also king.

10. Luigi Gritti, son of Doge Andrea Gritti (1523–38), was born in Constantinople during his father's imprisonment (he was then the *bailo* of the Republic). Luigi spoke perfect Greek (his mother was Greek) and Turkish and was able to gain the favour of the Grand Vizier Ibrahim. He became his friend and also the friend of John Zapolyai, King of Hungary. When peace was concluded between Suleiman and Ferdinand, Gritti entered Hungary with 1,000 janissaries and 2,000 *sipahi* and had the Bishop of Varazdin, Cibaco, killed in front of his eyes. This crime was greeted with horror by the population and a terrible punishment was inflicted on

him: in the morning, his hands were cut off; at noon, his feet; and in the evening, his head. The Turks called him Beyoğlu (the son of the *bey*) and the district of Istanbul where he built his residence, among the vines of Pera, has also been known as such ever since.

11. J. von Hammer-Purgstall, *op. cit.*

12. Ibid.

13. See Chapter 1, note 5.

14. Young, *Constantinople*, London and New York, n. d.

15. See Chapter 5, page 134.

16. Quoted in H. Inalcik, *op. cit.*

17. Quoted in R. Mantran, *Istanbul dans la seconde moitié du XVII siècle*, Paris, 1962.

18. See Chapter 12, pages 293–4.

19. *De la République des Turcs*, 1560, III.12.

20. *Voyages*, Paris, 1649, III.4.

21. See the description of Istanbul at the time of Suleiman's death in Chapter 9.

Chapter 3

1. The electors gave the title 'King of the Romans' to the prince who would succeed the reigning emperor. There was a college of seven electors, with three religious and four lay members: the Archbishops of Mainz, Trier and Cologne and the King of Bohemia, the Palatine Count of the Rhine, the Duke of Saxony and the Margrave of Brandenburg.

2. See Chapter 5, page 136.

3. P. Giovio, *Turcicarum Rerum Commentarius*, Chapter XXX.

4. Letter from the Prince of Croy, 2 September 1532.

5. That is to say, the Peloponnese.

6. Cardinal Ximenez de Cisneros, who was the counsellor of Queen Isabella the Catholic, inspired and sustained him during 'the final crusade' against the Moors.

7. See Chapter 4, pages 100ff.

8. B. Jacquart and J. Benassar, *Le XVIe Siècle*, Paris, 1972.

9. See Chapter 2, note 1.

10. The dervish orders, which were attached to different schools sprung from Sufism, appeared in the Orient in the 10th century. They played a considerable role in the Turkish occupation of Asia Minor, as important as that of the *gazis*, with whom they were often confused. Under the Ottoman Empire, they became a force which the ruling

powers had always to bear in mind. A list of them is given in Appendix 7.

11. The Conqueror's unexpected death, when he was carried off by a mysterious disease, was thought to be related to these measures, taken, essentially, to fill up a treasury which had been depleted by military expenses.

12. Selim is said to have executed several tens of thousands of them.

13. 'The term Kizilbaş ('Red Heads') appeared at the time of Ismail's father, Sheikh Haidar, who was born in 1460 and killed in 1488. It referred to the supporters of the first Safavids, who wore red headgear. At first a political title, the term later, as a result of the religious propaganda of the first Safavids, began to designate a special Turkoman form of Shiism. This was certainly linked to the cult of the Twelve Imams but also revealed all the signs of Shiite extremism: belief in the *tedjelli* or manifestation of God in human form; belief in *tenassuh*, that is, metempsychosis or, more exactly, transformation and multiplicity of forms; intense devotion to the Safavid sovereign as a reincarnation of Ali, himself the *mazhar* of God – the manifestation of God in human form. Later, the Safavid dynasty had to purify itself of such elements, typical of Kizilbaş Shiism, to create a religion better suited to the Iranian mentality' (I. Mélikoff, 'Le problème Kizilbach', *Turcica*, VI, page 50.)

14. The Hanafi rite is one of the four rites or legal schools making up orthodox Islam. The others are the Maliki, Shafi'i and Hanbali.

15. Portugal and the Pope had both, on several occasions, sent emissaries to the shah, offering him help against the Ottomans. Ambassadors also came from Charles V, by way of Poland or the Cape, to the court of Tahmasp – evidently on a mission hostile to Suleiman. In 1548, the Portuguese sent twenty pieces of artillery to Tahmasp, to be used against Suleiman.

16. The Uzbek hordes, of Turkish race, appeared at the end of the 15th century in Transoxania. They had occupied Bukhara and Samarkand, then Kwarezm and the basin of the sea of Aral. They compelled Babur to abandon the country – it is then that he set off to conquer India. Shah Ismail fought against them and finally made peace with them. Now they were powerful and well-established in Turkestan, they could have joined up with the Ottomans to form a pincer movement round the Persians, but perhaps they did not wish to become the immediate neighbours of the Porte.

17. See Chapter 8.

18. An entire chapter is devoted to Istanbul (Chapter 9).

19. Several sultans were deposed in this way, including Ibrahim in 1648 and Ahmed III in 1730.

Chapter 4

1. We can speak here of a 'synchronous conjuncture' whereby two enemies desist from combat at one point in order to fight better later. 'The Christian withdrew from the combat: the Turk likewise, and at the same moment; he was concerned with the Hungarian frontier or a naval war in the landlocked sea, and no less with the Red Sea, India or the Volga. From epoch to epoch the centre of gravity and lines of action of the Turk changed according to the modalities of a "world" war. At certain points, Christians and Muslims fought and then turned their backs on each other to resume their internal conflicts' (F. Braudel, *La Méditerraneé . . ., op. cit.*, Volume 2).

2. In J. von Hammer-Purgstall, *op. cit.*

3. Did Suleiman and Barbarossa dream of flying the flag of the Prophet over Saint Peter's? Ibrahim had spoken of this more than once in the presence of foreign envoys, and the Venetian ambassador reports that 'the sultan Suleiman said: "To Rome! To Rome!" '

4. To feed its population, the Republic had to import immense quantities of wheat. In some years, from the Ottoman Empire alone, it obtained 500,000 hundredweight, bought officially or through smugglers in the Aegean, who operated with the complicity of the leading Turkish dignitaries. (The Grand Vizier Rustem Pasha built up his fortune partly from this illegal traffic.) Ottoman ships were built especially to transport wheat, almost exclusively to Venice.

Only at the end of the 16th century did Venice start 'to turn away from commercial adventuring' by improving the land of its continental possessions – a first step towards the self-sufficiency it achieved, with great difficulty, only much later.

5. See Chapter 2, note 10.

6. See Chapter 5, page 141.

7. E. Charrière, *Négociations de la France dans le Levant*, Paris, 1840, Volume I.

8. Francis had refused to take part in this league and claimed that Charles's only motive was to weaken the Venetians, who often interfered with his plans.

9. It was later discovered that the Turks had been informed by Francis I of the instructions the Venetian negotiators at Constantinople had been

given. These instructions, dated 1 May 1540, laid down: 'If the lord pashas ask us to hand over the towns of Napoli de Romania [Nauplia] and Napoli de Malvoisia, we allow you to give up Malvoisia or, if they do not want it, Nauplia alone. You ought to insist on this with the greatest finesse and skill you can command. But if you see that not granting both of the towns would make all hope of peaceful settlement disappear, and that, without ceding them, they will refuse to make peace, in that case we give you permission to accept, in the name of God, such a concession and conclude a peace treaty' (O. Ferrara, *Le XVIe siècle vu par les ambassadeurs vénitiens*, Paris, 1954).

The Turks were therefore on velvet since they knew the Venetians wanted peace at any cost. Francis I received this information from his ambassador in Venice, Guillaume Pellissier, who had got it from a certain Agostino Abondio, who was in contact with Constantino and Nicolas Cavezza, respectively first secretary of the Council of Ten and second secretary of the Senate, two of the most secretive organizations which had ever existed. When he learnt that he was under suspicion, Abondio sought and was granted refuge at the French Embassy. The Council of Ten, furious, ordered their troops to force a way into the embassy and seize Abondio, which they did despite the protests of the ambassador. The two secretaries, who had long been committing acts of treason, were betrayed by Girolamo Mattarossi, the lover of Abondio's wife. They were naturally executed along with him. Such acts of treason are extremely rare in the history of the Venetian Republic.

10. F. Braudel, *La Méditerraneeé . . ., op. cit.*, Volume 2, page 227.

11. J. de la Gravière, *Les Corsaires barbaresques*, Paris, 1887.

12. Ibid.

13. Report of an agent to Francis I (E. Charrière, *op. cit.*, Volume I).

14. Letter from the Bishop of Montpellier to Francis I (E. Charrière, *op. cit.*, Volume I, page 525).

15. 'One day, he went so far as to order that a Muslim woman caught in debauchery should be mutilated with a razor in a part of the body politeness does not allow me to mention. The indecency and barbarity of this punishment revolted everyone. Lutfi Pasha was married to a sultana, the sister of his master. The princess, in a fury, reproached him forcefully and bitterly. How could he have invented such a cruel and degrading punishment? It was a punishment befitting the crime, the vizier replied, and would henceforth be inflicted on all who dishonoured themselves and showed contempt for religion and law. At these words, the sultana hurled

insults at him and called him a barbarian and a tyrant. Overcome with anger, the monster picked up his mace and rushed at her; but when his victim cried for help, her slave girls and eunuch guards rushed to her aid and chased the vizier out of her apartment with punches. Such an extraordinary event led to the fall of Lutfi Pasha. Suleiman openly criticized his conduct, ordered his separation from the sultana, deprived him of his rank and sent him into exile in Demotika, where he ended his life' (J. von Hammer-Purgstall, *op. cit.*, Volume V).

16. J. von Hammer-Purgstall, *op. cit.*

17. Cited in ibid.

18. Kenneth Setton, 'Lutheranism and the Turkish Peril', *Balkan Studies*, 3 (1962).

19. Prayers were offered at intervals in the mosques of Istanbul that the Christians of Europe should remain divided.

Chapter 5

1. Francesco Guicciardini (1483–1540), counsellor of the Medicis and historian.

2. E. Charrière, *op. cit.*, Volume I.

3. Winczerer, the King of Bavaria's ambassador.

4. E. Charrière, *op. cit.*

5. Ibid.

6. Ibid.

7. See Chapter 4, page 105.

8. His description of the Ottoman Empire at the time of Suleiman is one of the best we possess.

9. Cf. J. Ursu, *La politique orientale de François Ier*, Paris, 1908.

10. Saint Blancard arrived with his fleet the day before Suleiman's departure from Corfu. He and Marillac (who represented Francis I) were very well received and their entourage was showered with presents; they obtained all they required from the sultan to continue their voyage. But that proved to be in vain. Saint Blancard returned to France the next year after spending the winter in the Levant and Constantinople. The account he left of his wanderings and the interviews he had with Suleiman and the viziers is one of the liveliest and most colourful we possess from that period (it is included in E. Charrière, Volume I).

11. Rinçon was a Spanish noble in the service of Francis I.

12. On his return to France, Rinçon had stopped in Venice to urge the Serene Republic to join the Franco-Turkish alliance. Even though the

Venetians had refused, this had enraged the imperial forces. But since it was known that the emperor wished to do away with Rinçon, a Venetian armed guard was, at Suleiman's request, put at his disposition.

13. Montaigne speaks of him in his *Essays*.

14. A district governed by a pasha.

15. P. Giovio, *Epistolarum turcicarum*, IX, page 1, Paris 1598.

16. 'Married women, nubile girls and even nuns who left their religious houses and cloisters forgot their sense of honour and plaintively asked the first person they met in the street during the hours of darkness that he show them the route to the nearest gates and carry a light before them' (Paolo Giovio).

17. Cited by J. de la Gravière, *op. cit*.

18. Nice belonged to Charles of Savoy, an ally of Charles V.

19. The archives in Toulon contain long lists of products of every kind supplied to the Turkish fleet. But, contrary to the views of Sandoval, Charles V's chronicler, and later Michelet, the local population was not mistreated. There are no traces in the French archives of the stories of men, women and children being carried off which Michelet records as fact. There does exist a report, on the other hand, indicating a murder of two Turks at Conil, near le Bausset (reported by J. Deny and J. Laroche, *Turcica*, I, 1969).

20. Translated by J. Deny and J. Laroche, ibid.

21. Jérôme Maurand, *Itinéraire d'Antibes à Constantinople*, 1544.

22. J. Chesneau, *Le voyage de Monsieur d'Aramon ambassadeur pour le roi au Levant*, Paris, 1887.

23. See Chapter 4, page 125.

24. Henry VIII and Luther both died a few weeks before him. Barbarossa was also to die in the same year.

Chapter 6

1. 'Consisting in 815 farms, 476 watermills, 1,700 slaves, 600 saddles decorated with silver, 500 embellished with precious stones and gold . . . 130 pairs of stirrups in gold, 760 sabres covered in precious stones, 800 copies of the Koran, 32 precious stones worth 11 million aspres, and coins to the value of 100 million aspers (or 2 million ducats)' (cited in A. G. de Busbecq, *op. cit.*).

2. Or, according to some historians, at Aktepe, near Konya.

3. Mustafa was himself the author of three *divans* in the *gazel* form.

4. A. G. de Busbecq, *op. cit*.

5. In Western Europe as well, the *beau seizième siècle* had finished. Land under cultivation and agricultural techniques no longer matched population increases – which led to subsistence crises and increases in food prices. The combination of unchanging salaries and increasing tax burdens led to social tensions. And the start of the 'little ice age' was not without its effect on agricultural production.

6. See M. A. Cook, *Population Pressure in Rural Anatolia, 1450–1600*, London, 1972.

7. His love of strong drink was to cost him his life. When he went to visit the baths he had just had built in the palace after drinking a bottle of wine, he lost his balance and slipped on a wet tile. Eleven days later, he was dead.

8. J. von Hammer-Purgstall, *op. cit.*

9. Alberi, *Relazioni degli ambasciatori veneti durante il secolo XVI*, Florence, 1839–63.

10. Suleiman was also, no doubt, beginning to understand that another danger was on the horizon in the North-East: the Tsars of Moscow who had just seized Kazan and Astrakhan. The idea began to take root of an offensive in that direction to put a stop to Russian expansionism in the region of the Volga estuary and the North of the Caucasus and to safeguard the route taken by pilgrims from Central Asia to Mecca. In 1563, he informed the khan of the Crimean Tartars, Devlet Giray, of his plan to attack Astrakhan and build a canal between the Volga and the Don, which would facilitate trade and allow him to move troops and ammunition more easily. The Grand Vizier Sokullu was the principal spokesman for the canal project – a project which failed in 1569, however, probably because of insufficient preliminary studies and the lack of support from Devlet Giray, who was hardly keen to see Ottoman garrisons installed in an area to which he also had claims.

Chapter 7

1. The *sambuca* (sambaque) was a sort of flying bridge that was lowered on the walls of the fortress under attack.

2. One of the reasons, and perhaps the main one, for the Spanish desire to expel the Ottomans from the Central Mediterranean was the presence of *Moriscos* (or *mudejares*) in the peninsula who had remained in Spain after the *Reconquista* and had, in theory, converted to Catholicism. In fact, they had revolted on several occasions and the policy of Christianization had failed completely. The Muslim hope of regaining their land and perhaps

even expelling the Spanish was encouraged by Ottoman successes in Europe and the Mediterranean. There was thus a 'fifth column' in Spain which, with the help of the Ottomans and the many Muslims who had taken refuge in North Africa, could create major problems for the men who had brought about the *Reconquista* fifty or sixty years earlier. These Spanish fears continued until the time of the complete expulsion of the *Moriscos* in 1609, and they were not empty fears, since documents exist which indicate the Porte's desire to co-ordinate its efforts against the Christians with those of the Spanish Muslims.

3. F. Balbi de Corregio, *Verdadera Relación*.

4. Sokullu Mehmed Pasha became Grand Vizier in 1565, eighteen months before Suleiman's death, and remained so for the next fourteen years, under Suleiman, Selim II and Murad III (see Appendix 10).

5. According to information which reached the French court.

6. In the Munich museum.

7. By Nigari.

8. Minor military operations continued for a while in the region of Croatia, but the war was over. The greatest disappointment was felt in Paris, where it had been hoped that the Habsburgs would be yet again tied down for some time in Central Europe. A few months later, Selim and Maximilian signed a peace treaty.

Chapter 8

1. The North of India was then in the hands of Babur, a Turk descended from Tamerlane. In the South, where there was already a good deal of Turkish penetration, there was complete anarchy. There were many Ottomans (as bodyguards and gunners) in the court of the Muslim princes.

2. Later, Murad III was not able to seize the chance he was offered.

3. At the Mamluk court, all the utensils, even in the kitchen, were made of gold, and the great palace was paved in gold and marble, the walls incrusted with gold. Even private individuals lived in extraordinary luxury: mosaics, inlaid ivory and ebony, sculptures, were piled up in an abundance to be seen nowhere else. The arts and letters were as flourishing there as in the towns of the highest civilization in Europe and Asia. The most famous names in Arabic literature, the best architects, all lived there. Although it was only a provincial town, Damascus yielded nothing to Cairo. A fount of high culture, magnificent buildings and vast numbers of artworks were signs of a prosperity only increased by its

situation at the edge of well-watered and always flourishing gardens. The other towns in the empire were not neglected: Jerusalem, Mecca, Medina and others of lesser importance all enjoyed great prosperity.

4. Kansuh was replaced by Tuman, the last of the Mamluk sultans, who was defeated by Selim I a few months later.

5. Firichta.

6. At the beginning of the 17th century, they abandoned Abyssinia.

7. F. Braudel, *op. cit.*

8. Preface to the *Travels and Adventures of the Turkish Admiral Sidi Ali Reis*, Lahore and London, 1899, 1975, VI–VII.

Chapter 9

1. The name 'Istanbul' is probably derived from the Greek expression *eis tin polin* ('to the city'), altered and Islamicized into Islambol ('full of Islam') and then into Istanbul, which only became the city's official name after the Ataturk revolution. Under the empire, the capital was called Konstantiniyya, Constantinople.

2. A. H. Lybyer expressed his opinion of the Turkish slave state in the following terms: 'There are reasons for thinking that human history has never known a political institution which was ruled by pure intelligence for so long and thus achieved its aims so successfully as the Ottoman institutions of government' (*The Ottoman Empire in the Time of Suleiman*, New York, 1913).

3. Muslim Turks went so far as to pay Christians to take their sons and pass them off as their own at the time of recruitment. 'There was a considerable number of volunteers,' writes the historian L. V. Schloezer. 'Boys dreamed of being able to call themselves servants of the Great Lord, of seeing the marvels of the Seraglio or having access, perhaps, to the chamber of pages, and becoming rich and famous.'

4. The important persons of the empire also had *kullar* in their palaces. They received a refined education and could obtain *timar* in the provinces their masters governed. The system functioned thus at all levels of the civil and military administration. Everybody obeyed the rules, up to the sultan himself, who claimed to infringe none of the *kanun* of the 'slave state' that he and his predecessors had established.

5. *The Selected Letters of Lady Mary Wortley Montagu* (edited by Robert Halsband), London, 1970.

6. See Chapter 11.

7. 'This anxiety was so deep-seated that it constituted a genuine affair

of state to which the highest authorities – the Grand Vizier especially and sometimes even the sultan – paid an immense amount of attention' (R. Mantran, *La Vie quotidienne à Constantinople au temps de Soliman le Magnifique et de ses successeurs*, Paris, 1965). For more details, see the same author's *Istanbul dans la seconde moitié du XVIIe siècle*, Paris, 1962.

Chapter 10

1. To use Lutfi Pasha's expression.

2. F. Braudel, *op. cit.*

3. In the 14th and 15th centuries, Venice had obtained from the Porte certain commercial privileges, particularly the right to import cereals from the Ottoman Empire and, later, the right to establish warehouses there. These concessions were renewed and augmented and had thus given the Venetians an almost total dominance of trade in the Levant, especially since the Mamluk sultans had also granted them privileges in Egypt and Syria. The Catalans and the French had benefited later from similar concessions. Selim I, after the conquest, and later Suleiman, at the time of his accession to the throne, had confirmed them; they formed the basis for the 1535 accord which established the status of the King of France's subjects (see Appendix 15).

4. I. Sunar, 'Economie et politique dans l'Empire ottoman,' *Annales E.S.C.* (3–4), 1980.

5. Clandestine exports, not only of wheat but of ore and timber (the sale of which to foreigners was permanently prohibited), developed on a large scale in the following century, when the central government had become much weaker and the minorities, particularly Greeks and Jews, had become more enterprising.

6. It was the age of the Field of the Cloth of Gold.

7. L. Tiepolo (cited by Braudel, *op. cit.*). See also H. Inalcik, *The Ottoman Empire: Conquest, Organisation and Economy* (London, 1978) and *The Ottoman Empire: The Classical Age* (London, 1973).

8. Transylvania imported more than 300 hundredweight of pepper each year from Wallachia, a trade worth 35,000 florins (S. Paul Pach, *Mélanges Braudel*).

9. J. B. Tavernier, *Les six voyages en Turquie, en Perse et aux Indes*, Paris, 1717.

10. 'The country is safe and there are no reports of kidnappers or highwaymen on the major roads. The emperor does not tolerate any

highwaymen or thieves,' wrote an anonymous Frenchman in 1528 (quoted by Braudel, *op. cit.*).

11. They were even preceded by the railway in Ottoman Turkey, which opened up Anatolia in the 19th and 20th centuries. Roads were only used on a large scale from around 1960, after the Menderes government had established a policy of developing the road network in the 1950s. A diplomat posted in Ankara published a pamphlet in 1939 describing his journey from there to Istanbul. Even around 1950 it took about twelve hours to cover that distance (560 kilometres) – it now takes only five or six.

Chapter 11

1. Normally from the *sipahi*, who received an 'entry tax' from the new occupant.

2. In the next century, maize, which reached Eastern Europe and Asia Minor from the West, was also cultivated and eaten. It was known as *misir* (the 'Egyptian' food).

3. They spoke an Indo-European language (Iranian).

4. J. Thévenot, *Relation d'un voyage du Levant*, Paris, 1917.

5. J. B. Tavernier, *op. cit.*

6. In wealthier circles, spoons were used for eating soups and vegetables.

7. Busbecq mentioned this on several occasions: 'They think so little of the pleasures of the table that if they have bread and salt and a little garlic and onion, they ask for nothing more. Even in wealthy circles their meals consist only of cakes, pastries and sweet things of every kind, with rice cooked in many different ways and mutton or poultry added to it . . . If they have a little honey or sugar in their water, they would not envy Jupiter his nectar.'

8. See Chapter 12, page 291.

9. In 1527–8, the total tax receipts of the Ottoman Empire came to 537,929,006 *akçe* (about 10 million gold pieces), of which 276,977,724 (51%) was considered part of the state treasury, with 37% used for military endowments (*timar, zeamet* and *has*) and the remaining 12% as revenue for the *vakf*. Since the weight of a gold piece, at the beginning of the century, was 3.59 grammes and the price of a gramme of gold was stabilized in February 1983 at 100 new francs, the total value of the Ottoman budget can be put at about 4,000 million (4 US billion) francs (very roughly £400 million or $600 million).

This is not an enormous amount of money, even if we take into account its much greater buying power in those days: around 1530, a *kile* (25.65 kg or 10.2 lb) of wheat cost about 2.5 francs (i.e. 25 pence or 38 cents), the same quantity of rice twice as much; an *okka* (1.283 kg or 5.5 lb) of honey cost 3.5 francs (i.e. 35 pence or 53 cents) and the same weight of fat about the same. Divided – although far from equally, of course – between the 30–35 million inhabitants of the empire, the tax burden was by no means excessive, at least in that era.

10. J. B. Tavernier, *op. cit.*

11. At the time Smyrna hardly existed. Its economic take-off began at the end of the century and it became, as Tavernier said, 'the most famous town of the Levant, and the largest trading post for all merchandise carried from Europe to Asia, and from Asia to Europe' (J. B. Tavernier, *op. cit.*).

12. H. Inalcik, *op. cit.*

13. *The Complete Letters of Mary Wortley Montagu*, edited by Robert Halsband, Volume I, 1708–1720 (Oxford, 1965), pages 354–5 (with spelling and capitalization modernized).

14. F. Braudel, *op. cit.* For more details, see B. A. Cvetkova, 'La vie économique dans les villes et les ports balkaniques aux XVe et XVIe siècles', *Revue des études islamiques*, XXXVIII, 1970 and N. Todorov, *La ville balkanique aux XVe et XVIe siècles*, Bucharest, 1980.

Chapter 12

1. His five sons also wrote poetry, although of very unequal merit: the best were those by Selim (the Sot), but the most touching were the work of the unfortunate Bayezid, who was executed by his father.

2. J. von Hammer-Purgstall, *op. cit.*

3. Only ruins survive of the palace at Edirne, which was almost completely destroyed in the 19th century, but it too was composed of several different buildings.

4. Koran, LV, 26.

5. R. Mantran, *op. cit.*

6. R. Ettinghausen makes a curious comparison between the Turkish adaptation of Christian art and the Ottomans' use of their Christian subjects: 'One could say that the idea of Saint-Sophia, transformed, is the equivalent in art to the system of *devşirme*, by means of which elements of the Christian population were drawn into serving Ottoman ends' (*Turkish Miniatures*. New York, 1965).

7. The Turks always admired Saint-Sophia enormously. A writer of the 16th century composed the following couplet:

'If you are looking for Paradise, O Sufi,
The heaven of heavens is Aya Sofy.'

Another wrote: 'It is a dome such as to rival the nine celestial spheres' (Tursun).

8. The prayer recess, which indicates the direction of Mecca.

9. U. Vogt-Göknil, *Architecture de la Turquie ottomane*, Fribourg, 1965.

10. See ibid. and S. T. Yetkin, *L'architecture turque en Turquie*, Paris, 1962.

11. In literature as well as the visual arts, because of the differences in language.

12. This passion went so far that an age in Turkish history at the start of the 18th century was known as the 'tulip period' (*lale devri*). Unusual tulip bulbs were sold for dizzying prices and men ruined their families to buy them. A leading dignitary was given the post of 'master of the flowers'.

13. In the collections of the Victoria and Albert Museum, the Sèvres Museum, the British Museum, the Musée des Arts Décoratifs and the Benaki Museum in Athens.

14. The chaplain to Maximilian II's ambassador wrote as follows in his journal: 'The ambassador has just written to the Bishop of Salzburg to ask him to pay 1,000 thalers for bricks from Nicaea used by the pashas to cover their rooms. These bricks are made of a material as white as chalk. Arabesques and flowers are painted on them. Some of them – to the value of over 100 ducats – have been sent to Venice' (cited by Migeon and Sakisian, *La céramique d'Asie Mineure*, Paris, 1923).

15. See O. Grabar, *The Formation of Islamic Art*, Yale, 1973.

16. Islamic sculpture in the round is almost non-existent. This is not true, however, of relief sculpture of men and animals, specimens of which can be found in the museums. Ince Minare in Konya, for example, possesses several from the Seljuk era: two winged figures thought to represent Ormuz and Ariman; two Turkish soldiers wearing helmets and chainmail; a bearded man bearing a falcon on his right, gloved, hand, etc.

17. There, are, however, erotic miniatures in the library in the Topkapi Palace.

18. Busbecq, *op. cit.*

19. 'The superiority of the Turkish language appeared as clear as that of the blood-drenched Ottoman sword' (Atai, cited by F. Köprülü in *Les Origines de l'Empire ottoman*, Paris, 1935).

20. In *History of Ottoman Poetry*, London, 1900–09.

21. A *gazel* is a poem of five or six couplets, two of whose lines rhyme; a *kaside*, considerably longer, is a kind of eulogy; *rubai* are quatrains. A *divan* is a collection of poems written, and usually put together, by a single author.

22. *Gazel* 20, 29, 150 and 201 in A. Bombaci, *Histoire de la littérature turque*, Paris, 1968.

23. In ibid.

24. F. Köprülü, *op. cit.*

25. A. Bombaci, *op. cit.*

26. The origins of the Turkish shadow theatre are unclear. According to some people, it must have come from China and been brought by the Turks of Central Asia and the Moghuls; according to others, it must have penetrated into Central Asia by means of Buddhist propaganda or have come from India. It would seem rather, according to Turkish specialists, to have been created by the Turks of Central Asia themselves. Known among the Abbasids before the 10th century and in Cairo and Damascus in the 13th and 14th centuries, it had certainly been introduced in the Ottoman Empire before the 16th century. It was still, it seems, a dumb show, which only used shadows moving across a cloth screen. It only took on the aspect it has retained to this day in the 17th century; in the 19th century, its extremely varied repertoire even included whole scenes from Molière, incorporated almost word for word.

27. See Chapter 8.

28. The first Seljuks created these teaching centres from as early as the 11th century, with the aim of forming a body of men who were educated in the Sunni orthodoxy. There was at the time a powerful Sunni reaction against Shiism and the many heterodox groups which had flourished in the previous century. The Seljuk dynasty took over the leadership of this movement and developed it. The *medrese* then played an essential role in the triumph of orthodox ideas, since civil administrators and *kadi* were both educated there. The Ottoman sultans developed these schools, which continued to be the principal basis of education. In Iznik in 1331 a former convent was transformed into a *medrese*. Murad I built one in Bursa as soon as the town became his capital; his successors did the same, in Bursa and in their new capital, Edirne. In Istanbul, all the Ottoman sultans built more or less important *medrese* beside and depending on the 'imperial mosques' and provided them with revenues so they could function.

Three Centuries of Decline and Fall

1. Peter von Sivers – *Annales S.C.I.* May–August 1980.

2. The Mohacs campaign in 1526 took place in torrential rain from the time of departure from Istanbul. In June, the army 'had difficulty crossing the water courses and swollen brooks'. The same problems arose in Asia during the Two Iraqs Campaign of 1534; there was snow in Anatolia in mid-August.

In 1563 in the region of Istanbul, there was the most terrible flooding recorded in the annals of the empire. Aqueducts were destroyed, buildings near the Bosphorus and Golden Horn swept away. Suleiman, who happened to be out of the city at the time, could well have drowned if an exceptionally tall man had not lifted him up on to his shoulders.

Violent storms did great damage in the sultan's last campaign in the Danube territories in 1566: bridges were swept away and hundreds of camels drowned.

The 'little ice age', brought about by a drop in the average temperature of 1 degree, lasted from about 1540 to 1850, but the first half of the century also saw a sequence of cyclonic years which led to poorer harvests and many famines. Were these rainstorms and cold summers a sign of the change in climate soon to come?

3. One might add that the sultan's army was made up of *gazi* whose role was to fight Infidels and not Muslims, even if they were heretics.

4. If we consider the details, the picture is much less clear-cut: prices did not increase to the same extent across the whole of Europe nor in direct proportion to the increased amounts of money in circulation.

5. F. Braudel, *op. cit*.

6. Carried out by O.L. Barkan.

7. According to O.L. Barkan, 'The Price Revolution of the Sixteenth Century', *International Journal of Middle East Studies*, 6 (1975).

8. Notably S. Lahib in 'The Era of Suleyman the Magnificent: a Crisis of Orientation', *Journal of Middle East Studies*, 10 (1979). Toynbee also believed that it was an error on Suleiman's part not to have been able to resist 'the temptation to enroach on the neighbouring territories of Iran and Western Christianity'.

Appendix 1
The Pre-Ottoman Turks

In the 8th century, the *Samanids*, who were of Iranian origin, replaced the Arab conquerors in Transoxania, but then their power went into a slow decline and the *Ghaznavids*, the Turkish 'pretorian guards' (whose support had been called upon against the other Turks or Qarakhanids), eventually supplanted them in Khorasan (999). Mahmud founded a great empire which eventually included the whole region from Ray (Tehran) in the West, and from the Oxus (Amu-Darya) in the North to the mouth of the Indus in the South.

The *Qarakhanids* – the dominant power in Kashgaria, further to the East, at this time – took prisoner the Samanid sovereign, Abdel Melik, and annexed Transoxania. The Samanid territories ceased to exist. Kashgaria and Transoxania were 'Turkified'. Later, the Ghaznavids and Qarakhanids, who had both been converted to Islam, were conquered in turn or reduced to vassal status and replaced by Seljuk rulers.

A branch of the Oğuz tribe, the *Seljuks* were led by Togrul and soon became masters of all Iran. Togrul entered Baghdad and was given the title of 'King of the Orient and Occident' by the caliph. His successor, Alp Arslan, defeated and captured the Byzantine Emperor at Manzikert (1071). Armenia, Cappadocia and the whole of Eastern Anatolia lay open to the Turks. Melik Shah, Arslan's son, organized the conquest with Nizam el-Mulk, but in the wake of his death a period of anarchy (*Fetret Devri*) ensued and the empire split up. The Persian sultanate and those in Damascus and Aleppo collapsed, but the sultanate in Asia Minor, with Konya as capital, continued for two centuries and 'Turkified' the country. It formed the basis of modern Turkey.

Appendix 2
Turkish Civilization before the Ottomans

The men who seized Constantinople were not, as has long been claimed, barbarians from the depths of Asia come to destroy 'the New Rome'.

When the Turks reached the walls of Byzantium in the middle of the 15th century, they had behind them several centuries of brilliant civilization. Central Asia had long ceased to be the huge steppe, described by ancient writers, where uncultured and smelly tribes roamed. Even in the 5th and 6th centuries the Tabghaç had brought to Northern China a flourishing artistic tradition which renewed Chinese art. (These Tabghaçs were Turks, although they became 'Sinified' in the 9th century.) Turkish art is to be found in the Uighur manichean painting of Turfan, Turkish literature in Buddhist writings (using the Sogdian alphabet). Two centuries later, the Ghaznavid frescos of Lashkari-Bazar discovered by Daniel Schlumberger are directly descended from the Turkish frescos in the Gobi desert. And all this is quite apart from the often important remains we possess of the Great Seljuks and the Seljuks of Rum in Iran and Anatolia, notably in the beautiful museum at Konya. Like the names of their sultans – Keykavus, Keykubad – their art was steeped in Persian culture. Yet this is no way alters the fact that the towns of the Great Seljuks – Hamadan, Ray, Isfahan – as well as those of the sultanate of Rum (Niğde, Konya, Divriği and others) were all Turkish towns. It was at Konya that Celaleddin Rumi, one of the world's greatest mystical poets, lived, wrote and died; he also founded the Mevlevi order of dervishes.

At the time of the Great Seljuks (the end of the 11th century), Mahmud of Kashgar published his *divan*, a collection of 200 extracts from Turkish poets which he translated into Arabic. Some of the poems are stamped with a spirit of experimentation, sincerity, feeling for nature and popular morality that makes one regret that Turkish poetry in subsequent centuries did not pursue its own native genius and was deeply influenced instead by the more conventional motifs of Persian verse. By the end of the 14th century, Turkish poetry was essentially court poetry, of a mystical erotic nature, which had been influenced by both Persia and

Islam. It nonetheless produced great writers like Mir Ali Şir Nevai in the following century, who created an immense volume of work in Çagatai Turkish at Herat, the court of the Timurid ruler, Husein Baykara. He himself claimed to have impressed his artistic stamp on the Turks all the way from Khorasan to China.

At more or less the same time, at the start of the 16th century, Babur, the conqueror of India (a descendant of Tamerlane on his father's side, Genghis Khan on his mother's), wrote his *Baburname* (or *Book of Babur*), the memoirs of a turbulent and audacious life and one of the liveliest books in Turkish literature.* Alongside the court poety influenced by the Persians, there was also another kind of popular and mystical poetry best represented by Yunus Emre, a poet of very various and original talent.

The list of major poets and writers in the Turkish language is long, although no doubt shorter than the list of monuments – mosques, *medrese*, tombs, caravanserai – erected throughout the Orient by the Turks from the 13th to the 15th centuries; many magnificent examples still exist.

* A new edition by M. J. -L. Bacqué-Grammont has recently been published in French.

Appendix 3
The Janissaries

The creation of the janissaries dates back to the very start of the Osmanli dynasty. The army of Osman, the founder, was made up mainly of horsemen, and the foot soldiers were few in number and little valued. It was Murad I, the third sultan, who, after the occupation of Thrace, decided to create a regular troop of infantry – given the name of *yeniçeri* (new troops) – almost a century before the first permanent army was established in France.

The empire's 'foreign legion' was closely linked with the order of Bektaşi dervishes which was founded in Central Anatolia by Haci Bektaş, a mystic who came from Khorasan in the 13th century and whose heterodox doctrines and practices were always regarded with suspicion by the official theologians (see Appendix 7). According to legend, Haci Bektaş blessed the first recruits by placing the sleeve of his robe on their heads and saying: 'May the faces of these soldiers be always white [i.e. strong], their arms sturdy, their swords sharp and their arrows lethal.' Thus the young Christian converts to Islam were placed under the protection of an order which was to become one of the most powerful in the whole Muslim world; they received as a head-dress a high white bonnet with a long piece of felt hanging down the back, just like Haci Bektaş's sleeve.

This legend is actually false, since Haci Bektaş was dead before the janissaries came into being. It was probably the sultan who ordered them to wear the white bonnet, although with the approval of the Bektaşi order, who were also dressed in white. On joining the corps of janissaries, the young Islamicized Christians were also initiated into the order. The so-called Bektaşi 'fathers' (*baba*) lived permanently in the janissaries' barracks and went with them into battle. On parade days, eight of them processed by the side of the mounted *ağa*. When a new Bektaşi superior (*dede*) was appointed, he was enthroned in the barracks by the *ağa*. The janissaries have been described as the Bektaşi 'fighting order'.

About 1,000 in the 14th century, 5,000 in the 15th, the janissaries numbered 12,000 in the days of Suleiman. Later on, they became yet more numerous, admitted those who were Muslim by birth and often practised professions as well. They thus became the scourge of the Turkish nation and, in the 19th century, a sultan – Mahmud II – had to use force to destroy them.

In the 16th century, such developments were still far away. The elite of the elite, spearhead of the Turkish army, the janissaries were fed by their father the sultan. The symbol of the regiment, its 'mascot' on parade and almost its 'flag', was the brass pot (*kazan*) around which the men assembled once a day for their only meal, just like the Turkish nomads of Central Asia. To tip over the pot was a sign of revolt, to take refuge next to it assured immunity. The men carried a wooden spoon attached to their bonnet by a metal ring. Ranks were based on cooking: the colonel was the *çorbaci başi* (chief soup-maker), followed by the steward (*vekil harc*), etc. The janissary corps was known as the *ocak* (hearth). It was divided into *orta* ('milieu' or company) with a fixed number of men – 196 in Suleiman's day – and each had an emblem which the men made it a point of honour to tattoo on their arms and legs. They could only be punished by their officers. Advancement was based entirely on seniority and janissaries only left the corps when they came to retire.

They possessed considerable prestige. Their commander-in-chief – *yeniçeri ağasi* – was one of the highest ranking officers in the hierarchy. Only the cavalry commanders – the *ağa* of the *sipahi* and *silahdar* – ranked above them, because their corps had been founded earlier. Even the Grand Vizier had no authority over the janissaries, who obeyed only their officers. Yet their obedience was total. When one of them was given a *falaka* (bastinado, i.e. a beating with a stick), he had to submit to his punishment and then go and kiss the hand of the officer who was present.

When they were not on campaign, the janissaries had the responsibility of maintaining order in Istanbul and the major towns of the empire. Units were stationed in the provinces, then in the capital, in another province, and so on. In later centuries, when their numbers had greatly increased, their presence in the provinces posed problems – both financial and political – which were never to be resolved, since soldiers scattered throughout the country inevitably enjoyed an excessive independence.

Appendix 4
The Law of Fratricide

In Turco-Mongol law, every member of the family possessed equal rights, although the eldest son nonetheless took precedence. This always had the same effect: heirs came to blows, the empire crumbled and collapsed – and they had to wait for a strong leader to arise and put it together again. Then *his* possessions would in turn split up, the empire would be shattered and the cycle begin anew.

The Ottoman sultans, whether from native genius or because of their contact with Byzantium and Western states which had long recognized the need for a single heir to the throne, understood the danger and soon came to regard the maintenance of the empire's unity as their overriding aim. The customary arrangements which formed the basis of their legal system could not actually be abolished, but they circumvented them with brutal realism. They decided that whichever member of the imperial family became sultan had the right to do away with anyone who posed a threat to his power. Mehmed II formalized this tradition of the early sultans in a decree worded as follows: 'Most legalists have declared as permitted that whichever of my illustrious sons or grandsons attains supreme power can sacrifice his brothers to maintain the peace of the world; they should take the appropriate measures.'

Thus, we see Murad III, Suleiman's grandson, sending his 5 brothers to their death; Mehmed III, his successor, did the same with his 19 brothers and their 15 pregnant concubines. The execution of Suleiman's two sons, Mustafa and Bayezid, and their sons was based on the same principle: the sultan had the right to use any means, including the death of his closest relatives, to retain power.

Towards the end of the 16th century, this Law of Fratricide was abandoned, and the *kafes* (or cage) replaced it. Although this was less bloody than legal execution, it was almost equally cruel. When a sultan died, the new occupant of the throne would not kill his brothers but lock them away for the rest of their lives in a building in the fourth court of the Seraglio. In this 'cage', they were treated more like prisoners than princes and were given only miminal instruction; although they also received a harem when they came of age, every precaution was taken to prevent them producing heirs. Occasionally, however, when a sultan died or was deposed, one of these men might come to the throne; despite their upbringing, some of them proved astonishingly capable of governing an empire.

Raison d'état – or rather of the House of Osman – was thus predominant. The empire only existed because of it, authority resided in the sultan of that dynasty and no one would have dreamt of trying to install an outsider, however prestigious, on the throne. Nobody believed that the Grand Vizier Ibrahim seriously planned to supplant Suleiman, an idea which would have occurred only to a madman. Even in the following centuries, when degenerate or perverted sultans occupied the throne, there was never any question of replacing them by the skilful and energetic Grand Viziers who on several occasions succeeded in keeping afloat a collapsing empire which had become a prey to rival powers. Deprived of a sultan who was heir to the House of Osman, the empire – which only existed through him and whose foundation and motive force he was – could only collapse.

Appendix 5
The *Timar* System

The *timar* system, with military, economic and social elements, traced its origins far back into the Anatolian past. The Byzantine Empire had, since the 6th century, established soldier-peasants called *stratiots* on each plot of land. The Seljuks of Rum and the Anatolian principalities had also used the system before the arrival of the Ottomans. From the time of Orhan and under all his successors, it was a prominent feature of Ottoman life, although the details were reorganized and codified several times, notably by Mehmed II and Suleiman.

The *timar* was established on the principle, which formed the basis of the Ottoman state, that all cultivable land belonged to the crown (i.e. the state) and that people could enjoy the right of possession only in return for services rendered. Such an 'endowment' could be handed down from father to son or might *not* be, as often happened in the early days. It could also be withdrawn for various reasons, or for no reason: everything belonged to the sultan, who could take back just as easily as he had granted. The right to land could obviously be neither sold nor given away. There were three levels: the state owned the land; the peasant (*reaya*) cultivated it; and the soldier received the revenue from it and possessed an extra portion (*hasa*) which he either farmed or got someone else to farm.

The *timar* could also be granted as recompense to people who had no connection with the army: certain functionaries, judges (*kadi*), governors, tutors of princes, etc. Some of them, nonetheless, were reserved for military purposes or to cover the expenses of soldiers and equipment. When the granting of non-military *timar* became more widespread in the 17th and 18th centuries, it had a deleterious effect on the system itself and was one of the causes of its decline.

The *sipahi* or military *timariotes* took on the role of village leaders in the countryside while the empire was at peace. They had to keep order and reside there, although they were not allowed to cultivate any more than their special portion of land. The peasants had to perform minor services for them and give them presents at the time of certain festivals, but this was nothing to compare with the obligations the rural classes lived under in most Central and Western European countries at the time. In each *kaza*, the *subaşi* played the role of police officer, collecting fines, carrying out the penalties imposed by the *kadi* and so on. Yet the *timariotes* also had a role, at each level of the hierarchy, in the collection of certain taxes (others were farmed out). These taxes, in whole or in part, constituted their 'endowment'. They were made up of religious and customary (common-law) duties and were only fixed after a cadastral commission had worked out in precise detail how much it was possible to exact from the peasants. Cadastral rolls were compiled so that the central authorities possessed accurate information about land ownership as well as population. The censors registered all revenues, in town and country, from fields, etc. 'The law laid down that the large and small *timariotes*, the delegates of the imperial domains, the people who enjoy the use of the *sancakbey* domains, the *zaim*, the *timariotes* and the people enjoying franchises must all assemble in the presence of the censor and the local *kadi*. It is obvious that no one could avoid the census, neither simple nor grand *timariote*, nor the *reaya*. Such regulations, applied as much to the lords as to the villeins or serfs, were inconceivable in the West at this time.' (N. Beldiceanu)

Ottoman society was divided into two classes. The *askeri* (or military) included the sultan's military personnel and slaves (*kul*) as well as the *timariotes* (*sipahi*) and their families, slaves etc. They were subject to the *Şeriat* – but under the jurisdiction of the *kazasker* rather than the *kadi* – as well as a special code, the *Kanun-i-sipahiyan*, which dealt with administrative, fiscal and juridical issues. In theory, membership of the *askeri* class was not hereditary, although in practice, at least from the 17th century, it almost always was. Yet since this was not established by right, the class did not constitute a true aristocracy.

The *reaya* included the peasants and town dwellers, although the term could also be used to refer only to the peasants. They were subject to the *Şeriat* and the laws of the empire (*kanun*). They were not allowed to ride a horse, bear arms or receive military endowments (*timar*). Nonetheless, it was possible to move from the *reaya* class into the *askeri*, or vice versa.

Appendix 6
The *Divan*

The Grand Vizier had a very large staff responsible to him, in both Istanbul and the provinces. In all matters of domestic and foreign policy, and the maintenance of public order, he had three viziers to assist him, although their precise spheres of competence were not clearly established. The two *defterdar* (treasurers) for Rumelia and Anatolia were the empire's Ministers of Finance, with many offices and a complex organization responsible to them. Each office dealt with both the receipts and expenses in a particular field, receiving the tax revenue and laying down how it should be spent. The *nişanci* was the Chancellery chief who authenticated documents and confirmed that the instructions and orders handed down by the *Divan* were in accordance with the laws currently in force. He would then affix the reigning sultan's *tuğra*. The *kazasker* of Rumelia and Anatolia had the whole judiciary under their authority.

These leading functionaries – 'the Pillars of the State' – all had direct access to the sovereign and were responsible only to him.

In his role as the sultan's representative, the Grand Vizier presided over the *Divan*. Until Mehmed II, the sultan himself had presided, but the Conqueror increased the powers of the Grand Vizier and gave him authority over the Council – although the sultan could, if he wished, listen in by using a window which had been inserted in one of the walls to ensure that 'each man did his duty'.

The Council was held four times a week or, if necessary, even more often. The viziers, *defterdar, kazasker, nişanci* and the Rumelian *beylerbey* took part as of right; from the time of Barbarossa, the *kapudan pasha* (commander-in-chief of the fleet) also attended, once it had become established practice for him to be appointed from the ranks of the viziers. The *ağa* of the janissaries and other dignitaries could also be called upon in certain circumstances.

As both the supreme court and the council of ministers, the *Divan*'s field of competence had almost no limits. All political and military issues, any law suit, could be submitted to it. It controlled administration and justice and gave its approval to laws (*kanun*). The pivot of the empire, it dominated all the other institutions.

Everything proceeded from the Grand Vizier and everything was reported back there; directly responsible to him, in the first instance, were the thousands of dignitaries, scribes and other employees who kept the great empire's administrative, military and judicial machine – whose origins date back so far into the Ottoman past – functioning in both Istanbul and the provinces. It seems highly unlikely that the system was largely borrowed from the Byzantines, as some have claimed. The Turkish gifts for command and organization were recognized throughout the Orient. In this respect, the Seljuk state could be used as a model, together with the inheritance from the Sassanids and Abbasids, who had themselves drawn inspiration from the empires of the old Orient, notably the Achaemenids. The Ottomans drew on all these sources and brought what they had borrowed to perfection.

Appendix 7
The Dervish Orders

The *Melematis*, one of the numerous groups of Sufis, were notable for their total rejection of all 'religious hypocrisy': merely observing the *Şeriat* was not enough, they believed, for the most rigorous form of Islam. In the 16th century, the movement took off again and was adopted by the Porte *sipahi* in imitation of the janissaries, adepts of the *Bektaşi* doctrine.

The doctrine and practices of the order founded in the 13th century by Haci Bektaş were very ambiguous: a syncretic form of religion based on Turkish and Islamic elements, it placed great stress on devotion to Ali and the martyrs of Kerbela and had undergone a diverse range of Yezidi and even Christian influences, although the latter have been exaggerated. The Ottoman sultans tried to use the order as a means of channelling the heterodox beliefs which were widespread in Anatolia, although they failed to eliminate them; the Bektaşi themselves, meanwhile, became more and more influenced by such ideas. In any event, the Bektaşi continued to exert an important influence in the social and intellectual domain, even after the order was suppressed in 1826.

The *Kalenderi* were openly heretical and nearer to pantheism than orthodox Islam. They were particularly numerous among the tribes who fought on the frontiers of Islam in the early centuries. The Ottomans had to take vigorous action against them to establish their own authority.

The *Hurufi* were close in outlook to the Shiites, while the *Kadiri* and *Nakşibendi* were more orthodox.

The *Mevlevi* – whom we refer to as 'the whirling dervishes' – bear the name of the great mystical poet Mevlana Celaleddin Rumi, whose successors founded the order at Konya in the 13th century. They flourished under the Ottoman sultans and formed an orthodox Sunni counterbalance to the Bektaşi.

The *Halveti* were numerous and very influential at Istanbul – and even in the Palace – in the 16th and 17th centuries; the *Rifai*, who have been called 'the howling dervishes', slashed themselves and burnt their bodies in the course of their religious practices; then there were the *Şadhili* and countless others, scattered throughout the empire, notably in Egypt and North Africa. Mouradgea d'Ohsson put their number at 36, but the traveller Evliya Çelebi counted as many as 140, other chroniclers 80 in Egypt alone.

Appendix 8
The Ottoman Fleet

The Ottoman fleet was made up almost entirely of oar-powered boats. Huge sailing vessels were little used in Mediterranean combat and only made their appearance towards the end of the century, with the *barça* or 'round boats' built by the Venetians as combat vessels. They were first to be seen in the sultan's fleet at the beginning of the 17th century, although Piri Reis did use 4 of them in the Red Sea in 1552. The *barça* (known as the *barza* in Venice) developed into galleons, veritable floating fortresses which were only taken up by the Ottomans later, in the second half of the 17th century, when they realized that their galleys and *barça* combined were no match for the Christian fleets. But by then it was too late: the Venetians, with their enormous ships, were able more than once to hold the sultan's fleet in check. One might add that the Ottomans, even at the apogee of their empire, were rather wary about the use of sailing fleets, no doubt because they never fully understood how to control them.

At the time of Suleiman, galleys (of more or less the same kind) were the warships most widely used by both Christians and Muslims. Their Turkish names varied according to the number of banks of oars: *kalite* (19–24), *kadirga* (25 or 26), *baştarda* (up to 36). The final group were used as flagships or to carry the sultan (*baştarda-i-humayun*). The *mavna* was a large and heavy galley used for commerce or as a provision ship in battle fleets. When sails were added, fewer oarsmen were needed: the three men with an oar each were replaced, around 1560, by teams of three rowers wielding a single oar in the Venetian style. Besides the oarsmen, each galley had six to ten officers and several dozen soldiers, *timariotes* or janissaries. It was they who attacked the enemy ships, usually by boarding them after cannons had done as much damage as possible. Some of the boats carried artillery and others, horses.

The galleys were light, easy to manoeuvre and fast. In theory, they could be used even in calm weather and did not, like galleons, require wind, but their very lightness put them at the mercy of storms and so they were only used in the summer. Naval campaigns took place from the spring to the autumn equinox: Christians and Muslims alike returned to base in winter. The galleys also had another major weakness: for their comparatively low tonnage, they needed large numbers of men on board to act as a 'motor'. Huge quantities of food and water were required for 200–300 crew and soldiers. This meant that a fleet needed provision ships, which sometimes had to shuttle to and fro in the high seas between galleys and ports: it was thus very difficult ever to go far from Turkish or friendly coasts, which was one cause of Ottoman setbacks in the Western Mediterranean. They never managed to achieve complete dominance there, any more than in the Indian Ocean, where conditions were very different. Quite apart from the fact that the political will was lacking, the galleys had great difficulty defeating the tall, heavy and powerfully armed Portuguese *caraques*.

When there was a reasonable wind and circumstances did not require the squadron to make full speed, sails – usually a triangular sail on a single mast – were sufficient. But when time was pressing and ships were retreating or rushing to attack the enemy, it was galley slaves with oars who propelled the boats forward. Some were condemned common-law criminals, others were volunteers from coastal areas or even from further away, when a naval expedition, for example, meant that more men were needed. Such volunteers were attracted by the modest yet regular rates of pay they received. They were generally required also to spread the sail and do maintenance work. The crews were officered by a special corps of professional sailors (*azab*), who worked as helmsmen and topmen and oversaw the galley slaves. Such men could be promoted, sometimes even to the rank of ship's captain or commander of a section of the fleet. Valour was the quality most needed for advancement.

The forced conscription carried out in villages in certain areas, usually near the sea, also provided a large contingent of oarsmen each year. One man was required for every 23 households, each of which had to give him a month's salary (100 *akçe*). The number of foreign galley slaves, carried off in raids on Christian coasts, captured from ships or taken prisoner in combat, was much smaller than has sometimes been claimed. Christian prisoners were usually needed for tasks more suited to their professions or skills; on the galleys, they were very much the exception.

The fleet – although, like the army, nominally under the emperor's command – was put under the orders of the chief admiral. Although he ranked as the supreme leader of all the naval squadrons, his powers on land were fairly restricted. Apart from Barbarossa, he was not a member of the *Divan* (unless he happened to be a vizier as well), to which he had to submit all the important decisions he took, including promotions and nominations. He oversaw the arsenals, but it was the central administration which allocated credit and directed the enrolment and forced conscription of the galley slaves. He was not always even the commander-in-chief of expeditions.

In Malta, Piyale (one of the greatest admirals of Suleiman's reign) was under the orders of the incompetent and limited vizier Mustafa, who was chiefly responsible for the setback on that campaign. More often the admirals were men who had had no experience at sea before their appointment; like all the dignitaries, they had usually been trained at the Pages' School. When Barbarossa died, he was replaced by Sokullu Mehmed Pasha, whose title, on the day he was appointed, had been 'Guardian of the Palace Gates'. His successor Sinan Pasha was the brother of the Grand Vizier Rustem Pasha and had never before commanded a fleet at sea. Piyale was also a man of the Palace, although this did not prevent him from being a great sailor and from emerging victorious at Jerba and at Chios. Yet after him came Muezzinzade Ali Pasha, who was chiefly responsible for the defeat at Lepanto.

Appendix 9
The Army on Campaign

The army set off on campaign amid solemn ceremony and with clearly established marching orders. The troops assembled either at Davud Pasha (for expeditions to the North) or at Uskudar (when they were going East), the sultan took command of the expedition and they moved off at once. At the front were the squadrons of reconnaissance cavalry, followed by the mounted advance guard and then the bulk of the army and artillery; on the flanks, the *sipahi timariotes* formed a protective rearguard.

When they reached the enemy and the leading unit commanders had been consulted, the sultan – or the Grand Vizier, if he was leading the expedition – gave the orders to attack. The *akinci* and *azab* were told to join combat and spread disorder in the enemy ranks. The cavalry harassed the enemy, infiltrated his flanks and rear, feigned retreat and returned to the attack. A powerful concentration of artillery would be used to throw the enemy into confusion. Then the whole cavalry would advance together for the final assault and the battle would end in a merciless pursuit of the enemy soldiers by Turkish soldiers and irregulars who could usually not be restrained from massacring and pillaging.

On the following day, the sultan held a *Divan*, in the course of which he was congratulated by the army chiefs and handed out awards. Letters of victory were sent to provincial governors and leading dignitaries, to members of the imperial family and foreign rulers. The last of these responded with warm congratulations even when the extension of the domains conquered by the Great Turk was the last thing in the world they would have wished for. When the victory was less complete than had been hoped or even when it had been necessary to beat an inglorious retreat, it was still announced that the campaign had ended in the flight of enemies who had not dared face the *padishah*'s powerful armies.

The return to Istanbul was equally triumphant, and preparations began at once for the next campaign. The Turks possessed the Asiatic talent – Genghis Khan is often cited as the supreme example – for not giving up, for trying again after a setback to achieve an important objective, just as if nothing had happened.

In his book *De la naissance, durée et chute des Estats* (On the Birth, Survival and Fall of States) (1588), René de Lusinge laid down 17 reasons for the Turk's successes in the 16th century: '1) He devoted himself to war above all else. 2) He always took the offensive in war. 3) He gave little consideration to fortresses. 4) He trained up bold and valiant soldiers. 5) He used discipline and military justice to keep his powerful armies under control. 6) He never depended on forces other than his own. 7) He used ruses and deceptions as well as sheer power in battle. 8) He was served by excellent commanders. 9) He made no mistakes in his undertakings. 10) He did not waste time on unimportant amusements. 11) He took advantage of his opportunities. 12) He carried out his plans speedily. 13) He went to war in person, 14) well-equipped, and 15) at the right time of year. 16) He refused to divide up his forces and 17) did not carry on fighting against a single adversary.'

Appendix 10
A Grand Vizier's Career: Sokullu

Sokullu was born in the early years of the 16th century in Sokoloviçi, Bosnia, where his family were probably members of the minor peasant nobility. He had started his religious studies and attained the rank of deacon before being recruited into the *devşirme* system at the age of 18. Some accounts claim that his father and uncle, a monk, tried in vain to release him from his 'conscription' by offering the man who came to 'collect' him a large sum of money.

He quickly rose through the ranks to the post of Grand Chamberlain. He was then appointed commander-in-chief of the fleet in 1546, when Barbarossa died. Three years later, he became *beylerbey* of Rumelia. He took part in almost all Suleiman's military campaigns and rallied to the support of Prince Selim at the time of his dispute with Bayezid. When Selim came to the throne, he retained Sokullu as his Grand Vizier and virtually handed over the government of the empire to him. He had the difficult task of rebuilding the Turkish fleet after Lepanto. More a man of peace than of war and an administrator of the first rank, he carried through the conquest of Cyprus in 1571 with great efficiency, although he had hardly been a fervent supporter of the plan. He was extremely rich, but believed to be almost incorruptible. He died in 1579, stabbed by a man disguised as a dervish whose *timar* he had withdrawn.

Badoero described him at the end of his life: 'He was tall in stature and of solemn countenance; his beard added to his majestic air. He was very vigorous for his age and a very skilful negotiator, experienced in difficulties and firm in his resolve.' Antonio Tiepolo spoke of him as follows: 'I have rarely held discussions with him where he did not reveal an almost smiling sweetness of temper even on topics where he had decided in advance to refuse us.'

Appendix 11
Henry II and Suleiman

No sooner was he on the throne than Henry II of France faced a situation full of dangers – for himself and for the whole of Europe. Charles V had crushed the Elector of Saxony at the Battle of Mühlberg and was only a step away from doing the same to the Protestant princes. If he were not stopped, he would soon control all Europe. The Turkish alliance was needed more than ever.

Like his father, Henry II did not allow himself to be swayed by the now familiar criticism that he was betraying Christendom. He immediately sent to Istanbul two gentlemen in his entourage, the Baron de Funel and the Sieur de Lucson, to announce his accession to the throne and to tell the sultan that the King of France wished to maintain and develop the alliance between their two countries. A few weeks later, Henri de Codignac set out on a mission to prepare a new plan of campaign with the Porte. A third envoy, d'Huyson, followed not far behind with the same instructions. Henry believed that Turkish attacks on the Danube only had the effect of closing German ranks, which was clearly not at all what he wanted.

But Suleiman was at the time more concerned about his war with Persia. Once he had settled accounts with the Sophy, he could deal with 'the King of Spain'. Yet to show that his amity with the French king remained intact, he took Henry's ambassador, Gabriel d'Aramon, with him on campaign. This was unquestionably a great honour for France, although it was one that d'Aramon could well have done without and proved exhausting for a man no longer in his first youth. 'What glory for that ambassador and the French nation,' wrote Brantôme, 'to be given such a position in the entourage of the greatest monarch in the world!'

Suleiman took his time in Persia, and with good reason. Charles V showed himself less dangerous than had been feared, since the Habsburgs spent most of their time disputing among themselves about who should succeed him; the emperor, aging and ill, thought of little else. The victory at Mühlberg was already a long way in the past and Henry's position was improving. He had disentangled himself from his war with England. (Henry VIII had seized Boulogne, and France replied by intervening in Scotland, where Mary of Lorraine was regent. According to the subsequent peace, signed at Ardres, Boulogne was restored to France in return for 800,000 crowns and an undertaking not to intervene again in Scottish affairs.) Henry could now spend his time in plots aimed at breaking up Suleiman's truce with the Habsburgs. French agents were in action on all sides. All sorts of plans were laid: Suleiman would expel 'the King of Spain' from Naples and Sicily and hand them over to Henry. D'Aramon returned to France and then came back to Istanbul. The Turks laid siege to Tripoli, which was in the hands of the Knights of Malta and made little effort to resist. D'Aramon's presence among the Turkish troops there emphasized the continuing co-operation between France and the Porte. Although he managed to bring about the release of the Knights who had been imprisoned, the Grand Master of the Order accused him, with some justification, of complicity with the 'barbarous infidels'.

The fall of Tripoli, although it deeply affected Europe, was far from being Henry's primary concern. He wanted the Ottomans to attack Hungary and to join with the French fleet in the Mediterranean. Both of these projects in fact took place, but the first did Henry little good and the second failed either because of the lack of co-ordination between the two commanders or because of ill will on the part of certain Turkish chiefs; at all events, an exceptional opportunity to destroy the imperial fleet and perhaps to conquer the Kingdom of Naples fell through. The Turks indeed were preoccupied with other matters at the time: the war with Persia and the quarrel between Suleiman and Mustafa, the heir to the throne, which was just reaching its climax.

In the following year, 1554, the same mistakes were made. The Turks, who had promised booty 'good and large', were disappointed by the spoils they gained from the expedition, although the French managed, temporarily, to seize Corsica from the Genoese. In 1555, another expedition also came to naught. Two years later, following an appeal from Henry to Suleiman, a Turkish fleet of 111 galleys under Piyale Pasha's command set out again for the Western Mediterranean. Whether he had been bribed before departure by Genoese agents or actually instructed to take his time, he merely devastated the Balearic Islands and then returned to Nice and Toulon. He refused to accede to French requests that he attack Bastia. When he got back to Istanbul he was deprived of his rank at the French ambassador's request and new plans for co-ordinated attacks were discussed.

It was at this point that France and Spain patched up their long dispute, when they signed the peace of Cateau-Cambrésis on 5 April 1559. France recovered Calais and the fortifications on the Somme but gave up Savoy, Piedmont and Corsica. It renounced all claims in Italy, which now fell under Spanish domination. A page of history had been turned.

Now that peace had been made with the Habsburgs, the Turkish army and fleet were no longer so important to Henry. In any event, he died shortly afterwards, and Suleiman soon followed him to the grave. The Wars of Religion enfeebled France and turned its attention away from ambitious foreign schemes. The Franco-Turkish alliance became far less important, although relations between the two countries remained good (and sometimes excellent) until the early 17th century. The capitulations were renewed in 1569 and again in 1581, 1597 and 1604, with extended privileges accorded on each occasion to the Most Christian King, his ships and his traders. Those in 1581 laid down that the French ambassador would in future take precedence over those of all other Christian sovereigns.

Appendix 12
Suleiman's Death

On 25 October 1566, the viceroy of Naples handed over to Philip II a letter sent on 24 September from Constantinople to Ragusa in which 'those who were present there' announced the death of Suleiman and Selim's accession to the throne. Some of the details have never been published before, so it is here given in full (although the stylistic flourishes considered appropriate in the writings of 16th-century Spanish diplomats have been removed):

'On 15 September, a *çavuş* arrived in Constantinople who had left the Turk's camp seven days earlier; he brought the news that the Turk had died after the capture of Szeged and Gyula and that this had happened on the 6th of the said month.

'On the 24th, the Sultan Selim, who had heard news of the Turk's death, came to Escufareto [probably Uskudar], opposite Constantinople, with 6,000 men; another 15,000 were following behind. He at once sent instructions by sea to Iskender Pasha, the Governor of Constantinople, for him to give orders for the entry he wished to make into the town, since he had heard that his father was dead. The said pasha, who had received the same news, therefore gave orders to this effect and armed two galleys, two imperial brigandines and many other vessels to go and fetch the said Sultan Selim. He thus arranged for the sultan to reach Istanbul with the guard he needed and with so much secrecy that he had already arrived there before the people knew anything about it.

'Later, when Selim had entered Constantinople, the news spread through the town and was received with great joy; it displeased nobody, although it was feared that the town and Pera might be sacked. When he entered the Seraglio, he was proclaimed emperor and many boats were sent at once to collect the entourage of the said Selim.

'The sultanas, sister and aunt of the sultan then came to kiss his hands, lamenting the Turk's death and rejoicing that he [Selim] was now at the head of the empire.'

On 25 and 26 September, letters from Constantinople had given the viceroy the following information (which he also transmitted to Philip II):

'The Sultan Selim II has determined to set out on campaign on the 26th so as to meet up with the army in Hungary in 30 days.

'He has confirmed in his post of Governor of Constantinople Iskender Pasha, the man who had held the office in his father's time.

'The former French ambassador* and the new one, as well as the Venetian ambassador, came to kiss Selim's hand on the following day; he had also ordered Juan Micas [a Portuguese Marrano, otherwise known as Joseph Nasi, whom Selim was later to appoint Duke of Naxos and who dreamed of becoming King of Cyprus] to come to the Seraglio and told him he would become very powerful because he was very dear to him.

'On 26 September, a *çavuş* arrived who had left the camp 8 days ago and was much astonished by the news, since the army did not know the Turk was dead; a whole month had gone by without them finding out.

'He described all that the Turk's camp had done so that no one should learn of the Turk's death before Selim's arrival.

'On the same day, the 26th, a great display of artillery was held in the town as Selim rode by; he then left the town by the Adrianople Gate, where the aforesaid ambassadors kissed his hands and spoke approvingly of the peace which had been made with his father. He replied that he would respect it and spoke at greater length with the Venetian ambassador than the French king's.

'Selim took with him a mere 3 or 4 thousand men, and it was said that the new emperor would be back with his army within 3 months, if the Christians posed no further problems for him, since he is personally much more in favour of peace than of war.'

(Simancas, Eo 1055, fo 198; *ibid* fo 215)

* This was either Antoine de Petremol – who was technically a 'resident' and not an ambassador – or rather, according to Charrière, Monsieur Bonnet, sent by the French court mainly to clear up one particular problem. This concerned two young Turkish girls captured in 1557 by a squadron belonging to the Grand Prior François of Lorraine in the Western Mediterranean. They were probably on a pilgrimage to Mecca at the time and had been handed over to Catherine de' Medici and baptised Catherine and Marguerite. This matter, which took 25 years to settle, had a notably chilling effect on Franco-Turkish relations at one point. In the end, the girls remained in France, but an allowance was given to their mother in compensation. For further details, see the article by S. Skilliter in *Turcica*, VII (1975).

The new French envoy, who did indeed bear the title of 'King's ambassador', was Grantrie de Grandchamp.

Appendix 13
The Turkish Baths

Lady Mary Wortley Montagu, whose husband was the English ambassador to the sultan (Ahmed III) in 1717–18, left letters to her friends during her stay in Turkey which undoubtedly rank among the truest and best observed accounts of life in the Ottoman Empire. This extract is a description of a Turkish bath for women in Sofia:

'I went to the bagnio about ten o'clock. It was already full of women. It is built of stone in the shape of a dome with no windows but in the roof, which gives light enough. There was five of these domes joined together, the outmost being less than the rest and serving only as a hall where the porteress stood at the door . . . The next room is a very large one, paved with marble, and all round it raised two sofas of marble, one above another. There were four fountains of cold water in this room, falling first into marble basins and then running on the floor in little channels made for that purpose, which carried the streams into the next room, something less than this, with the same sort of marble sofas, but so hot with steams of sulphur proceeding from the baths joining to it, 'twas impossible to stay there with one's clothes on. The two other domes were the hot baths, one of which had cocks of cold water turning into it to temper it to what degree of warmth the bathers have a mind to . . .

'The first sofas were covered with cushions and rich carpets, on which sat the ladies, and on the second their slaves behind 'em, but without any distinction of rank by their dress, all being in the state of nature, that is, in plain English, stark naked, without any beauty or defect concealed, yet there was not the least wanton smile or immodest gesture amongst 'em. They walked and moved with the same majestic grace which Milton describes of our General Mother. There were many amongst them as exactly proportioned as ever any goddess was drawn by the pencil of Guido or Titian, and most of their skins shiningly white, only adorned by their beautiful hair divided into many tresses hanging on their shoulders, braided either with pearl or riband, perfectly representing the figures of the Graces . . .

'To tell you the truth, I had wickedness enough to wish secretly that Mr Jervas [a portrait painter] could have been there invisible. I fancy it would have very much improved his art to see so many fine women naked in different postures, some in conversation, some working, others drinking coffee or sherbet, and many negligently lying on their cushions while their slaves (generally pretty girls of seventeen or eighteen) were employed in braiding their hair in several pretty manners. In short, 'tis the women's coffee-house, where all the news of the town is told, scandal invented, etc. They generally take this diversion once a week, and stay there at least four or five hours without getting cold by immediate coming out of the hot bath into the cool room, which was very surprising to me. The lady that seemed the most considerable amongst them entreated me to sit by her and would fain have undressed me for the bath. I excused myself with some difficulty, they being all so earnest in persuading me. I was at last forced to open my skirt and show them my stays, which satisfied 'em very well, for I saw they believed I was so locked up in that machine that it was not in my own power to open it, which contrivance they attributed to my husband."*

* Included in *The Selected Letters of Lady Mary Wortley Montagu*, edited by Robert Halsband (London, 1970), pages 90–91.

Appendix 14
The Mendes Family

The Mendes family, headed at the time by Doña Gracia, controlled most of the spice trade in Europe. Their economic and financial power was so great that they have been compared to the Fugger banking dynasty.

Since it was the sultan's consistent policy to help anyone who could enrich the empire establish himself within its borders, Suleiman encouraged Doña Gracia to set up shop in Istanbul. She did so in 1553. Joseph Nasi (or Juan Micas) was her nephew, a close friend of the Sultan Selim II and well known for his love of strong drink. He was therefore granted a monopoly in the empire's wine trade and entrusted with the task of administering Naxos and the neighbouring islands, a major centre of viniculture. Selim even appointed him Duke of Naxos. Yet his commercial activities also extended to the countries beyond the Danube, notably Poland, where King Sigismund had borrowed the immense sum of 150,000 ducats and given him a monopoly in the export of beeswax. He also lent 150,000 ducats to Henry II in 1555, when the French king was trying to arrange a large loan. Repayment of this sum and the complications which ensued, although rather obscure (Braudel describes Nasi as an 'extortioner'), helped produced a major crisis in Franco-Ottoman relations. French ships were seized in Alexandria in 1568.

Nasi-Micas was also one of the people who agitated in 1570 for the anti-Venetian attack on Cyprus (where he hoped to become king), although the Grand Vizier was opposed to the scheme. Sokullu Mehmed Pasha would have preferred to obtain Cyprus by negotiation and, it is said, to come to the aid of the Moors of Granada, who were in revolt against Spain. Yet it was the faction composed of Nasi, Lala Mustafa Pasha (Selim's former tutor), Hoca Sinan and Piyale Pasha (the third vizier and *kapudan pasha*) which won the day. Nicosia fell on 9 September 1570. On 25 May in the following year, however, the foundation of the Holy League was proclaimed in St Peter's, Rome; on 7 October, the Battle of Lepanto 'broke the spell of Turkish power'.

Appendix 15
The Capitulations

With the exception of the treaty of 1536, the capitulations were always concessions granted by the sultan for the benefit of a particular foreign power. The *aman* could be withdrawn if the sultan felt that the *mustamin* (foreign resident) had not behaved in 'a friendly and benevolent manner'. At least until the middle of the 18th century, the capitulations had to be renewed each time a new sultan came to the throne, which led to long negotiations and gave the Porte a chance to increase or reduce the privileges granted in accordance with the state of relations between the Ottomans and the relevant Christian power. In general terms, their contents were similar to those of the treaty made with France in 1536, although there would always be specific additional clauses, more or less favourable, for each individual nation.

Under Suleiman, only France, Poland and Venice were granted capitulations, but towards the end of the century the efforts of Queen Elizabeth and the English traders bore fruit: Murad III, who needed an ally against Philip II's Spain as well as metal for weaponry, granted them the same concessions as the French. The English soon acquired a preponderance in the Levant, with consulates in Beirut, Syrian Tripoli and Alexandria. Their exports consisted particularly of textiles, knit-wear, paper, sugar, dyes and spices. England imported wool, leather, cotton, wax, silk and hemp. In 1612, the Dutch were also granted capitulations and the long period of three-power rivalry in the Levant began. The French first gained the upper hand, then the English. In the middle of the 18th century, the French once again received important privileges and the level of trading reached a new peak. They retained a major outpost in Turkey right until the end of the 19th century.

Yet the Ottoman Empire became weaker and the Habsburgs and Russia, and then almost every European country, were granted similar capitulations. They ended up as 'an instrument of domination in the hands of Europeans'. Not only were the privileges extended beyond all measure, they were granted to thousands of people who had no right to them. The *dhimmis* (non-Muslim subjects of the empire: Greeks, Armenians, Jews) obtained, at a price, letters from ambassadors or European consuls which offered them posts as dragomans or interpreters.

They themselves, their sons and their servants thus became beneficiaries of all the privileges enjoyed by foreigners. There were thousands of false interpreters who avoided the requirements of Ottoman law and commercial regulations in this way.

In addition, the great powers each had many protégés who, again for a fee, were given the status of foreign traders. Thus Russia even claimed, at the time of the Crimean war, that all the Orthodox subjects of the empire counted as its protégés. With concession after concession, Turkey became a semi-colonial state, where all the public services – electricity, gas, banks, railways, ports and even the post – were in foreign hands, where Europeans and their protégés bought and sold merchandise freely. This led to the death of the infant Turkish industries and to economic stagnation. In the 19th century, foreigners were the masters of the country. It was only in 1923, after the Ataturk revolution, that the Treaty of Lausanne abolished the capitulations once and for all.

Appendix 16
Islam and Painting

Painters were greatly honoured and by no means regarded as men who systematically infringed the Prophet's Law; artists worked quite openly. In Istanbul, quite apart from those who worked at the palace for the sultan and princes, *nakkaş* and *musavvir* practised their crafts without concealment. How was this possible in a society controlled by narrow-minded Sunni *ulema* and ruled by a sultan extremely anxious to maintain religious orthodoxy? In his essay on the aesthetics of Muslim art, A. Papadopoulo offers an explanation.*

The Prophet's *hadith* did not ban the artistic reproduction of the human form but 'a representation resembling a real individual being'. Everything depended therefore, Papadopoulo claims, on 'the manner of representing living beings'. By aiming not for resemblance but only for *the concept of man* (although this could take a wide variety of different forms), the artist would never infringe any religious interdictions. This would also apply if he abstained from representing 'images in shadow' since representation was considered to consist in 'the impression of relief communicated by shadowing'. This explains the absence of light and shadow in Muslim miniatures. Art historians often criticize Islamic art for being 'flat', but this defect is entirely voluntary. If the colours are sometimes inadequate and if depth is suggested by representing standing objects 'as if they appeared vertical while the rest of the scene is viewed partly at eye level and partly from above', this is because painters were actually *trying* to create pictures which lacked verisimilitude.

Historians of Muslim art are mistaken, claims Papadopoulo, when they speak of 'lack of skill' and say, for example, that painters 'did not yet understand how to represent perspective or achieve modelling'. This so-called 'lack of skill' was deliberate and had a precise objective: to avoid lifelike imitation. Theologians accepted the existence of the *Karagoz* not only because 'by showing vice it taught virtue' but also because the images used, which required 'a hole to put string through', were not real men.

*A. Papadopoulo, 'Esthétique de l'Art Musulman, La Peinture', *Annales E.S.C.* (May-June 1973).

Genealogy of the Sultans of the House of Osman

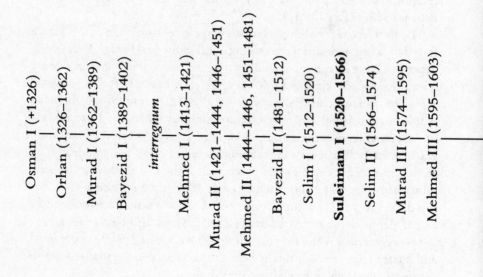

Osman I (+1326)
|
Orhan (1326–1362)
|
Murad I (1362–1389)
|
Bayezid I (1389–1402)
|
interregnum
|
Mehmed I (1413–1421)
|
Murad II (1421–1444, 1446–1451)
|
Mehmed II (1444–1446, 1451–1481)
|
Bayezid II (1481–1512)
|
Selim I (1512–1520)
|
Suleiman I (1520–1566)
|
Selim II (1566–1574)
|
Murad III (1574–1595)
|
Mehmed III (1595–1603)
|

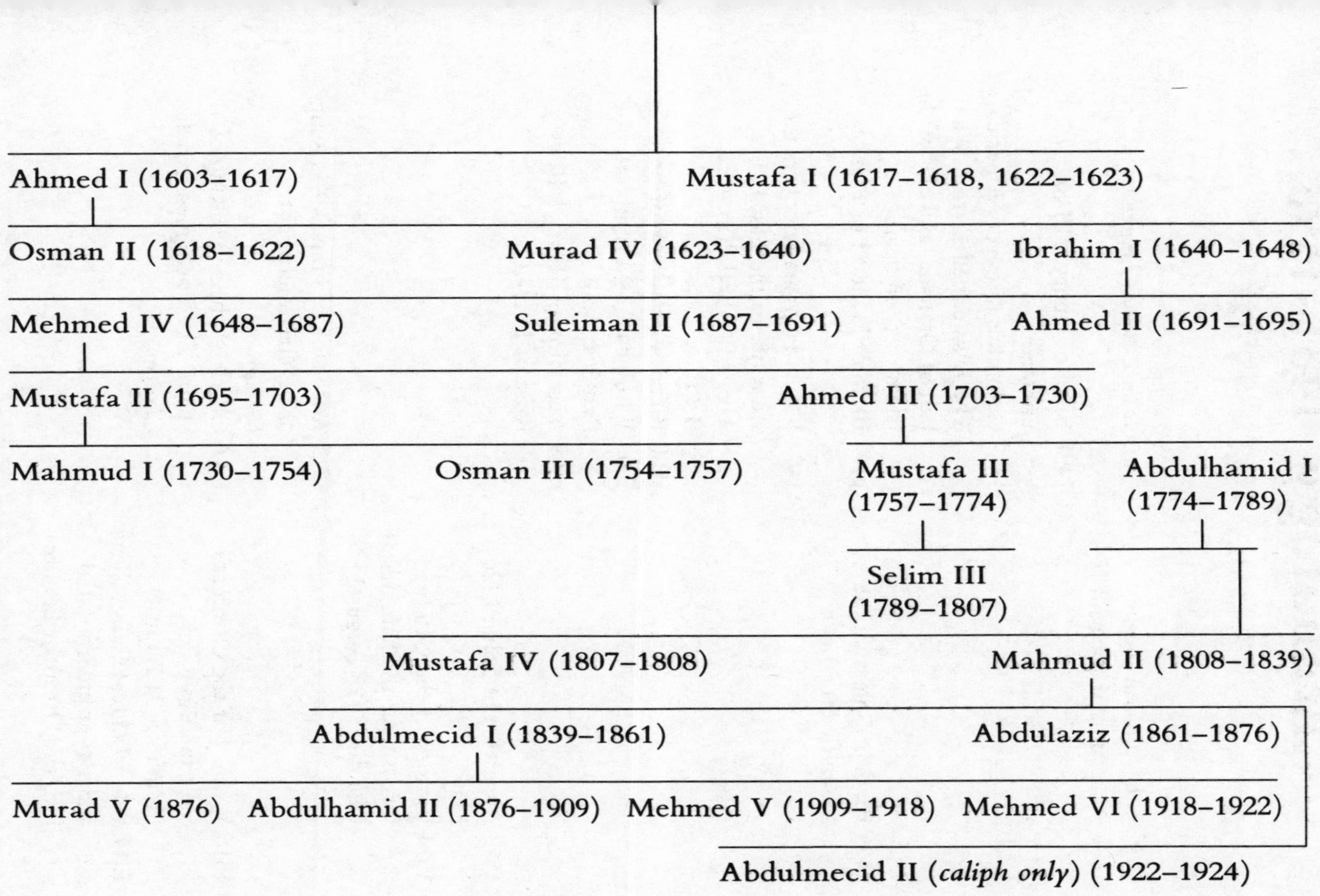

Ahmed I (1603–1617)
Mustafa I (1617–1618, 1622–1623)
Osman II (1618–1622)
Murad IV (1623–1640)
Ibrahim I (1640–1648)
Mehmed IV (1648–1687)
Suleiman II (1687–1691)
Ahmed II (1691–1695)
Mustafa II (1695–1703)
Ahmed III (1703–1730)
Mahmud I (1730–1754)
Osman III (1754–1757)
Mustafa III (1757–1774)
Abdulhamid I (1774–1789)
Selim III (1789–1807)
Mustafa IV (1807–1808)
Mahmud II (1808–1839)
Abdulmecid I (1839–1861)
Abdulaziz (1861–1876)
Murad V (1876)
Abdulhamid II (1876–1909)
Mehmed V (1909–1918)
Mehmed VI (1918–1922)
Abdulmecid II (*caliph only*) (1922–1924)

Chronology, 1481–1598

Within the Ottoman Empire	*Outside the Ottoman Empire*
1481 Accession of Bayezid II	
	1491 Birth of Henry VIII of England
	1492 Columbus discovers America. The Jews expelled from Spain. Fall of Granada, and end of the Islamic era in Spain.
1494 Birth of Suleiman the Magnificent	1494 Birth of Francis I of France
	1497 Vasco da Gama discovers the sea route to the East Indies. Alvares Cabral discovers Brazil
	1500 Birth of Charles V of Spain
	1502 Vasco da Gama completes the Red Sea route
	1509 Accession of Henry VIII as King of England
1512 Accession of Selim I (26 May)	
1514 Victory of the Ottoman forces over the Safavids at Chaldiran (23 August)	
	1515 Accession of Francis I as King of France. Victory at Marignano
1516 Victory of the Ottomans over the Egyptian Mamluks (24 August)	1516 Charles V becomes King of Spain. The Portuguese reach Canton
1517 Selim I enters Cairo. Syria and Egypt incorporated into the Ottoman Empire	

Within the Ottoman Empire	*Outside the Ottoman Empire*
	1519 Charles V elected Emperor
	1519–21 Magellan circumnavigates the earth. Cortés conquers the Aztec Empire, Pizarro the Inca Empire
1520 Death of Selim I (21 September). Accession of Suleiman (30 September)	
1521 Suleiman takes Belgrade. Canberdi al-Ghazali's revolt in Egypt is crushed	1521 Luther excommunicated
1522 Suleiman conquers Rhodes	
1523 Ibrahim becomes Grand Vizier	
1524 Ahmed Pasha's revolt in Egypt	1524 Death of Shah Ismail of Iran; accession of Shah Tahmasp
1525 Ibrahim pacifies and reorganizes Egypt	1525 Battle of Pavia; Francis I taken prisoner
1526 Battle of Mohacs (29 August). Louis II killed. Zapolyai created King of Hungary	1526 Battle of Panipat. Babur founds the Moghul dynasty in India
	1527 Sack of Rome by Charles V's troops
1529 Barbarossa takes control of Algiers. Suleiman lays siege to Vienna	1529 Treaty of Cambrai (The Ladies' Peace)
	1530 Charles V crowned Emperor
	1531 Henry VIII breaks with Rome. Protestant Schmalkaldic League
1532 Austrian campaign; siege of Güns	1532 Peace of Nuremberg
1533–34 Two Iraqs Campaign. Conquest of Baghdad	1533 Accession of Ivan the Terrible
1534 Barbarossa takes Tunis	

Within the Ottoman Empire		*Outside the Ottoman Empire*	
1535	Charles V recaptures Tunis. J. de La Forest's mission to Suleiman		
1536	Execution of Ibrahim (5 March). Ayas Pasha becomes Grand Vizier. The Franco-Ottoman alliance; capitulations		
1537	War with Venice. Siege of Corfu		
1538	Hadim Suleiman Pasha's expedition to Diu. Naval battle of Preveza.	1538	Truce of Nice; Charles and Francis meet at Aigues-Mortes
1539	Death of Ayas Pasha; Lutfi Pasha becomes Grand Vizier		
1540	Peace with Venice		
1541	Suleiman at Buda; annexation of Hungary. Charles V's disastrous expedition to Algiers. Lutfi Pasha deposed; Suleiman Pasha becomes Grand Vizier	1541	Assassination of Rinçon
1543	Barbarossa's expedition along the French coast; siege of Nice. Suleiman in Hungary		
1544	Suleiman Pasha deposed; Rustem Pasha becomes Grand Vizier	1544	Peace of Crespy
1545	Truce between Suleiman and Ferdinand	1545	Opening of the Council of Trent
		1546	Death of Luther (18 February)

Within the Ottoman Empire	*Outside the Ottoman Empire*
1547 Peace of Constantinople. Occupation of San'a and Ta'izz	1547 Battle of Mühlberg. Death of Francis I (27 January). Death of Henry VIII (31 March). Henry II becomes King of France
1548 Suleiman's campaign in Iran	
1550–56 Construction of the Suleimaniye mosque	
1551 Turgut Reis takes Tripoli. Piri Reis's expedition	1551 Assassination of Martinuzzi
1553 Sidi Ali Reis's expedition. Execution of Mustafa (16 October)	1553 Death of Edward VI of England; Mary Tudor becomes queen
1554 Suleiman's campaign in Iran	1554 The Russians take Astrakhan
1555 Execution of Ahmed Pasha; Rustem Pasha again becomes Grand Vizier. Peace of Amasya	1555 Peace of Augsburg
1556–59 Hungarian campaigns	1556 Abdication of Charles V; Ferdinand becomes Emperor, Philip II King of Spain. Accession of the Moghul emperor Akbar
	1558 Death of Charles V (21 September). Death of Mary Tudor; Elizabeth I becomes Queen of England
1559 Struggle between Bayezid and Selim; Bayezid escapes to Iran	1559 Peace of Cateau-Cambrésis. Francis II succeeds Henry II as King of France
1560 Capture of Jerba by Piyale Pasha	1560 Charles IX becomes King of France, Catherine de' Medici regent
1561 Execution of Bayezid	

Within the Ottoman Empire	*Outside the Ottoman Empire*
1562 Peace treaty with Ferdinand. Death of Rustem Pasha; Ali Pasha becomes Grand Vizier	1562 Start of the Wars of Religion in France
	1564 Death of Ferdinand I; his son Maximilian succeeds him
1565 Siege of Malta. Death of Ali Pasha; Sokullu Pasha becomes Grand Vizier	
1566 Ottoman campaign in Hungary. Siege of Szeged. Death of Suleiman (6 September); Selim II becomes sultan	
1569 Expedition to Astrakhan. Failure of the Don–Volga canal project	
1570 Cyprus expedition	
1571 Battle of Lepanto	
1574 Definitive conquest of Tunis by the Ottomans. Death of Selim II; accession of Murad III	1574 Death of Charles IX; Henry III becomes King of France
	1576 Death of Shah Tahmasp
1578 Assassination of Sokullu Pasha	
1580 Capitulations granted to the English	1580 End of Portuguese independence
	1584 Death of Ivan the Terrible; 'the Time of Troubles'
1585 Financial crisis; devaluation	
	1587 Accession of Shah Abbas II
	1588 Defeat of the Spanish Armada
1589 Revolt of the janissaries	1589 Assassination of Henry III of France
1595 Death of Murad III; Mehmed III succeeds him	
	1598 Death of Philip II

Glossary

Note: Unless a plural form is indicated, the same form has been used for both singular and plural.

acemi oğlan: young Christian recruited by the system of *devşirme* for the sultan's service in the palace, either in administration or the Porte regiments

ağa: chief (for example, *yeniçeri ağasi*: janissary general)

ahi: member of a semi-religious co-operative association (*futuvva*) under the Seljuk and first Ottoman rulers

ak ağa: white eunuch

akçe: coin long used in the Ottoman Empire; 50–60 *akçe*, in the middle of the 16th century, were worth a gold ducat

akinci: troops stationed in frontier regions

akritai: Byzantine warrior on the frontiers of the Islamic world

askeri: soldier, person belonging to the military (as opposed to the *reaya*) which consisted essentially of the Porte and *timar* armed forces and the functionaries in the sultan's service

avariz: exceptional tax levied on the *reaya*

azab: soldier serving in the provinces, a garrison or a fortress; naval officer

baba: father superior in a dervish community (notably the Bektaşi)

Bab-i Ali: Sublime Porte

bailo: Venetian ambassador to Constantinople

baş kadin: first lady of the palace, mother of a son

baştarda: large galley

bedesten: covered or closed market, where precious objects were stored and sold

Bektaşi: member of the order founded in the 14th–15th centuries by Haci Bektaş Veli, to which the janissaries were affiliated

bey (pl. *beys*): prince, vassal sovereign of the sultan, governor

beylerbey: '*bey* of *beys*', governor of a province

beylerbeylik: province governed by a *beylerbey*

birun: exterior section of the Seraglio

bostanci başi: chief gardener of the sultan (a leading functionary)

cami: mosque
çavuş: emissary of the sultan who carried out his orders
cebeci: armourer
cebelu: soldier armed with a breastplate and taken on campaign by a *timariote sipahi*
celali: rebel, in the 16th century
çift: unit of agricultural land of 60–150 *donum* in area (which could be worked by a pair – *çift* – of oxen)
çiftresmi: land tax payable by Muslim peasants
ciziye: poll tax payable by non-Muslims (*dhimmis*)
çorbaci: colonel (of janissaries) or, literally, the man who makes the soup

damga resmi: stamp/registration duty
dede: grandfather, chief of a dervish community
defterdar: Minister of Finance for the empire (member of the *Divan*) or treasurer (of Egypt, the Asian provinces, etc.)
dervish: member of a Muslim religious order
devşirme: the system of conscripting Christian children to serve in the sultan's administration or one of the Porte regiments
dhimmi (pl. *dhimmis*): non-Muslim subject of a Muslim sovereign
divan: collection of verse by an Ottoman poet
Divan-i humayun: Imperial Council, chief organ of the Ottoman Empire
donum: land measure (940 sq. m)

emin: functionary who administered the financial services of the imperial bureaucracy
emir: prince, chief
enderun: interior of the Seraglio
esnaf: corporation or, by extension, the members of a corporation
eyalet: province

ferman: decree of the sultan
fetva: opinion expressed by the *şeyhulislam* (or a *mufti*) in response to a question about the Prophet's Law
fusta: light galley
futuvva (or *futuvvet*): popular semi-religious association or brotherhood

from which the corporations originated; 'craftsmen's pact of honour' (L. Massignon)

gaza: Muslim holy war
gazel: poem consisting of five or six couplets
gazi: warrior of the Muslim faith against the Infidels
gulam: slave (of the sultan or a member of the ruling class)
gureba: one of the six regiments of Porte cavalry

hadith: the body of traditions about the Prophet which make up 'an oral law to supplement the written law' (H. Massé)
hahan başi: chief rabbi at the head of the Jewish 'nation'
hammam: Turkish bath
han: hostelry
Hanafi: one of the four schools of Sunni Islamic law to which the Turks belonged; the others are the Hanbali, Shafi'i and Maliki schools
Harem: women's apartment
Harem ağasi: chief of the black eunuchs
has oda: the sultan's private chamber
haseki: the favourite of the sultan
hass: endowment (granted to a member of the imperial family, a *beylerley*, a *sancakbey*, etc.) worth over 100,000 *akçe* a year
hazine: the treasury
Hazine-i Amiri: the Imperial Treasury
hutbe: the Friday sermon

içoğlan (pl. *içoğlanlari*): young slave of the sultan who received his education at the palace
ihtisab: the body of regulations about commercial transactions in Istanbul and other towns
imam: he who leads the prayers; priest in charge of a mosque; descendants of Ali (among the Shiites)
imaret: complex of buildings founded for charitable and religious purposes and maintained by the *vakf*

janissaries (*yeniçeri*): Porte infantry recruited by the *devşirme*

kadi: judge and chief administrator of a *kaza*
kadiasker: one of two deputies in the judicial administration

kadin: one of the sultan's four privileged wives
kadirga: galley
kafes: cage; part of the Seraglio in which the royal princes were locked up
kanun: law laid down by the sultan
Kanunname: code of law
Kapi: the Porte or government
kapi ağasi: chief of the white eunuchs of the palace
kapikulu: Porte slave (from the *devşirme*), palace functionary
kapudan: captain (at sea)
kapudan pasha: chief admiral
kapudan-i derya: chief admiral of the fleet
kaymakam: governor
kaza: administrative and judicial subdivision of a *sancak*
kazasker: supreme chief of judicial administration in Rumelia or Anatolia
kethuda: representative, agent of or to a government; assistant; leader of a corporation
Kizilbaş: 'red head'; member of one of the heterodox and generally pro-Safavid sects in Anatolia

lala: tutor, private teacher
lale devri: Tulip period (1718–30)
levend: vagabond, brigand, corsair

mavna: galley with three masts and thirty-two (or more) banks of oarsmen
medrese: advanced educational establishment
millet (pl. *millets*): 'nation' or community based on religion
miri: state possession
mufti: doctor of Islamic law who was allowed to interpret it
muhtesib: inspector of the markets and corporations, who kept an eye on public morals and the observance of Koranic duties
mulk: private property
muteferrika: elite corps formed of the sons of vassal princes and *beys*

naib: substitute for the *kadi* who exercised the same functions as him in districts (*nahiye*), villages or small towns
nişanci: chief of the Chancellery; secretary of the *Divan* (of which he was a member)

ocak (lit. 'hearth'): corps of janissaries

okka: measure of weight (1. 283 kg)
orf: the sovereign's prerogative, which allowed him, in particular, to pass his own laws (*kanun*) to fill the gaps in the *Şeriat*
orta: company (of janissaries)

pashalik: area governed by a pasha
pir: chief of a community of dervishes

reaya: subjects of the Ottoman Empire who had to pay tax and were not members of the military class (*askeri*)

sancak (lit. 'banner'): administrative area governed by a *sancakbey*; subdivision of a *beylerbeylik*
sancakbey: governor of a *sancak* and commander of the *sipahi* within it
seğban: provincial militiaman provided with firearms
serasker: commander-in-chief
Şeriat: the sacred law of Islam
şeyh: 'chief', 'aged person'; superior of a Muslim community; tribal chief
şeyhulislam: supreme chief of the *ulema* in Ottoman Turkey, the highest Muslim dignitary in the empire
silahdar: guardian of the sultan's arms; one of the six Porte cavalry corps
sipahi: horseman; horseman who held a *timar* in return for service in the army
subaşi: holder of a *timar* and commander of a detachment of *sipahi*; responsible for policing within his area
sunna: 'theory and practice of Muslim orthodoxy' (H. Massé)
Sunni: orthodox Muslim
surgun: deportation

tarikat: religious order; religious brotherhood
tekke: dervish monastery
timar: military endowment of less than 20,000 *akçe* a year, in return for the holder's participation in war
timariote (pl. *timariotes*): holder of a *timar*
topçu: gunner
tophane: cannon foundry; arsenal. A district of Istanbul
tuğra: monogram used by the sultan to confirm the legality of a document
turbe: tomb

uc: march, frontier region
ulema: Muslim theologian and jurist
ulufeci: horsemen of one of the six Porte cavalry regiments
usta: master artisan (in the corporations)

vakf: religious foundation to which revenues were assigned to assure its continued operation
valide sultan: mother of the reigning sultan
vizier: minister of the sultan and member of the *Divan*

yuruk: Turkish nomad from Anatolia or Rumelia

zaviye: religious foundation by a road or in a small town established by a *şeyh* or a dervish to provide lodging to travellers
zeamet: military endowment worth 20,000–100,000 *akçe* a year, in return for the holder's participation in war

Bibliography

Collected Works and General Histories

The Cambridge History of Islam (Cambridge)
Encyclopedia of Islam I, 1913–1938 (Leiden)
Encyclopedia of Islam II, 1960– (Leiden)
Histoire de France, by E. Lavisse (Paris)
Histoire Générale, ed. by L. Halphen and P. Sagnac (Paris)
Islam Ansiklopedisi (Istanbul, 1940)
The Koran, transl. by M. Pickthall (Harmondsworth)
The New Cambridge Modern History (Cambridge)
Recueil des Instructions Données aux Ambassadeurs de France, XXIX

ALBERI, *Relazioni degli Ambasciatori Veneti durante il Secolo XVI* (Florence, 1839–63).
E. CHARRIÈRE, *Négociations de la France dans le Levant* (Paris, 1840–60), 4 vols.
E.J.W. GIBB, *A History of Ottoman Poetry* (London, 1900–09), 6 vols.
N. JORGA, *Geschichte des Osmanischen Reiches* (Gotha, 1908–13).
J. PIRENNE, *Les Grands Courants de l'Histoire Universelle* (Neuchâtel, 1947–52).
J. VON HAMMER-PURGSTALL, *Histoire de l'Empire Ottoman depuis son Origine jusqu'à Nos Jours*, transl. from German by J.J. Hellert (Paris, 1835–48), 18 vols.
J.W. ZINKEISEN, *Geschichte des Osmanischen Reiches in Europa* (Hamburg-Gotha, 1840–63).

Studies

P. ACHARD, *La Vie Extraordinaire des Frères Barberousse* (Paris, 1939).
A. ADIVAR, *La Science chez les Turcs Ottomans* (Paris, 1939).
A.D. ALDERSON, *The Structure of the Ottoman Dynasty* (Oxford, 1956).
W.E.D. ALLEN, *Problems of Turkish Power in the 16th Century* (London, 1963).
O. ASLANAPA, *Turkish Art and Architecture* (London, 1971).
J. AUBIN, *Le Monde Iranien et l'Islam* (Paris & Geneva, 1971).
F. BABINGER, *Mahomet II le Conquérant et son Temps* (Paris, 1954).

J.L. BACQUÉ-GRAMMONT, 'Études Osmano-Safavides. I. Notes sur le Blocus du Commerce Iranien par Selim Ier', *Turcica VI* (1975).
— 'Notes sur une Saisie de Soies d'Iran en 1518', *Turcica VIII* (2) (1976).
— 'El Apogeo del Imperio Otomano', *Historia, Universal Salvat* (Barcelona, 1982).
M. BANDELLO, *Novelle* (London, 1791–3).
Ö.L. BARKAN, 'Essai sur les Données Statistiques de Recensement dans l'Empire Ottoman aux XVe et XVIe Siècles', *Journal of the Economic and Social History of the Orient* (1958).
— 'L'Organisation du Travail dans le Chantier d'une Grande Mosquée à Istanbul', *Annales*, E.S.C., 6 (1962).
— 'Les Mouvements des Prix en Turquie entre 1490 et 1655', *Mélanges Braudel* (Paris, 1973).
— 'The Price Revolution of the Sixteenth Century: a Turning Point of the Economic History of the Near East', *International Journal of Middle East Studies*, 6 (1975).
— 'The Ottoman Budgets', *Revue de la Faculté des Sciences Économiques d'Istanbul*, XVII.
V.V. BARTHOLD, *Histoire des Turcs d'Asie Centrale* (Paris, 1945).
— *La Découverte de l'Asie*, transl. by B. Nikitine (Paris, 1947).
— *Four Studies on the History of Central Asia* (Leiden, 1962).
I. BAŞGÖZ, 'Earlier References to Kukla and Karageuz', *Turcica III* (1971).
BAUDIER, *Inventaire de l'Histoire Générale des Turcs* (Paris, 1617).
L. BAZIN, 'Turcs et Sogdiens: les Enseignements de l'Inscription de Bugut (Mongolie)', *Mélanges Benveniste* (Paris, 1975).
N. BELDICEANU, *Le Monde Ottoman dans les Balkans, 1502–1566* (London, 1976).
— *Le Timar dans l'État Ottoman (début XIVe-début XVIe)* (Wiesbaden, 1980).
— and C. VILLAIN-GANDOSSI, 'Gecim: une Armure pour Homme et Cheval', *Turcica XII* (1980).
I. BELDICEANU-STEINHERR, 'Le Règne de Sélim Ier: Tournant dans la Vie Politique et Religieuse de l'Empire Ottoman', *Turcica VI* (1975).
F.A. BELIN, *Relations Diplomatiques de la République de Venise avec la Turquie* (Paris, 1877).
P. BELON, *Les Observations de Plusieurs Singularitez et Choses Mémorables Trouvées en Grèce, Asie, Judée . . .* (Paris, 1553).
B. BENASSAR and J. JACQUART, *Le XVIe Siècle*, coll. V (Paris, 1972).
M. BERINDEI and G. VEINSTEIN, 'La Présence Ottomane au Sud de la

Crimée et en Mer d'Azov dans la Première Moitié du XVIe Siècle', *Cahiers du Monde Russe et Soviétique*, XX (34).
N. BERK, *La Peinture Turque* (Ankara, 1950).
J.K. BIRGE, *The Bektashi Order of Dervishes* (London, 1965).
L. DE BOISGELIN, *Malte Ancienne et Moderne* (Marseilles, 1905).
A. BOMBACI, *Histoire de la Littérature Turque*, transl. by I. Mélikoff (Paris, 1968).
J. BORDIER, 'Journal' (unpublished).
J. DE BOURBON (le Bastard de Bourbon), *La Grande et Merveilleuse et Très Cruelle Oppugnation de la Noble Cité de Rhodes* (Paris, 1527).
V.L. BOURRILLY, 'L'Ambassade de la Forest', *Revue Historique*, LXXVI (1902).
— 'Antoine Rinçon et la Politique Orientale de François Ier', *Revue Historique*, CXIII (1913).
E. BRADFORD, *The Sultan's Admiral. The Life of Barbarossa* (London, 1968).
G. BRANDI, *Charles Quint et son Temps* (Paris, 1951).
BRANTÔME, *Vies* (Paris, 1858–95).
F. BRAUDEL, *La Méditerranée et le Monde Méditerranéen à l'Époque de Philippe II* (Paris, 1966).
— *Civilisation Matérielle, Économie et Capitalisme, XVe-XVIIIe Siècles* (Paris, 1979).
[The above 2 works are published in English as:
F. BRAUDEL, *The Mediterranean and the Mediterranean World in the Age of Philip II*, transl. by S. Reynolds (London, 1972), 2 vols.]
H. BUCHANAN, 'Luther and the Turks', *Archiv für Reformation Geschichte*, 47 (1956).
A.G. DE BUSBECQ, *Lettres* (Paris, 1748).
C. CAHEN, *Pre-Ottoman Turkey* (London, 1968).
— 'Baba Ishak, Baba Ilyas, Hadji Bektach et Quelques Autres', *Turcica I* (1969).
'Charles Quint et son Temps', symposium (Paris, 1959).
P. CHAUNU, *Conquête et Exploitation des Nouveaux Mondes* (Paris, 1969).
J. CHESNEAU, *Le Voyage de M. d'Aramon*, travel writings edited by Scheffer (Paris, 1887).
A.N. ST CLAIR, *The Image of the Turk in Europe* (New York, 1973).
P. COLES, *The Ottoman Impact on Europe* (London, 1968).
— *La Lutte contre les Turcs* (Paris, 1969).
M.A. COOK, *Population Pressure in Rural Anatolia, 1450–1600* (London, 1972).

B.A. CVETKOVA, 'La Vie Économique dans les Villes et les Ports Balkaniques aux XVe et XVIe Siècles', *Revue des Études Islamiques*, XXXVIII (1970).

DEFONTIN-MAXANGE, *Eudj'Ali* (Paris, 1930).

J. DENY and I. MÉLIKOFF, 'L'Expédition en Provence de l'Armée de Mer du Sultan Suleyman sous le Commandement de l'Amiral Hayreddin Pacha dit Barberousse (1543–1544)', *Turcica I* (1969).

J. EBERSOLT, *Constantinople Byzantine et les Voyageurs du Levant* (Paris, 1919).

L.T. ERDER and S. FAROQHI, 'The Development of the Anatolian Urban Network during the XVIth Century', *Journal of the Economic and Social History of the Middle East*, XXIV.

R. ETTINGHAUSEN, *Turkish Miniatures* (New York, 1965).

EVERSLEY (Lord), *The Turkish Empire* (Lahore, 1959) (reprint).

S. FAROQHI, 'Rural Society in Anatolia and the Balkans during the Sixteenth Century', *Turcica IX/I & XI* (1977 & 1979).

G. FEHER, *Miniatures Turques des Chroniques sur les Campagnes de Hongrie* (Paris, 1978).

O. FERRARA, *Le XVIe* Siècle Vu par les Ambassadeurs Vénitiens (Paris, 1954).

S.A. FISCHER-GALATI, *Ottoman Imperialism and German Protestantism* (Harvard, 1959).

J. FONTANUS, *Ad Adrianum Pont. M. Epistola Missa e Rhodo* (Tübingen, 1523).

P. DU FRESNE-CANAYE, *Voyage au Levant* (H. Hauser, Paris).

A. GABRIEL, 'Les Étapes d'une Campagne dans les Deux Iraq d'après un Manuscrit Turc du XVIe Siècle', *Syria, IX* (1928).

H.A.R. GIBB, 'Lütfi Pasha on the Ottoman Empire', *Oriens*, 15 (1962).

— *The Arab Conquest of Central Asia* (New York, 1970) (reprint).

— and H. BOWEN, *Islamic Society and the West* (Oxford, 1950–57).

P. GIOVIO, *Turcicarum Rerum Commentarius* (Rome, 1531; London, 1546).

R. GIRAUD, *L'Empire des Turcs Célestes* (Paris, 1960).

A. GÖKALP, 'Une Minorité Chiite en Anatolie: les Alevi', *Annales E.S.C.*, 3–4 (1980).

T. GÖKBILGIN, 'Süleyman I', I.A.XI.

G. GOODWIN, *Ottoman Turkey (Architecture)* (London, 1977).

— *Sinan: Ottoman Architecture and its Values Today* (London, 1992).

O. GRABAR, *The Formation of Islamic Art* (Yale, 1973).

J. DE LA GRAVIÈRE, *Doria et Barberousse* (Paris, 1886).

— *Les Corsaires Barbaresques* (Paris, 1887).
B. GREKOV and A. IAKOUBOVSKI, *La Horde d'Or* (Paris, 1939).
F. GRENARD, *Grandeur et Décadence de l'Asie* (Paris, 1947).
R. GROUSSET, *L'Empire des Steppes* (Paris, 1939).
— *La Face de l'Asie* (Paris, 1955).
F. HACKETT, *Henry VIII* (Paris, 1930).
Haci HALIFA, *The History of the Maritime Wars of the Turks*, transl. by J. Mitchell (London, 1831).
F.W. HASLUCK, *Christianity and Islam under the Sultans* (Oxford, 1929).
A. HESS, 'The Moriscos: an Ottoman Fifth Column in 16th Century Spain', *American Historical Review* (1968).
— 'The Evolution of the Ottoman Seaborne Empire in the Age of the Oceanic Discoveries', *American Historical Review* (1970).
— 'Piri Reis and the Ottoman Response to the Voyages of Discoveries', *Terrae Incognitae*, VI (1974).
W. HEYD, *Histoire du Commerce du Levant* (Leipzig, 1936).
E. HOMSY, *Les Capitulations et les Chrétiens aux XVIe et XVIIe Siècles* (Paris, 1956).
C.H. IMBER, 'The Navy of Süleyman the Magnificent', *Archivum Ottomanicum* (1980).
H. INALCIK, *The Ottoman Empire. The Classical Age 1300–1600* (London, 1973).
— *The Ottoman Empire. Conquest, Organisation and Economy* (London, 1978) (collect. studies).
N. IORGA, *Histoire des États Balkaniques* (Paris, 1925).
M. IZZEDIN, 'Les Eunuques dans le Palais Ottoman', *Orient 24* (1962).
H. JENKINS, *Ibrahim Pacha. The Great Vizir* (New York, 1911).
IBN JOBAIR, *Voyages*, transl. by Gaudefroy-Demonbynes (Paris, 1949–65).
Kanuni Armağanı (Ankara, 1970).
H. KARPAT, *The Ottoman State and its Place in World History*, symposium (Leiden, 1974).
L. KEHREN, *Tamerlan. L'Empire du Seigneur de Fer* (Neuchâtel, 1978).
KEMAL PACHA ZADEH, *Histoire de la Campagne de Mohacs*, transl. by Pavet de Courteille (Paris, 1869).
H.J. KISSLING, 'Chah Ismail, la Nouvelle Route des Indes et les Ottomans', *Turcica VI* (1975).
F. KÖPRÜLÜ, *Les Origines de l'Empire Ottoman* (Paris, 1935).
M. KORTEPETER, *Ottoman Imperialism during the Reformation. Europe and the Caucasus* (New York, 1972).

J.H. KRAMERS, 'Historiography among the Osmanli Turks', *Analecta Orientalia*, 1 (1954).
E. KÜHNEL, *Islamic Arts* (London, 1970).
B. KÜTÜKOGLU, 'Les Relations entre l'Empire Ottoman et l'Iran dans la Seconde Moitié du XVIe Siècle', *Turcica VI* (1975).
S. LABIB, 'The Era of Suleyman the Magnificent: Crisis of Orientation', *International Journal of Middle East Studies*, 10 (1979).
A. LANE, *Early Islamic Pottery* (London, 1947).
— *Later Islamic Pottery* (London, 1957).
S. LANE-POOL, *The Mohammadan Dynasties* (Beirut, 1966) (reprint).
— *Turkey* (Beirut, 1966) (reprint).
H. LAPEYRE, *Les Monarchies Européennes du XVIe Siècle et les Relations Internationales*, coll. Nouvelle Clio (Paris, 1967).
A. LEFAIVRE, *Les Magyars pendant la Domination Ottomane en Hongrie, 1526–1722* (Paris, 1902).
L. LÉGER, *Histoire de l'Autriche-Hongrie* (Paris, 1920).
C. LEMERCIER-QELQUEJAY, *La Paix Mongole* (Paris, 1970).
E. LE ROY-LADURIE, *Les Paysans de Languedoc* (Paris, 1966).
— *Histoire du Climat depuis l'An Mil* (Paris, 1967).
— *Le Territoire de l'Historien.*
M. LESURE, *Lépante. La Crise de l'Empire Ottoman* (Paris, 1972).
— 'Notes et Documents sur les Relations Veneto-Ottomanes, 1570–1573', *Turcica VI* (1972) and *VIII/I* (1976).
M. LEVEY, *The World of Ottoman Art* (New York, 1975).
B. LEWIS, *Istanbul and the Civilization of the Ottoman Empire* (Norman, 1963).
— *The Emergence of Modern Turkey* (London, 1968).
— 'Ottoman Observers of Ottoman Decline', *Islamic Studies*, 19.
R. LEWIS, *Everyday Life in Ottoman Turkey* (New York, 1971).
LONGWORTH DAMES, 'The Portuguese and Turks in the 16th Century', *Journal of the Royal Asiatic Society*, 1 (1921).
R. DE LUSINGE, *De la Naissance, Durée et Chute des Estats* (Paris, 1588).
A.H. LYBYER, *The Government of the Ottoman Empire in the Time of Süleyman the Magnificent* (New York, 1913).
— 'Constantinople as Capital of the Ottoman Empire', *Annual Report of the American Historical Association* (1916).
M. MALOWIST, 'Le Commerce du Levant avec l'Europe de l'Est au XVIe Siècle. Quelques Problèmes', *Mélanges Braudel* (Paris, 1973).
E. MAMBOURY, *Istanbul Touristique* (Istanbul, 1951).
R. MANTRAN, *Istanbul dans la Seconde Moitié du XVIIe Siècle* (Paris, 1962).

— *La Vie Quotidienne à Constantinople au Temps de Soliman le Magnifique et de ses Successeurs, XVIe–XVIIe Siècle* (Paris, 1965).

L. MASSIGNON, *Parole Donnée* (Paris, 1962).

J. MAURAND, *Itinéraire de J. Maurand d'Antibes à Constantinople, 1544* (Paris, 1901).

I. MÉLIKOFF, 'Le Problème Kizilbach', *Turcica VI* (1975).

E. MERCIER, *Histoire de l'Afrique Septentrionale* (Paris, 1891).

M. MERCIER, *Le Feu Grégeois* (Paris & Avignon, 1962).

J.B. MERRIMAN, *The Rise of the Spanish Empire* (New York, 1918–34).

— *Süleiman the Magnificent* (New York, 1944).

G. MIGEON, *Manuel d'Art Musulman* (Paris, 1927).

— and SAKISIAN, *La Céramique d'Asie Mineure* (Paris, 1923).

A. MIQUEL, *L'Islam et sa Civilisation* (Paris, 1977).

J. MONLAÜ, *Les États Barbaresques* (Paris, 1964).

Lady M. MONTAGU, *L'Islam au Péril des Femmes* (Paris, 1981).

MOURADGEA D'OHSSON, *Tableau Général de l'Empire Ottoman* (Paris, 1788–1824).

A. NAVARIAN, *Les Sultans Poètes* (Paris, 1936).

N. DE NICOLAY, *Les Quatre Livres de Navigations et Pérégrinations Orientales* (Lyons, 1568).

R.W. OLSON, 'The Sixteenth Century Price Revolution and its Effect on the Ottoman Empire and Ottoman-Safavid Relations', *Acta Orientalia*, 37 (1976).

T. ÖZ, *Turkish Ceramics* (Ankara, n.d.).

A. PALLIS, *In the Days of the Janissaries* (London, 1951).

A. PAPADOPOULO, 'Esthétique de l'Art Musulman, La Peinture', *Annales E.S.C.* (May–June 1973).

N.M. PENZER, *The Harem* (London, 1936).

X. DE PLANHOL, *Le Monde Islamique, Essai de Géographie Religieuse* (Paris, 1957).

— *Les Fondements Géographiques de l'Histoire de l'Islam* (Paris, 1968).

G. POSTEL, *La Tierce Partie des Histoires Orientales* (Poitiers, 1560).

— *De la République des Turcs* (Paris, 1575).

R. PUAUX, *François 1er Turcophile?* (Paris, n.d.).

L. VON RANKE, *Histoire des Osmanlis et de la Monarchie Espagnole pendant les XVIe et XVIIe Siècles* (Paris, 1839).

J. REZNIK, *Le Duc de Naxos* (Paris, 1936).

C.D. ROUILLARD, *The Turks in French History, Thought and Literature* (Paris, n.d.).

J.P. ROUX, *La Turquie* (Paris, 1953).
— *Turquie* (Paris, 1968).
— *Les Barbares* (Paris, 1982).
RÜÇHAN ARIK, 'La Maison Turque d'Anatolie', *Objets et Mondes*, T. 21 (1982).
M. SANUTO, *I Diarii* (Venice, 1889).
J. SAUVAGET, *Alep* (Paris, 1941).
— *Introduction à l'Histoire de l'Orient Musulman* (Paris, 1961).
— *Introduction à l'Étude de la Céramique Musulmane* (Paris, 1966).
A. SCHIMMEL, *Islamic Calligraphy* (Leiden, 1970).
R.B. SERJEANT, *The Portuguese of the South-East Coasts* (Oxford, 1963).
K. SETTON, 'Lutheranism and the Turkish Peril', *Balkan Studies*, 3 (1962).
S.J. SHAW, *History of the Ottoman Empire and Modern Turkey*, 2 vols. (Cambridge & London, 1976–77).
SIDI ALI REIS, *The Mirror of Countries*, transl. by Vambery (London, 1899).
E. SIVAN, *L'Islam et la Croisade* (Paris, 1968).
M. SOKOLNICKI, 'La Sultane Ruthène: Roksolanes', *Belleten 23* (Ankara, 1959).
S. SOUCEK, 'Certain Types of Ships in Ottoman Turkish Terminology', *Turcica VII* (1975).
W. SPENCERS, *Algiers in the Age of the Corsairs* (Norman, Okla., 1976).
I. STCHOUKINE, *La Peinture Turque*, 2 vols. (Paris, 1966–71).
A. STRATTON, *Sinan* (London, 1972).
G.W.F. STRIPLING, *The Ottoman Turks and the Arabs, 1511–1574* (Urbana, 1942).
I. SUNAR, 'Économie et Politique dans l'Empire Ottoman', *Annales E.S.C.*, 3–4 (1980).
T. TALBOT-RICE, *The Seldjuks* (London, 1961).
J.B. TAVERNIER, *Les Six Voyages en Turquie, en Perse et aux Indes* (Paris, 1681).
J. THÉVENOT, *Relation d'un Voyage du Levant* (Paris, 1717).
A. TIETZE, *The Turkish Shadow Theater and the Puppet Collection of the L.A. Mayer Memorial Foundation* (Berlin, 1977).
N. TODOROV, *La Ville Balkanique sous les Ottomans* (London, 1977).
J. URSU, *La Politique Orientale de François Ier* (Paris, 1908).
D.M. VAUGHAN, *Europe and the Turk. A Pattern of Alliances, 1300–1700* (Liverpool, 1954).
P. VILAR, *Or et Monnaie dans l'Histoire* (Paris, 1974).

C. VILLAIN-GANDOSSI, *Contribution à l'Étude des Relations entre Venise et la Porte* (Munich, 1967–70).

U. VOGT-GÖKNIL, *Architecture de la Turquie Ottomane* (Fribourg, 1965).

N. WEISSMANN, *Les Janissaires* (Paris, 1957).

P. WITTEK, 'De la Défaite d'Ankara à la Prise de Constantinople', *Revue des Études Islamiques* (1938).

— *The Rise of the Ottoman Empire* (London, 1938).

S.K. YETKIN, *L'Architecture Turque en Turquie* (Paris, 1962).

— *L'Ancienne Peinture Turque* (Paris, 1970).

Index